The Deans' Bible

Anyone who treasured his or her college experience will find this book compelling and captivating. Through the eyes of its five featured pioneers—and these deans were indeed pioneers in the sense they broke new ground in the ways that students were served, supported, and inspired while in college—the author gives us a moving and memorable sense of the sights, sounds, and passions of life on American college campuses from the 1930s to the present.

TOM RUDIN
Senior Vice President, the College Board, Washington, DC

The Deans' Bible celebrates a collegiate history that informs leaders about how to move any organization past a turbulent and distraction-filled time toward a system where organizational goals take center stage. Leadership requires self-awareness, an exhaustive inventory of local assets, and knowledge of the organization and national trends. The deans excelled in each one of these areas because of their core value to make a positive difference. Leaders, no matter the industry, will learn how to craft a legacy—strategically navigating changing trends with a welcoming and inclusive spirit.

RAYMONDA L. BURGMAN
Director, HERS Institutes, University of Denver

Student affairs at Purdue University came alive on the first deans' watch. They were bold in demonstrating how the "old girls network" could work as well as the one belonging to the "old boys," and they were, to a woman, regarded in deans' circles for their equanimity and strategic aplomb. In telling the deans' story, the author showcases the roles these remarkable leaders played on the national stage of higher education.

JANE A. HAMBLIN
Executive Director,
Mortar Board National College Senior Honor Society

Angie Klink has woven the lives of these remarkable, courageous women educators into an inspiring narrative—scrupulously researched, wonderfully written. A compelling story and a joy to read.

ILENE BECKERMAN
Author of *Love, Loss, and What I Wore,*
adapted for the stage by Nora and Delia Ephron

The Deans' Bible superbly chronicles the indelible impact of five courageous, passionate, and caring women who led and fought for the advancement of women and higher education. This is the account of leaders who shared of themselves generously and set an example of professionalism for all they touched. These women were "leaning in" long before others recognized that women could take their place in a leadership position.

RUSTY RUEFF
Chairman, the GRAMMY Foundation

The Founders Series

Also by Angie Klink

Kirby's Way: How Kirby and Caroline Risk Built their Company on Kitchen-Table Values

Divided Paths, Common Ground: The Story of Mary Matthews and Lella Gaddis, Pioneering Purdue Women Who Introduced Science into the Home

The Deans' Bible

Five Purdue Women and Their Quest for Equality

By Angie Klink

Purdue University Press
West Lafayette, Indiana

The author and publisher gratefully acknowledge the support of friends and admirers of the deans depicted in this book. Without their generosity, the writing and production of this book would not have been possible.

Paperback ISBN: 978-1-55753-765-2
ePDF ISBN: 978-1-61249-325-1
ePUB ISBN: 978-1-61249-326-8

The Library of Congress has cataloged the earlier hardcover edition as follows:

Klink, Angie, 1959-
The dean's bible : five Purdue women and their quest for equality / Angie Klink.
pages cm. -- (The founders series)
Includes index.
ISBN 978-1-55753-676-1 (hardback) -- ISBN 978-1-61249-325-1 (epdf) -- ISBN 978-1-61249-326-8 (epub) 1. Purdue University--Faculty--Biography. 2. Women deans (Education)--United States--Biography. I. Title.
LD4672.K54 2014
378.772'95--dc23

2013048869

Cover design by Natalie Powell.
Cover photo: Deans Helen B. Schleman, M. Beverley Stone, Barbara I. Cook, Betty M. Nelson, and Dorothy C. Stratton in July 1987. Photo by Dave Umberger.

In memory of my mother,
Rosemary Lawhead Rhodes Lipp,
because no one told her she could.

CONTENTS

	Foreword	xi
	Preface	xiii
	Author's Note	xix
	The Deans' List	xxi
1	Celestial Chicken Salad	1
2	Carolyn Shoemaker, a Faraway Look	3
3	Artists of Life	13
4	Far Horizons	23
5	Dorothy Stratton Finds a Bible	31
6	Helen Schleman, Born in the Right Moment	39
7	If Walls Could Talk	47
8	Amelia Earhart, Cabbages and Kings	55
9	Lillian Gilbreth, the One Best Way	69
10	Ladies' Agreement	79
11	Beverley Stone, a Lovely Light	93
12	Your Best Foot Forward	101
13	Be Interesting	111
14	Don't Be a Spare . . . Be a SPAR!	121
15	Meanwhile, Back at the Ranch	135
16	In Sheep's Clothing	145
17	Barbara Ivy Wood Cook, 'Tis a Gift to Be Free	157
18	Bible Bequeathed	167
19	Gospel of the Go-to-Hell Fund	179

20	B-Squared	187
21	Dean of Women Punch	195
22	At the Service of the President	205
23	Mixed Messages	217
24	Winter's Death Rattle	233
25	Betty Mitchell Nelson, Message in the Hollow Oak	243
26	'Twas Ever Thus	253
27	The Quiet Crisis	261
28	Uncharted Waters	267
29	Peace, Love, and a Bible Passage	279
30	Off Guard	285
31	Sit In, Stand Out	293
32	In Walks the Pantsuit	303
33	Hip Women	313
34	Entitled to Title IX	323
35	The Hand That Rocks the Cradle Can Rock the Boat	333
36	Easier to Move a Cemetery	339
37	And She Did It!	349
38	Deanie Weenies	357
39	Bible Holding Pattern	365
40	Chicken Salad Reprise	379
41	The Main Thing	383
42	To Understand More Than One Knows	393
43	Hearing What Is Not Said	403
44	Helen's Hankie Club	415
45	Betty's Blast Off and Bible Hand Off	421
46	Hugging the Purdue Campus	427
47	By Your Leave, Sirs	435
48	The Place Just Right	441
49	Epilogue	445
	Index	447
	Reading Group Guide	461

Foreword

We must always take sides. Neutrality helps the oppressor, never the victim. Silence encourages the tormentor, never the tormented.

—Elie Wiesel, Holocaust survivor, author of *Night*
Nobel Peace Prize acceptance speech, 1986

Five remarkable women enlivened and enhanced Purdue University from 1933 to 1995. They shared profound concern for students and the educations they were receiving. In addition, they also were united by their efforts to expand opportunities for women, both at Purdue and nationally.

Purdue itself benefited immensely from their service, including their forceful and direct efforts to convince their boss, typically the university president, to modify policies that would make Purdue a stronger university. Often, though not always, they were successful.

Who was this quintet? They were the deans of women and then deans of students from 1933 to 1995: Dorothy C. Stratton, Helen B. Schleman, M. Beverley Stone, Barbara I. Cook, and Betty M. Nelson. In their early years they were part of a mere handful of adult women in positions of responsibility at Purdue. Thus, their concerns for women transcended student life to include opportunities for women as professors and senior administrators. Not surprisingly, many of their male colleagues did not share their enthusiasm.

Angie Klink has recorded their experiences in this lively volume, *The Deans' Bible: Five Purdue Women and Their Quest for Equality.* This is not simply a tale of five beloved servants of Purdue. Rather, Klink has embedded their efforts in the larger tale of women's changing role in American society in the twentieth century. She places these women—from Missouri, Indiana, Virginia, Tennessee, and West Virginia—in the national events influencing women's experience as well as the service of three of them in the military during World War II.

This is a book for Boilermakers to remember some of our most impressive leaders. I am fortunate to have known and admired all of the deans as a child in West Lafayette and as a Purdue student (BS, 1955; MS, 1958; Litt.D., 1980). Additionally, it is a book for those who have not had the privilege of a Purdue education to learn about this dedicated group who sought and achieved improvements, both in women's opportunities and in university education.

—PATRICIA ALBJERG GRAHAM
Charles Warren Professor of the History of Education Emerita
Harvard University

Preface

For nearly a century, six Purdue women deans passed down a secret Bible. The Bible was the clandestine emblem of their shared profession and a symbol of their sisterhood. The many-layered story of their interwoven lives and their pursuit of equity for all people rings of fiction, but because it is true, the tale is relevant and inspiring today. We hunger to learn from women like Dorothy Stratton, Helen Schleman, Beverley Stone, Barbara Cook, and Betty Nelson. I was privileged to channel these women's astonishing lives into this book.

Over the course of several years when I attended a University "women's event" in the Purdue Libraries Archives and Special Collections, I saw the same photo of five women striding shoulder to shoulder in a grassy meadow. Repeatedly, the photo was printed on programs or posters to signify "women of Purdue." It was as if this image was *the* representation of powerful women in Purdue's history. The photo became iconic. I didn't know much about the five, but every time I saw the picture, the women walked toward me, and I thought, "There's a story."

Then I was told of the secret Bible, originally held by Carolyn Shoemaker who became Purdue's first part-time dean of women in 1913. When I heard of the hand-me-down Testament, I knew—there *is* a story, and I would love to write it.

While not all of the women were devoted churchgoers, each dean passed the Bible to her successor. The book remained tucked in the acting dean's desk drawer where it emitted a quiet, formidable reminder that when the dean on duty met with obstacles, injustice, or good fortune, the deans were always there for one another in presence and in spirit, shoulder to shoulder in forward momentum.

The story of the five deans is a tale of women helping other women. The deans abetted each other, female students, faculty, and administrators. These women of great substance aided minorities, people with disabilities, and any student—male or female—who needed a good listener and a word of hope.

The Deans' Bible spans one hundred years of women's rights, women at Purdue University, and women in America. The book is about equality for all people. Dorothy, Helen, Bev, Barb, and Betty were cut from the same progressive, broad-minded cloth and wore the same mantel of parity and integrity throughout their lives.

Dorothy and Helen were friends with Amelia Earhart and Lillian Gilbreth. The aviatrix and engineer were profound influences on Dorothy and Helen who, into the twentieth century, carried forth the famous women's philosophies that females can accomplish great feats.

Dorothy, Helen, and Bev enlisted to serve during World War II. Captain Dorothy Stratton was the founder and director of the women's reserve of the United States Coast Guard, which she named the SPARs. Captain Helen Schleman was Dorothy's "right-hand woman." Many who knew Beverley Stone may not have realized that this ultrafeminine woman who wore pearls and fur coats had been a WAVE, a member of the women's reserve of the United States Navy. Time spent in the SPARs and the WAVES proved to these three that females could accomplish anything; however, when the war ended, women were told to go back home, take care of their men, have children, and forget thoughts of careers. This cultural pressure for women to marry, stay home, and not pursue their dreams was something that the deans challenged on Purdue's campus for decades.

Throughout her lifetime, Dorothy Stratton was honored as the director of the SPARs. Her contribution to America's women and minorities spanned from her association with Eleanor Roosevelt, beginning in the 1940s, to her posthumous association with Michelle Obama in the 2000s, when the first lady christened and commissioned a United States Coast Guard cutter in Dorothy's name. The *USCGC Stratton* protects America's shoreline today.

I thank the staff of the Purdue University Virginia Kelly Karnes Archives and Special Collections for their steadfast assistance during my research for *The Deans' Bible*. University Archivist and Head of Archives and Special Collections Sammie L. Morris was most helpful in opening the "vaults" for me to peer inside. A special thank-you goes to Stephanie Schmitz, the France A. Córdova Women's Archivist, and Jonathan K. McConnell, graduate assistant, for their prompt attention to my many queries to find a particular letter or newspaper clipping.

Each dean has her share of papers and ephemera housed in the Purdue Libraries Archives and Special Collections, but Helen was the queen saver of them all. I read through thirteen archival boxes filled with Helen's papers. She saved every letter she received and carbon copies (written back in the days of carbon paper) of the correspondence she sent. It was as if Helen knew that she must document the continual battles to bring women equal opportunities at Purdue and in the country, and that I would come along sixty years later to write down her trials for the world to see and learn from her efforts and fortitude.

Often, when I left the beautiful research area of the Purdue Libraries Archives and Special Collections, where I had been cloistered for an afternoon surrounded by the rich wooden cabinets housing every *Debris* yearbook since the 1800s, I would feel the weight of Helen's struggles. The continual oppression that she and the female students endured weighed heavily upon my shoulders; however, I also went away with such awe for her persistence and that of her sister deans. They never gave up. Even in retirement during the early 1990s, Helen, in her eighties, handwrote a four-page letter to the president of Purdue expressing her concern that there were not enough women in administration at the University. She then listed potential candidates and their qualifications.

I thank two very special women for their immeasurable help in writing *The Deans' Bible.* Dean of Students Emerita Betty M. Nelson is the dean "holding down the spiritual fort" here on earth for her predecessors. The deans considered themselves a "chosen family," and Betty's stories of her lineage of deans gave much insight to the tapestry of their connections, the challenges they faced individually and collectively, and the fun they had in the journey. To know Betty is to know a woman of class, depth, and energy. She's funny, intuitive, and brilliant.

I thank another member of the "chosen family," Captain Sally Watlington. Sally was the daughter Helen Schleman never had. Sally was equally close to Dorothy Stratton. Dorothy, Helen, and Bev influenced Sally in her decision to join the navy. Sally and Betty cared for the deans as they aged. (Sally affectionately called them "the Deanie Weenies" and "the Girls.") In the spirit of the Bible's symbolic undertone of women advocating for one another, Betty and Sally were there for the deans, to the end. Most recently, the two cared for Barbara Cook until her passing in April 2013.

The day after Barb passed away, I was at Betty's house to interview Purdue alumna Teresa Roche, who knew all of the deans and is especially close to Betty. As Teresa and I sat at the kitchen table, Betty headed for the front door to leave for an errand. As if something came to her suddenly, she stopped, turned her head to the side, and said rather cryptically, "Be prepared for your life to change." Then she opened the door and scurried off. Her words wafted prophetically in her wake.

People have asked me if my books change me during the process of writing. They all have left their marks, even the children's books with their sparse number of words. But *The Deans' Bible* has transformed me the most, for these distinguished women have "removed the scales from my eyes."

Each dean chose a favorite passage to write down in the front matter of Carolyn Shoemaker's Bible. Similarly, I am selecting a verse for this book—Acts 9:15–18, referred to as the "Conversion of Saul." It reads:

> But the Lord said, "Go and do what I say. For Saul is my chosen instrument to take my message to the Gentiles and to kings, as well as to the people of Israel. And I will show him how much he must suffer for me."
>
> So Ananias went and found Saul. He laid his hands on him and said, "Brother Saul, the Lord Jesus, who appeared to you on the road, has sent me so that you may get your sight back and be filled with the Holy Spirit." Instantly something like scales fell from Saul's eyes, and he regained his sight.

After receiving his sight, Saul spent time with other believers to learn of the teachings of Jesus, and then he embarked on a ministry to preach the truth to others. When Saul spoke to others, his words were powerful because he was a brilliant scholar, yet most convincing was the evidence of the way he lived. It's important to know the Good Book and how to defend one's faith, but words need to be backed up with a changed life.

For nearly two years I conducted research and wrote *The Deans' Bible*. I have spent much time with the believers. It's important that the efforts of the deans are written down to proclaim their faith in the potential of all people and their gospel of women helping other women. Scales must fall from more eyes. I hope my words can be backed up with a changed life—yours and mine.

—ANGIE KLINK

Publisher's Note: In addition to the photographs in the center of this book, further images can be found on a connected website hosted by the Purdue University Archives and Special Collections at collections.lib.purdue.edu/womens-archives/quest-for-equality.

Author's Note

Deans of women at universities and colleges across the United States were once connected as a nurturing network of mentors by their own professional organization, founded in 1916 as the National Association of Deans of Women (NADW). The early founders worked diligently to professionalize the position of dean and to legitimize their roles on predominantly male college campuses. The organization metamorphosed through the twentieth century, changing its name three times before shuttering in 2000.

Deans of women opened doors and opportunities for female students, faculty, and administrators throughout American campuses. Their scholarly journal, research monographs, symposia, and conferences provided evidence of the immeasurable contributions that the association and its members made to higher education and women's voices in that education.

At the 1956 NADW annual conference in Cincinnati, Ohio, President Eunice Hilton declared a new name for the forty-year-old association.

It became the National Association of Women Deans and Counselors (NAWDC).

In 1973, the name changed again as the word "administrators" was added. The organization became the National Association for Women Deans, Administrators, and Counselors (NAWDAC), a name it would hold until 1991, when the group moved into a new identity.

In 1990, a fundraising consultant hired by NAWDAC recommended a name change using the ideas of "women in education" and "women's leadership" as a guide. The membership of NAWDAC voted to change the association's name to the National Association for Women in Education (NAWE). The word "dean" was no longer part of the seventy-five-year-old organization's distinctiveness.

By the turn of the twenty-first century, NAWE experienced increased competition for membership from other professional organizations. Society had also shifted away from supporting single-sex groups; NAWE came to an end in 2000. The association's legacy and immense contributions to the advancement of female students, faculty, and administrators in higher education live on through its historical contributions—contributions that are of the utmost importance still today.

In 2012, the American Council on Education's (ACE) survey of college presidents found a profession dominated by white men—a portrait that has hardly changed since the NADW was founded in 1916. Today, 26 percent of institutional leaders are female. No doubt, the deans of women would encourage females to persevere, for there is still work to be done for the issue of women's educational equity and advancement—still a goal to be attained in the twenty-first century.

Today, the National Student Affairs Archives (NSAA) at the Center for Archival Collections at Bowling Green State University, Bowling Green, Ohio, comprises the institutional papers of numerous national, regional, and state professional student affairs associations. The NSAA also is home to "The Student Affairs History Project," a website devoted to the history of the student affairs profession. The NSAA was a helpful resource in the writing of The Deans' Bible.

The Deans' List

Carolyn E. Shoemaker
Born: 1865
Died: March 2, 1933
Dean of Women: 1913–1933

Dorothy C. Stratton
Born: March 24, 1899
Died: September 17, 2006
Dean of Women: 1933–1942
WWII leave of absence: 1942–1947

Helen B. Schleman
Born: June 21, 1902
Died: February 5, 1992
Dean of Women: 1947–1968

M. Beverley Stone
Born: June 10, 1916
Died: April 16, 2003
Dean of Women: 1968–1974
Dean of Students: 1974–1980

BARBARA I. COOK
Born: December 8, 1929
Died: April 10, 2013
Dean of Students: 1980–1987

BETTY M. NELSON
Born: March 17, 1935
Dean of Students: 1987–1995

Deans Helen B. Schleman, M. Beverley Stone, Barbara I. Cook, Betty M. Nelson, and Dorothy C. Stratton at Purdue's North Golf Course (today named Kampen Course) in July 1987. Betty had been Purdue's dean of students for two weeks when she was invited to lunch at the Cook-Stone home flanking the golf course. Much to her surprise, Betty was presented with Carolyn Shoemaker's Bible, a symbol of the women's shared profession. Photo by Dave Umberger.

1

Celestial Chicken Salad

On a verdant July day in 1987, a camera clicked and a roll of 35-millimeter film advanced to record a moment in Purdue University history. Five women were captured in a photograph that represented six decades of striving for the advancement of women, a quest for equality for all beings, and an interweaving of lives that formed a chosen family. The photograph became known as "Five Deans Walking."

Betty Nelson, age fifty-two, had just completed her first two weeks as Purdue's dean of students when her predecessors, Beverley Stone, age seventy-one, and Barbara Cook, age fifty-eight, invited her to lunch at the white two-story colonial they shared on Western Drive in West Lafayette, Indiana. Betty thought she merely was invited to a nice lunch with the women who had become like family since she first worked in the Office of the Dean of Women twenty years before. Bev and Barb said the meal would be "something small, just a little salad." And, as an afterthought, "Oh, Helen and Dorothy might be there, too."

Neighbors and friends had nicknamed Western Drive "Deans' Row." Down the block from the "Cook-Stone" home, Dorothy Stratton, age eighty-eight, Purdue's first full-time dean of women, shared a contemporary house with her successor, Helen Schleman, age eighty-five. The four former Purdue deans lived their retirement years, houses apart, along the edge of the emerald bunkers and bays of Purdue's North Golf Course (today named Kampen Course).

Betty arrived and noticed that the deans were dressed in summer suits, pastel skirts, and crisp blouses. Helen wore her gold Purdue pendant watch around her neck. Dangling from Bev's ears were her signature faux pearl earrings. The table in the breakfast nook with a panoramic view of the golf course was set in style, and the women were in high spirits. Celestial Chicken Salad was served nestled in crisp lettuce cups.

Celestial Chicken Salad was a recipe handed down to Barb from her mother, Thelma Wood. Thelma told her daughter it was a dish to be served when one wanted to impress. The chicken salad was aptly named, for it was heavenly, indeed. The five deans sat at the kitchen table feasting and chatting. The lineage of their common chosen professions was nearly palpable.

CELESTIAL CHICKEN SALAD
Dice cooked chicken (always white meat, of course). Toss lightly with celery, whole mushrooms (whole, *not* sliced), toasted pecans, fried bacon, mayonnaise (*must* be Hellman's—this is important), sour cream (*not* low fat), and lemon juice. Garnish the luncheon plate with halved cherry tomatoes.

Dessert was served, and at the invitation of Barb and Bev, Dave Umberger, Purdue's senior photographer, arrived. The women knew Dave loved Key lime pie, and Bev's southern recipe was a refreshing favorite. It was then that the reason for the gathering was revealed. Barb pulled out a tattered brown leather Bible.

Betty watched, hands folded and resting on her poplin skirt, still thinking she was simply there for a pleasant noontime meal. She loved to hear these women's stories, some captivating and new, others familiar and deep-rooted like family fables. Betty sat waiting, glancing at the old book in Barb's hand. It was then that the four past women deans shared with the new woman dean their long-standing secret—the tale of the deans' Bible.

2

Carolyn Shoemaker, a Faraway Look

Carolyn Ernestine Shoemaker possessed a Bible, an American Standard. The cover was supple, cocoa-hued leather. The end of the word "HOLY," embossed with gold lettering on the spine, curled cheerily upward. The spine read:

HOLY BIBLE
REFERENCES
SELF-PRONOUNCING
NELSON

The term "References" indicated that throughout the text, the Bible contained mentions of other passages of Scripture on the same subject. A "Self-Pronouncing Bible" is one where difficult names are broken into syllables and accented by diacritical marks to help the reader pronounce them correctly. "Nelson" referred to Thomas Nelson Bibles, one of the oldest Bible publishers in the world.

Perhaps the Bible was given to Carolyn as a gift when she was baptized or when she graduated from high school and entered Purdue University. Carolyn graduated with a bachelor of science degree in 1888, less than twenty years after the University opened. Two of her classmates were George Ade, an author and humorist, and John T. McCutcheon, the "Dean of American Cartoonists" and Pulitzer Prize winner.

Carolyn was quiet, composed, and cheerful. People said she had perfect poise. Mrs. Mindwell Crampton Wilson, in "A Tribute to Dean Shoemaker" during Carolyn's memorial service, said that she "loved truth, seeking it above material things." She had an open mind; she valued friends, loved her two brothers, Jesse and Charles, lived simply, and found joy in work. One of the few photos of Carolyn shows her looking wistfully through her wire glasses, her dark hair in a finger wave, a popular style of the time, with a long strand of pearls accenting her dark, scooped-neck dress with lace sleeves.

Carolyn was a student in the first class Stanley Coulter taught after he arrived at Purdue to teach zoology. Later, he would become Purdue's first dean of men. Coulter spoke fondly of Carolyn, the student he would grow to know more deeply as a colleague in the following decades. During Carolyn's memorial service, in a speech titled "Dean Shoemaker, The Woman," Coulter said: "I recognized in her case I was to deal with an exceptional personality. She had at all times a faraway look in her eyes, which only the years interpreted to me."

Emma Montgomery McRae was a professor of English literature at Purdue who nurtured Carolyn's love of language. The two women had studied together and shared a trip to Europe. Carolyn said that Emma was the greatest influence of her adult life.

Emma was a solid, broad-faced woman with hair loosely piled atop her head. She had been a high school teacher and principal in Muncie, Indiana, and she was the first woman in the state to be chosen as president of the State Teachers Association.

A group of women created the Muncie McRae Club in Emma's honor in 1894 for "intellectual and cultural pursuit" of "education in art, science, literature, and music." This was during a time when many women did not have the opportunity for education, and the club was an answer to that academic void. The club also discussed social concerns such as suffrage, child labor, and race relations. A program booklet contained the motto, "Study to be what you wish to seem" with a tribute to Emma, "our honorary member—eminent as teacher and lecturer, a woman of rare character and great influence."

The McRae Club history goes on to describe Emma as a woman who ". . . filled her niche in life to the fullest, and with it all, remained so gentle, so plain, so unassuming and yet so dignified. Wherever she walked, people were wont to say, 'A queen has passed this way.' [Her] lectures were always masterpieces, her travelogues were unsurpassed [and] couched in the King's best English."

When Purdue President James H. Smart hired her in 1887, Emma became the "unofficial" dean of women. She was known as "Mother McRae," and because there were few female faculty members and a small number of female students, she served as a counselor on every academic and personal problem these students experienced. Emma epitomized high character, delivered masterful speeches, and garnered immense respect. With Emma, the die was cast.

Ladies Hall was the epicenter of every academic and social activity for Purdue's female students and where all of the home economics classes were held. In the early years, home economics was the "foot in the door" to higher education for women. Often, females were "not allowed" to take other courses seen as "unwomanly." It was the rare woman who bucked the stereotypes and took engineering or agriculture.

The building also was a residence hall where the women and Emma lived. Ladies Hall was a striking redbrick building with imposing twin towers. An iron fire escape wove a path from a third-floor arched window onto a veranda rooftop, then down a ladder that scaled the side of the building to the lawn. The fire escape was a popular place for photographs, with women students posing in a line on each stair step or clinging to the ladder, smiling, in their hats, gloves, black fur-collared coats, and high-button shoes. Each window bore a roller shade with a dangling string to pull for privacy. When it was constructed in 1872, Ladies Hall was the first permanent building north of State Street, the dirt thoroughfare that divided the Purdue campus.

Put in context, it is remarkable that any woman obtained a college degree during the late 1800s, for society severely challenged women's efforts for an education. When Lucretia Mott and Elizabeth Cady Stanton organized the first Women's Rights Convention in 1848, in Seneca Falls, New York, grievances were documented in the "Declaration of Sentiments" and set the agenda for the women's rights movement. One of the sentiments stated, "The history of mankind is a history of repeated injuries and usurpations on the part of man toward women. . . . He had denied her the facilities of a thorough education, all colleges being closed against her." An outcome of the convention was a demand for higher education for women.

Through the 1890s, "scientific" reports were released that showed that too much education could seriously hurt the female reproductive system. Commonly known as the Progressive Era, 1890 to 1917 was a watershed in women's intellectual history. There was a genuine fear that a good education would make a woman unfit for marriage and motherhood. In fact, nearly half of the first generation of college women did not marry or delayed marriage. They turned their energies to social reform and careers. Society offered educated women two choices—marriage or work, and many chose work. Remarkably, this cultural commandment to choose between career and marriage persisted well into the first half of the twentieth century.

When Carolyn Shoemaker was twenty-one, she obtained her master's degree from Purdue with plans to embark on a teaching career; however, as happens to many women, she put her personal goals on hold to care for someone she loved. Carolyn tended to her invalid mother for eleven years. Emma McRae hired Carolyn, age thirty-five, as an English literature instructor in 1900, the same year Carolyn's mother passed away.

Carolyn was an inspiring professor who infused a love of literature and drama into her teaching. She was a dynamic orator, on and off campus, and gave book reviews and speeches to clubs and organizations throughout Indiana.

Carolyn's office was in University Hall, today the oldest building on Purdue's campus. In his speech during Carolyn's memorial service, titled "Miss Shoemaker, The Teacher," Professor H. L. Creek, head of the Department of English, described Carolyn in this manner:

> She would enter the English Department office to get her mail, smile a greeting to anyone who might be present, and go back to her own office, perhaps without speaking. Ordinarily she seemed quite composed, with something of philosophic calm in her face and manner. Then sometimes there would come a sudden revelation of emotion—deep determination to accomplish something she thought important, a touch of indignation at some wrong, a bit of sorrow at the failure of others to reach her ideals, a flash of sympathy for someone who did not seem to be having a fair chance in life. At such moments we felt that Miss Shoemaker, calm as she might seem, had a deeply emotional life, and that her power as a teacher and as a woman lay in the warmth of her feelings.

Carolyn enjoyed studying human character. The teaching of drama appealed to her the most because she was interested in the interplay of purpose and personality. She relished mortal complexities found in fiction, biography, and autobiography.

As a member of Central Presbyterian Church, Carolyn taught "Bible Class in the Sabbath School" to a large group of Purdue coeds. The Bible was filled with the literary concepts Carolyn loved—drama, mortal complexities, purpose, and personality.

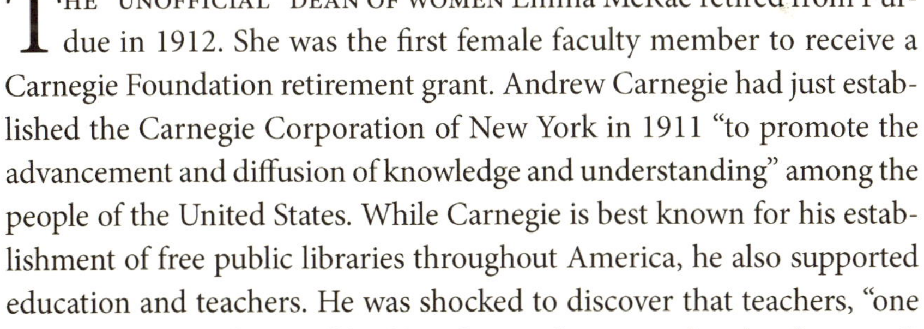

The "unofficial" dean of women Emma McRae retired from Purdue in 1912. She was the first female faculty member to receive a Carnegie Foundation retirement grant. Andrew Carnegie had just established the Carnegie Corporation of New York in 1911 "to promote the advancement and diffusion of knowledge and understanding" among the people of the United States. While Carnegie is best known for his establishment of free public libraries throughout America, he also supported education and teachers. He was shocked to discover that teachers, "one of the highest professions," had less financial security than his former office clerks. His teacher retirement accounts are now called TIAA-CREF.

The year after Emma retired, Purdue President Winthrop Stone called Carolyn, age forty-eight, into his office and offered her the newly created appointment of part-time dean of women. Many universities were establishing similar positions, and as Stone said, almost begrudgingly, he guessed

Purdue should, too. Female students had lost their confidante and counselor when Emma retired. Shoemaker was surprised and in awe of the responsibility; she said she was not sure she could handle such a job. The story repeated in countless chronicles of Purdue history for the last century is that Stone bellowed, "Be a man, Miss Shoemaker! Be a man! Do not let this or any other task worry you." Carolyn accepted the position of part-time dean of women in 1913, but she served Purdue very much like a woman.

Student Marion L. Smith (in her memorial speech for Carolyn, titled "The Dean of Women") described her:

> High aims and high ideals alone were not enough for Miss Shoemaker. One of the significant characteristics to which practically every coed made reference was her willingness to help—no problem brought to her by a coed was too small for her to consider; another characteristic was her desire to be reached easily by the coeds—she tried to be in her office whenever possible, and she was never too busy to see one; another trait was her sympathetic and understanding nature. She realized how important those problems were and what they meant to the girls who brought them, and she sincerely tried to solve those problems. Girls have actually gone into her office weeping and come out smiling.

Female faculty members in colleges across the United States were asked to serve a dual role as deans of women from the 1890s to the 1930s. The deans were to oversee the women who were the minority population on campus. They would insulate the women from the "maleness" of the campuses and, in turn, protect and guide the women. The deans were scholars who were concerned about the intellectual development of women, especially in competition with men.

The presence of women on campuses made university presidents and male faculty members uneasy. Women in colleges raised concerns about propriety, delicate matters of health, and female "problems," as well as the institutional responsibility to families to protect the safety, sexual virtue, and reputations of daughters far from home. For the uncomfortable males, appointing a dean of women to handle all those "unpleasant" female needs was the perfect solution.

Yet Carolyn helped the less than one hundred females on Purdue's campus with much more than matters of propriety. When women did not have enough money to finish their degrees, Carolyn gave them financial assistance from her own pocketbook. She also abetted social troubles, "scholastic adjustments," rooming house supervision, and general overseeing of all coed organizations and activities. The Young Women's Christian Association (YWCA) was one of the oldest campus institutions. The YWCA sponsored the Big Sister Movement, by which the women in the upper classes familiarized the freshmen females with activities and customs. In later years, this program at Purdue would be named the "Green Guard."

Carolyn became Purdue's first part-time dean of women the same year Alice Paul and Lucy Burns formed the Congressional Union (later named the National Woman's Party) to work toward the passage of a federal amendment to give women the right to vote. Paul, age twenty-eight, "cut her teeth" as a suffragist in England. While there, she met Burns in London.

On March 3, 1913, one day before President-elect Woodrow Wilson's inauguration, Paul and Burns organized a strategically timed, majestically staged women's suffrage parade with more than 5,000 marchers striding down Pennsylvania Avenue. Stunning and confident, Inez Milholland, a lawyer, led the parade. Draped in a cream cape that billowed in the breeze, she rode astride a snow-white horse. Holding a place of honor, immediately following, were women from seventeen countries that had already enfranchised women. Then came the "Pioneers," women who had been struggling in the American suffrage movement for sixty-five years to secure the right to vote.

The next section of the parade celebrated workingwomen, grouped by occupation and wearing the appropriate garb. There were nine bands, twenty-four floats, and a section for male supporters. The marchers waved American flags and bore signs and sashes in suffrage colors of purple, white, and gold that bore the words "Votes for Women." About 500,000 spectators gathered along the route.

Everyone was welcome to participate, with one exception. In a city that was southern in both location and attitude, where the Christmas Eve rape of a government clerk by a black man had percolated racist sentiments, Paul was convinced that some white women would not march with black women. In response to several inquiries, she had quietly discouraged blacks from participating.

Aware they were not wanted and in spite of fear that they may be attacked, a new Howard University African American sorority, Delta Sigma Theta, joined the procession. African American activists believed that if white women needed the vote to secure their rights, black women needed it even more. They faced discrimination on two levels—sex and race. The parade was the group's first public act. Today, Delta Sigma Theta is one of the largest African American women's organizations in the country, with an estimated 300,000 members around the world and a chapter at Purdue University.

Meanwhile, panicky reports came from white suffragists in Chicago that Ida B. Wells-Barnett, an African American journalist and suffragist who led an antilynching campaign, planned to join the procession. When the Illinois unit assembled in the parade line, leaders of the group instructed Wells-Barnett to walk with an all-black group rather than under the flag of her home state. With tears in her eyes, Wells-Barnett refused to participate in the procession unless "I can march under the Illinois banner."

Wells-Barnett stood from the sidelines watching the cavalcade until she decided to solve the issue herself by defiantly walking, mid-parade, from the sidelines into the Illinois group, matching their stride and ignoring their stares. Wells-Barnett once said, "I felt that one had better die fighting against injustice than to die like a dog or a rat in a trap."

Few would notice Wells-Barnett's bold move for the parade was about to turn to mayhem. Some of the onlookers, mostly men in town for the presidential inauguration, jeered, "Go back home where you belong." Men surged into the street, making it difficult for the parade to pass. They snatched banners, grabbed at clothing, and tried to climb onto floats. Women were tripped, grabbed, shoved, spat upon, and many heard "indecent epithets" and "barnyard conversation." The men marching in the parade were met with degrading remarks, such as, "Where are your skirts?"

Rather than protecting the marchers, some of the police were amused by the sneers and laughter and joined in. A mass of humanity filled the streets, wearing bowlers and wide-brimmed hats, bundled in coats and gloves. While many policemen turned a blind eye to the marchers' degrading and frightening circumstances, the unexpected heroes of the march were 1,500 Boy Scouts of America.

The Boy Scouts had been invited to the parade in full uniform—knickers, boots, hats, and staves—as volunteers to help with law enforcement. Their organization had been founded just three years earlier. Little did the Boy Scouts know when they agreed to assist the police, they would have to actually defend marchers from police *inaction*. The boys attempted to hold back the crowds and assisted the two ambulances that traveled to and from the hospital for six hours shuttling the one hundred injured. Eventually, Secretary of War Henry L. Stimson authorized the use of a troop of cavalry from nearby Fort Myer to help control the crowd.

Boys' Life magazine featured a four-page article about the Scouts' deeds in its April 1913 issue. The magazine reported that while the police initially told the Boy Scouts to stay behind their lines, the crowd soon overwhelmed law enforcement. Police were begging scouts for help and borrowing their staves. As a young organization, the Boy Scouts of America relished the good press. The *Boys' Life* article concluded, "Washington and its respectable visitors will not soon forget the spectacle of boys in the uniform that stands for learning the principles of good citizenship actually restraining grown men from acting the part of brutes."

Even with the numerous difficulties, many marchers completed the parade route, which ended at the Treasury Building.

The mistreatment of the marchers by both the crowd and the police led to Senate subcommittee hearings with more than 150 witnesses recounting their experiences. The superintendent of police for the District of Columbia lost his job. The committee heard multiple mentions of the heroic Boy Scouts.

Despite the anger and violence, the suffragists considered the march a success, for it was the first national expression of demand for an amendment to the United States Constitution enfranchising women. The public outcry and press coverage after the event helped the suffragists' cause.

The parade reinvigorated the suffrage movement and aided in propelling the country toward the Nineteenth Amendment's ratification on August 18, 1920. With a parade, a vision, and courage, Alice Paul and Lucy Burns reignited a national ardor for the women's vote.

This was America for women when Carolyn Shoemaker became the first dean of women at Purdue University.

3

Artists of Life

Six years after Carolyn Shoemaker was appointed Purdue's first dean of women, Stanley Coulter, Carolyn's former instructor, was named Purdue's first dean of men. Slowly, universities in the United States added the Office of the Dean of Men during the 1910s and 1920s. Administrators were jittery about women on campus, so they made rules and regulations for them and thought a dean of women was needed to guide the girls. The male students were left to their own devices with few rules, so at the outset, administrators didn't think they needed a dean of men.

In 1916, the deans of women united officially and founded the National Association of Deans of Women (NADW), a branch of the National Education Association (NEA). The first annual meeting, organized by Kathryn Sisson Phillips, dean of women at Ohio Wesleyan University, was entitled "What a Dean of Women Is—What Her Duties Are." Gertrude S. Martin gave the key address at the first program and pinpointed poetically what a dean does:

> We are trying to *define* the dean. Some say the dean is just a chaperone—a nice, ladylike person. Others say the dean is a necessary evil, a concession.... Others say the dean is a sort of adjunct to the President, because the President usually lacks at least one of the qualifications for the dean.
>
> The fact is the dean of women is unique! She is expected to teach and do a great many other things. She is preeminently a teacher of the *art of living*. She asks: How many of us are *artists of life* ourselves?

Often when a group of women come together, there is a sisterhood formed that can facilitate change. The collecting of deans of women was no different. In the decades to follow, the NADW would prove to be a lobbying powerhouse and a force of nature as it connected deans of women throughout the country in common goals for females everywhere. Their discussions and resolutions were on cutting-edge topics. They came to define themselves as humanists. Future Purdue deans of women would make their marks and become known throughout the United States through the NADW, later named the National Association of Women Deans and Counselors (NAWDC).

The early deans of women established the foundations of professional practice for student affairs and higher education administration. They developed a body of professional literature, which included journals, research reports, and books. The deans of women at Purdue would write many papers for such periodicals.

The pioneering women of NADW worked hard to "professionalize" the position of dean and to legitimize her role. The deans of women were early champions of the scientific methods of guidance for students. After World War I, their vocation would be termed "student personnel work." They often challenged each other and their campuses to "do the right thing" by women. During their first informal meeting in Chicago in 1903, the country's collective deans of women passed a resolution condemning "gender segregation" in higher education. This cause to condemn gender segregation in universities perpetuates still today.

In "How the Deans of Women Became Men," printed in *The Review of Higher Education*, Robert A. Schwartz wrote candidly of the unfair, demeaning, and stereotypical views of deans of women: "Many of their significant accomplishments have been lost or ignored in compilations of the modern history of higher education. What remains is an unfortunate caricature of deans of women as 'snooping battle axes'—prudish spinsters who bedeviled the harmless fun seeking of their students."

Schwartz also gave his opinion as to why the achievements of deans of women have been disregarded: "This inaccurate view results from the male voice's domination of written and oral histories of American colleges and universities . . . the accomplishments of deans of women have rarely received honest evaluation, validation, or appreciation. Rather, they have been discounted, discredited, or ignored."

Schwartz then imparted women deans their due: "In reality, the deans of women were consummate professionals who anchored much of their work to the academic principles of rigorous research and scholarly dissemination of their findings. Many of the significant and well-established practices of student affairs work and higher education administrations that exist today were first put in place through the work of the deans of women."

Additionally, the deans of men gathered as a group but with a very different mind-set and direction. The first recorded meeting of deans of men took place casually in 1919 "for a discussion of our problems." The men came together because of a concern about student discipline. (Since the male students had few rules, unlike the females who had many, it is understandable that discipline would be a concern.)

Two years later, the gathering formerly organized under the name of the National Association of Deans of Men (NADM). The meetings were social and club-like, sounding almost like a men's society where they could imbibe and smoke cigars, in contrast to the professionalism of the national conferences of the deans of women. According to Schwartz: "The deans of men enjoyed the opportunity to converse, to enjoy local hospitalities and activities, and to regale each other with tales from their campuses. Over time, issues of professionalism, graduate study, and the role of the dean of men were topics of discussion, but they were addressed in a more affable, informal manner with less emphasis on scholarship and research than the deans of women demonstrated in their sessions."

Purdue's own Dean of Men Stanley Coulter revealed his sense of humor when he described his position. Coulter said:

> What is Dean of Men? I have tried to define him. When the Board of Trustees elected me Dean of Men, I wrote to them very respectfully and asked them to give me the duties of the Dean of Men. They wrote back that they did not know what they were but when I found out to let them know. I worked all the rest of the year trying to find out. I discovered that every unpleasant task that the president or the faculty did not want to do was my task. I was convinced that the Dean of Men's office was intended as the dumping ground of all unpleasant things.

CAROLYN'S LOVE OF LANGUAGE AND LITERATURE blossomed in her speeches. The creation of a Community Center for Women began through her articulated words.

During World War I, when women sewed bandages and knitted socks, gloves, and hats to be sent overseas to the men in battle, fifteen sewing machines belonging to war relief organizations were hauled around the city of Lafayette because they had no permanent resting spot where women could congregate and work for civic causes. Carolyn not only thought of the welfare and needs of her Purdue women, but she wanted to help women of her community.

Lucy Eunice Coulter (wife of Purdue's Stanley Coulter) was superintendent of the Industrial School and Free Kindergarten in Lafayette. Members of the Purdue faculty volunteered their services there.

On Valentine's Day that year, Carolyn was asked to speak to the women on the board of this organization. The title of her speech was "Civic Needs." She talked about the necessity of a central meeting place and shelter for girls and women. Carolyn was concerned about women who visited the city from rural farms who spent time on the streets or in a lonely boarding house. There was no common meeting place open to them. Her speech was inspiring and roused the board to purchase a building to serve the community.

The group found a home to purchase at 617 Ferry Street. Carolyn paid $800 into a fund to create the Community House. The Community House Association was formed, and with her large donation, Carolyn was made a life member of its board of directors.

Eventually, the Industrial School and Free Kindergarten became a part of the public school system, and the Community House was used solely for women's society meetings and rented sleeping rooms for women. The YWCA held its first meetings there. In subsequent years, Carolyn's dean of women successors would also heed the call to help women and families of the Lafayette community and foster strong connections to the YWCA.

AS EARLY AS 1913, Purdue's female students were longing for a new residence hall and classroom building to replace the decaying Ladies Hall. Yet it would be years before they would see a new women's residence hall built on Purdue's campus. In the 1919 *Debris* yearbook, a poem called "The Coed's Plea" was printed. In lighthearted rhyme, the women students lamented their need for a new building and how other new structures on campus, such as a new horse barn, received precedence over providing an adequate facility for women.

Inside Ladies Hall, the walls were cracking and chunks of plaster fell into the bread dough the women mixed; the coeds were forced to work in dim light because many of the gaslights were inoperable; and dishpans were scattered around the building to catch leaks from the water pipes. The poem ended with these lines: "And now, Purdue, you wonder why / We're sour and cross today. / It's all because we coeds few / Are treated in this way."

Accompanying the poem printed in the 1919 *Debris*, Carolyn wrote an essay titled "Woman's Building." She said, "The number of girls enrolled in the University has been more than doubled in the past few years." There were 247 women registered, and she attributed the increase to the fact that the women were offered courses that appealed to them, and "we have taken care of our girls." Carolyn continued, "This, in fine, is the Purdue spirit. Progressive? Yes. And we have accomplished it all with no place that is peculiarly our own. But with a Woman's Building with headquarters for our various activities,—well, just watch us and see!"

In 1920, the women were still waiting for their new building, so Carolyn wrote another essay in the *Debris*, ending with words of empowerment: "With the advent of a Woman's Building there will be a new order of things. And with a Dormitory we could beat the world."

Carolyn had established a rapport with the women students she affectionately called "my girls," as is evident in a tribute they wrote to her: "She is sympathetic to the popular activities of the University and is ready to march across the levee at the head of the coeds whenever a college demonstration is to be made—and never is too weary to chaperone a campus dance, even into the 'wee sma' hours.'"

In 1920, women gained the right to vote and Prohibition was instituted. The next year, the Indiana General Assembly passed a bill requiring the governor to select at least one woman among the six appointments to the Purdue University Board of Trustees. The women's suffrage movement had put pressure on all public institutions to appoint qualified women when board positions became available. Indiana Governor Warren T. McCray selected Virginia Claypool Meredith, age seventy-two, as the first female member of the Purdue University Board of Trustees.

Virginia had been a "lady farmer," managing a 115-acre farm in Cambridge City, Indiana, after her husband passed away. She was a nationally known agricultural writer and speaker. At the age of forty, Virginia became a single mother when she adopted the children of her late best friend. Her adopted daughter was Mary L. Matthews, who would become Purdue's first dean of home economics. Mary and her graduate students taught at the Industrial School and Free Kindergarten where Carolyn was a lifetime board member.

During the Roaring Twenties, Virginia was the grand dame of Purdue. With so few women on campus and a rather small University population of approximately 3,200 students, her presence was noticeable at meetings and functions; photos show her with an understated regal air. Nearly always depicted as the only female standing with the other male trustees, she dressed in an ankle-length black dress, a cape, and a matching hat with plumes softly cascading over the brim. She wore black gloves and a scarf with a hefty tassel. Her layers of clothing seemed to weigh her down, for she stooped slightly with her head bowed; however, perhaps, rather than her strata of clothing, it was the enormity of being the first woman on the Purdue University Board of Trustees that pressed upon her. The first woman of any endeavor must set the pace and the example for those who follow in her stead.

At her initial meeting as Purdue's first female trustee, Virginia voted with the board to authorize the construction of the Home Economics Building, a structure that five decades later would be named after her adopted daughter. Once the Home Economics Building was completed, Virginia turned her attention to creating a much-needed women's residence hall.

Carolyn's annual reports during the 1920s referred repeatedly to the need for scholarships, dormitory accommodations, and a women's gymnasium. She continually expressed concern for the number of female students living in town for whom the University made no provision. In 1925, she urged the establishment of housing that would accommodate all freshmen women and thus do away with sorority rush, which she considered one of the worst aspects of college life. Often, women who were not selected for sorority membership withdrew from the University and returned home in humiliation and despair. Later, her successor, Dorothy Stratton, would share Carolyn's aversion of rush and make a change in its structure.

Because women students could not find housing close to campus, they often walked great distances, and in the winter, they walked in the dark in their high-top, heeled shoes. The women often were physically uncomfortable and vulnerable to exhaustion, especially in hot weather. The average outfit a woman wore back then, with its layers of garments, took nineteen yards of material and weighed almost twenty-five pounds.

Virginia and a committee she established to study women's housing recommended to the Purdue University Board of Trustees that Ladies Hall be renovated and used as a temporary dormitory until an adequate women's hall could be erected. The board consented but put just enough money into the project to keep the building serviceable, and Ladies Hall housed fewer than fifty women.

Five years later, the cost for more repairs exceeded what the board was willing to spend, and Ladies Hall was demolished. One of the last of Purdue's five original buildings disappeared. Virginia thought that the demise of Ladies Hall would speed up the construction of a women's dormitory. After all, fifty women had been displaced. She pointed out that most land-grant colleges in the Midwest already offered modern residence halls for women; however, Purdue administrators again leased rooms for female students in local homes, and even Dean of Women Carolyn Shoemaker had to follow suit.

One of the homes was the George Dexter house on Marsteller Street where today's Marsteller Parking Garage is located. This was where Carolyn made her office and home with some of her students.

In 1928, Frank Cary offered $60,000 to build a residence hall for women, which was to be named in memory of his wife who had passed away. The Carys previously had given money for the building of a men's dormitory in memory of their late son. Today, that building is named Cary East, part of Cary Quadrangle.

Virginia was appreciative and thanked Frank Cary for his gift in a heartfelt resolution read to the board. The group assured Frank that they would borrow sufficient additional funds necessary to complete the construction of the women's residence hall. With the go-ahead for the project, Virginia and the other trustees decided they would no longer lease the home for women students on Marsteller Street. As a result, Carolyn lost her office and was given a temporary space in the Engineering Administration Building. It would turn out to be not so "temporary."

The plan was that the women's dormitory would be built on property on what is today called Russell Street. Purdue expected to acquire this land from owner Phillip Russell. Years before, Phillip's parents had donated land to John Purdue for the construction of the University; however, Phillip was not as generous as his parents and did not want to donate the land. The Women's Residence Hall project faced suits and countersuits as Purdue tried to gain control of the Russell property. Frank Cary grew tired of waiting and eventually found another project in which he memorialized his late wife. He built the Jessie Levering Cary Home for Children in Lafayette.

Though Frank would not donate funds to build a women's dormitory, he agreed to give money to build another men's dormitory near Cary Hall. Not wanting to lose a chance at a donation, the Purdue board, including Virginia, agreed that the money would be accepted for the construction of another men's dorm.

The male administration did not place a high priority on bringing female students to Purdue. Virginia had spent nine years working for better housing for women with nothing to show for her efforts, and Purdue's enrollment of women was in jeopardy. Why would women choose to attend Purdue if adequate and safe housing was unavailable? It appears excuses were made. Bids came in "too high," the designated land was caught in a legal battle, and the men in administration wondered how many women would actually be able to afford and want to stay in the new dormitory. Virginia, Carolyn, and the female students they fostered were left in limbo.

While Virginia spent much of her energy on women's residential concerns, she also headed the effort to build Purdue's Memorial Union. Just two months after she was appointed to the board, Virginia was named president of the Purdue Memorial Union Association Board of Governors. She was the principal figure in the design, construction, financing, and management of the building dedicated to the more than four thousand alumni who had served in the Civil War and World War I. Raising money to build the Memorial Union was an ongoing, agonizing process. She led the groundbreaking for the building in 1922, but it was not completed until 1930 when Virginia was eighty years old. This long gap was due to donors who were not honoring their commitments to pay their pledges to finance the construction; however, Carolyn made a handsome donation of $5,000 (the equivalent of $65,000 today), the largest contribution made by a woman.

4

Far Horizons

After the Nineteenth Amendment was passed and women received the right to vote, many suffragists "retired" from activism, but Alice Paul, the famed suffragist who organized the march on Washington in 1913, continued to toil for women's equality. In 1923, Alice announced a new constitutional amendment she authored and named the Lucretia Mott Amendment. It stated. "Men and women shall have equal rights throughout the United States and every place subject to its jurisdiction."

Like Alice, Lucretia Mott was a Quaker. She and Elizabeth Cady Stanton were the organizers of the Seneca Falls Convention in New York "to discuss the social, civil, and religious condition and rights of women." Lucretia was a fluent, moving speaker for human rights who remained composed even before hostile audiences. She was the consummate role model for Alice, and it was fitting that Alice named the amendment after her. In the decades to follow, Alice would work assiduously for the passage of the Lucretia Mott Amendment, which would be reworded and named the Alice Paul Amendment, before it would be termed the Equal Rights Amendment (ERA).

The ERA was introduced in every session of Congress from 1923 until 1972. After Congress passed the amendment nearly fifty years after Alice first introduced it, the ERA ultimately was not endorsed by enough states to be ratified. Every step of the way, each year the ERA was presented and debated in Congress and at statehouses, the National Association of Deans of Women steadfastly supported its ratification.

During this time, female students in higher education sought equality with regard to honor societies. Since women were not considered for membership in most of the men's honor societies, women began forming their own local groups. At Purdue, the Home Economics Society was renamed the Virginia C. Meredith Club in the spring of 1925 to esteem the revered first and only female trustee.

Honor societies and other forms of recognition are vital for a woman's development of ambition. In *Necessary Dreams: Ambition in Women's Changing Lives*, psychiatrist Anna Fels wrote of the two emotional engines of ambition: the mastery of chosen skills and the essential recognition of that mastery by others. In *The Good Girls Revolt* by Lynn Povich, Fels is quoted as saying that women are "subtly discouraged from pursing their goals by a pervasive lack of recognition for their accomplishments." For centuries, women have feared that seeking recognition will open them up for ridicule about how they live their lives, with attacks on most anything, including their popularity, femininity, and motherhood.

Povich states in her book, "But recognition in all its forms—admiration from peers, mentoring, institutional rewards, and societal approval—is something that makes us better at what we do." Fels explained that without it, "people get demoralized and ambitions erode." Thus, on college campuses, women's honor societies were and are crucial to foster female ambition and success.

Mortar Board was the first national organization honoring senior college women. It began with a chance meeting of two women from separate societies wearing identical pins. In the fall of 1915 on the campus of the University of Chicago, a member of the Ohio State University honor society, called Mortar Board, met a member of the Pi Sigma Chi honor society from Swarthmore College. Both women wore lapel pins in the shape of a mortarboard, the tasseled academic cap with a square, flat top worn at graduation ceremonies. The women remarked of their identical pins and realized each represented a different honor society for women with similar ideals and traditions. The main difference between the two honor societies was the name.

Three years later, a founding meeting for the Mortar Board National College Senior Honor Society took place at Syracuse University. Female representatives at the meeting were from Cornell University, the University of Michigan, the Ohio State University, and Swarthmore College. Representatives from Syracuse University also were in attendance, but this university did not choose to join the national organization when it later became Mortar Board.

Years later, Barbara Cook, who would become a Purdue University dean of students, gave her theory on why Mortar Board came to be: "My guess is that women in the early twentieth century were not taken very seriously as scholars or as leaders. In 1916 [*sic,* 1915], women were not yet allowed to vote. So perhaps Mortar Board originated from a feeling of being excluded and isolated as women in higher education."

Many of the traditions established for Mortar Board were taken from the original Ohio State Chapter, including the name, their initiation rituals, and the pin in the shape of a mortarboard with the insignia of three Greek letters—ΠΣΑ (Pi Sigma Alpha)—meaning service, scholarship, and leadership. Barbara Cook said:

> Service as a concept has always been familiar and appropriate to the feminine domain, but surely there was something adventuresome about suggesting to college women in 1916 [*sic,* 1915], that scholarship and leadership were achievable qualities for women.
>
> Although the collegiate fashion of the day was that of secret societies bathed in mysticism and meeting by the hoot of an owl at midnight, there is no evidence that Mortar Board was ever intended to be anything but open and available to both public and academic scrutiny.

With Carolyn Shoemaker's impetus, the thirty-sixth chapter of Mortar Board was chartered at Purdue University in November 1926. Carolyn became an honorary member. That year 631 women were enrolled out of the approximately 3,500 students. A russet suede commemorative scrapbook with leather ties at the binding and a metal Purdue medallion affixed to the center of its cover contains the original handwritten petition for a charter. The mellow gold pages are filled with particulars and photographs about the University. Under the lovely handwritten words "Purdue Facts," the text eloquently states the mantra of the land-grant institution: "Purdue's sole cause for existence is service to the people of the state, not only in the training of young people here on the campus, but in the carrying of information out to residents of the state unable to come to the institution for its advantages."

The scrapbook contains black and white photographs of each "active" and a listing of her activities. Each woman smiles from under her Roaring Twenties hat and drop-waist dress.

The group would provide scholarships to many women who would otherwise be unable to obtain a college education. The money for the scholarships was raised through Mortar Board-sponsored events, such as the "coed bid dance" and the Gingham Gallop held each spring. In subsequent years, each succeeding Purdue dean of women and dean of students would be a member and advisor to Mortar Board.

Today, the national headquarters for Mortar Board is located in Columbus, Ohio, as an affiliate of Ohio State University. In 2014, Mortar Board's third executive director is Jane Hamblin, a Purdue University graduate who formerly worked in Purdue's Office of the Dean of Students.

At the encouragement of the men's athletic booster group, the Gimlet Club, the Purdue Mortar Board organized a junior and senior women's athletic booster club called the Gold Peppers. Adorning their heads, the Gold Pepper women wore gold felt beanies called "pots." The Gold Peppers served as Purdue's pep club.They attended football and basketball games where they sold candy and led the crowds in cheers

In the early years, a newly elected pledge wore a black pot, one gold and one black bobby sock, and a black and gold armband. She carried a cigar box filled with candy and, dangling from a ribbon, a real green pepper gilded in gold leaf. The pledge carried the pepper for days, and often it would rot. After the pledge became a full-fledged active member of the group, she turned her beanie inside out and displayed the celebrated gold side that was decorated with an image of a pepper.

In the stands and on the bleachers the audience was "peppered" with gold pots. After World War II, the women organized veterans' dances known as "Pepper Shakers."

In the 1960s, the Gold Peppers celebrated the end of their yearly activities with a "Smarty Party" to honor high-achieving sophomore women and award an annual scholarship to one of those entering graduate school. The Gold Peppers disbanded in the 1970s. Women and society had changed. Wearing a gold pot was outmoded, and by then, the term had taken on a new meaning in the slang prevalent on college campuses.

Sarah Ely was a member of the Community House Association in Lafayette, where Carolyn was active. Sarah married her boss, Thomas Duncan, who founded the Duncan Electrical Manufacturing Company in 1901 in Lafayette. Duncan Electric produced electrical meters that were used in homes and businesses around the world. Thomas Duncan was an inventor and industrialist who held 150 patents. He traveled to Europe and took a safari tour of Africa in 1922. Upon his return, he wanted to entertain his wide circle of friends with his movies and a lecture about his adventures. He engaged the entire first floor of the Community House for his travelogue, but he found it too small. It was then that he decided to make provisions in his will for the creation of "an adequate hall" for the people of Lafayette. When he died in1929, Duncan left money to the Community House Association to construct a new building where the Victorian house once stood.

A new two-story, redbrick Georgian colonial with stone trim and a slate roof was constructed in 1931. The structure boasted walnut panel walls, marble floors, a balcony overlooking a ballroom, richly decorated meeting rooms, a tearoom, and live-in hostess quarters. As stipulated in Duncan's will, a board of thirty women was to be elected to manage the facility. The regal building still graces Ferry Street, where citizens hold wedding receptions, piano recitals, quilt shows, concerts, art shows, club meetings, and teas. Duncan provided the money for the hall, but it had been Carolyn who originally energized the idea of a community hall back in 1914 through her speech, "Civic Needs."

On March 1, 1933, Carolyn was scheduled to speak at Duncan Hall to the educational and social group called the Twentieth Century Club, but she failed to show. Members of the club attempted to locate her, calling her office and her home in Varsity Apartments, located a block from the Purdue Memorial Union. Unable to contact Carolyn, club members became alarmed, for she seldom missed a meeting in which she provided the program reviewing the latest current literature. The club contacted the office of Purdue's President Edward C. Elliott and spoke with Helen Hand, Elliott's secretary. Helen checked the University calendar and determined there was no record of any engagement to account for the dean's absence. Helen then contacted a janitor at the Varsity Apartments to check Carolyn's home.

The janitor unlocked Carolyn's door that afternoon and found the dean lying on her bed, unconscious. It appeared that she had been stricken while she prepared to retire the prior evening. The newspaper account read: "The lights were burning. The morning milk bottles had not been taken in, and papers at her office, placed under the door, had not been disturbed. Nor her mail touched. She had only one class in English scheduled for 11 a.m. Thursday, and her absence from it had not been reported."

Physicians were summoned, and Carolyn was rushed by ambulance to St. Elizabeth Hospital in Lafayette. The newspaper stated that after her arrival at the hospital, Carolyn uttered a few words to one of the Catholic sisters on staff, which indicated she was partly conscious for a time, but she never spoke again. Carolyn died of apoplexy and acute uremia that night.

Today, apoplexy is referred to as a stroke. Uremia is a condition that results from kidney failure. Some accounts say that Carolyn passed away from nephritis, which is inflammation of the nephrons in the kidneys caused by infections, toxins, or autoimmune diseases. Carolyn had not complained of feeling ill and had gone about her numerous duties as usual, so her sudden passing stunned all who knew her.

The newspaper headline the day after Carolyn's death stated, "Community Shocked by Death of Dean Carolyn Shoemaker." Carolyn's funeral was at Central Presbyterian Church, where she had taught Sunday school. Pastor W. R. Graham said, "The key to the amazing life of service of Dean Shoemaker was selflessness." She was referred to as "a student, teacher, executive, club woman, alert citizen, and 'foster mother' to an ever changing and ever increasing host of young people."

The newspaper said of Carolyn: "She was a deep student of human nature, sympathetic and helpful to all. Her philanthropies were so numerous and extensive that she seemed to overlook completely her own comforts and convenience. From her vast store of literary information and understanding, was able to act as guide and interpreter of books and writers. At the same time her own personality served to awaken new interest in the subjects she discussed."

Carolyn's casket was covered with a blanket of red roses, a tribute from the University she loved. All of the student organizations of Purdue honored their cherished dean with a huge spray of calla lilies and roses. Relatives and University officials asked that all others omit flowers and instead give to the newly established Carolyn E. Shoemaker Scholarship fund. Carolyn was buried in Springvale Cemetery in Lafayette.

Purdue held a memorial service in Eliza Fowler Hall on April 19, 1933. President Elliott presided. He and Harry G. Leslie, the governor of Indiana who was born in West Lafayette, spoke to the crowd of their personal loss.

Marion L. Smith, a student, recounted a story that Carolyn had told during a speech to a group of coeds the previous October. Paraphrased, the story describes a morning when Carolyn was walking down State Street, the main avenue through Purdue's campus, when a child and her mother approached. As they were about to pass, the child recognized Carolyn and spoke to her. The mother did not know the dean. Perhaps the child knew Carolyn from time spent at the New Community House and Industrial School and Free Kindergarten. The mother asked the child who the passing woman was, and the youngster looked up in surprise and said very emphatically: "Why, Mama, she is the mother of all the Purdue girls!"

Dean Emeritus Stanley Coulter spoke of Carolyn, whom he had known since she was a student nearly forty-five years before. He had watched Carolyn metamorphose from student to professor to dean of women. He said:

During all of those years that "faraway' look in her eyes deepened, and those same years brought its interpretation to me. You may have visited Atlantic City. . . . You may have wearied of its meaningless monotony and turned your eyes seaward following the long line of a great pier. There, at its uttermost limit, you may have seen a few, perhaps only one or two, who, utterly unmindful of the gay throngs, gazed steadfastly seaward, seemingly striving to penetrate far, far horizons. What lay beyond those horizons of opportunity for growth and service?

Dean Shoemaker was one of those who constantly gazed upon far horizons. Apparently removed from the bustle and confusion round her, she gazed steadfastly into the future. What did it have for her of opportunity and service and growth? But it loomed larger and larger before her, and she grew into and became a part of those far horizons.

5

Dorothy Stratton Finds a Bible

It was during the Great Depression, as thousands of Americans were unemployed and a decade-long drought helped to create the Dust Bowl, when Dorothy Stratton, age thirty-four, received a phone call. She had just finished her PhD at Teachers College of Columbia University in New York City and was happily employed as dean and vice principal of girls at Sturges Senior High School in San Bernardino, California. The president of Purdue University in West Lafayette, Indiana, was on the line.

Edward C. Elliott invited Dorothy to interview for the position of Purdue's first full-time dean of women. Soon after that fateful call, Dorothy journeyed by train across the parched countryside to Purdue where she was introduced to, as she said, "everybody from the president to the janitors."

It is not clear how Elliott knew of Dorothy. One speculation is that Elliott obtained Dorothy's name through mutual Columbia University connections. Elliott had received an honorary degree from Columbia in 1929. Dorothy received her PhD from that institution in 1932. Perhaps

President Elliott asked his friends at Columbia to recommend someone for the position of dean of women to replace Carolyn Shoemaker.

Decades later, Dorothy said good-naturedly, "I came from California to be looked over." She met with R. B. Stewart, vice president for finance, and Mary L. Matthews, the dean of home economics and the only female dean at Purdue. Dorothy accepted the offered position and became Purdue's first full-time dean of women.

Dorothy was outdoorsy, easygoing, and attractive, with short, dark, wavy hair, thin lips that smiled pleasantly, and confident almond-shaped blue eyes. She wore the latest dresses or two-piece, knit business frocks with cowl necks and shin-length skirts or a herringbone wool blazer over a white blouse. To look at Dorothy was to see a woman comfortable in her own skin.

After Dorothy was offered the dean of women position, she purchased her first car, a $200 secondhand Dodge. Her parents, Reverend Richard Lee and Anna Troxler Stratton, lived with her. The three drove from California to Indiana in the used car, which sporadically lost its brakes during the cross-country trek. The trio discovered late in the trip that "a suction cup had been put in the wrong way."

Dorothy was born on March 24, 1899, in Brookfield, Missouri. Her broad-minded father was a Baptist minister who had been born in Rothville, where Dorothy's grandfather had a large plantation during the Civil War. Her mother was a homemaker from Louisville, Kentucky, who met her husband when he was attending a Baptist seminary there. When Dorothy was growing up with her brother, Richard, the family moved every three or four years to small communities throughout Missouri and Kansas as her father ministered from church to church.

Dorothy entered grade school a year earlier than the average child back then. She said, "I was always very fond of school. In fact, my father took me to visit when I was only five, and I was so crazy about it, they never could get me away. So the teacher finally gave up and let me enroll." Dorothy was a bookworm, spending time in the library rather than with groups of friends who may have seen her as the minister's daughter who would put a damper on their social lives.

Dorothy was a lifelong learner, and her love of reading and knowledge would continue as she lived into the twenty-first century. Her academic prowess was combined with a fervent independence likely fostered as she moved from town to town, school to school, always the new girl in the classroom.

Dorothy had a strong devotion to her parents. She said, "From my father I learned to have an abiding interest in people and to want to be of service to my fellow man. He taught me the importance of intangibles. From my mother I learned to make the most of simple things. She was able to create a happy home atmosphere and to make you physically comfortable on very little. Ours was a typical minister's family. We actually received 'missionary barrels' in Kansas, although none of my friends will believe it. They were good barrels, too."

The term "missionary barrel" is synonymous with used clothing and hand-me-downs. The contents were cast-offs from donors or even foodstuffs. The filled barrels or packages were gifts to help missionaries survive in their work that afforded them little money.

Dorothy was five years older than her brother. She said, "I had to look after him, iron his blouses, take care of him during church services, and final humiliation, occasionally take him out with me on dates!"

As an undergraduate, Dorothy had attended Ottawa University, a Baptist college in Ottawa, Kansas. Dorothy said, "Of course, nobody in (other parts) of the country ever heard of Ottawa University. They think it's in Canada. I've just given up on trying to correct that impression." Dorothy wanted to learn to dance, but dancing was not something that the daughter of a Baptist minister was allowed to do. She managed to pick up a few dance steps where she wasn't supposed to—at her Baptist college. She would go on to chaperone so many dances during her career that she claimed dancing "lost its glamour."

Known in her neighborhood as a tomboy, Dorothy loved to play ball and tennis, with no interest in cooking or sewing. At Ottawa, she played on the school basketball team and won the women's tennis championship in the Kansas Collegiate Athletic Conference. She served on the staff of the school newspaper, the yearbook, and as a member of the student council.

Though most of her friends did not go to college, Dorothy always knew she would pursue higher education. "It was never a question," she said. "I was very academically oriented." After she graduated in 1920, Dorothy was offered a position on the Ottawa newspaper. As a young avid reader, she had dreamed of writing the proverbial great American novel. She said, "I don't know what gave me the idea, but it was there. I don't recall that I expected to go through any apprentice period. I just expected that said masterpiece would spring full-blown from the head of Zeus."

Dorothy turned down the newspaper job in favor of the field of education and moved to Renton, Washington, to teach physical education. She said, "My reception there was a trifle sour. When I arrived, the principal took one look and told the superintendent, 'We surely have picked a lemon this time.'"

During the Great Depression, Dorothy worked to pay off her parents' debts and to put her brother through medical school. "Baptists ministers didn't make much in those days," she explained.

With her zest for learning and her abiding interest in others, Dorothy wanted to discover why people behaved the way they did. In 1923, she enrolled at the University of Chicago for a year of graduate study in psychology. She left with her master's degree and the realization that not even psychology can explain all the "whys" of the human race. She recalled, "I found that employers wanted firstly, a man with a PhD degree; secondly, a man with a master's degree; thirdly, a woman with a doctoral degree, and very fourthly, a woman with a master's degree. Having no money to continue my studies, I went to San Bernardino, California, as dean of girls and vice principal of the high school. I was working under my former principal of the 'lemon' quotation."

In California, Dorothy learned to love the outdoor life in a way that had never been possible before. She soaked in the desert, mountains, and seashore. She loved to look from her office window at Mount San Bernardino, gaining strength and serenity from the peaceful view.

After several years at San Bernardino, Dorothy traveled to Teachers College of Columbia University to study student personnel administration. During her year at the university, she stayed in the International House with students from fifty-seven countries. Early in 1933, she received her PhD and returned to San Bernardino. That's when President Elliott called.

She came to Purdue not only as dean of women, but also as an associate professor of psychology. Her salary was $3,300 a year, about $100 more than she was paid in California.

Even before Dorothy became dean of women, she had accomplished much in a time when few females attended college, worked outside the home, or made a respectable living. Yet for Dorothy, still in her mid-thirties, the best was yet to come. Her life would be filled with accomplishments that inspired other women.

When Dorothy and her parents arrived at Purdue, they were lodged at the Fowler Hotel across the Wabash River in Lafayette. She said, "After having lived in beautiful California, I moved to a seared state [referring to drought-devastated Indiana]. I thought to myself, 'I can't stand it.' The minute I got across to West Lafayette, the people were so nice—so really nice—I changed my mind."

Dorothy was appointed dean in August 1933, and she was given what had been the office of the part-time dean of women located on the top floor of Fowler Hall.

Dorothy said, "The dean preceding me was Carolyn Shoemaker, who must have been a very fine person. I never met her. She had great respect from people on campus."

Dorothy climbed to the top of Fowler Hall carrying a box of her workplace goods and discovered that the Office of the Dean of Women was more like the *Closet* of the Dean of Women. The room was about six-by-eight feet. Tucked away from the accesses of student life, it was a tiny room about to be inhabited by a world of a woman. Dorothy set about moving her files and papers into her new desk. Someone had been given the task of emptying the desk after Carolyn's sudden death. As Dorothy began to arrange pens and paperclips, she opened a drawer and found in its shadowy recesses a book.

Dorothy pulled the book from the drawer, feeling the nubby texture of the cover; the scent of leather preceded the exhumation. It was a Bible. She thumbed through the soft, India paper. The title page indicated that the Bible was a 1901 standard edition, "Translated out of the original tongues." Dorothy thought of her predecessor, whom she had never met but had heard mentioned with great reverence.

Was the Bible inadvertently left inside of Carolyn's desk? Or did the person with the unpleasant task of clearing elect to leave the testaments for the next dean of women?

As the daughter of a Baptist minister, Dorothy was no stranger to the Holy Bible. An analytical thinker, she had her questions regarding its stance on such topics as women and their place. She wrote in 1971 letter, "Aside from the Adam and Eve story, Paul has done more to set back the progress of women than almost any other person. Many people are greatly influenced by Bible references. Probably, we all are, even though unconsciously."

Dorothy placed the Bible back into the drawer and continued her task of cultivating the Office of the Dean of Women.

DOROTHY AND HER PARENTS obtained a house at 825 Salisbury in West Lafayette. Her father worked as a representative for the Equitable Life Assurance Society in the Lafayette Life Building on the courthouse square in Lafayette.

Dorothy's first goal as dean of women was to campaign for a more accessible office. She said of her out-of-sight, out-of-mind alcove, "Students would really have to want to see me to find me." She accomplished the relocation of her office by the "Elliott method," which President Elliott himself described: "First, you ask the president for something, and he says, 'no.' Then you come back and ask again—and he says 'no' again. The third time you come back to ask, you pound on his desk, and he says, 'Oh, go ahead and do it!'"

Dorothy explained that her experience was a bit different than Elliott's take: "Well, it turned out just the other way; it was the president who yelled, and I was the one who went and did it. I was never much of a pounder, but I learned how to operate with Elliott."

Apparently, Dorothy was, indeed, a quick study of the Elliott method, for her office was moved to the ground floor of the Engineering Administration Building, next to the office of the much-revered Dean of the Schools of Engineering Andrey A. Potter and across the hall from Dean of Men Martin L. Fisher, who had succeeded Stanley Coulter. Dorothy said she made every effort to furnish the Office of the Dean of Women to create a friendly, informal, and cheerful atmosphere.

At a 1988 Mortar Board Leadership Conference, recorded on a videotape now stored in the Purdue Archives, Dorothy, then age eighty-nine, spoke to a group of students about her first days as dean of women:

> When I came to Purdue in 1933, of course we didn't have all the things that you have now. We were very simple, and we didn't have very much of anything for women. No university housing, no placement service for women, no bachelor of arts degree in the University. So it was a lot of fun to start from scratch and see what could be done.
>
> The Dean of Women's Office consisted of me, period. No secretary, no staff, just me. I wanted to have the image of the dean of women not to be one of discipline. I thought no intelligent person would spend her life in a job that had discipline at its core, and I didn't want students to say when they left, "I was never called into the dean's office once while I was in the University" and be proud of that.

There were 500 female students at Purdue when Dorothy assumed her deanship. That was about one woman to seven men. She said of the campus, "It was like the old definition of an island—a small body of women completely surrounded by men."

Years later, Dorothy reminisced about what she and her women students lacked, yet also what they possessed in abundance: "We didn't have anything fancy like career counseling. We didn't know what it meant. We didn't have television, drip-dries, or power steering. What we did have was trust in each other, and that was very important."

In Dorothy's 1933 annual report, she shared her most frequently asked question, "Just what does the dean of women do?" Dorothy said her office had two main functions: the first was to ensure that the environment in which female students lived, worked, and played was conducive to development and growth. The second was to be of assistance to the individual student. In short, her office was a clearinghouse for matters pertaining to the welfare of female students. Her annual dean of women report was the first to refer to female students as "women" rather than "girls."

In her leisure time, Dorothy enjoyed shooting baskets in the women's gym. It was there that she befriended a newly arrived graduate student named Helen Blanche Schleman. Helen worked part-time in the Department of Physical Education, refereeing women's basketball games at twenty-five cents an hour while she earned her master's degree in psychology and education. The two women had a lot in common. They had both arrived at Purdue the same year and were well educated, brilliant, athletic—both golfers—and forethinkers. Maybe that's why some people often mistook one for the other. Helen said, "I appeared on campus and everybody sort of bowed and scraped. They were nice and friendly to me. I soon found out that they were confusing me with Dorothy Stratton!"

The National Youth Administration (NYA) had just been established on Purdue's campus. During the Great Depression, many young people could not afford the cost of even a high school education. Taking stock of these grim statistics, Eleanor Roosevelt remarked that she often had "moments of real terror when I think we might be losing this generation." She persuaded President Franklin D. Roosevelt to create the NYA, a New Deal program established by an executive order in June 1935.

The NYA created part-time jobs for high school and college students, and it provided relief and job training to unemployed young people. The goal was to prevent students from dropping out of high school and college due to financial hardship by providing grants in return for part-time work in such places as libraries and cafeterias.

For the female students at Purdue, the NYA initiative was assigned to the Office of the Dean of Women. Dorothy needed a part-time staff member to organize and administer the program. She hired her new acquaintance, Helen Schleman, for the position that paid seventy-five cents an hour. At the time, Dorothy had no idea she was mentoring the next dean of women and fashioning a friendship that would span six decades.

6

Helen Schleman, Born in the Right Moment

Helen B. Schleman said she was born fifty years before her time. What she meant was that she lived during an era when women were not given the same opportunities afforded to men. Yet Helen seemingly grabbed with gusto every life prospect that appeared before her, and her "progressive" thinking about what women could do arrived at the perfect time—when women needed her convictions most.

Helen was born in Francesville, Indiana, on June 21, 1902, to William and Blanche Hollett Schleman. In the summer of 1912 when she was ten, Helen moved with her parents and two brothers, Herbert and Delos, to Valparaiso, Indiana. Her father had been in the harness, buggy, and farm implement business and owned Gas-well Farm. He sold the business and purchased an eight-hundred-acre farm called Breyfogle Ranch. The Schlemans were active in the Methodist Church. Every Sunday morning from spring through fall, Helen's mother brought one or two bouquets of flowers from her garden to adorn the church altar.

Helen's father also owned a real estate and insurance business, the Schleman-Morton Company, and the Valparaiso Home Ice Company, but his real interest was in land development. In the 1920s, he opened several housing developments including, with great pride, Forest Park, a subdivision with several wooded homesites surrounded by a seven-hole golf course. Helen was essentially weaned on golf, and she would live near a golf course for most of her life. She was athletic, as was her younger brother, Delos, who died of a heart problem at age eighteen. Delos was described as a "tall, lanky boy, a good student, but a better golfer."

The Schlemans donated Forest Park Golf Course to the city of Valparaiso in 1947, with the stipulation that it be restored and operated as a municipal facility. Two years later, the course was expanded from seven to nine holes with a clubhouse, and a dedication ceremony was held. William was asked to tee up the first ball. Thirty years later, land was purchased to create an additional nine holes. Another dedication ceremony was held, and among those teeing off that day in 1973 was Helen Schleman.

Helen had a broad, open face with blue eyes. She swept her brown hair away from her high forehead, and when she smiled broadly, her inner zest was unmistakable. To look at Helen was to see woman standing on solid ground.

In 1920, the year women won the right to vote, Helen entered Northwestern University in Evanston, Illinois, because it was relatively close to home and was easy to reach. She claimed that young people didn't receive much guidance as to college selection back then. Helen said, "I had a marvelous four years—garnered two majors, one in English literature and one in philosophy—had a terrible time with organic chemistry—had plenty of time to play tennis, field hockey, baseball, basketball, and golf." Helen was president of the Women's Athletic Association, and she worked with the YWCA, student government, and Mortar Board. The organizations she enjoyed and believed in early on would continue to remain close to her heart throughout her life.

As student president of Northwestern's Women's Athletic Association in 1922, Helen, age twenty, attended the national Athletic Conference of American College Women, held at the University of California over Easter weekend, where she gave a "splendid report." Her talk was on the successful launching of the official national publication of the *Newsletter of the Athletic Conference of American College Women*. Helen was an assistant editor of the student publication and would become the editor the following year.

A newspaper account of the convention tells of Helen's future goals for the Women's Athletic Association and foreshadows what would become her career philosophy for decades to come: "One of the highlights toward local progress, which Miss Schleman advocated for the association, was the taking of a bigger place in shaping campus ideals. 'The WAA has a definite place in campus activities,' she advised. 'We must not only maintain our present standing, but show a marked development at the next national conference in 1927 at Cornell University.'"

Helen's youthful vocal stance on increasing the visibility and power of the Women's Athletic Association for every American college and "shaping campus ideals" occurred at the same synergistic moment when Virginia Meredith and Carolyn Shoemaker were speaking out in the struggle for a women's residence hall to be built at Purdue. Across America, women were plodding along and joining forces to bring females' collective needs to the forefront of higher education.

Helen graduated in 1924 with, as she said, an "AB degree." AB is an abbreviation of the Latin name (artium baccalaureus) for the bachelor of arts (BA) degree. Yet Helen was not actually expected to do something with her degree. Years later, she said in a speech:

> Nobody—not the dean of women, not any of my professors, not anyone in my residence hall—no one, and least of all, I, myself, expected me *to do* anything with my college education. Exposure to higher education was just supposed to make you a better person for your traditional role as wife and mother. No one asked me what I was going to do when I graduated. As far as I know, no one expected me to do anything except to get married, raise a family, be an upright citizen, volunteer my services wherever needed, and live happily ever after.

With these expectations, or *lack* of expectations, Helen graduated from Northwestern with her future in question. Helen recounted, "I had no plans to marry. I had no plans to work. I had no plans—period. What was more, I didn't have a marketable skill in the world. One of my favorite gym teachers suggested that since I liked sports so well, I might go to

Wellesley and do two years of satisfactory graduate work in hygiene and physical education for which I would get a certificate. With that in hand, I might get a teaching job in physical education. So, that's what I did!"

Helen claimed that she had no "marketable skills," but in her position as president of Northwestern's Women's Athletic Association and the speech she gave at their 1922 convention, the seed of her talents was sown. She just did not yet see her own burgeoning abilities. It would take another person to help Helen recognize her potential: Dorothy Stratton.

Helen's two-year graduate course in hygiene and physical education at Wellesley College also had a marked influence on her future career and principles. Wellesley is a highly selective private women's liberal arts college founded in 1870 by Henry and Pauline Durant, who were passionate about the higher education of women. Located in Wellesley, Massachusetts, west of Boston, the organization is a member of the original Seven Sisters, a loose association of seven liberal arts colleges in the Northeastern United States that are historically women's institutions.

Founded with the intention to prepare women for "great conflicts, for vast reforms in social life," Wellesley is known for cultivating women as global leaders and for its influential alumnae, many of whom are among the most accomplished women in the world in a wide variety of fields. Alumnae include writer Nora Ephron, news reporters Diane Sawyer and Cokie Roberts, and Secretaries of State Hillary Rodham Clinton and Madeleine Albright.

Helen became close friends with three other female students in the hygiene and physical education graduate course. They shared a house in the village close to the five-hundred-acre Wellesley campus, verdant with evergreen and deciduous woodlands, open meadows, and scenic Lake Waban. The women wore black stockings and full bloomer gym suits, and they were required to learn precision marching and strenuous Swedish gymnastics. One of the women owned a two-seater, open-air Model T Ford that they all shared. The Model T had to be hand-cranked to start. The four Wellesley women would pile in and make a trip into Boston for Boston Pops concerts or rattle up to Rockport to enjoy the ocean.

This was the Jazz Age, famous for flappers and bathtub gin, but conversely, Helen spent time playing on the Wellesley College Hockey Team and the Boston team in international competition. She and her three roommates shared joint custody of an Irish Terrier named Old Fuzzer, who Helen said "distinguished himself by leading the sedate Wellesley May Day Parade—uninvited!" Helen loved dogs, and Old Fuzzer was one in a long line of furry best friends yet to inhabit her life.

Wellesley did not give a master's degree for the completion of the two-year hygiene and physical education certificate, so Helen completed coursework during two additional years and earned a master of science degree in 1928. Her first job after graduation was at Ohio State University, where she taught in the Department of Physical Education for Women. Some of Helen's summers were chocolate-box, with time spent in stunning settings. She lived the summer of 1929 at Ogontz White Mountain Camp in New Hampshire teaching tennis. Ogontz was a camp for "privileged girls," with log cabins, spacious lodges, and clay tennis courts framed by mountain vistas.

The summer of 1930 was one of Helen's most memorable. She took a trip to Europe. One might say she "drove" from Columbus, Ohio, to England. She and her car were ferried across the Atlantic Ocean and the English Channel. An article about Helen stated, "A car, she discovered, would cover a lot more of Europe than a bicycle."

Two summers later, Helen worked as an assistant manager of one of her father's businesses, Valparaiso Home Ice Company, which made daily deliveries of blocks of ice for the family icebox, the predecessor to the electric refrigerator. Additionally, the company delivered glass bottles of cold milk and cartons of freshly churned ice cream that were placed into small tin boxes kept on customer's front doorsteps and porches.

The stock market had crashed the year after Helen graduated from Wellesley, and America was in the midst of the Great Depression. Jobs were scarce, yet that fact did not deter Helen from shifting gears and looking to other goals. Unlike most, Helen had the backing of her father and his many businesses. After six years at the Ohio State University, Helen decided that physical education was not what she wanted as a permanent career. She quit her position and went home to Valparaiso to work with her father and brother in various business enterprises, but perhaps, ultimately, to finish writing a book.

Practically born with a golf club in her hand, Helen, age thirty-one, penned her knowledge and experience onto paper and, in 1933, wrote, *Group Golf Instruction,* which was published the next year by A. S. Barnes and Company of New York. The manual was considered pioneering in the theory of teaching golf to large groups. Looking back, Helen said, "That was at a time when golf was just beginning to be a very popular game for a great many people. It had always been a rich man's game up to this point, but physical education departments were beginning to teach it to many people in groups, and there needed to be some methods worked out for group instruction."

Helen operated her family's Forest Park Golf Course during the summer of 1933, and she held volunteer classes in group golf instruction for high school girls. She may have been testing the teaching methods she was writing about in her book. That October, after deciding she had better "get back into education," she drove forty miles south to Purdue to enroll as a graduate student in psychology and education.

For many Americans, despair peaked in 1933. It was the worst year for unemployment in the history of the United States. Tens of thousands traveled the road and rail looking for work. Hobos camped in shanties and knocked on families' doors for handouts. The country's banking system was propped up with the United States Banking Act in an attempt to stop panicking people from withdrawing their money. Adolf Hitler became the chancellor of Germany and opened the first concentration camp at Dachau. The country's collective sadness resonated in newspaper headlines, Philco radios, and newsreels that preceded the showing of movie house films like *Little Women*, staring Katharine Hepburn.

Yet an hour's drive from Helen's family home in Valparaiso, the opulent 1933 Chicago World's Fair had opened that summer to celebrate the windy city's hundredth anniversary. A Century of Progress International Exhibition became a "break in the clouds" of America's overcast economy and gave the world a ray of happiness and pomp as people looked toward the future of innovation along the shores of Lake Michigan.

It was during the autumn of 1933 that Helen Schleman, age thirty-one, arrived at Purdue University with degrees from Northwestern and Wellesley, plus a soon-to-be-published book under her belt. She found a part-time job refereeing women's basketball games—a position she said she was lucky to find—and she met thirty-four-year-old Dorothy Stratton. Together, the two women would begin making what would become wide, sweeping marks in history for Purdue and America.

7

If Walls Could Talk

When Helen Schleman arrived at Purdue University in 1933, a residence hall for women was under construction. Set in a peaceful, wooded parcel three blocks west of campus, the long-awaited building became a joyful reality because of a nation's sorrow—the Great Depression. The Women's Residence Hall was built with funds from the Federal Public Works Administration (PWA) and the sale of farmland donated to Purdue by Ophelia Fowler Duhme. Today, the dormitory is named Duhme and is part of an enclave of like residences, a quadrangle, known collectively as Windsor Halls.

The PWA was part of the New Deal, a series of economic programs designed to heal the effects of the Great Depression. The PWA was created through the National Industrial Recovery Act and fostered the building of large-scale public works, such as dams, bridges, hospitals, and schools. It created infrastructure that generated national and local pride in the 1930s and remains vital decades later. The PWA had a rival agency with a confusingly similar name, the Works Progress Administration (WPA), which focused on smaller projects and hired unemployed skilled workers.

Frances Perkins first proposed the idea of a federally funded public works program to President Franklin D. Roosevelt. Perkins was an economist and social worker who became the first female cabinet member in United States history when Roosevelt appointed her Secretary of Labor, a position she held throughout Roosevelt's presidency. Perkins was avant-garde for her day, refusing to take her husband's name when she married in 1913, and subsequently defending her right to her own name in court. As part of her social services career, Perkins surveyed appalling living and working conditions in New York's Hell's Kitchen and witnessed the horrific 1911 Triangle Shirtwaist Factory fire, where trapped young women leapt off window ledges into the streets below. She was appointed to the Committee on Safety of the City of New York and visited workplaces to expose hazardous practices and champion legislative reforms.

Frances' PWA idea, in turn, advanced the realization of a women's residence hall at Purdue University. When Purdue University's Board of Trustees voted in October 1933, authorizing President Edward C. Elliott and board president David Ross to complete plans for the Women's Residence Hall and to apply for financial assistance under the PWA, the vote was unanimously in favor. After thirteen years of striving for a women's residence hall, Virginia C. Meredith, the sole woman on Purdue's nine-member board, was very pleased. And after waiting all those years, work on the dormitory had to commence immediately to fulfill a PWA requirement. The Women's Residence Hall would be built quickly in six months.

The new hall would need a capable and vibrant manager. Dean of Women Dorothy Stratton selected Helen Schleman as director. Dorothy had come to know Helen's strengths and potential as Helen worked in the Office of the Dean of Women, heading up the National Youth Administration initiative. Dorothy said, "Helen lacked self-confidence. She didn't know what she was capable of. If I made any contribution to Helen's life, it was that I gave her some confidence. I helped her know that she could do what she set her mind to doing."

Those who knew Helen throughout her life would not have guessed she ever lacked confidence. Even though she was shy, she became a candid powerhouse with a worldview of equality for all persons, male and female, all colors, races, nationalities, and disabilities. She hated discrimination of any kind, and she would battle against it all of her life.

The Women's Residence Hall was slated to open in fall of 1934. During the preceding spring, an executive memorandum was sent from Elliott's office to the officers and heads of departments of the University to explain the ins and outs of the hiring and overseeing of the director of the hall. The memorandum stated: "It will be appreciated if those interested in the welfare of the women students at Purdue University will cooperate to the fullest extent with the Dean of Women and the Controller in dealing with their respective problems arising from the operation of the new hall."

The flowchart of Purdue's hierarchy was compact in those days. A hand-drawn, updated version was included with the memorandum. The dean of women, dean of men, and controller were on equal ground and reported directly to the president, who reported to the Board of Trustees. Dorothy's immediate and only boss was Elliott. Years later, Dorothy said of the order of command during her time: "The organization was very simple—I reported directly to the president. There were some advantages in those days. None of this going through this one and that one and the other one before you can get to the president. I reported directly to him, and I was an officer of the University."

Helen, on the other hand, had two bosses: Dorothy and Robert Bruce (R. B.) Stewart, the controller and chief financial officer. Dorothy selected Helen as director and jointly, she and Stewart recommended her. Helen had just completed her master's degree when she accepted the position. She would be responsible to Stewart for the business management of the hall and to Dorothy for its social and educational programs. Decades later, Helen spoke to a group of women at a Mortar Board leadership conference and said, "I had two bosses. I had the dean of women and I had the controller of the University, but don't be afraid of that. You have to work a little harder, but you learn twice as much. If you have a chance to take two jobs or have two bosses on the job, take it."

Stewart was Purdue's chief financial officer from 1925 to 1961. He made a striking impact with his excellent management and unquestionable integrity in the handling of Purdue's resources during a time of growth and evolution for the University. Stewart Center, formerly Memorial Center, was named in his honor after his retirement.

Karl H. Kettelhut, whose Lafayette construction company built many campus buildings, worked with architect Walter P. Scholer to design the Women's Residence Hall, which cost approximately $250,000. Scholer visited several colleges and women's schools before drawing up his plans, which used the latest ideas in dormitories to house 125 women.

An *Exponent* article described the hall:

> Of English Tudor design in brick with Indiana limestone trim, the new residence hall will be of fireproof construction throughout and modern in every way. . . . All out-of-town freshman girls will be expected to live in the new girls' residence hall, which will provide among other features, laundry, shampoo room, lounge and reception rooms. . . . The laundry is to be equipped with electric washers and driers. . . . The shampoo room will contain electric hair driers, and the sewing room is to be equipped with machines for those who wish to do their own sewing.

As the construction was underway for the Women's Residence Hall, Stewart's wife, Lillian, was in charge of the interior decorating and selection of furnishings. Lillian had studied interior design at the University of Wisconsin. Years later, R. B. said, "She really helped us. We couldn't afford to hire a decorator." Evidently, Lillian donated her services.

The couple met for five days in Chicago with D. Robertson Smith, a designer from the American Furniture Company of Batesville, Indiana. Smith was an Englishman who had designed the nursery furniture for the Prince of Wales (who became Edward VIII and later the Duke of Windsor, perhaps best known as the King of England, who abdicated the throne for the woman he loved in 1936). The Stewarts did not want the heavy blond furniture used in many public buildings, and instead they selected furnishings with a combination of Tudor and Jacobean design. It appears that Smith's English heritage and the architect's design influenced the Stewarts' decorating choices.

Helen's beginning salary was $1,750 per year. Dorothy arranged for her to have a suite of rooms on the first floor of the residence hall, and Helen paid $350 a year for room and board. Student residents paid about the same. Years later, Helen said, "I'll always remember that R. B. said the reason that he and Dorothy could agree on me [for the position] was that Dorothy thought that I could do the job, and R. B. thought I didn't know anything about it, so he could tell me how he wanted it done."

Being a numbers man, Stewart was happy when Helen kept costs at bay. Helen said, "As long as I could report to R. B. that the daily food costs were less than $1.00 for three meals a day, I got along pretty well. The only difference that R.B. and I ever had on residence hall management was about how much had to be set up in reserve . . . after paying the expenses. My theory was that anything left over should go into social and educational programs within the hall. His theory was that you ought to save more of it. That was our only point of difference."

The day before the semester was to begin in the fall of 1934, the Women's Residence Hall was ready to open barring one detail: the furniture had not yet arrived. Helen, Lillian, and R. B. waited nervously for delivery trucks to appear outside the arched front door. The scent of newly hewn oak and fresh plaster permeated the air. Adding to their angst was the rain that pelted against the diamond-paned windows. Sidewalks had not yet been constructed, and mud surrounded the hall's exterior. Finally, at 5 p.m., truckloads of furniture began to arrive.

Helen, the Stewarts, and a few others worked through the night to arrange the furnishings in nearly 100 rooms. For years, R. B. repeated a story that on that occasion at 4 a.m., he went into one of the rooms and stretched out on a bed. He claimed to be the "first man to sleep in a women's residence hall at Purdue." R. B. was joking, but just the next year another man would actually sleep several nights in the hall—George Palmer Putnam, the husband of Amelia Earhart. Amelia stayed in the Women's Residence Hall when she spent time on campus as an advisor.

The hall was filled beyond capacity, so two small annexes were created to house the overflow, and twenty students had to be turned away. Female students were enthusiastically streaming to Purdue and staying in the hall that looked like a storybook English manor.

In 1937, through PWA funds and donations, a duplicated women's dormitory was created near the first and referred to as "North Hall," making the original building "South Hall." A third women's building was built two years later. By 1951, there were five identical women's halls nestled together on the same plot of wooded land and connected with cave-like tunnels. Collectively, the stately five were named Windsor Halls. Individually, each hall was named after a woman or family who contributed money for construction: Duhme, Shealy, Warren, Wood, and Vawter.

Windsor was designed so that nearly every room in each hall received sunlight at some point during the day. Another distinctive architectural detail of four out of five of the Tudors is that they line up like soldiers. When the lobby doors of Duhme, Shealy, Warren, and Vawter are opened concurrently, one could, hypothetically, shoot an arrow in a straight line through them all.

WHEN DOROTHY BECAME DEAN OF WOMEN, she experienced the culture of sororities and fraternities for the first time. The effects of sorority rush on the female students were difficult for her to watch. "Rush" is a term that comes from a time when sorority and fraternities literally "rushed" to invite "desirable" incoming freshman to live in their houses before another organization got to them first. Dorothy said of sorority rush:

> There are always those who are chosen and those who are not chosen, and I had to deal with those who were not chosen, and this, to put it simply, broke my heart. I just couldn't take this. Here a student came to the University looking forward to it. It is terribly important what your peers think of you when you are seventeen. Either your skirt looks too short or your hair isn't cut right or somebody didn't like you, and you didn't get in. I just didn't think it was fair that a student would come to the University and be treated that way.

At the objection of the National Panhellenic Conference, Dorothy made the decision to establish deferred rush at Purdue. Rush would not take place until the second semester, allowing incoming freshman time to become acclimated to academic life, make friends, and get to know themselves to determine if being a member of a sorority really was something they wanted.

Members of the sororities saw Dorothy's deferred rush plan as a tactic to fill the women's residence halls, but this was not the case. Deferred rush was Dorothy's way of limiting the number of women with bruised self-esteems and increasing the number who garnered self-knowledge. Deferred rush became an example that other universities followed and remained in practice at Purdue for more than seventy years until it ceased in the early 2000s.

Many of the social regulations at Purdue and on most campuses during the first half of the twentieth century were aimed at female students and stemmed directly from the "protectionist" concept, which implied subtly that control of women meant control of men. One of the purposes of the Women's Self-Government Association (WSGA) was the design and enforcement of regulations for women. All female students were automatically members of WSGA. There was no counterpart organization for the men. It appears that there were few rules for the male students and none regarding a curfew calling them in at night. In *Cary Hall, The First Half Century*, a history written in 1984, the first male dormitory of the early 1900s is described as "so despicable that residents 'sneaked in after dark to sleep, and left as soon as possible in the morning.'"

The new Cary Hall was built in 1928, and Lloyd M. Vallely, the first manager, called a meeting of all residents the night before Orientation Week. The historical account conveys Vallely's message to the male residents: "He spelled out his hopes that Cary would become a 'free' organization, with no restrictions placed on members except those necessary for the welfare of so many individuals living together."

Conversely during the mid-1930s, the WSGA printed a handbook with regulations for females that included: "No woman student shall be permitted to leave town to be gone overnight unless given permission by the Dean of Women. Permission to stay away from residence houses overnight shall be limited to two nights per month unless further permission is granted by the Dean of Women. No daytime social engagements with men shall be permitted in residence houses except on Saturday or Sunday. Women students leaving residence houses to be gone after 7:00 p.m. shall be required to fill out in full a W.S.G.A. blank provided for that purpose."

The booklet's introductory sentence was an attempt of the association to pat itself on the back for its "leniency." It stated, "Rather liberal are these rules by which you live, as you'll find by comparison with regulations of other universities." The words are laughable by today's cultural standards.

One may wonder what hard and fast rules beset the women at the "other universities." The practice of "locking up" the women students in order to control the men students would continue into the 1960s, and Helen would be the one to voice the battle cry of change.

The book of regulations for women ended with this declaration: "Landladies and housemothers shall be responsible to WSGA for the enforcement of these rules." Unfairly, one conjures an image of "the enforcer," a matronly woman in a washed out floral cotton dress standing at the door of the residence hall, scowling at her wristwatch as the clock strikes 7 p.m.

In actuality, housemothers were often widows who had a strong desire to do something useful with the second half of their lives. Dorothy instituted "Housemother Training School" at Purdue in 1939, the only one of its kind in the United States. Helen helped organize and implement the training. It was for women in midlife, without family responsibilities, who were looking for a new direction and eager to train for a career to help others. Housemother Training School was directed particularly to women who were asking themselves, "What can I do with the rest of my life?" Women came to Purdue from across the country to learn how to become housemothers during two-week summer sessions. They lived in the Women's Residence Hall while in training. The women would then be hired in sororities, fraternities, cooperative houses, and residence halls on campuses throughout the United States.

In the first half of the twentieth century, widows at the midpoint of their lives had few options for employment. Purdue's Housemother Training School filled a much-needed void for women who had no working experience and were often frightened of where their lives would go next. Housemother Training School gave women confidence, a career, housing, and companionship. "The enforcer" was actually "the empathizer," for the housemother was often like a student's second mom far from home.

8

Amelia Earhart, Cabbages and Kings

Often it takes a brave man in power to step outside the traditional modes invented by males to make possible the advancement of women. Purdue President Edward C. Elliott was the father of two daughters, and he was exceptionally interested in the education of women. Female faculty members at Purdue and most American universities were scarce. Elliott realized that the more professional women to revere and admire amid the redbrick and limestone buildings of Purdue, the more female students would be drawn to its campus. If those role models were world-famous, that would be an added coup.

Purdue had its first full-time Dean of Women Dorothy Stratton, a grand Women's Residence Hall with dynamic Director Helen Schleman, and now the University needed a woman to advise and teach science and put the campus on the atlas around the globe. What better woman than one who piloted her own plane across that globe—Amelia Earhart.

It has been said that Elliott had a flare for the dramatic and was always on the alert for ways to stimulate and inspire students to greater aspirations and accomplishments. A meeting with Amelia sparked a flash of brilliance.

In 1934, Amelia was a speaker at the annual Women and the Changing World Conference sponsored by the *New York Herald Tribune*. By then, Amelia had claimed many flying firsts. She was the first woman to fly the Atlantic Ocean as a passenger. She piloted over the Atlantic alone, and she became the first person to cross twice. Additionally, she set the women's record for fastest nonstop transcontinental flight. Amelia was a successful author and little-known poetess, who took Eleanor Roosevelt on a night flight to go "skylarking" and became a beacon of hope to unemployed struggling families during the Great Depression.

Elliott also was a speaker at the conference, and he was seated next to Amelia at Mrs. Ogden (Helen) Reid's luncheon. Ogden Reid's family owned the *New York Herald Tribune*. Mrs. Reid was the vice president of the newspaper and a good friend with Marie Mattingly Meloney, who introduced Amelia before she spoke. Meloney was one of the leading United States female journalists, having written for numerous renowned publications including the *Washington Post* and the *Herald Tribune*. Both she and Mrs. Reid ran in the same circles as magnificent, powerful women. In the 1920s, Meloney organized a fund drive to buy radium for Marie Curie, the first woman to win a Noble Prize, and she was a friend and confidante of Eleanor Roosevelt. Meloney announced Amelia: "I present to you evidence against a 'lost generation.' For I remind you that no generation which could produce Amelia Earhart can be called a lost generation. She has set the pace for those of her age and her time. She has never been content to rest on her laurels. She has worked, and is working, and will continue to work hard to further the science to which she has dedicated her life."

Amelia's introduction alone could have been the flicker to fan a flame in Elliott's mind. An idea crystallized, and later that evening Elliott dined with Amelia and her husband, George Palmer Putnam, at the Coffee House Club in New York. The private social club was located in the Hotel Seymour, where the couple lived in the theater district. Established in 1914, the name of the club was a nod to the coffee houses that first appeared in London and were "patronized by all the wits and talent of the town." The club was not pretentious but intentionally "very simple and cheap." Some of the early members were Winston Churchill, Douglas Fairbanks, Herbert Hoover, and Purdue alumnus George Barr McCutcheon.

Putnam described Elliott in his book, *Soaring Wings,* written in 1940 after Amelia's death. In the chapter he titled simply "Purdue," Putnam states: "He is a lean, powerful man who combines the brisk attributes of a dynamo with the important qualities of scholarship and human vision. He has a habit of referring to himself, with humorous deprecation, as just a Hoosier schoolmaster, but no gentleman from Indiana ever knew his way about more competently than Dr. Elliott."

Putnam goes on to write about the Coffee House Club setting in which a fateful deal was struck between Amelia and Elliott: "That evening we three had to ourselves what I imagine is the most civilized and homely clubroom in America. We sat at a little table in that first-floor front room with its books and paintings, the grand piano and diminutive stage where some of the most lively capers of theatrical tomfoolery in our time have been presented . . . the setting was superlatively pleasant for the launching of any project."

After the three ate dinner, Putnam and Amelia sat on a clubhouse couch while Elliott sat in a chair facing the couple. He smiled and got to the point: "We want you at Purdue."

"I'd like that," Amelia said, without hesitation. "If it can be arranged. What do you think I should do?"

Elliott told Amelia that Purdue had six thousand enrolled students, of whom eight hundred were women. He said, "We've a feeling the girls aren't keeping abreast of the inspirational opportunities of the day nearly as well as might be."

For two hours into the night, the three discussed the idea of Amelia coming to Purdue and how she could work with the female students. Then Elliott had to catch a midnight train from Grand Central Station to head to a morning conference. The plan was settled. Amelia would spend as much time as she was able at Purdue, which for such a busy woman would total about six to seven weeks out of the academic year. For Amelia, one of the attractive qualities of Purdue was that it was the only university in the United States with its own fully equipped airport for day and night flying. Amelia would have a free hand in "ventilating" her philosophies to Purdue's women students as a counselor and also as an advisor in aeronautics.

In June 1935, Elliott announced the appointment: "Miss Earhart represents better than any other young woman of this generation the spirit and the courageous skill of what may be called the new pioneering. At no point in our educational system is there greater need for pioneering and constructive planning than in education for women. The University believes that Amelia Earhart will help us to see and to attack successfully many unsolved problems."

That fall, Amelia became a visiting faculty member at Purdue University and began her friendship with Dean of Women Dorothy Stratton and Women's Residence Hall Director Helen Schleman. Years later, Helen said of Elliott's methods:

> We used to joke, albeit very respectfully, that sometimes President Elliott hired a person he knew would be great to have on campus and then wrote the job description later. Sometime this aspect of the agreement between the university and the new personality, if it happened to be a feminine one, fell to the Dean of Women to fashion. This was largely true in the case of Miss Earhart. Dean Stratton, with her rapport with student groups of all kinds, saw to it that women students had all possible opportunities for contacts with Amelia Earhart.

On September 21, 1935, Dorothy wrote a letter to President Elliott outlining how she believed the aviatrix could be most effective on campus. She suggested that Amelia meet informally with students as well as talk to groups. Amelia could be of service through conferences with individuals and with families, where she could highlight new progress and opportunities for women. Dorothy penned:

> It seems to me that one of the best ways to provide for informal student contacts with Miss Earhart would be for her to live in the Women's Residence Hall during at least part of her stay on the campus. . . . In order to introduce Miss Earhart informally to the campus, it would be my suggestion that the Women's Self-Government Association and the Student Senate arrange a meeting in the Union Building. . . .
>
> Miss Earhart has no doubt made considerable study of the careers for women and would welcome opportunities to discuss this problem with students.

Helen wrote Amelia at her home at the Hotel Seymour in New York City on September 7, 1935, inviting her to stay in the Women's Residence Hall. It is curious that Helen corresponded with Amelia prior to Dorothy sending her letter to Elliott that suggested Amelia live in the residence hall. Helen sent copies of her letter to President Elliott and Dorothy. She wrote:

> My Dear Miss Earhart,
>
> The Women of the Residence Hall should like to extend to you an invitation to be their guest while you are in Lafayette. We have a very nice guest room with private bath, located on the first floor, and we should be very glad to have you use this room at your convenience while you are with the University. We thought perhaps that such an arrangement might give you the opportunity of knowing the freshman women particularly well and we are sure that they would gain much from whatever casual contact they might have with you while you are in the house as a guest.
>
> All of the women of the University are looking forward to your coming and we of the Residence Hall should feel most pleased to have the privilege of entertaining you.

Helen secured a garage on campus to house Amelia's eye-popping car. Decades later, Helen described Amelia and commented on her automobile, which had been manufactured by the Auburn Automobile Company in Auburn, Indiana:

> Those of us who lived in the only women's residence hall at the time . . . were the luckiest of all. The opportunity to know her, even a little bit, is one of my most cherished memories. What was she like? What endeared her to all of us? . . . I always think of her as a beautiful woman—tall, willowy, and very graceful in movement. She could and did wear any kind of clothes with grace and ease, but I remember best in her everyday clothes that she wore on campus and round the hall at mealtime.
>
> She was probably the first woman who ever wore slacks on the Purdue campus with impunity. I see her in my mind's eye in impeccably tailored brown flannel slacks, a small figured "coordinated shirt, open at the collar, and a brightly colored handkerchief knotted around the throat. The shoes were soft brown leather, low-heeled. If it were cool, she wore a

> soft brown leather jacket. In those days, this was considered somewhat "mannish" attire, but Amelia came across as feminine and attractive. In fact, whether she was in a long evening dress or in this typical workday outfit, the word one heard was "glamorous." It fitted perfectly. I've also thought, too, that the long, sleek grey Cord sports car that she drove enhanced this image. And flying, of course is still glamorous, even though we are apt to take it for granted.

The Auburn Automobile Company, with its stylish headquarters in northeastern Indiana, formed Cord Corporation in 1929. The Cord was marketed as a world-class car that provided performance and style. Clark Gable and Babe Ruth also owned Cords.

Amelia saw her role at Purdue as an exploration in professional needs and the development of new fields for women students. She was a proponent of matching a student's natural skills with his or her course of study and profession, and she voiced her resolve to Purdue faculty. Amelia expressed her hope that the time would come when psychologists would determine a child's bent at preschool age so as the child wouldn't waste time studying and working in the "wrong direction."

Though not a mother, Amelia sensed that in the heart of every child, the seed of their future germinated. This deep understanding may have come from her girlhood experiences. As a youngster, Amelia played in her backyard on a flying Dutchman, a leg-propelled merry-go-round; she zipped down steep, icy hills on a sled; and she built her own roller coaster—all in an attempt to satisfy a calling that summoned action steadfastly from her core.

Amelia was glad to be associated with Purdue. She said, "It is my kind of school, a technical school where all instruction has practicality, and where a progressive program for women is being started, too." Amelia's office was set up near Dorothy's in the Office of the Dean of Women, which was "attractively furnished," where she would meet female students for "heart-to-heart" career discussions.

Amelia sent out a questionnaire to women students to explore their post-scholastic plans. She wanted to help Purdue's faculty to develop appropriate courses and to help the women clarify their thinking about goals. Student Miriam Beck described Amelia: "Tall, skinny, handsome, tousle-headed, smiling, the students were transported with delight, and even the most skeptical of older residents charmed."

Purdue's first annual career conference for female students was held in 1935, and Amelia spoke on the findings from her questionnaire. She began her talk by referring to a previous speaker's remarks—negative words that women still hear in the twenty-first century. Amelia said, "Mrs. Woodhouse apologized last evening for ending her talk on 'Why Women Fail in Business.'"

Amelia continued with some positive reflections from the questionnaire. She said that 92 percent of the women who answered planned to work after leaving college, and the reasons given for seeking employment were not economic necessity, as one might think during the Great Depression years, but to achieve professional success. The second most popular reason for working after college was to attain personal independence; and the third was economic necessity.

Amelia said, "These results are very interesting, since women as a whole have not had enough experience to know the joy of independent work as men know it. All too often women have had to bury what they had of the creative in routine tasks which have not brought them even the reward of a little spending money of their own."

Amelia also learned that those women who did not have the experience of earning their own money voted more strongly for personal independence than those women who had earned money. Amelia said, "Working for pay gives a truer measurement of the individual outside the sympathetic circle of the home, a measurement women have been escaping a long, long time."

In all likelihood, Dorothy and Helen sat in the audience as Amelia spoke at Purdue's career conference. Amelia's remarks foreshadow the career that was yet to be for Helen. In decades to come, Helen would conduct surveys, give speeches, and create strategies to help Purdue's female students think about their lives and plan their career goals. Amelia said of her feedback:

> The fifth question was, "If you were the wage earner and your husband ran the home, would you consider his work financially equivalent to yours?" Sixty-seven percent said yes, thirty-three percent said no. . . . I wonder if the wife would not soon think her husband had the easier task. Imagine yourself, every one of you who answered the question

> affirmatively coming home from a long day's work and saying to your husband, "Well, my dear, what did you do today?" "Oh," he would reply, "I washed the dishes, dusted, planned the meals, made a cake, and was just going to do some ironing, when Mr. Jones came by on his way to market. He asked me to go along, so I did, and bought some new towels. Then I called up Mary's teacher and told her she was marking Mary too low in arithmetic. Then I fed Junior, and dinner's ready now."
>
> The only estimate I have on the value of a housewife's services, just as a housewife, mind you . . . is $500 a year.

Only 21 percent of Purdue's women students planned to work after marriage in 1935. The reason given for not working was that it would interfere with managing the home. Amelia took the opportunity to pointedly address the reasoning behind the statistic to her captive audience of women: "Again, I know it is very hard to look ahead and see yourselves as married women of forty, with your children away at Purdue, your husband busy with his work, and you with no particular interest but the four walls of your home. My hope is that none of you who decide so positively that women should under no circumstances work after marriage will not be victims of your present outlook."

Amelia ended her talk with a paragraph that rings familiar today and causes one to think the world is a slog for change: "A secondary answer to question ten was the large vote for the husband's taking an equal part with the wife in running the home, if both were employed outside. This last reply may point a prophetic finger to what may be the ideal state, that is, when both husband and wife earn and are jointly responsible for the home (of course, with credit on the ledger for the wife who bears children)."

Helen was unaware of her destiny as she sat in the audience of the career conference listening to the brilliant, brave, prophetic Amelia Earhart. Helen would carry Amelia's mantle far into the twentieth century, urging Purdue's women students to plan the full span of their lives and realize their potential, long after the aviatrix would be lost at sea.

Women students came to know Amelia personally during mealtimes in the Women's Residence Hall. Her husband wrote in *Soaring Wings* of the fun she had "with a different group of girls sitting at her table each time." The young women vied for dining spots close to their heroine, and they peppered her with questions. Putnam also noted, "She had a room in one of the halls, too, and was right among girls 'where they lived,' more senses than one."

Dinner was a formal affair. Helen led the women, clad in their dresses and nylons, into the dining room, and a prayer was delivered in song. James R. Brown, a 1938 mechanical engineering graduate, worked in the dining room. Years later he said, "I still recall the first night, as it was my duty to start the singing. The waiters were stationed around the room and were taught to sing also. It seemed as though I was singing a solo. It took several days before the girls joined in."

People wondered how Amelia, so independent, could fit into the rigid life of a women's dormitory, yet, according to her husband who also stayed in her suite, she enjoyed every minute of her sojourn with the coeds. Putnam wrote in his book, "Sometimes she absent-mindedly broke the rules. She came to dinner once in her flying clothes, and the freshmen waited ecstatically to see if she wouldn't be sent back to get properly dressed for dinner. Very early in the proceedings she asked if she could have buttermilk—whereupon calls from the student body for buttermilk increased fortyfold overnight."

The buttermilk was ordered from the Purdue Creamery, and the sudden increase in demand caused some quick reordering of supplies. Formal dining called for proper etiquette. Helen recalled, "One thing you were supposed to do was keep your elbows off the table. Amelia's posture at table, when she was deep in conversation, was apt to be sitting forward on the edge of her chair—both elbows on the table and chin cupped in hands. Naturally, the question was, 'If Miss Earhart can do it, why can't we?' The stock reply was, 'As soon as you fly the Atlantic you may.'"

Students were not allowed to leave the dining room until all had finished eating. After dinner, many followed Amelia into Helen's suite of rooms, just outside the dining room. Amelia sat on the floor, and the women gathered around to talk and listen. She was "adaptable, easy, and informal." This was the time when Helen and the students came to know the real Amelia—her beliefs, hopes, and dreams.

The conversations invariably centered around Amelia's conviction that women had choices about what they could do with their lives. She said women could be engineers or scientists; they could be physicians as well as nurses; they could manage businesses as well as be secretaries to the managers. She believed in women's intelligence, their ability to learn, and their ability to do whatever they wanted to do. Amelia saw no limitations. On pages 228–29 of *Soaring Wings*, she is quoted:

> After all, times are changing, and women need the critical stimulus of competition outside the home. A girl must nowadays believe completely in herself as an individual. She must realize at the outset that a woman must do the same job better than a man to get as much credit for it. She must be aware of the various discriminations, both legal and traditional, against women in the business world. . . . If you want to try a certain job try it. Then if you find something on the morrow that looks better make a change. And if you should find that you are the first woman to feel an urge in that direction—what does it matter? Feel it and act on it just the same. It may turn out to be fun. And to me fun is the indispensable part of work.

In the next decade, both Dean of Women Dorothy Stratton and Director Helen Schleman would "find something on the morrow" and make unprecedented career changes. Dorothy and Helen would experience their share of firsts. And they would most certainly have fun.

Helen said of Amelia, "There was no question that she, through her own achievements and persuasiveness, was an effective catalyst to heretofore unthinkable thoughts for all of us."

In *Soaring Wings*, Putnam wrote of his wife's "favorite thesis that men have need—among other things—of domestic education." Amelia said to women students:

> You may find your own fun in what is called "a man's work." I don't like these discriminations between men's work and women's work. There is too much arbitrary division between the two. But we have to accept these separations until women catch up with the procession. . . . As it is, men enter into marriage with little training in domestic economy, know little

> about food and how it should be prepared, little about child-training and their duties as parents. What, I wonder, is going to be done about all that. Perhaps some of you will have an idea.

These voiced "unthinkable thoughts" were not wanted by some. Word spread around campus as to what Amelia was telling female students. A "prestigious men's senior honorary group" (perhaps Iron Key) asked for a meeting with Amelia. The purpose of the meeting was to protest her counseling practices. Amelia pressed the young men for their reasons as to why she shouldn't talk about high aspirations, many choices, and such for women. Their reply: "It's hard enough to get the girls to marry us, as it is."

It was student Marian Frazier who Putnam said "drew a picture of [Amelia] as I like to think of her in her university tour of duty." Frazier said:

> One night I was sitting in my room studying, and Miss Earhart stuck her head in the door and asked if she could borrow my pen. She said, "I'll bring it back in a sec," just like any girl would do. I guess I couldn't keep it to myself, because, when she did bring it back, there was a bunch of girls in my room—just to get another look at her. But really, you know, I don't think she gets enough sleep. She's terribly busy. I often hear her typewriter clear up to midnight.

Amelia's self-contained dream was to become a poetess and writer. She savored words as much as she did soaring airborne. When she wrote of flying, she melded her loves: "After midnight the moon set, and I was lone with the stars. . . . The lure of flying is the lure of beauty, and I need no other flight to convince me that the reason flyers fly, whether they know it or not, is the esthetic appeal of flying."

Often, the reason writers write, is the esthetic appeal of writing.

By the time she was at Purdue, the artistic and progressive Amelia had written two nonfiction books, chapters for several children's tomes, and stories on aviation for numerous magazines and newspapers, such as the *New York Times* and the *New York Herald Tribune*. For a short interval, she was aviation editor for *Cosmopolitan* magazine, answering readers' questions about flying. But her cloistered poems and short stories were her heart's fancy. She had written many drafts before she became a famed aviator. A treasure-trove of Amelia's papers is now housed in the George

Palmer Putnam Collection of Amelia Earhart Papers at Purdue University. Putnam wrote of his wife's writing: "At one time and another, [Amelia] wrote many fragments of verse, for she found deep pleasure in building little images with words. That aspect was very private—almost secret."

After Amelia's first stay on Purdue's campus, her husband, who was also her promoter, typed Helen a letter on December 9, 1935, on headed stationary printed simply with capitalized words: AMELIA EARHART. Putnam wrote:

> Dear Miss Schleman:
>
> Miss Earhart has asked me to write and thank you on her behalf for your hospitality and for all your friendly helpfulness. Unfortunately this last week she has been ill—laryngitis which compelled the cancellation of three lectures—and today she is shoving off for a fortnight in New England. So . . . she at least wants you to know how greatly she appreciates all you did for her and has asked me to pitch-hit as a correspondent.
>
> By the way, I note in a *Kansas City Star* interview that some of your girls "felt sure this was the first night Mr. Putnam had ever spent in a woman's dormitory." You can assure them that they are correct!

STUDENT HELEN HALL, who was president of the Women's Self-Government Association (WSGA), had frequent talks with Amelia. Hall said to a reporter for the *Indianapolis Star*, "You should have seen her at the waffle supper at Dean Stratton's one night. She curled up before the fireplace just like one of the girls."

There was no dining service at the residence hall on Sunday evenings, so often Dorothy invited Amelia to her home for dinner, even though Dorothy did not cook. Dorothy and Amelia had much in common and developed a friendship, both being bright, independent advocates for women. Amelia was one year older than Dorothy. In later years, when Dorothy's good friend Sally Watlington heard Dorothy invited Amelia for dinner, she was fascinated. Sally knew Dorothy disliked cooking. Sally said, "Dorothy, you did not have her over for dinner." To which Dorothy replied, "I did, too. I cooked waffles."

Waffles, it appears, were Dorothy's specialty. Perhaps she used Amelia's recipe. An October 1936 *This Week* magazine issue ran an article entitled "Ace-High Dishes: Amelia Earhart, Feminine Ace of the Air, Takes a Successful Flyer in Waffles and Sunday Night Suppers." It included Amelia's recipe for sour cream waffles. The article states that Amelia likes to cook but has little time to do so and, "'She makes extremely good waffles,' says Miss Earhart's husband."

When people asked, "What did you talk about with Amelia?" Dorothy would invariably say, "cabbages and kings." Ever lean with her words and always to the point, Dorothy was secretive about her conversations with Amelia. Although in a 1999 interview on her one hundredth birthday, Dorothy revealed an intriguing tidbit: "[Amelia] was interested in a lot of things including extrasensory perception. She believed it was possible."

"Cabbages and kings" is a phrase from the poem "The Walrus and The Carpenter" in *Through the Looking-Glass and What Alice Found There* by Lewis Carroll. The verse reads:

> "The time has come," the Walrus said,
> "To talk of many things:
> Of shoes—and ships—and sealing-wax—
> Of cabbages—and kings—
> And why the sea is boiling hot—
> And whether pigs have wings."

Oh, to have been a fly on Dorothy's wall, when she and Amelia ate waffles and talked of many things.

9

Lillian Gilbreth, the One Best Way

The same year Amelia Earhart became an advisor at Purdue, another famed woman came to campus—Dr. Lillian Moller Gilbreth. President Edward C. Elliott had heard Lillian speak at the same Women and the Changing World Conference where he had seen Amelia. Lillian and Amelia often found themselves in the same spheres, as both were admired around the world. They appeared together in Ida Tarbell's September 13, 1930, "Fifty Foremost Women of the United States," a list of women defined as having done the most to advance the country's welfare. The list also included suffragist Carrie Chapman Catt and birth control pioneer Margaret Sanger.

Alas, most accounts of her initially focus on the number of children she bore, but Lillian, while loving and rearing her gaggle of Gilbreths, also birthed extraordinary milestones in engineering, even by today's standards. Lillian would become Dean of Women Dorothy Stratton's greatest influence.

Lillian was a model of acumen and caring as one of the world's few female authorities in industrial engineering and management. She was internationally known for her contributions in the field of motion study, work simplification, and psychology as it applied in industry, the home, and the world of the physically disabled. Her quest—as she studied individuals' actions in the workplace and the home environment—was to find "the one best way," the most efficient time- and work-saving method to complete a task. This was breakthrough work that she and her husband had shared before his death.

"Anyone can make a problem complicated," Lillian said. "The real achievement is to make it simple."

The Gilbreths developed the concept of "therbligs," a term that is "Gilbreth" spelled backward. Therblig is the name the couple gave to the smallest unit of work motion. For example, to check off a box on a form, you need to look for a pencil, reach for the pencil, pick it up, adjust your grip, move the lead to the paper, make a check mark, move the pencil to its resting place, and put it down. Each of these tiny steps is a therblig. The Gilbreths defined eighteen different therbligs, each with its own symbol and color, which they used to produce motion charts. They were the first to use motion pictures to study timed units of work and find ways to eliminate unnecessary therbligs from tasks.

In 1915, as a mother of seven children, Lillian earned a PhD in philosophy from Brown University. From 1911 to 1920, between having babies, she collaborated with her husband to write several classic books on management, which incorporated Lillian's knowledge of psychology along with engineering, including *Motion Study, A Primer of Scientific Study,* and *Fatigue Study.* Frank shopped for publishers and resented the fact that the manuscripts with only his name were quickly accepted, but manuscripts with both his and Lillian's name found no market. Macmillan finally published their co-authored books, provided Lillian's name was represented only by initials and the publicity would not include the fact that she was a woman. In her book *As I Remember,* written in 1941 and published in 1998, Lillian wrote, "This disturbed feminist Frank more than it did Lillian."

Lillian would be designated as the American Women's Association's "First Lady of Engineering" and "Woman of the Year" in 1948, and she was the first woman to receive the Western Society of Engineers' Washington Award, given previously to such men as Orville Wright, Herbert Hoover, and Henry Ford. Lillian was the first woman elected to the National Academy of Engineering in 1965. Yet this scholar, industrial pioneer, and author, who was recognized by more than twenty universities with honorary doctoral degrees, seems today to be most widely known for one thing: she was the mother of twelve children. At age eighty-one, the Industrial Management Society named her "Mother of the Century."

Lillian's organized and regimented family life was humorously depicted in the book *Cheaper by the Dozen*, written by two of the Gilbreth children in 1948. The successful book became a movie two years later with Clifton Webb, an Indianapolis native, playing Frank Gilbreth and Myrna Loy portraying Lillian. A remake decades later staring Steve Martin and Bonnie Hunt was radically different from the original best-selling book and charming film. Lillian's accomplishments after her husband died unexpectedly in 1924 are only suggested at the end of the original movie.

Lillian was thin, yet vigorous, with red hair and an easy, compassionate smile. She met Frank while studying for a doctorate in psychology in Boston. They were married in 1904 when Frank, a mechanical engineer, was thirty-six years old and a prominent contractor-builder who had started as an apprentice bricklayer. He had already invented the gravity mixer for cement and the moving scaffold that keeps bricks and wall always in line. Today, Frank is considered the "Father of Management Engineering."

In the first weeks of their marriage, Lillian became intensely interested in Frank's work in time and motion study. Ever the planner and precision man, Frank spelled out to "Lillie" on their honeymoon what he wanted in offspring.

Lillian said, "When my husband first told me he wanted to have six sons and six daughters, I asked how on earth anybody could have twelve children and continue a career. But my husband said, 'We teach management, so we shall have to practice it.' Over a seventeen-year period we had our children—all planned, I assure you."

Time management was instituted to raise the Gilbreth children. As *Cheaper by the Dozen* expresses so endearingly, at the "old but beautiful Taj Mahal of a house" in Montclair, New Jersey, where the family lived, there was a daily assembly call. On Sundays, "family council" was held to work out the collective budget and take offers from the children on who would perform household tasks, with pay to the child who submitted the lowest bid. When several of the children had tonsil troubles, the Gilbreths put efficiency into action, and all "twelve" of the children had their tonsils removed at the same time. Twelve was the operative word, yet the number is deceiving.

Everything about the book plays on the "dozen" theme, from the title, the jokes, the dialogue, to the symmetry—six boys, six girls. While Lillian and Frank did have a dozen children, there never were twelve children at one time. Mary died of diphtheria in 1912 at age six, five days before the sixth child was born.

There's no mention of Mary's death in *Cheaper by the Dozen.* Authors Frank B. Gilbreth, Jr. and Ernestine Gilbreth Carey tiptoe around mentioning the passing of their sister, and it takes an alert reader to notice. Perhaps Mary's death is not mentioned outright because neither Lillian nor Frank mentioned it in real life. In *Time Out for Happiness,* Frank Jr.'s account of his parents, he wrote, "Neither Frank nor Lillie ever discussed Mary again, at least in the presence of the children. . . . For years thereafter, if one of the younger children asked Mother about Mary, she'd do her best to answer calmly, and then retire hastily to her room, with her shoulders shaking in sobs."

In *As I Remember,* Lillian wrote that Mary's death "was an experience an understanding psychologist might possibly have adjusted, but it was not adjusted, and left a permanent scar."

In the 1949 biography *Frank and Lillian Gilbreth: Partners for Life,* Edna Yost wrote of Frank's grieving, saying it "was not the normal reaction of a man to death, for this death was his first forced admission of failure in a project to which he had given his utmost." A theme in *Cheaper by the Dozen* is that illness was considered a weakness. Thus, Frank headed illness off at the pass, and he had all the children's tonsils removed at one time, even if all did not have tonsil plights.

Lillian wrote of her husband's response to Mary's passing: "Frank insisted on trying his techniques, but it was no use. . . . For the first time in his life [he] faced a situation which he could not master."

The death of his daughter and his attempt to engineer his grief may have been Frank's greatest perceived failure in finding "the one best way."

Frank had a heart condition and carried "stimulants" with him at all times in case he had an "attack." Both he and Lillian were to attend conferences in Europe the summer of 1924, where Frank would speak: the Power Conference in London and the First International Management Congress in Prague. Three days before he was to sail to Europe, Frank walked to catch a commuter's train for New York to update their passports. Before he left, Lillian brushed specks of dust from his coat, and Frank said in his usual chipper style, "The pat of finality!"

A short time later, Frank telephoned from the station. He had forgotten their passports. Lillian put down the phone to look for the documents. Frank said, "All right. I'll wait." When Lillian returned, the line was silent. She jiggled the receiver but heard nothing. Frank Gilbreth had collapsed in the phone booth and died.

Two days after Frank's death, shell-shocked Lillian called a meeting of the "family council." She told the children, who ranged in age from two to nineteen, that they did not have much money. Most of it had been invested in the couple's business. The family could move to California to live with Lillian's mother, or there was an alternative. If the children could pull together, sacrifice, and take care of themselves and each other, Lillian could go ahead with their "father's work." The vote was unanimously in favor of Lillian carrying forth the couple's shared professional passion in the research of motion study.

In June of 1924, Lillian, age forty-six, sailed for Europe with a group of eminent American engineers and their wives. Lillian would give Frank's scheduled speeches at the overseas conferences. Unlike the other women on board wearing their long white summer dresses, Lillian wore black. Her life had changed in a phone booth.

Lillian's future floated on the waves before her. For the next fifty years, she would carry on the Gilbreth scientific mission of motion study, which dovetailed with family life.

In *Cheaper by the Dozen,* Frank Jr. and Ernestine wrote:

> There was a change in Mother after Dad died. A change in looks and a change in manner. Before her marriage, all Mother's decisions had been made by her parents. After the marriage, the decisions were made by Dad. It was Dad who suggested having a dozen children and that both of them become efficiency experts. If his interests had been in basket weaving or phrenology, she would have followed him just as readily.
>
> While Dad lived, Mother was afraid of fast driving, of airplanes, of walking alone at night. When there was lightning, she went in a dark closet and held her ears. When things went wrong at dinner, she sometimes burst into tears and had to leave the table. She made public speeches, but she dreaded them.
>
> Now suddenly, she wasn't afraid anymore, because there was nothing to be afraid of. Now nothing could upset her because the thing that mattered most had been upset. None of us ever saw her weep again.

DURING HIS CAREER, Frank had been an occasional lecturer at Purdue University, invited to campus by A. A. Potter, dean of the schools of engineering. In the early 1900s while he was a student at Massachusetts Institute of Technology (MIT), Potter began a friendship with Frank and Lillian that lasted a lifetime. Frank had built an MIT building in an unbelievably short time. Potter attended a lecture Frank gave on "the one best way" to lay bricks. In the following years, Frank would be a lecturer at Kansas State when Potter was on faculty there, and then at Purdue after Potter was hired as dean in 1920. Potter had joined the Gilbreths as guests at the White House. The three became personal friends of President Herbert Hoover and his wife, Lou.

Lillian filled in for Frank as a visiting lecturer at Purdue after his death, and in 1935, she took the first salaried job of her life there. She became a full professor of management in Purdue's School of Mechanical Engineering, the first woman in the United States to hold such a title. Perhaps because of the time commitment and her children, Lillian may have first said no to the position. Decades later Dorothy Stratton wrote to Ernestine and told of the day that she invited, yet again, another famous friend over for waffles—the woman she called "Dr. G."

> Your mother came to the Purdue faculty shortly after I became Dean of Women at Purdue. It was understood by me, although never mentioned by Dr. G., that Dr. Elliott had offered her the position and that she had refused it. I knew that Dr. Elliott would be decisively influenced in his opinion of me by what Dr. G. thought. I was new to the university circles as a staff member, new to Indiana, and to being a D. of W. I was also relatively young—34. And of course, I was overawed by your mother's reputation.
>
> In due course, I invited your mother to a luncheon. There were just four of us—my mother and father and Dr. G. and I. We were having waffles and bacon. Period. The waffles stuck (in the waffle iron). Cooking has never been my strong suit. I didn't know what I was going to do. There was nothing else to eat. In desperation, I took the (waffle) iron to the kitchen, explained to it what the dilemma was, asked for its cooperation, brushed out the crumbs, uttered a brief prayer and took it back to the table. It worked. Throughout your mother chatted along as though unaware of any crisis. I still wonder what I would have done if the [waffle] iron had not cooperated.

Lillian also admitted she couldn't cook. She spent little time in the kitchen unless it was to analyze therbligs to decrease the user's motions and improve the layout of the galley. Lillian referred to Dorothy as one of "her girls." Dorothy was special to Lillian, and she would give Purdue's young dean of women much sage advice in years to come. The two women's lives would intertwine in weighty endeavors until their deaths.

Lillian talked to her children about moving to West Lafayette, but they did not want to leave Montclair and their friends, so she went without them. It was Potter who suggested that Lillian become a staff member, and it was Elliott who arranged her salary and accommodations in the Women's Residence Hall. Her son Bill was a student at Purdue during this time. When Lillian was told she would be working on the same campus as Amelia Earhart, Lillian said, "I'm so glad, because I'm one of her ardent admirers."

Long before she, herself, became famous, Amelia was a fan of the Gilbreths. She had pasted a photograph of the couple in her 1924 scrapbook.

For two years, Lillian spent three weeks of every month during the academic year at Purdue. Lillian's daughter Martha, age twenty-nine, ran the family on a day-to-day basis back home. Lillian supervised from afar. She once wrote a letter to Eleanor Roosevelt on Purdue notepaper asking if her daughter's middle school class could visit the White House during a field trip to Washington. Eleanor instructed her secretary to invite the class to tea. While at Purdue, Lillian also acted as a consultant at Duncan Electric Company in Lafayette. This was the company founded by Thomas Duncan, who gave the funds to build Duncan Hall, which had been the vision of Dean of Women Carolyn Shoemaker.

Dorothy said that Lillian's hands were never still. "She was always knitting, crocheting, or tatting something for someone's birthday or anniversary." She kept an extensive birthday book and sent notes to an astonishing number of people. According to Dorothy, Lillian had a great capacity for caring. Perhaps the loss of a child and a husband, and loving a dozen children had increased her empathetic ability. Dorothy said, "Most of us have, I think, a limited capacity as to the number of people we can care for. Dr. G. seemed to be able to take a personal interest in and care for many. She could reach across educational barriers, social barriers, race barriers, sex barriers, age barriers, and find common ground. Some of my experience was too personal to be shared with the public. I am thinking of how Dr. G. visited my father when he was in his final illness."

Amelia Earhart garnered much attention in the Women's Residence Hall where Lillian also resided. Dorothy said that Amelia was "a glamorous figure to all, especially to the students," and Lillian had a "sense of balance" about it. She continued, "Dr. G. took Amelia's popularity in stride, went her own quiet way influencing many lives by her interest and wise counsel." As director of the Women's Residence Hall, Helen Schleman was in the right place at the right time to play the gracious hostess to two of the most prominent, enchanting women of the time. Helen said of Lillian: "Those of us who were lucky enough to be her fellow residents, or work closely with her on campus every time she came to Lafayette, loved her not so much because she was great, but because she was appealingly human."

Lillian would rise early in the morning and send postcards to her children before breakfast. Students learned that they could enjoy time with her if they, too, arrived when the dining room doors opened at 6:30 a.m.

Nearly all of her life she walked a mile a day. If Lillian met a student who wanted to talk to her in the Purdue Memorial Union, she said, "Walk with me. I need to pace my daily number of steps." Lillian walked much, for she never learned to drive.

Dorothy talked of Lillian's "intellectual curiosity" and the variety of departments she influenced on campus: "I think she probably saw a wider cross section of people than anyone else on campus. She met with professors from the School of Management, other Schools of Engineering, School of Home Economics, Division of Education, Department of Psychology, and with staff from the residence halls, Office of the Dean of Women, Placement Services for Men and for Women, and goodness knows how many others. At the same time, she kept up contacts with women's groups in the town and often would speak with them and to them."

It was not always easy for Lillian as the only female in Purdue's male engineering environment. She collaborated with a younger professor, Marvin Mundel, who was an abrasive character. He repeatedly attempted to embarrass Lillian in front of other engineers, calling on her to complete mathematical calculations. Math was not her strong suit. Frank had always done the calculations needed for their motion studies. However, there may have been more personal reasons as to why Mundel caused difficulty for Lillian. She had liked Mundel's first wife and was affronted by his divorce. Yet, on the whole, Lillian's Purdue experience was a happy, successful one—so much so, that she donated her papers to Purdue University, where today the Frank and Lillian Gilbreth Collection is archived.

Lillian was an ambassador of feminine knowledge, compassion, and punctuality. A. A. Potter described Lillian as "a master of the art of conducting free discussion until mutual understanding was achieved." Her natural gift of free discussion was recognized on a grand scale, as she would serve on presidential committees during the presidential administrations of Hoover, Roosevelt, Eisenhower, Kennedy, and Johnson. The committees included civil defense, war production, women in the services, aging, and rehabilitation and employment of the physically disabled. These committees and Lillian's knowledge gathered therein would influence the lives she touched, from students to women like Dorothy and Helen.

Decades later, Helen gave a speech to honor Lillian at the 1978 Lafayette YWCA Salute to Women dinner. Lillian had passed away six years earlier. Helen said:

> To me, one of the characteristics of a "good" feminist is strong support of other women. Too many of the relatively few successful women in the past have had a tendency to shrug their shoulders and say, "Oh, any woman can make it if she's just good enough and is willing to work." Dr. Gilbreth did not hold with this. She knew that it took caring, understanding, and support on the part of women who had arrived in the professional and work world of men to make opportunities for other women—if very many were ever to be successful at breaking the age old barriers. She understood "sisterhood" long before it was popular.

10

Ladies' Agreement

For women, Purdue was firing on all cylinders at the end of the 1930s. The synergy of Amelia Earhart, Lillian Gilbreth, Dorothy Stratton, and Helen Schleman beckoned bright-eyed young women who wanted to be a part of the internal combustion that was propelling women forward.

By 1937, Dorothy and her parents lived at 1007 Ravinia Road in West Lafayette. During Dorothy's tenure, the enrollment of women at Purdue tripled. Dorothy recalled, "Dr. Elliott brought Amelia Earhart and Doctor Gilbreth to the campus, which was simply overwhelming. I have never known exactly why he did, and I'm not sure that he knew, but he did and it was great. It was wonderful. These two had a tremendous impact on all of us. For a lack of something better to put them in, they were attached to the Office of the Dean of Women. This was a great treat for me."

Amelia and Lillian were concerned that there was no bachelor of arts degree offered at Purdue. Many women who came to Purdue in the 1930s wanted what would basically be a liberal arts degree, but for the most part, they were pigeonholed into home economics. Some female students were enrolled in the School of Science, and just a couple of women majored in engineering or agriculture. There was no bachelor of arts degree offered at Purdue because of a "gentlemen's agreement." Decades later, Dorothy explained: "At the time, David Ross, president of the Board of Trustees, told me at least fifty times that there was a gentlemen's agreement with Indiana University that Purdue would never give the BA degree. I still don't know what happened. When I tried to find out who the gentlemen were who made this decision, I never could find out, but of course gentlemen stick by their decisions."

The "gentlemen's agreement" was an understanding between Indiana University and Purdue University regarding the academic degrees each would offer. Indiana, located in the southern part of the state, would offer a liberal arts curriculum, while Purdue, as the land-grant university in the northwest part of the Hoosier landscape, would offer the sciences, engineering, and agriculture.

Often Dorothy was invited to the summer home of Purdue University Trustee and benefactor David Ross. He named his three-story house and surrounding wooded terrain "The Hills," located in the country south of Purdue's campus in what is today Ross Hills Park. Dorothy also would visit his home on South Seventh Street, which was across the street from President Elliott's home in Lafayette. At The Hills, Dorothy played hostess during various Ross functions. She always visited the summer home with a chaperone; while in town, she would call on Ross alone.

There's a photograph of Dorothy standing by steps that lead to an entrance of Ross's summer cottage. She looks quite jaunty wearing jodhpurs—riding breeches—and riding boots, as if she rode a horse while visiting Ross. But friends say Dorothy was not a horsewoman, and perhaps she simply looked the part, as she was always superbly put together for any event. One can imagine Dorothy and David Ross sitting in his living room with the wall of windows facing the thickets that led down to the Wabash River. Perhaps they talked of the "gentlemen's agreement" and how a Purdue curriculum could be instituted to attract more female students.

President Elliott and David Ross gave Dorothy the most resonating bits of philosophy to carry throughout her life. Elliott's motto was, "No great deed was ever done by falterers asking for certainty." From Ross, Dorothy learned the importance of releasing the creative energies of young people and giving them a chance to do things on their own—a philosophy that would serve her well in the myriad of careers she would enjoy throughout the twentieth century.

In 1937, at Dorothy's urging, President Elliott appointed the Committee on the Education of Women to consider the problem of Purdue's lack of a bachelor of arts degree. Professor Helen Hazelton, head of women's physical education, led the group. The committee's first report stated, "Much could be done on women students' behalf simply by making the effort to either supplement or circumvent entrenched academic and administrative structures designed primarily to serve the vocational interests of men."

In other words, Purdue should offer design classes and majors to appeal to women's interests and concerns. Now the finding seems obvious, but alas, even today, entrenched male-oriented ideologies prevail for many disciplines like engineering.

Purdue, along with most universities of this era, felt duty-bound to prepare women for marriage and family life *in loco parentis*. While young women were away from the family nest, it was thought that universities were to be substitute parents, watching over female students, instilling societal expectations, and implementing rules and regulations. This philosophy persisted into the 1960s.

The committee recommended a course on the physical and psychological relations of marriage, problems of home management, economic aspects of marriage, child development, and community involvement. The report stated, "Such knowledge is as essential to effective living today as a knowledge of mathematics or the science of economics."

Women were to be educated at Purdue, but not at the expense of family life. The course was not required of male students. Presumably, it was assumed men did not need such knowledge for "effective living" as husbands and fathers.

Dorothy explained the committee's groundbreaking pronouncement: "This committee decided they would try an experiment. It was a small experiment, but we set up a curriculum for women. It was as close as we dare to come to a liberal arts degree."

The new degree was developed as "liberal science." One could have termed the new program a "ladies' agreement."

A curriculum was created with an emphasis on the sciences, as well as the opportunity to take a broad range of classes from any school in the university. Forty women were permitted to register in the School of Science for the first experimental semester. They were a select group, chosen on the basis of outstanding high school records, test scores, and recommendations, as well as personal interviews. Later, enrollment increased to about one hundred women.

Dorothy, Professor Hazleton, and Professor Dorothy Bovee, the program director, were determined to admit only women capable of meeting rigorous academic standards. In some campus publications, the students were referred to as "the guinea pigs." Most of the women were explicitly not interested in home economics or technical scientific training. Women who wanted a liberal education and normally would not have considered Purdue learned of the curriculum and sought admittance. This was proof that the liberal science program was serving the audience for which it was created.

The course material presented fundamental scientific principles from an historical and philosophical perspective, and then raised questions about the role of science in contemporary life. The cover on the program brochure carried this subtitle: Modern Training for Modern Women. The women were enthusiastic and found the classes challenging and stimulating, taught by outstanding faculty who welcomed the chance to work with such capable and committed students. Former "guinea pigs" said of Professor Sol Boyk: "He'd have us running around the classroom, pretending to be electrons. He asked questions that set our heads spinning and challenged our traditional thinking methods. We learned to question, not just to be contrary, but to rethink our answers and the possibilities of new solutions. Chemistry was fun when we learned from him, but we learned so much more."

Another professor who taught the women was Cornelius Lanczos, a shy refugee from Eastern Europe who had worked with Einstein and gave piano recitals for the students. Disheartened by the misconception that mathematics was thought to be a dry subject, he strived to give the women an appreciation of the imaginative and artistic character of mathematical thinking.

Professor Bovee sponsored the class "Women and Women's Work," a forerunner of women's studies courses. The class highlighted important events in women's history and encouraged students to value the importance of women's varied roles as paid professionals and community volunteers, as well as homemakers responsible for raising the next generation. The course discussed vocations open to women, the choice between marriage and employment outside the home, the possibilities of combining both, and the possible means of maintaining the best balance between them—all hot topics still debated in the twenty-first century.

In the speech "Guinea Pigs: The Experimental Curriculum for Women at Purdue, 1939–1947" by professor of history Sarah Barnes, she states: "Above all, students in the experimental curriculum were encouraged to think of themselves as leaders—leaders with an awareness and understanding of the critical role of science in modern life, a clear perception of present-day social, economic and political problems and the resolve to confront and solve those problems in an objective and democratic fashion."

Still today, women are encouraged to have faith in their abilities and think of themselves as "leaders." The time has not yet come when it is simply an understood fact with no discussion necessary: women are leaders.

The women in the liberal science course were high achievers and felt privileged to be part of a rather elite group. After World War II, Purdue would be teeming with veterans returning to college thanks to the GI Bill. With its selective standards for admission, small class size, demanding courses, and outstanding faculty, the liberal science curriculum developed a reputation as an honors program. Male students clamored for admission. The first group of men selected by the same criteria as the women was admitted in 1947.

In 1985, Dorothy said of the program she helped create: "We really had something going on trying to offer at least a group of women something that was better adapted to what they needed and wanted than had been available before. That [liberal arts degree] got dropped, I must say, after President Hovde came."

By 1953 under the Presidency Frederick L. Hovde, the School of Science would morph into what would be named the School of Science, Education, and the Humanities, with new separate departments of psychology and sociology, and—what seems misplaced today—a Division of Intercollegiate and Intramural Athletics, at that time a male-dominated entity. In *A Century and Beyond*, author Robert W. Topping states: "Hovde was always aware of the need to (as he put it) 'educate the whole man.' To him that meant exactly what it said: Purdue would achieve greatness only when its topflight scientific, engineering, and agricultural programs were accompanied by first-class undergraduate programs in the humanities and social sciences."

Topping goes on to write: "One of the requirements for Hovde's 'educated man' was that he at least try to understand or recognize the philosophical, cultural, political, emotional, spiritual, and traditional factors involved in the complex processes that underlie the society in which he would be expected to participate."

It appears that women were no longer part of the equation that had begun as a liberal science program for exemplary females to learn about the role of science in contemporary life. The "ladies' agreement" had been superseded by another type of gentlemen's agreement.

In 1959, Purdue trustees approved the bachelor of arts degree. In *The Hovde Years* by Topping, he states: "A year later Hovde agreed, though it seemed with no great enthusiasm, to seek from the trustees 'in principle' approval of a Master of Arts degree. But he made it clear that Purdue's involvement in such arts programs should be limited to bachelor's and master's degrees. This would not, Hovde felt, raise the ire of his I.U. colleagues."

The stigma of the "gentlemen's agreement" between Purdue and Indiana Universities that began at the turn of the twentieth century perpetuated into the 1960s, seemingly edging out women in the process, because as Dorothy stated, "gentlemen stick by their decisions."

In a 1970 interview with Helen Schleman conducted by Professor R. B. Eckles of Purdue's Department of History, the two discussed the liberal science program. Eckles revealed this telling piece of information about the dean of the School of Science, Education, and Humanities: ". . . may I say for the record that Dean W. L. Ayres destroyed every piece of paper relating to those wonderful women and girls; destroyed them in my presence. The record of their achievements was not kept purposely by the dean. I shall say no more than this, that his inability to support the program and his refusal to, in the terms of staff and of, shall we say, financial encouragement, was why the liberal science program was discontinued."

Speculating on what could have been with a statement that rings true today, Helen replied: "One can't help wondering what would have been the final outcome if the liberal science curriculum could have continued and could have expanded. It was ahead of its time; there's no doubt about it. If we had in this country now great numbers of women who had the kind of background in science that that curriculum provided, we might not be in the difficulty that we're in, in terms of our environment."

The original intent of the liberal science degree—to answer the varied interests of women—had been lost to the winds of time. In the 1950s and into the 1960s, most Purdue female students would be enrolled in the School of Home Economics, and Dorothy's dean of women successor, Helen, would carry the torch, ever vigilant in her attempt to break women out of the traditional mold.

In 1988, Dorothy Stratton, then age eighty-nine, spoke to a group of Mortar Board National College Senior Honor Society members. At that time, liberal arts at Purdue had been given a mouthful of a name: Humanities, Social Science, and Education (HSSE, pronounced "hissy"). It seems the University still feared repercussions if they called the offering "liberal arts." Dorothy told the students in the audience her tale of liberal arts at Purdue and ended on a high note, saying, "I'm told . . . [our liberal science program] was the acorn into which the great school HSSE has grown. I think it's great that Purdue now can give to its students the bachelor of arts degree."

Purdue has walked a long and crooked path to a liberal arts degree since Amelia Earhart and Lillian Gilbreth encouraged its establishment, and Dorothy Stratton took on the initiative to beckon more women. Today, this field of study is available through Purdue's College of Liberal Arts.

PART OF PURDUE'S ATTRACTION for Amelia was the school's airport, the first to be owned and operated by a university. The campus airfield was made possible with land donated by Purdue Trustee David Ross. He believed that, along with the theory of aeronautics, Purdue should provide practical flight training. Amelia admired Purdue for offering reasonably priced flying instruction for students. In *Soaring Wings*, George Palmer Putnam wrote of his wife: "The matter of flying-lesson expense worried her. Whereas most girls were not able to earn as much money as boys—no one wanted feminine grease-monkeys around hangars to do the odd jobs which often pay a good part of a young man's rudimentary training—they had to pay the same price as the boys for their lessons."

Amelia especially valued how conclusions from laboratory tests conducted in the aeronautics department at Purdue could be immediately put into practice at the airfield southwest of campus. In George's *Soaring Wings*, Amelia is quoted: "You see, my interest in aviation goes into every part of the industry. It isn't flying alone. To be interested exclusively in pilots would be like being interested solely in the engineer in the railroad industry. It takes from forty to a hundred men on the ground to keep one plane in the air. That is from forty to a hundred jobs per plane—and I don't think all those jobs need forever be held by men!"

It was George who first planted the idea of a "Purdue flying laboratory" in President Elliott's mind. In the early part of 1935, Elliott asked George what he thought Amelia desired most in the field of research and education beyond the classroom. George recounted, "I told him she was hankering for a bigger and better plane, not only one in which she could go to far places farther and faster and more safely, but to use as a laboratory for research in aviation education and for technical experimentation."

Amelia said of her husband, "Mr. Putnam, a practicing believer in wives doing what they do best, is an approving and helpful partner in all my projects."

The January before Amelia came to Purdue, she flew from Honolulu, Hawaii, to Oakland, California, in her Lockheed Vega in eighteen hours and fifteen minutes, the first person to make this flight. A few months later, she flew from Burbank to Mexico City in thirteen hours and thirty-two minutes for a new record. That fall, Amelia unassumingly drove her steel gray Cord onto Purdue's campus with her neck scarf billowing and two newly acquired world records under her belt, the belt that held up her avant-garde slacks.

Amelia yearned to pilot the longest flight of her aviation career, a world flight. While on the expedition, she wanted to test human reactions to flying—responses involving diet and altitude, fatigue, the effect of the stratosphere on people conditioned to lower altitudes, and the differences in the reactions of men and women to air travel, if any.

In the autumn of 1935, Elliott held a dinner party at the University-owned president's home, a gray stucco, Spanish eclectic-style house with arched windows and entrance canopy, located many blocks from campus on South Seventh Street in Lafayette. At the party with several Purdue-connected guests, Amelia talked of her dreams for women and aviation. Before the evening was over, David Ross offered to donate fifty thousand dollars toward the cost of a plane that would be Amelia's flying laboratory.

Additional donations in cash and equipment were received from J. K. Lilly of Eli Lilly Drug Company, Vincent Bendix, and manufacturers Western Electric, Goodrich, and Goodyear. A total of eighty thousand dollars comprised the Amelia Earhart Fund for Aeronautical Research. The manufacturers hoped Amelia's female example of flight would help their cause in promoting aviation to women, who at that time displayed "sales resistance" to air travel.

Last Flight is a book published in 1937 and written nearly entirely by Amelia from an accumulation of journals, logbooks, and letters scribbled in the cockpit as she flew her last flight over four continents. The narrative of her journey was also compiled from cables and telephone conversations. Originally, the book was to be named *World Flight.* Because she had promised her publishers that she would produce the manuscript promptly, Amelia mailed her written documentations to her husband from along her route as she traversed the globe. Amid the clouds, Amelia recalled her quest for the very airplane from which she wrote: "Where to find the tree on which costly airplanes grow, I did not know. But I did know the kind I wanted—an Electra Lockheed, big brother of my Vegas, with, of course, Wasp engines. . . . Such is the trusting simplicity of a pilot's mind, it seemed ordained that somehow the dream would materialize. Once the prize was in hand, obviously there was one flight which I most wanted to attempt—a circumnavigation of the globe as near its waistline as could be."

In the sky, her ship's twin engines a droning backdrop, Amelia poetically penned her dream for girls: "I have harbored a very special ambition. The imaginary file card reads, 'Tinkering For Girls Only.' The plan is to endow a catch-as-catch-can machine shop, where girls may tinker to their heart's content with motors, lathes, jigsaws, gadgets, and diverse hickies of their own creation. Where they may sprawl on their back, peering up into the innards of engines, and likely as not get oil in their hair. . . . And emerge somewhere in the scale between grease monkeys and inventors."

Amelia's thoughts were also on Purdue. While in the midst of her world-circling project cultivated by Elliott and Ross, she wrote, "The flight was to be the forerunner of activities at Purdue, where miraculously, there exists a real comprehension of the quaint viewpoint I have tried to indicate. Practical mechanical training, engineering and the like, is available without discouragement to women students there. . . . Which perhaps explains my enthusiasm for Purdue, womanwise as well as aviation-wise."

Amelia took formal delivery of her Lockheed Electra on July 24, 1936, her thirty-ninth birthday. It was a standard commercial plane that Amelia had modified to her specifications. "It's simply elegant," Amelia said to mechanics who crowded around the gleaming all-metal craft, with its smooth curvatures and duel propellers poised to add sway like anticipant, graceful butter knives. "I could write poetry about this ship."

President Elliott traveled to Los Angeles for a scheduled inspection of the flying laboratory in August. The "twin-motored ship" had been repainted in Purdue's colors, gold and black.

Years later when Helen was in her eighties, she would give talks about Amelia and what it was like to know her and have her at Purdue. In 1984, Helen said, "When plans were announced for what turned out to be Miss Earhart's last flight, there was tremendous interest and excitement on campus. We went out to the Purdue Airport to see the plane when Miss Earhart flew it in from California. We followed preparations for the world flight. We followed all of the changes in plans and delays in planning the trip. Finally, in March 1937, Miss Earhart left Purdue for California and then on to Honolulu."

One can visualize Dorothy and Helen, colleagues and friends, assembling their charges, young women standing in their sweater sets and wool skirts, as the Indiana March wind whipped the grassy fields surrounding hanger number one at the Purdue Airport. They would gaze, blinking, at the polished Lockheed Electra, a metallic condor of the sky, and watch the gentle woman who would settle into the cockpit and study her maps that were, to Amelia, like adventures in and of themselves.

Reporters and admirers asked Amelia why she decided to attempt an around-the-world flight. Her answer was always, "Because I want to."

In *Last Flight*, she expounded upon her usual brief answer, perhaps because she could express her reasoning best with pen and paper: "Here was shining adventure, beckoning with new experiences, added knowledge of flying, of peoples—of myself. I felt that with the flight behind me I would be more useful to me and to the program we had planned at Purdue."

Helen goes on to explain the ups and downs of Amelia's start to her circumventing the globe "at its waistline": "Again a change in plans—a tire blew and a strut collapsed and the plane had to come back to California for repairs. The route of the flight was reversed. In May the plane was flown to Miami for a 'shakedown cruise.' Finally, on June 1, 1937, the long flight began. As the flight progressed, we all followed whatever scraps of information came via radio and in the press with the intense personal interest and concern."

The mood on the Purdue campus must have been eager and electric. It was, in a sense, Purdue's plane. Purdue's Amelia. Purdue's world flight. It was March 20, when Amelia's plane "ground looped" and she crashed taking off in Hawaii, headed for Howland Island. As Helen said, Amelia returned the plane to the Lockheed factory in California for repairs.

President Elliott sent a telegram of encouragement to Amelia. On March 25, he wrote a letter to George, who was at Union Air Terminal in Burbank, California. Evidently, to help buoy his wife, George had suggested the telegram idea to Elliott. By this time the two men had become close, as indicated by the salutation of familiarity:

My dear G.P.:

Thanks for the clippings and for the suggestion of a special message for A.E. when she lands today. This has gone and reads as follows:

YOU ARE COMMISSIONED AND CHARGED TO GIVE A.E. A SPECIAL PURDUE GREETING WHEN SHE LANDS TODAY STOP HER COURAGEOUS EXPLOIT HAS GIVEN THRILL TO EVERY MEMBER OF THE BOILERMAKERS GUILD STOP THEY ARE ALL WITH HER TO THE SUCCESSFUL END OF THE FLIGHT

I hope it contains pep for her.

Four months later, Lae, New Guinea, would be Amelia's final stop, where she reveled in the native tongue. She wrote on July 1, 1937, in *Last Flight:*

> My only purchase at Lae besides gasoline has been a dictionary of Pidgin English for two shillings. I was well worth the price to discover that all native women are called Mary. The natives have their own name for everything. For instance airplanes are called "balus," or "birds." . . . My plane has acquired special distinction over other metal ones here, which have corrugated surfaces. The Lockheed is smooth and to the native resembles tins in which certain biscuits are shipped from England. Therefore it is known as the "biscuit box."

Amelia and her biscuit box would attempt to cross eastward over the Pacific to land on Howland Island, along a route never traveled before by airplane. She wrote before taking off, "Shall be glad when we have the hazards of its navigation behind us."

Rather than behind her, the hazards would forever be Amelia's mystery and legacy.

Decades later, Helen described hearing the news that Amelia was lost at sea: "On July 2, the final radio message came. It was picked up by a New Guinea radio station: 'circling . . . cannot see island . . . gas running low.' There was no more word."

The Purdue community collectively displayed shock. Yet hope. There was always hope. Maybe Amelia would be found. Helen continued: "We were all sad and unbelieving. It did not seem possible that the vibrant, beautiful person we had known would not return. She will always be a symbol of high courage to those of us who were fortunate enough to know her."

Until she passed away in 1992, Helen kept a newspaper clipping with the headline "Earhart's Radio Mixed Bared." Dorothy had scrawled a note at the top and evidently given it to Helen. She wrote, "Have you seen this explanation? Certainly tragic and apparently needless."

The July 8, 1937 news story stated that the tragedy was due to a communication failure with a coast guard cutter, which cruised along one of the loneliest stretches of the earth's surface to guide Amelia:

> Far from the scene of the search for Amelia Earhart and her navigator on the coral reefs and watery wastes of the Pacific, maritime radio experts today piece together the story of a radio mixup which may spell the doom of the fliers.
>
> Briefly the mixup was this:
>
> The coast guard cutter *Itasca* stationed near Howland Island as a safety measure when the Earhart plane zoomed across the sea from New Guinea expected Amelia would broadcast in code on 500 kilocycles. The *Itasca* was equipped to take a directional bearing on the plane only if Miss Earhart was sending in code over 500 kilocycles.
>
> But Amelia, before leaving on her globe-circling flight, had scrapped her 500-kilocycle equipment. She could send only on high frequencies.

Amelia was quoted regarding the scrapping of the 500-kilocycle equipment: "It means we would have to take along a 250-foot trailing antenna, which would have to be reeled out after every takeoff and reeled in before each landing. . . . The antenna would be one more thing to worry about, and we have enough things to think of already."

The commander of the Itasca was unaware that Amelia's cherished Lockheed Electra could not receive the signal sent from his ship.

On July 16, President Elliott sent a Western Union telegram to George, who was in Burbank, California, the text of which read:

> SHE WOULD NOT WANT US TO GRIEVE AND WEEP YET WE ARE IN THE DEEPEST DEPTHS OF SADNESS STOP WE SHALL

> LONG MOURN THIS GALLANT ONE WHOSE LIFE WAS A COURAGEOUS ADVENTURE SHE WOULD HAVE A HEROINES PART IN ANY AGE STOP WHEN YOU ARE ABLE PLEASE LET ME KNOW YOUR PLANS SO THAT WE MAY MEET TO CONSIDER HOW TO CARRY ON

Nearly forty years later, Dorothy told her friend Sally Watlington where she was on July 2, 1937, a moment etched in time, just prior to America's most patriotic of celebrations, Independence Day. Dorothy was at a meeting in the Purdue Memorial Union when word came—Amelia Earhart was lost at sea. Those in the meeting sat dazed, then mechanically and without a word, they gathered their papers. Still not speaking, Dorothy and the group left the room, walked down the terrazzo tiled hallways of the Union, where Amelia had once walked, and out into the summer sunshine.

When asked how she felt upon hearing Amelia was missing, Dorothy thought of her famous, fearless friend whom she had hosted in her home with waffles and talks of "cabbages and kings." She gave a one-word answer: "Devastated."

11

Beverley Stone, a Lovely Light

As Dorothy Stratton and Helen Schleman were spiriting women through their education and Purdue campus life amid the corn and hayfields of Indiana, Beverley (Bev) Stone, a woman they would come to know as a friend and colleague, was beginning her formative years at a woman's college at the foot of the majestic Blue Ridge Mountains near the Appalachian Trail—Randolph-Macon.

At Randolph-Macon Woman's College in Lynchburg, Virginia, Bev majored in chemistry. Years later, Bev recalled her girlhood visions of her professional goals. She said, "I had three dreams—to be a movie star, a doctor, or a schoolteacher." All of her life, Bev dressed like a movie star in pearls, high heels, and furs. She used her chemistry degree to become a schoolteacher, but the physician dream she voiced as a child never came to pass.

Several of Bev's family members were doctors, and they discouraged her from becoming a physician, fearing that it would be too difficult a career for a woman, or as Bev said, "They decided a female doctor would be inappropriate." Financial hardships brought on by the Great Depression also made medical school an unrealized dream.

At Randolph-Macon, Bev was influenced by female deans and instructors who, unbeknownst to her at the time, gave her the underpinning for her future calling as a guide for students, encouraging them to follow their innate gifts and capabilities. Deanship was a dream, not yet formed. Bev said:

> In 1932, when I entered Randolph-Macon at age sixteen from the small town of Crewe, Virginia, I was probably the most naïve and unsophisticated freshman there. When I was assigned seating at Dean Sallie Payne Morgan's table for the semester, I assumed that this occurred by chance. It turned out to be prophetic! From her I learned many things beyond the academic. Throughout my experience on campus, there was an atmosphere of caring about individual students. The faculty helped students discover and enhance their capabilities in an environment of personal attention, encouragement, and support.

Personal attention, encouragement, and support would become Bev's trifecta of student care.

Feminine, ash-blond, and blue-eyed, Marguerite Beverley Stone was born in Norfolk, Virginia, on June 10, 1916. She had an "old Virginia voice," described by a newspaper reporter as "soft and warm as the mellow glow of antique silver." Bev's parents were her heroes. Her father was an electrical engineer, and her mother was a schoolteacher. Her maternal grandmother was a higher education pioneer. Araminta Elizabeth Sims, "Miss Minty," was one of eight women, along with nine men, to graduate from Indiana University in 1883. So even though she was a "southerner," Bev grew up with a warm connection to the Hoosier state.

Bev recalled, "The basis to my life has been growing up in a loving family who had reasonable expectations." Bev's sister Mary entered Randolph-Macon three years after her older sister. Their parents believed that "anyone who was of reasonable intelligence had a responsibility to do something worthwhile for the sake of others." Bev would forever carry that parental mantra into her daily life and profession.

When Bev graduated from high school, a friend of her mother's gave her a book by Edna St. Vincent Millay. That's when Bev adopted a lifelong love for Millay's poetry. Millay was five when she began to write poems, and by 1912, when she was just eighteen, she was quite famous. She won a Pulitzer Prize in 1923. Millay read her poems aloud on her series of nationwide radio broadcasts. English novelist and poet Thomas Hardy once said that the two great things about America were its skyscrapers and the poetry of Edna St. Vincent Millay. Bev's favorite Millay poem was "A Few Figs from Thistles," which she could recite by memory:

First Fig

My candle burns at both ends;
It will not last the night;
But ah, my foes, and oh, my friends—
It gives a lovely light!

Second Fig

Safe upon the solid rock the ugly houses stand:
Come and see my shining palace built upon the sand!

Little did youthful Bev know when she memorized Millay's poem, that one day as dean of women at Purdue University, she would feel as if she was burning her candle at both ends while building a "shining palace" upon what may have felt like sand. Yet Bev's students would only see her lovely light.

Millay visited Randolph-Macon to give a lecture while Bev was a student. Bev would forever remember that day. It seems that Millay lived up to her reputation. She was known to drink, party, and have affairs, making her the envy of some during the days of Prohibition, particularly young women. Millay's poetry was described as "wild, cool, elusive," and it "intoxicated the Jazz Babies." Bev described the day she saw Millay: "She had on a green velvet dress with a train on it. She may have done a little too much imbibing because, though she read beautifully, her papers kept dropping on the floor. And her husband in the receiving line pinched some of the students' behinds."

Miss Clara Davidson taught courses in religion and character education at Randolph-Macon. She was a stimulating and challenging professor who influenced Bev's life with her genuine concern for others and her desire to bring out the best in people. Bev remained close to Davidson until the teacher's death in 1951. Bev said: "[Randolph-Macon] was a small college—750 students. I was invited into the home of all my professors—not once, but many times. That close relationship was the most meaningful part of my college experience. Many times in my career, I have felt Miss Davidson looking over my shoulders! Clara Davidson was my special mentor, role model, and friend through my first teaching experiences. Her moral, spiritual, and ethical values shone like a beacon for countless students."

When Bev graduated in 1936, three public schools offered her a job teaching mathematics and chemistry. She chose the highest paying at $90 per month with no benefits at a high school in Norfolk, Virginia. Bev said, "I loved high school teaching, but my first day was a disaster. I told the class everything I knew about chemistry. I looked at my watch, and ten minutes had passed."

Bev's position acquainted her with the wide range of needs of teenagers in Norfolk. She saw that many needed counseling during the difficult days of the Depression, and she was frustrated at her lack of expertise in the field. Some had personal problems, and she was not equipped to help. One such student was Freddie. He was intelligent, yet he did not like school and missed classes. Freddie had contracted a bad case of trench mouth from smoking cigarette butts that he had found on the ground.

Bev helped Freddie, putting into practice the examples she had been shown by Miss Davidson and the deans and counselors at Randolph-Macon. She saw a smart, likeable young man who was not living up to his fullest potential, and she wanted to change that. Bev helped Freddie, but also Freddie helped Bev, for it was because of him that Bev realized she wanted to serve others as a counselor rather than teacher. She returned to school for a master's degree in student personnel administration, studying in the summers at Teachers College of Columbia University (where Dorothy Stratton had earned her PhD in 1932) and graduating in 1940.

While at Columbia, Bev made what would become a profound, lifelong connection with one of her professors, Esther McDonald Lloyd-Jones. Esther was a legend in student personnel administration teaching at Columbia from 1928–1966. She wrote the first book on personnel work in higher education, *Student Personnel Work at Northwestern University* (1929).

Decades later, with a very full and sometimes tumultuous career as Purdue's dean of women and dean of students behind her, Bev, age sixty-three, wrote a letter to her beloved teacher:

> I suspect you have no notion of the extent of your influence you have had from the time I had the first course with you in 1937. You have been a constant inspiration during these intervening years. Your encouragement, support, affection, and warmth have been qualities I have always counted on, and I hope that I may have imparted some of these same qualities to others. Many students I may have reached may not be aware that a part of you has influenced my reaching out to them. Nonetheless this is true.

Esther believed in a holistic approach. She became an advocate for deans of women and deans of men to be educators in an unconventional and new sense, which she called "deeper teaching." The Lloyd-Jones approach was to help students and staff learn skills for their fulfillment as whole persons, facilitating their personal growth. She believed in creating environments where everyone could feel worthy of receiving and giving respect. She believed students learned through enriched interactions with others, and this learning would best take place in small, natural communities on campus. Esther's concepts countered the view that student personnel work was a collection of services from which students would select, such as career counseling, academic advising, and testing.

In a sense, Bev became a Lloyd-Jones protégé, who in the coming years would take the holistic approach in her career. Through her model of caring, Bev would teach thousands of students how to form bonds with others.

Bev's first position where she would begin to emulate Esther was as the headship of Virginia Hall and assistant professor of history at Tusculum College in Greeneville, Tennessee. While Bev ultimately would teach chemistry, a letter from the college president stated that she was to be in the history department.

At the foothills of the Great Smoky Mountains, Tusculum is the oldest college in Tennessee. The college is famous for its landmark, "The Arch," a stone archway built at the front of the shady campus after the American declaration of war in 1917.

An August 21, 1941 letter from Tusculum President Charles Albert Anderson to Bev stated that she was to have added responsibilities as hostess in the dining hall in charge of service during mealtimes. He wrote that Bev's room was to be on the first floor opposite the stairs with a bed, dresser, two tables, and two chairs, and that it had "just been freshly papered with yellow." He provided the dimensions of the room's windows so that Bev could obtain curtains.

President Anderson also suggested that Bev participate in some meetings prior to the arrival of the students for the academic year and, "It would help to have you direct a woman who will clean Virginia Hall." At age twenty-five, Bev's life was taking shape as she settled in to preside over the women's hall baring the name of her home state, deciding the perfect drapes to match her yellow-papered walls.

It appears that Bev turned a lemon of a situation during Freshman Week into some southern lemonade, and her superiors noticed. A letter to Bev from Dean Leslie K. Patton states: "I want to take this opportunity to express my genuine appreciation for the splendid way that you handled the problem of scoring the tests during Freshman Week. From my observation and from what I hear from others, I think that you just about 'worked a miracle.' . . . In the name of the college I want to tell you that we are very grateful."

Whatever "miracle" Bev worked, the dean went on to ask that Bev prepare in writing a plan for scoring the tests and a report on how she believed the job should be done for future exams. It appears that Bev had gone above and beyond her duty and solved a scoring glitch in the freshmen testing. It must have been a shining, memorable event for Bev, for she saved the letter of commendation from Dean Patton for the remainder of her life.

The Japanese attacked Pearl Harbor in 1941, and the United States entered into World War II. When the head of Tusculum's chemistry department left to accept a position in military research at Johns Hopkins, Bev was called to the office of the president. He asked her if she would teach quantitative analysis and organic chemistry to premed students. While Bev had taught chemistry at the high school level, all of her graduate work had been in student personnel administration, so she was uncertain about the proposed teaching position.

The president convinced Bev that it was her "patriotic duty" to accept the challenge. Most of her students were men. Bev said, "For the organic course, I worked harder than ever in my life. I spent fifteen hours preparing for each lecture. But all of the med students who applied were accepted for medical school."

Throughout her life, Bev was described as "a lady." She often wore her signature pearls with her favorite color—pink. She frequently wore a cardigan loosely draped over her shoulders, the sleeves dangling like angel wings. Bev was charming and sincere, able to command a meeting with the proper tone and grace, garnering respect from men and women alike. Perhaps to some, Bev's decision to enlist in the United States Navy was seen as out of character.

By the spring of the next year, America was in an all-out war, and male students received draft notices daily. Bev became convinced of her desire to serve in one of the armed services. Two female role models influenced Bev's desire to apply for the United States Naval Women's Reserve (the WAVES, "Women Accepted for Volunteer Emergency Service").

Bev had read about Mildred McAfee, a president on leave from Wellesley College (where Helen Schleman had obtained her advanced degree in hygiene and physical education in 1928). Mildred had been appointed director of the WAVES. When Bev arrived at Tusculum, she discovered that Mildred had been a faculty member there and was a campus legend, greatly beloved and respected. When Mildred was selected to head the WAVES, the news media gave great attention to Tusculum. Soon after, Mildred appealed to women in higher education to apply for commissions in the navy, and Bev wholeheartedly heeded the call from the woman she so admired.

The other role model who influenced Bev's attraction to the navy was her favorite aunt, who had been one of the 11,000 plus yeomanettes in World War I. A yeoman (or female nicknamed "yeomanette") is a member of the navy who manages the paperwork. Bev had been intrigued with photos and stories of her aunt and always was proud of her service. Women were employed as yeomanettes to meet severe clerical shortages during World War I. The Naval Reserve Act of 1916 (the year Bev was born) had conspicuously omitted mention of gender as a condition for service, leading to the enlistment of women in mid-March 1917, shortly before the United States entered the Great War.

The yeomanettes primarily served in secretarial and clerical positions, though some were translators, draftswomen, fingerprint experts, ship camouflage designers, and recruiting agents. The majority were assigned duties at naval installations in the United States, frequently near their homes, processing the great volume of paperwork generated by the war effort.

The yeomanettes wore wide-brimmed flattop hats with a band of ribbon imprinted with "U.S. Navy," white gloves, white blouses with navy blue neckties, blazers, and ankle-length skirts. The insignia for a yeomanette is a pair of crossed quills, symbolizing her clerical duties.

When Bev enlisted in the WAVES, her mother was supportive. Her father was opposed until he warmed to the idea and ended up rooting for his daughter. Bev said, "After I was in, my father was sure I was the one who had won the war."

Decades later, Bev spoke of her commissioning: "In September 1943, I entered Midshipman Training School at Smith College and was commissioned in November. I still remember Mildred McAfee's address when our class was commissioned, in which she said she did not worry about women officers performing well when the going was rough—but in wartime, when of necessity there would be occasions when there would be over-staffing—she was concerned about how we would handle responsibility when the going was dull."

While Bev was enlisting in the navy to become a WAVE, at Purdue University Dorothy Stratton was answering her own call to create a newly spawned women's reserve for the United States Coast Guard. Helen Schleman would follow Dorothy into the uncharted territory of women serving in World War II. And Mildred McAfee would be the common thread that would braid the lives of Bev, Dorothy, and Helen.

12

Your Best Foot Forward

When the initial shock of Amelia Earhart's lost flight progressed into a numb reality around the Purdue campus, it was as if lights dimmed in the Women's Residence Hall and pallor was cast over the University airport.

George Palmer Putnam continued his correspondence with Purdue President Edward C. Elliott. Putnam was left with the medals, scrapbooks, goggles, leather jackets, sprightly printed neck scarves, and mountains of papers and ephemera that had belonged to his wife. He had donated some of her artifacts to the World Center for Women's Archives (WCWA).

Historian Mary Ritter Beard had founded the WCWA out of frustration over the difficulty she encountered in trying to locate women's papers. The WCWA had its first organizational board meeting in New York in 1935. Prominent women such as Eleanor Roosevelt, Frances Perkins, Georgia O'Keeffe, Katharine Hepburn, Alice Paul, and Margaret Sanger endorsed the WCWA. "No documents, no history," was the motto of the

WCWA, reflecting Beard's conviction that women's history requires the preservation of women's papers. In a 1939 WCWA pamphlet now located in the Library of Congress, Beard is quoted: "What documents, then, have women? What history? (For without these records) women may be blotted from the story and the thought about history as completely as if they had never lived. . . . But what do the women of today know about the women of yesterday to whom they are so closely linked for better or for worse? What are the women of tomorrow to know about the women of today?"

Despite the wide publicity and initial support, the WCWA was unable to build a lasting future. By the end of the 1930s, the war in Europe preoccupied the WCWA's sponsors, overshadowing their interest in documenting the lives of women. With a lack of funding and the resignation of Beard, the center was forced to close on September 16, 1940. The hope was that after the war, the WCWA could begin again; however, the reawakening of such a "world" endeavor never came to pass.

Although the WCWA only existed for four years, the center's collections included an impressive assemblage of records, maps, and charts belonging to Amelia Earhart. Additionally, the WCWA left a lasting impact on colleges and universities, which began collecting materials for the study of women, raising awareness of the importance of preserving records of women's lives. One such university was Purdue.

In 1939, Putnam presented Purdue with a portrait of Amelia Earhart painted by Brynjulf Strandenaes, a noted Norwegian portrait painter. He created the portrait ten years earlier, following Amelia's solo flight across the Atlantic. President Elliott placed the portrait in the Women's Residence Hall, by then named South Hall, and today named Duhme, where Amelia lived when she was on campus.

The next November, Putnam received a letter from the WCWA telling him of their dissolution and suggesting Purdue University as one of the possible depositories of his wife's memorabilia. On November 7, 1940, Putnam, in Hollywood, wrote to Purdue's president:

> Dear Elliott:
>
> I am just in receipt of a letter from the World Center for Women's Archives telling me they are dissolving. It seems they have had financial difficulties.

At the time of their inception, I presented to them considerable records of A. E.'s last flight. They now ask me to whom I would like to have them pass on this material. They name three organizations to which they feel it would be proper to present them. Purdue, the 99ers, and the Society of Women Geographers. Neither the 99ers (women flyers) nor the Women Geographers have any permanent location or exhibition place. However, both were very close to A. E.'s heart.

Please give me your reaction. If you would like this material at Purdue I will see that you get it. In addition, I believe I would like to present to Purdue many other interesting souvenirs of Amelia's life including her decorations and her medals, of which, as you can guess, there is a considerable number. In all, I think an extraordinarily interesting collection which might be supplemented with a scrapbook or two, some newspaper mats, correspondence, maps, and the like. All I would ask is that they be properly and permanently safeguarded, and so far as desirable made available to those who might be interested in viewing them and perhaps gaining inspiration from them.

Sincerely,
G. P. P.

President Elliott responded a few days later: "While I do not want to appear selfish, it is my seasoned opinion that the best place for the records of A. E. would be Purdue. We are ready to assure you that these will be safely exhibited and so placed as to be a constant source of inspiration to our students. We shall expect to provide proper proof cases in the Library or in the Memorial Union Building or in the Women's Residence Halls center."

By the end of November the Amelia Earhart collection from the WCWA arrived at Purdue. Among the records were eight pages from Amelia's log of her world flight, the original manuscript of *Last Flight,* and the message she received at Lae that referenced the weather conditions before her ill-fated journey to Howland Island.

President Elliott gave Dean of Women Dorothy Stratton the task of examining the collection. Dorothy formed a small committee to do so. Then she wrote to Elliott:

> My dear President Elliott:
>
> Dr. Gilbreth, Miss Coolidge, Miss Schleman, Paula Zwierlein, and I have examined, as you requested, the Amelia Earhart material received from the World Center for Women's Archives. If this material represents the entire collection, which is to be available to the University, we recommend that it be turned over to the Library for preservation and for appropriate displays. The maps are very badly mounted and are warping now.
>
> If the material now available represents only the nucleus of a more complete collection of Earhartiana, it may be that the University would later wish to designate a special room in the Library or elsewhere for the display and preservation of this collection.

In addition to Dorothy, Lillian Gilbreth, and Helen Schleman, the other two women who helped examine Amelia's collection were Clare Coolidge, who was assistant dean of women, and Paula Zwierlein, a senior in home economics who was a Mortar Board member and president of the Women's Self-Government Association (WSGA).

It had been three years since the women heard Amelia was lost at sea. Had they reconciled with the belief that Amelia would not be found? Did touching Amelia's sketch of the Lockheed Electra's gasoline line and supply feel like touching the hands of fate? Although they may not have thought it at the time, the five women were privileged to have been chosen as the ones to assess what Dorothy so poetically termed "Earhartiana."

Today, the George Palmer Putnam Collection of Amelia Earhart Papers is housed in the Purdue University Libraries' Virginia Kelly Karnes Archives and Special Collections Research Center. The collection includes Putnam's original donation and a 2002 donation made by his granddaughter, Sally Putnam Chapman.

WHILE THE UNIVERSITY FOCUSED on preserving the past, Dorothy had been forging ahead, addressing the day-to-day needs of her female students. One such need was women's restrooms. Most buildings on Purdue's campus did not offer these facilities for women. This subtle demonstration of exclusion was quite obvious to Dorothy, and she worked to remedy the situation; however, her quest was difficult, and the lack of women's restrooms in several campus buildings would continue into the 1970s.

Women today have Ruth Steer to thank for restrooms in the present Heavilon Hall. When architectural drawings were created for the much-touted building, constructed in 1956, Ruth's husband, Max (Mack) Steer, brought home the plans for his wife to see. Mack founded Purdue's Department of Speech, Language, and Hearing Sciences, housed in Heavilon Hall. He began the speech pathology program in 1935. Ruth had a bachelor's degree in speech and a master's in psychology. Together, the couple conducted and published research in the field of psychoacoustics, the study of the perception of sound.

When Mack brought home the Heavilon Hall drawings to show Ruth, she took one look and noticed that there were no women's restrooms provided in the plans. Ruth pointed out the omission to her husband, and the architectural rendering was changed to accommodate Purdue's female students and visitors.

The lack of adequate facilities was an example of the sort of "sandpapering" of women's self-esteem and lack of inclusiveness that often occur in a male-dominated institution. It's what soft-spoken feminist icon Bernice R. Sandler in 1982 referred to as a "chilly climate." The chilly climate for women occurs when females are treated differently in myriad unconscious diminishing ways. For example, a teacher who calls on male students more than female students; a CEO who ignores what a woman says in a meeting but listens intently when a man makes the exact same point; a conference facilitator who introduces a female speaker by mentioning her appearance rather than her accomplishments, but feels no need to comment on the appearance of a male presenter.

These incidents may seem tiny and insignificant by themselves, but they add up and produce a cumulative "chilling" effect that makes women feel unwelcome. No women's restroom in a building translates to "we don't want you here." The effect is sometimes so subtle that women are not even consciously aware of it. They just have a nagging feeling of being "less than," unable to put a finger on why they feel that way. While today the law requires women's facilities in buildings, the climate for women still can be overtly cold due to subtle chills of discrimination.

THE 1930S BROUGHT AN INTENSIVE BUILDING PROGRAM for Purdue through funds obtained from the Public Works Administration. The Women's Residence Halls were constructed, as well as the Executive Building, today named Hovde Hall of Administration. President Elliott and the Offices of the Dean of Women and Dean of Men moved into the Executive Building in 1937.

Still today, the building is an imposing, colossal edifice with six massive stone columns standing sentry at the front doors that are entered from wide, soaring cement steps to the first floor, which is actually the second story. After Dorothy moved into the Executive Building, the Office of the Dean of Women would be located there for the next fifty years. The office had come a long way since the day four years earlier when Dorothy entered her "closet" space in Fowler Hall and found Carolyn Shoemaker's Bible tucked inside her desk.

According to Robert W. Topping, author of *A Century and Beyond*, President Elliott had asked the architects of the Executive Building to "include a private, back stairway leading to an unobtrusive exit so that young women students, occasionally in tears after a counseling session, could leave the building without having to display their emotions publicly in the main doors."

This reasoning for the back exit (which disappeared after the building was remodeled) doesn't align with the atmosphere Dorothy created in the Office of the Dean of Women. In the booklet "The Freshman Folio" for 1937–1938, a photo of Dorothy appears next to a message she wrote:

> To the New Women Students of Purdue:
>
> If you wish to be wise in the ways of Purdue, put this book first on your list of required reading for the summer! Miss Coolidge, the Assistant Dean of Women, and I are eager to meet all of you, and sincerely hope that you will not be awed by the imposing columns at the front of the Executive Building, but that you will walk right past them into our office and give us the opportunity of getting acquainted. Remember that we don't mind answering questions.

When Dorothy spoke at the 1935 annual meeting of the Kentucky Deans of Women (KADW) to address the problem of advising female students during times of economic uncertainty, she took the opportunity to remind her colleagues that many of these students, like some faculty and members of the general public, considered the dean of women solely a disciplinarian. She told a story of two young girls who saw a dean of women on a city street. Dorothy joked, "One little girl said to the other, 'Who is that woman?' and the other replied, 'I think they call her the demon of the college.'"

Dorothy told her audience that, particularly in times of financial stress such as in the Great Depression, young people needed their sense of security bolstered. The dean of women needed to reach out to female students and display understanding and discretion. She stressed that college women were an anomaly among their sex and faced puzzling questions concerning their career and marriage prospects. Dorothy believed that frank discussions of these issues would alleviate fear and establish bonds of trust and friendship between the dean of women and her students.

Decades later, Dorothy described her favorite accomplishment as dean: "The best was trying to create an image in the office that would be one of help to students—one where students would want to come, not where students would dread to come because they were going to be disciplined."

In a paper Beverley Stone wrote in 1974, entitled "Deans or Demons," she wrote of Dorothy and her "dean style": "The Dean of Women was not so much an executive or disciplinary officer as a friend. She was active in finding work for women students who needed to earn money. She inspected rooming houses, chaperoned social affairs. In short, she watched over the lives of women students with kindly care for their welfare."

The 1941 *Debris* yearbook put a different spin on what Dorothy did for female students. Under the heading of "Friendly Aid and Council are Found in the Dean's Office," the text states, "The Dean of Women's office handles some 3,000 interviews each year with students and parents . . . problems ranging from financial and housing troubles to love and indigestion."

Dorothy and Helen coauthored a paper that appeared in the *Harvard Educational Review* in 1938, entitled "Problems in Social Usage Which Puzzle College Students." The paper discussed their study of proper social graces for college students, research they were conducting to write a book. On page 485, the women state:

> Until recently . . . most colleges assumed that the students who came to their doors had already been well trained in the elements of social usage and that those few who had not would, by a process of osmosis, absorb good manners from those who had them. There are, however, signs that colleges are beginning to realize that neither of these assumptions is necessarily true for many of the students who come to college. . . . Such statements as . . . "three-fourths of the men who graduate from American colleges are barbarian" are none too comforting to college officials. Moreover, complaints of employers that students do not know the elements of courtesy, do not know how to conduct themselves in a business interview, cannot be trusted to use the correct fork or spoon, and are tongue-tied at important social functions are beginning to be heeded within the college walls.

To conduct their research, Dorothy and Helen quizzed a sampling of college students in nine coeducational colleges and universities throughout the country, obtaining participants through their networking with the National Association of Deans of Women. Students were asked to jot down questions about social mores that puzzled them. Dorothy and Helen explained in their preface: "It was suggested that the questions might include any areas of social behavior, such as 'dating,' dances, table manners, receptions, manners on the street, in public places, and so on."

Male and female students from Maine to California sent Dorothy and Helen more than 6,200 questions. Then the women solicited responses from Mortar Board student leaders from fifty-nine college campuses. Additionally, they discussed the questions and the manuscript with hundreds of Purdue students.

Dorothy and Helen titled their book *Your Best Foot Forward: Social Usage for Young Moderns.* Whittlesey House, a division of McGraw-Hill, published the text in 1940 with a tan, fabric-like cover and an understated line drawing by Alice O'Connor. The illustration shows a formally dressed couple—he in tails, she in a long flowing gown—stepping forward, as if dancing at a ball. The sketch is reminiscent of drawings by James Thurber, an American author and cartoonist most published in the *New Yorker* magazine.

In the acknowledgments, Dorothy and Helen thanked "Dr. Lillian M. Gilbreth . . . for her sustained interest in the project." Lillian had published several books and was probably an excellent source of advice.

In the first chapter, Dorothy and Helen wrote a prophetic paragraph: "If, seventy-five years from now, some young person were to brush the dust and cobwebs from this book and read of the customs of today, there is little doubt that they would appear more amusing and more outmoded to him than those of 1865 seem to us. So, of course, would our houses, our fashions, our automobiles, our subways, and our refrigerators seem, could this same young person of the twenty-first century see them. For us, however they are integral parts of our daily life and are, therefore important."

Your Best Foot Forward was very successful, selling well into the 1950s on college and university campuses across the United States. Deans of women and deans of men kept a copy in their offices to address questions. The copy of *Your Best Foot Forward* now preserved in the Purdue Libraries Archives and Special Collections was the copy that Dorothy gave to her parents. She and Helen both inscribed the book:

> To Papa and Mama Stratton with love and appreciation of their encouragement and assistance.
>
> Dorothy and Helen
> Nov. 24, 1940

Dorothy's father would pass away eight months after she and Helen lovingly signed the book.

One may wonder if Dorothy and Helen ever experienced some of the social intricacies that they discussed in their book. A "usage" that looms as a question is, "Did they date?"

Standards of conduct were strict for deans of women and females working in higher education. It may have been considered improper for a dean of women to have suitors, although Dorothy did spend time with Purdue Trustee David Ross, often with a chaperone.

"Deaning" combined with marriage was very unconventional for the time. Typically, women stopped working when they married, even if this meant ending a promising academic career. The convention was that men were the primary financial providers, and unfortunately, this standard "justified" lower wages for women, rationalized discriminatory hiring practices (especially for married women), and limited female career ambitions. A woman's education and professional experience were secondary to her husband's career.

In 1930, only 12 percent of married white women worked. A 1936 Gallup poll underlined public disapproval of married women's employment when 82 percent of respondents opposed women working if they were married and their husbands had jobs.

Looking back, the professional women of the first half of the twentieth century were victims of a double-edged sword. They were told they could not be married and have their careers, forced into an understood celibacy, and then branded with a scarlet letter that questioned their sexuality.

Dorothy and Helen were anomalies of their day. They had worked hard for their degrees, and they enjoyed their careers. Dorothy and Helen were light years ahead of "young moderns" in what they believed women could accomplish. Friends and role models Amelia Earhart and Lillian Gilbreth authenticated Dorothy and Helen's choices and views. Helen always said she was born fifty years before her time. Given the statistics, one can understand her lament.

The next decade would further validate Dorothy and Helen's beliefs in women's capabilities, including their own, as America went to war.

13
Be Interesting

In Purdue's 1941 *Debris* yearbook, Dean of Women Dorothy Stratton, age forty-two, is pictured writing at her desk. The headline reads, "Interesting," and the text states, "Dean Stratton's favorite theory is 'to be interesting, do interesting things.' In her spare time she reads, attends the theater, travels, and plays golf. Proving her own theory . . . she is an interesting person."

Another photograph shows Dorothy with her hair rolled in the 1940s pin curl style of the day, thumbing through a copy of *Your Best Foot Forward*. The text continues, "Dean Stratton's experimental project in education . . . the new curriculum for women in the science school, planned in off moments, has attracted the interest of progressive educators. And just off the press, *Your Best Foot Forward* . . . a book of etiquette by Dean Stratton and Miss Helen Schleman."

Dorothy's life was about to become even more interesting. The years 1940–1942 were pivotal. Dorothy had just become a published author after years of research and writing. The next year her parents, who lived with her, passed away within seven months of each other; her father died in July 1941, and her mother died the following February. Dorothy suddenly was living alone in her house on Ravinia Road. Losing her parents, sad as it was, gave Dorothy the freedom for a monumental shift. World War II came calling, and Dorothy was ready to answer.

The United States entered World War II in December 1941, after the Japanese attack on Pearl Harbor. In May of that year, Edith Nourse Rogers, a congresswoman from Massachusetts, had introduced a bill to create the Women's Army Auxiliary Corps (WAAC), a support entity, not part of the army itself. Once the United States was at war, the formation of the WAAC was approved by Congress and signed into law a year after its introduction. Oveta Culp Hobby was sworn in as the first director. She had been working in the War Department's Bureau of Public Relations and was a unanimous choice.

The WAAC was established "for the purpose of making available to the national defense the knowledge, skill, and special training of women of the nation." In 1943, the reserve became the Women's Army Corps (WAC) and officially was made part of the United States Army. Dorothy was asked to help recommend the first officer candidates for the WAAC. In a 1970 U.S. Naval Institute oral history interview, Dorothy, then age seventy-one, said, "I don't know how I happened to get the invitation, it just suddenly arrived, you know how things are. Mrs. Hobby was the director of the WAAC."

Lillian Gilbreth consulted at the Arma Plant in Brooklyn, New York, which handled navy shipyard defense contracts. Before Lillian arrived, it had been an all-male factory. As World War II heated up, Arma prepared to bring in female employees. The manager told Lillian, "We've never had women in the shop before. We don't know where to start. We're counting on you to tell us everything we have to do to get ready for them."

Lillian answered with a statement that became a byword in the War Manpower Commission. She said, "If that's all my job is, I can finish it with one sentence: Build separate restrooms."

Shipyard work was strenuous, and women would quit because of simple exhaustion. Lillian helped initiate an exercise program, which reduced absenteeism. Lillian, age sixty-five, participated, keeping up with "a suppleness and verve that put some twenty-year-olds to shame."

Lillian also was a member of the advisory group on the formation of the United States Naval Women's Reserve, the WAVES, who filled non-combatant jobs and released men for active duty overseas. Even before the legislation was passed to create the WAVES, Lillian was encouraging Dorothy to enlist. Dorothy said, "Dr. G. insisted that I should volunteer and do it early."

Dorothy headed to Chicago for a physical exam to see if she was qualified to become a WAVE. She said, "I was very much interested in the women's services and the fact that women were going to be given an opportunity to serve. I felt strongly that it was important that the United States should join the Allies and help win the war. To put it simply, it was important that we stop the Japanese and Hitler. If there was any opportunity for me to do my little bit, I wanted to do it."

Dorothy was commissioned in the WAVES and she requested a leave of absence from Purdue University. She remembered, "Dr. Elliott . . . was very generous about it. He thought it was the right thing for me to do, and he raised no objections whatsoever. In fact, I think he was glad I was going to do it. He always gave me wonderful support all through, not only during my years as dean of women at Purdue, but also while I was in the service."

During Dorothy's absence, the Assistant Dean of Women Clare E. Coolidge became Purdue's interim dean of women. President Elliott helped with the war effort by accepting a position as director of the Division of Professional and Technical Employment and Training of the War Manpower Commission. He traveled between Purdue and Washington, DC, serving eleven months. Through his work, Purdue housed and trained nearly three thousand marines, sailors, and soldiers in specialized war courses. The first day he left for Washington, on June 22, 1942, Elliott gave this message to the faculty: "Each and every one of you should be prepared to give not 100 percent but 110 percent of your effort for the success of the war program."

However, the only woman on Purdue's Board of Trustees, Kathryn McHale, thought Dorothy was making a mistake by leaving her position as dean of women to join the WAVES. McHale said, "Dorothy, you can't afford to do this," to which Dorothy replied, "I can't afford not to."

Dorothy knew she was taking a risk, and that her career and momentum for women at Purdue could be sidetracked, but she felt she had to enlist. Mapping new terrain for herself, for all women, and for the country was not completely new to Dorothy. She had already plowed fresh ground for females on a major university campus. Decades later, Dorothy said, "It was not always easy to be a pioneer. The public was uncertain about us. So were some of our civilian colleagues. I caught criticism from all sides."

Even though Dorothy no longer had her parents, she had her friend and mentor Lillian Gilbreth, who (at twenty years Dorothy's senior) may have been a motherly figure. Looking back, Dorothy said of Lillian: "She took a personal interest in me. When World War II broke out, she talked about going into the service, and she said I could go, too. So I did. It was a complete break; it determined my future life."

AS A SENIOR LIEUTENANT IN THE WAVES, Dorothy started with a high rank, called to duty on August 28, 1942. She explained it by saying, "I was pretty old." She was forty-three. Dorothy was sent with the first class of WAVES to the Naval Reserve Midshipmen's School in Northampton, Massachusetts. It was bare bones in the beginning. Dorothy explained, "We had no pillows and hardly any blankets. We didn't have anything to work with or any uniforms. We didn't have anything, except the shots we got, but we got along. I thought I had made the worst mistake of my life."

Yet in the end, Dorothy was glad for the initial disheartening experience. She continued, "Of all the directors of the services, I was the only one who went through this period of training. I was glad that I did because I knew what the others, the officers, were going to go through in their periods of indoctrination. I didn't learn to march, because a senior lieutenant apparently doesn't march, or didn't at that time. So I had to do only one thing, which was lucky for me. I only had to say, 'Platoon leaders take charge.'"

However, Dorothy inadvertently flubbed the one command she was to give. It was as if she had a premonition of the position she would hold during the 1950s as executive director of the Girls Scouts of America. Dorothy said, "I think I must have known then what my future job after the war was going to be. Instead of saying, 'Platoon leaders take charge,' I said, 'Patrol leaders take charge.' And the commander told me about it."

When Dorothy joined the WAVES, the Purdue *Exponent* ran a story with the headline, "Dean Stratton Joins the Women's Reverse [*sic*] of the Navy." Dorothy found the typographical error amusing; it seemed to have subconscious meaning.

After three weeks, Dorothy and two other WAVES were ordered to Washington, DC. Their uniforms had just arrived the night before. Mainbocher, a Chicago native, born Main Rousseau Bocher, designed the WAVE uniform gratis. He was the first American designer in Paris, and prior to that he was an influential fashion journalist. He designed the Duchess of Windsor's wedding dress. Mainbocher produced simple, elegant, expensive apparel that exuded luxury through cut, materials, and workmanship. His fashions were exquisitely finished inside and out, giving self-confidence to the women who wore them.

One of Mainbocher's clients was Josephine Forrestal, a former American *Vogue* writer who married Secretary of the Navy James Forrestal. She made suggestions for the initial uniform design. Some of her suggestions worked; some were impractical. Director of WAVES Mildred McAfee, who would become Dorothy's peer and good friend, said the initial blouse design was "simply impossible to iron." It would have worked for a socialite with a personal maid, but not for women who worked and ironed their own clothing. Nonetheless, the personal connection of a navy wife gave the enlisted women the chance to wear designer apparel for perhaps the only time in their lives.

The *Evening Independent* of St. Petersburg, Florida, ran a story on September 8, 1942, by Wide World Fashion Editor Dorothy Roe, titled "Clothes for 10,000 Best-Dressed Women." Roe wrote:

> Join the Navy and be dressed by Mainbocher.
>
> No such words have appeared on the recruiting posters, of course, but the psychological effect is the same. . . .
>
> They don't want to be surpassed by those snappy WAACs, and that's why Uncle Sam's sailor girls now can look the Duchess of Windsor in the eye and say:
>
> "I believe we have the same dressmaker."

> Neatest trick of the season is the lapel design, which is carried through all WAVES uniforms and coats: a rounded collar over peaked revers. The navy says this design is now the property of the U.S. government.
>
> The complete WAVES wardrobe consists of the following: Navy serge winter uniforms, reserve blue summer uniform, white summer dress uniform, victory blouse in white rayon, navy spun rayon and reserve blue cotton, navy serge raincoat and havelock, navy Melton greatcoat, hat with stitched navy serge brim and interchangeable navy or white tops, black calf shoes and handbag. The girls will select their own lingerie, the navy announces with a sigh of relief, and they will wear beige stockings of a uniform shade.

The revers is the turned back edge of a garment that reveals the reverse side or lining. A havelock is a cover worn over the military cap with fabric that extends downward to protect the neck from sun and weather. Melton is a heavy woolen cloth with a close-cut nap used in overcoats.

The Mainbocher uniform, along with its essential accessories, was understated perfection for the women of the navy. Each WAVE was given a $200 allowance for the purchase of her uniform. When the women first donned their uniforms and were seen in public, they turned heads. People were not accustomed to seeing women in uniform. During World War II, silk stockings were not available because all silk was used to manufacture parachutes. Stockings were made from other materials, such as cotton lisle made from a fine, smooth, tightly twisted thread. The flawlessly tailored deep blue jackets with gold buttons and six-gore skirts worn at mid-calf level, along with their jaunty side-brimmed hat, made every WAVE look and feel effortlessly powerful, ready to greet the world.

Dorothy remembered the trip to Washington with two of her fellow WAVES wearing their new Mainbocher uniforms. She said, "We traveled by train in those days. As we walked through the train to go to the diner, you could hear the whispers, 'The WAVES. The WAVES. The WAVES.'"

When Dorothy arrived in Washington, it was very crowded. The war had brought an onslaught of Americans to the area. Dorothy thought, "Dear Lord, preserve me from ever being ordered to duty in Washington during the war." Her prayer went unanswered as she would soon be assigned to Washington and rarely leave for the next three-and-a-half years.

For a very short time, Dorothy was assigned as the assistant to the commanding officer at the University of Wisconsin-Madison radio operators' school, the first such school for women. Because both WAVES and the radio operators' school were brand new, they all "stumbled along" trying to find their way. Dorothy's responsibility was to see that the women were "looked after." It was as if Dorothy was dean of women again. She was the one to find housing, food, and uniforms for the WAVES. Then she received a message that would change her life even further. Dorothy remembered:

> After I'd been there between three and four weeks, I got a telegram from the Naval Office of Personnel telling me to report by the fastest transportation possible to Washington. The fastest transportation I could get was a train. So, I reported . . . and I was promptly taken to the Coast Guard over on 1300 E. Street. There I was taken into a room full of admirals. I think that I probably had never seen an admiral before in my life, and here was a room full of them. Then I was asked a good many questions.

The admirals told Dorothy they were looking for a woman to direct the Women's Reserve of the U.S. Coast Guard, the nation's oldest sea service. One of the admirals in attendance was Commandant Russell Waesche, whom Dorothy would grow to admire for his impartiality. After the interview, Dorothy thought she would hear back in six weeks, but she received a response almost immediately. Dorothy recalled, "So, the navy lent me to the coast guard. There was no legislation yet."

Dorothy said of her new position to lead women in the coast guard: "It seems fitting for women to be connected with a unit that has as its main purpose the protection and conservation of life and property."

Looking back, Dorothy speculated that Mildred McAfee was the one to recommend her to be interviewed. Mildred had a gift for finding the right person for the right job. Dorothy had known Mildred when she was dean of women at Oberlin College. Dorothy quickly went back to Madison to tie up loose ends and returned to Washington to look for a place to live, but the city was so crowded that Dorothy could not find an apartment. She said, "Finally at the American Association of University Women, I got a sort of enlarged closet, which had a couch in it. It had nothing else, but it was all there was. I said, 'I'm not going to be here much, anyway. I'll take anything.' So I got this little room, which had a window opening on the shaft. You never could tell whether the sun was shining or it was raining."

Dorothy had numerous responsibilities to think about, but one loomed large. She said:

> Then came the question—what were we going to call this unit of the Women's Reserve of the Coast Guard? There wasn't anyone else except me to think about this. Everyone else had his mind on more important things. So I tossed on that hard bed many nights trying to think what we'd call this organization. Sometimes when you just absolutely have to do something, you do it. Suddenly, it came to me from the motto of the Coast Guard—"Semper Paratus—Always Ready—SPAR." I proposed it to the commandant and his assistants. They accepted it and that was it.

The nautical meaning of "SPAR" refers to a supporting beam of a ship. Dorothy said, "That is what we hope each member of the women's reserve will be." The enlisted women took over the men's stateside military jobs, freeing them to go to Europe and the Pacific for combat duty. The name was perfect: short, easy to remember, and imbued with double meaning. The SPARs were "always ready" as the supporting arm of the coast guard.

Mildred's father pointed out that the name also stood for four of the freedoms for which the United Nations were fighting—freedom of speech, press, assembly, and religion.

When she was selected as director, Dorothy knew nothing about the coast guard. She had never seen a coast guard officer. She said, "I felt if that was the place where I could work, that was fine with me. In other words, I only cared about being where I could feel I was doing something useful, and I thought this would be useful."

To indoctrinate herself into the ways of the coast guard, Dorothy asked that an officer be assigned to her to be available to answer questions and keep her from making mistakes. Dorothy said, "He was a very handsome coast guard officer, Commander Jewell. I don't know whether he liked the assignment, but he was tremendously helpful to me, because without him I would have made many more blunders than I did."

On November 23, 1942, legislation was passed creating the Coast

Guard Women's Reserve, SPARs. Dorothy was sworn in the next day as lieutenant commander, the same rank as the navy's Mildred McAfee, who attended the swearing-in ceremony. Mildred laughed and said, "I feel like the mother of the bride."

To save time, Dorothy asked Mildred if she could obtain a "nucleus" of the WAVE officers to start SPARs. Mildred and the navy agreed, so Dorothy returned to Northampton and made a plea to the women. Twelve WAVES volunteered to become the first SPARs.

Dorothy was authorized to select her own executive officer. The first person she thought of was Helen Schleman. From her glass-front office at the rambling brick coast guard headquarters, sitting at her walnut desk that displayed a clock in the shape of a ship's wheel and a new blue rug underfoot, Dorothy contacted Helen at Purdue's Women's Residence Hall where she was still the director. In a 1970 interview, Helen remembered, "Dorothy called me and asked me if I could come. She said if I was going to join one of the services at all, I had better come right then, because that was when I was needed. So, I did decide to go. I thought I should."

Without a day's military training, Helen was sworn into the coast guard over the telephone on December 14, 1942. She was the second officer to join the SPARs, becoming the executive officer with the rank of lieutenant, senior grade. She immediately left West Lafayette for Washington. The two Purdue friends, colleagues, and coauthors would lead the SPARs during World War II.

Helen talked of her initial task: "Our first job was to recruit. To get started we simply sat down at a desk and thought of all the women we knew who probably should come into the military service to help. We got in touch with them and tried to get them to come into the coast guard."

Dorothy and Helen telephoned their professional colleagues and said, "You have been recommended for a commission in the coast guard." The response was highly successful.

Next, the SPARs needed a uniform. Dorothy remembered:

> The WAVES already had a very good-looking uniform designed by Mainbocher. Somebody in the coast guard had also designed a uniform for the SPARs. So which one was going to be chosen?

> With great solemnity, a whole room full of admirals sat around and decided which uniform was the one to be worn. As I recall, it was one of my more amusing experiences—watching the admirals go through this process of deciding what the women were going to wear. I think I probably put in my nickel's worth, but I wouldn't say that it was the deciding voice. They finally decided on the WAVE uniform with the coast guard insignia, which was a good idea.

With the perfect name coined for coast guard women, Helen sworn in as her right-hand woman, the spiffy SPAR uniform selected, and recruits trickling in, Dorothy was making headway in her new position. She was accomplishing what she had said she wanted—to be useful. And she was doing "interesting things."

Dorothy understood that deep down the coast guard didn't want women any more than the navy did. So how did they arrive at the decision to include women? Dorothy was candid:

> Admiral Waesche, who was the commandant, was a very far-seeing man. It was a little hard to hold out after the army and the navy had accepted women. My biggest job in the beginning was to get some kind of acceptance. My first job, personally, was to convince the coast guard that the navy hadn't foisted off the worst they had on them, because the coast guard was pretty sure that the navy would give them the bottom of the barrel. So I had to live down the fact that I had been in the WAVES.

A story in the *Washington Times-Herald* was stinging in the approach taken. The headline read, "'Deserter' made head of SPARs, Dorothy C. Stratton Left WAACs, WAVES." The text stated, "Lieut. Comdr. Dorothy C. Stratton 'deserted' the Army and then the Navy to land in the Coast Guard as chief of the Women's group to aid that branch of the service in its paper and housework."

Mildred offered Dorothy some words of wisdom garnered from her own experience as director of WAVES. Mildred said, "I thought it was very important for me to keep the reins in my own hands, until I discovered that there were no reins."

14

Don't Be a Spare . . . Be a SPAR!

"Release a man to go to sea!" The SPAR recruitment poster encouraged women to join the coast guard to take over men's jobs so they could board ships and defend the coast. However, truth be told, some men did not want to be released to go to sea; they wanted to stay landlocked. So, the SPARs' presence was a double-edged sword. Some saw them as an asset; others saw them as a liability.

Dorothy Stratton brought prestige to her position as director of the SPARs, coming in as a dean of women of a large university. Yet her professional career brought another quandary for the coast guard, which did not want to project the "teacher image." Regardless, Dorothy's connection to Purdue and the National Association of Deans of Women drew many deans, teachers, and professors to join the SPAR ranks.

The requirements to become an enlisted SPAR included being between twenty to thirty-six years of age. A married woman could enlist, provided her husband was not in the coast guard. Marrying was prohibited during indoctrination or training. The coast guard wanted women of good character and required three references. The SPAR candidate was required to have at least two years of high school education; some classifications required that the woman be a high school graduate. She had to be at least five feet tall and weigh a minimum of ninety-five pounds, and "weight must be in proportion to your general body build." Vision had to be not less than 12/20 with each eye correctable with glasses to 20/20. Natural teeth had to be in sound condition or have "satisfactory replacements."

An apprentice seaman in the WAVES and SPARs earned $50 a month, and she could work her way up to chief petty officer, earning $126 a month. Food, housing, medical and dental care were all paid living expenses.

College women could earn commissions in the SPARs, with most qualifying as ensigns. By law, only a limited number were allowed to become lieutenants, junior grade and lieutenants, senior grade. They were paid the same allowances as male officers of equivalent rank. Officers had to meet the same requirements as enlisted women except in three respects: age could be twenty to forty-nine; they were to have a college degree or two years of college work plus at least two years of business or professional experience; and they had to have a minimum of eighteen "sound teeth, with at least two molars opposing each other on each side and four opposing front teeth." Evidently, it was assumed an older woman might have fewer teeth.

The WAVES officers were required to have two years of mathematics in high school or college. While Dorothy had always loved school and learning, mathematics was the one academic area she refused to embrace. Thus, the SPARs did not have the math requirement.

An aptitude test was given to all WAVES and SPARs. The recruitment brochure shared by the two women's reserves shows a young woman with her hand raised and a SPAR officer swearing her in as a member of the United States Coast Guard. The caption reads: "It's a proud moment when you raise your right hand and swear allegiance to your country. From then on, you step into a new life—in the service of Uncle Sam!"

The enlisted women were put to work as yeomen, responsible for accounting for supplies like clothing, commissary items, and spare parts necessary to keep the coast guard running. They were purchase agents and accountants. Dorothy's biggest job was to convince the service to accept women. She said, "If you could get the doors open so that the women could get a chance to do the jobs, they could do the jobs. But to get the doors open, that was not so easy. It took a good deal of personal contact, not only with the men officers, but also with their wives."

Dorothy understood that if the wives of the coast guard officers accepted the SPARs, half their battle was won. Dorothy felt there was a good chance of opposition from the wives on a number of bases. First, women were going to be immediately commissioned as officers, perhaps as lieutenant, junior grade, when it had taken the men ten years to obtain that rank. Secondly, the SPARs would be working directly with men, which could be perceived as a threat by their wives. And thirdly, there was the umbrella question of, "Why should women be in the coast guard anyway? This was a man's world, a man's job, and what were the women doing there?" With these three potential roadblocks in mind, Dorothy strategized her offense. She said, "We just tried to make friends. I suppose you could say by design, intentionally. Really, that isn't any different from what it is in a university. If the president' wife likes you, it helps a lot. I tell you who was a great help to us—Mrs. Forrestal."

Josephine Forrestal was the wife of Secretary of the Navy James Forrestal. She had influenced the Mainbocher uniform design, and because she was enthusiastic about women in the service, she swayed her husband.

After Dorothy became director, she was invited to take a ride on a coast guard cutter (even though she was susceptible to seasickness) and make a "test flight" in a coast guard plane. She also toured the training ship, *Denmark*, docked at the academy at New London, Connecticut.

At Mildred McAfee's suggestion, to save taxpayers' money, the first class of enlisted SPARs was trained at Hunter College with the WAVES. Later, the SPARs needed to separate from the WAVES. Each service has its own traditions, so for the sake of gaining acceptance within the coast guard, Dorothy parted from the navy training. By then, the army and navy were using most of the hotels in the country for training, and finding an available location was difficult for her latecomer group.

Dorothy and her immediate superior, Chief of Personnel Admiral Robert Donohue, took a train to the Biltmore, known as the "Pink Palace," in Palm Beach, Florida. The owner of the Biltmore, Colonel Henry Doherty, accompanied them and "wined and dined" them as enticement to choose his hotel as the first dedicated school for the SPARs—a way for Doherty to aid the war effort in a big way and garner positive public relations. Dorothy and the admiral found the location to be satisfactory, and 430 rooms in what was then reputed to be the most expensive building yet constructed in Florida were converted into training center space for the enlisted SPARs. Hotel furniture was replaced with "sturdy stuff" and walls were knocked out to accommodate six women per room, removing doors and luxury decorations.

Each morning a SPAR bugler tooted the wake-up call from the patio, and in the evening, *Taps* was played from the same perch. The boot camp included classes in organization, personnel, ships, and aircraft. Enlistees practiced deck swabbing in the hotel hallways. Disciplined physical training was held at the Surf Club, which gave the women exclusive use of the tennis courts and beach. Graduates become storekeepers, yeomen, cooks, bakers, commissary stewards, dental or pharmacist mates, or recruiters. The women were sworn in for the duration of the war and six months after.

Dorothy would fly down to Palm Beach with the commandant to meet each class of SPARs, often taking along a notable figure like Josephine Forrestal. Other training stations would be implemented on college campuses. In an interview by Robin J. Thomson, which was recorded on the coast guard website, Chief Storekeeper Mary Jane Klein said, "I began guarding the coast in the corn state of Iowa. Not a drop of salt water, nor a sailor in sight."

Dorothy reported directly to Admiral Donohue, but if there was a crucial need, she could see Admiral Waesche. Dorothy said, "Then I could get things ironed out very easily. He was a wonderful man to work for. He gave us all the help that he could, and that made all the difference in the world."

Overall, Dorothy's work with her male colleagues was pleasant. She said, "I didn't have any battles of any kind that I recall with the men officers. In fact, I enjoyed working with them very much. They were good to me."

One of Dorothy's biggest troubles was in finding recruits, which surprised her. She said, "I thought we'd have a rush to the colors, but we didn't. From early on we had to fight the propaganda—that women were just camp followers who weren't really in for any serious purpose. We did not get this from within the service, that I know of, but from the public."

The other women's reserve directors were Dorothy's mentors and cohorts in the cause to recruit more women and encourage them to prove their mettle. They had to counteract newspaper stories and hearsay. Military men and some civilians assumed that many women who joined the service were "loose" or of less than reputable character, except for the nurses, who were seen as angels of mercy as they cared for the wounded. After a particularly stinging story appeared, Oveta Hobby, director of WAACS, whose husband was a newspaperman, said, "I just thought I couldn't hold my head up again. I talked to my husband and he said, 'Oveta, never pay any attention to anything that isn't true.'"

If just one member of the SPARs, WAVES, or WAACS presented herself in an unfavorable light, then all women in the military were considered by the public to be like that one bad seed.

In 1970, Dorothy, always the progressive, said, "I should think we've become much more enlightened in the last twenty years, in civilian life, anyway. In terms of what's acceptable and accepted and what isn't."

Within the service the climate was good. Once the women and men worked together, they liked and respected one another. The men grew to realize that the women were there to work diligently and contribute. However, the media painted a different scenario. Dorothy explained, "We didn't get the favorable newspaper stories that could have helped us. The newspaper often would look for the lurid story, but I don't think we worried too much about it. We were too busy trying to get on with the job."

There was a need for public relations to aid recruitment. Dorothy said, "The director of public relations was a regular coast guard captain. We never had very good public relations. I would say that was a very weak area for us, very weak."

The lack of PR may have been one reason there were fewer SPARs than WAVES, and why today, many people are still unfamiliar with the term SPARs. The coast guard was very poor compared to the navy and had no money to spend on promotion. Yet they did have many photographs and appealing recruitment posters. The posters were designed in bold colors or soft, earthy hues with patriotic themes, catchy phrases, and the image of an attractive, wholesome SPAR in uniform. Some of the headlines read: "Your Duty Ashore . . . His Afloat"; "The Girl of the Year is a Spar"; "Make a Date with Uncle Sam"; and "Don't Be a Spare . . . Be a SPAR."

Black-and-white recruitment films were created that were shown in movie houses before feature films, including "Coast Guard Spars" (a video that today can be found online). As peppy marching band music plays behind images of coast guard women filing papers, typing on Underwood typewriters, and chauffeuring high-ranking coast guard men, a zealous announcer states, "There are many jobs the coast guard needs you for! The skills learned today could mean better jobs tomorrow. You won't get to be an admiral, but you may be the admiral's secretary!"

Recruiting brochures were distributed, newspaper and magazine articles were written, and books were authored, including the fictional *Patty Lou in the Coast Guard* by Basil Miller. It was a religiously oriented wartime story describing the adventures of Patty Lou, a missionary in the coast guard. There also was a stage show that became a movie. Dorothy said:

> We had the show *Tars and Spars*, which was kind of a morale builder that toured the country and went to the coast guard installations. It caused us a lot of headaches. The same kind you have on a college campus when the glee club rehearses after eleven o'clock at night. They just never lived by the regulations; they weren't that kind. The ones that go into something like a musical show are not exactly the kind that lives up to military regulations. But perhaps it was a morale builder. I hope so.

The "kind" to which Dorothy referred was the likes of comic actor Sid Caesar. Caesar enlisted in the coast guard in 1939 and was stationed in Brooklyn, New York, where he played in military revues and shows. He was ordered to Palm Beach, where Vernon Dukes, the famous composer of "Autumn in New York," "April in Paris," and "Taking a Chance on Love," along with Howard Dietz, who had worked for MGM and created the movie company's iconic mascot, Leo the Lion, were producing a service revue called *Tars and Spars*. At Palm Beach, where the SPARs were stationed, he met the civilian director, Max Liebman, who later produced Caesar's first television series. When his comedy received more applause than the musical numbers, Liebman asked him to do stand-up routines between the songs. The *Tars and Spars* revue became Caesar's first major gig as a comedian, and it toured nationally.

Columbia Pictures made a film version of *Tars and Spars* in 1946 (the video of which can be found online), and Caesar reprised his role. He would go on to be best known for his TV series *Your Show of Shows* and *Caesar's Hour*, winning an Emmy Award.

More than 10,000 women volunteered to become SPARs between 1942 and 1946. Statistically, it was the smallest women's reserve unit in the war. Initially, the navy limited the number of WAVES to 10,000, but by the end of the war there were nearly 90,000 WAVES on duty at 900 naval stations in the United States and Hawaii. Beverley (Bev) Stone, who would become an assistant dean of women at Purdue in the next decade, was one of them, stationed at the United States Naval Receiving Station in Charleston, South Carolina, as an assistant personnel officer. In a 1985 talk entitled "Women in the Navy," Bev described her duties:

> I was told I would have to serve temporarily as officer in charge of enlisted WAVES barracks. When I arrived at the newly constructed barracks . . . I discovered that there were no doors on the enlisted women's toilets and no curtains in the gang showers. As a new ensign with bright and shiny gold bars, I spent most of my first week going up the chain of command step by step until I finally got to the commandant of the navy yard, insisting at every step that enlisted women had to have privacy in their bathroom. A week later workmen arrived with doors for the toilets and curtains for the gang showers—my first success in my new career!

The barracks where Bev lived were on Noisette Creek. She said they were very well planned for maximum comfort with a "beauty parlor, linen room, and large lounge with piano, radio-victrola, books, and magazines." Behind the barracks was Wave Haven, a recreation house that was attractively furnished and equipped for parties and snacks. The women brought their dates to Wave Haven. A "specialist" was on duty to assist in planning refreshments or serving as hostess for special occasions.

As officer in charge of WAVES' barracks, Bev's duties included handling transfers and receipts of personnel, family allowances, and discipline. She also interviewed and assigned personnel to work billets, the military's term for accommodations. When she enlisted, Bev received a song booklet entitled "Marching to Victory." The cover shows the WAVES' color guard marching in their Mainbocher uniforms, complete with white gloves. A battalion of WAVES in formation is seen behind them on a grassy field, their white hats marking a dotted line in the distance. The songbook states, "Singing people are essentially happy people. And so the WAVES have a song for everything." One of the songs is "A Guy to Tie My Tie" with the beginning verse: "I don't need a man to give me sympathy. / Why I needed it before is a mystery / But there are things I can't do alone / No matter how I try. / High and dry, / I need a guy to tie my tie." The song ends with this verse: "Some day this will end / And I'll be back with you / And every morning you'll find / This little Wave is standing by / To comply / I'll be the guy to tie your tie."

The SPARs also liked to sing and had their own songbook to build camaraderie. It was as if the women were part of a 1940s musical where actors break out in song during the most ordinary of moments. Bev's songbook states: "When something good happens, when something not so pleasant comes along, when swinging up from drill on a glowing autumn day, when struggling on the icy hills to class on a bitter Saturday morning, when sitting waiting, just waiting, standing in a line, somewhere in the ranks a song starts and grows and swells in volume until all are singing."

THE AVERAGE SPAR VOLUNTEER was a single, twenty-two-year-old high school graduate. The women volunteered for various reasons. There were those whose husbands had been called to service and were lonely, those who wanted to get away from the routine, those who would make any sacrifice to contribute, and those who wanted to join the coast guard and "see the world."

The advertisements encouraging women to enlist touted "opportunities for advancement." Many women had been stuck in dead-end civilian jobs. In the services they obtained training, much of it technical, that they never could have obtained in civilian life.

While learning new skills, the women marched ten miles a day, marching to classes, dormitories, and the mess hall. Dorothy said, "A lot of energy went into marching, which a great many people thought was pretty foolish, and in some ways it was. In some ways I think it wasn't, because a certain feeling of unity did come out of marching together. The SPARs liked to march; they enjoyed it."

Even though Dorothy was the director of the SPARs and Mildred McAfee directed the WAVES, neither had command functions. Their commanding officer called the shots. Dorothy could only try to persuade her CO. She explained:

> There were those who thought that the Women's Reserve should be set up as a separate unit with a command function, with a director. There were those who felt it should be integrated into the regular service. And I think that was the better decision. While it made the job of the director a little more difficult, perhaps, it was much better. After all, if you can't persuade to your point of view, either you're not making a good case for it or you haven't got a good case to start with.
>
> It gave the women much more of a feeling of belonging to the coast guard, and the coast guard a feeling that the SPARs were part of the outfit. It made the position of the director very anomalous, but very few people knew it.

Dorothy and her SPARs followed the coattails of the WAVES, allowing them to take advantage of what the navy women had already set up. Mildred and her officers helped Dorothy tremendously, and Dorothy and her officers, in turn, helped the WAVES, either by telephone or in person. When the Marine Corps Women's Reserve was formed, the SPARs assisted them. It was women helping women. The WAACS helped the WAVES, the WAVES helped the SPARs, and the SPARs helped the Marines.

One of the first questions Dorothy had to answer was, "How was a female officer to be addressed?" The WAACS called the army woman "Ma'am." The WAVES addressed the navy woman by her name, as in, "Good morning, Miss Jones." Dorothy explained, "We just decided that since women were in the service, we could just say, 'Good morning, sir.' So we used 'sir' for everybody, men and women. That got us over one very awkward hump. Nobody liked 'ma'am,' and a lot of people didn't like 'sir' either, but you had to do something."

The Coast Guard Academy on the banks of the Thames River in New London, Connecticut, was the only men's academy to train female officers during World War II. None of the other armed services followed suit. The six-week training was tough on the first women, because the standards had been set for men. Many of these women were in their thirties and were performing physical activities, learning to shoot guns, and learning skills that they would not be called to use later.

Every six weeks, Dorothy attended the graduation ceremony at the Coast Guard Academy, which graduated more than 700 women during the war. She never missed a ceremony. Dorothy was compelled to be there to convey her genuine interest in the cadets. She believed in personal contact. Dorothy said, "It gave me a chance to chat with them informally and see how they were feeling about things. They could say, 'I feel some identification. I don't think Washington is just some place over there that never heard of me.' When you had to send women where the service wanted them to go and not where they wanted to go, it seemed to me to be extremely important to have some feeling of humanness and of individual interest. Furthermore, I enjoyed going."

Dorothy spoke to each graduating class, often taking an influential woman with her on the trip, like Congresswoman Margaret Chase Smith, whom she said was very helpful. Much like Lillian Gilbreth, Margaret continued her husband's work after his death. She was married to House Representative of Maine Clyde Smith, and Margaret assumed his position after he died unexpectedly in 1940. Known as the "Lady from Maine," she voted her conscience, not party line. An advocate for women's rights, she cosponsored the Equal Rights Amendment with Congresswoman Winifred Stanley in the mid-1940s. Margaret also worked on improving the status of women in the military. In 1964, she tried to become the Republican presidential nominee, but she lost to Senator Barry Goldwater.

IT WAS HELEN SCHLEMAN'S JOB to match the graduates' interests and abilities with their work assignments. She talked to the women individually to make a good position match for success of the individual and of the service. Helen kept extensive files on each officer. Most SPARs changed assignments during their enlistment time. Few kept the same job throughout their service.

SPARs became part of an initiative that was only spoken of behind closed doors—LORAN. The "long range aid to navigation" was a secretive monitoring station in Chatham, Massachusetts, which is believed to be the only women-run unit during the war. Dorothy was even kept in the dark. She said, "That was very hush-hush, and I know very little about it myself."

Commanding Officer Vera Hamerschlag, took a two-month LORAN operations course at Massachusetts Institute of Technology. The eleven enlisted SPARs took a one-week course in operations, and their mission was so secretive that not even the training officers knew what the duties of these women would be. When the commanding officer reported to Chatham, it was crewed solely by men. Within one month, it was turned over to 100 percent SPARs, except for one male radio technician, who joined his shipmates in overseas duty six months after the women arrived.

The LORAN women stood watch twenty-four hours a day recording measurements every two minutes of the radio signals transmitted from two shore-based stations. The signals were picked up by receivers on ships and planes, enabling sea and air navigators to calculate their exact positions.

The 50-by-30-foot station was complete with barracks, recreation room, office space, operations room, and all necessities for living and working around the clock. The station's antenna rose from the building on a 125-foot mast. Commander Hamerschlag said, "The human element of the work kept it from getting dull and routine for the operators. The thought that we were participating in a system that was playing such an important part in winning the war gave us a feeling of being as close to the front lines as it was possible for SPARs."

An article was written for the Girl Scout magazine, the *American Girl*, in October 1943, titled "Skipper of the Spars, a Spar writes her impressions of Lieutenant Commander Stratton, the dynamic woman who directs the Women's Reserve of the United States Coast Guard." Mary C. Lyne, a newly commissioned SPAR, wrote the article, giving her impressions of Dorothy when she met with Mary's graduating class at the Coast Guard Academy. The article appeared with a photo of Mildred and Dorothy in their uniforms, chatting as they sat at what looks like a military dinner. Lyne wrote:

> Somewhat bewildered Coast Guard officers nervously awaited the appearance of their skipper. What kind of person would our Commanding Officer be? We had waited for her all day long, expecting to be summoned any minute to a formal meeting in the boardroom. The day passed and we were at officers' mess, convinced that our skipper would arrive with due ceremony the following morning. Just as we were in the middle of the soup course, the door at the end of the dining hall was opened quietly and, completely unheralded by fanfare, in stepped Lieutenant Commander Dorothy C. Stratton, Director of the Coast Guard SPARs.

Dorothy slipped into a chair at the end of the table and put the new SPARs at ease with her smile. By the end of the day, she had interviewed all thirteen women individually. Mary continued, describing Dorothy:

> She had come aboard as unobtrusively as her lowliest ensign. And she was not only attractive and extremely competent, she also had a wonderful sense of humor. Miss Stratton is a slim, alert woman with the well-knit figure and the clear, tanned skin of an athlete. Her hair is brown, touched with gray, and she brushes it back from her face in two soft rolls. Her handclasp is strong and firm, and her eyes are remarkably expressive. When talking, she speaks in a low, earnest voice, and whatever she has to say sounds sincere and convincing. She is the kind of person you like instinctively and trust implicitly because she has rare sensitivity to the feelings of others.

Another of Helen's responsibilities was to oversee the building of barracks for the SPARs. Once again, Helen and Dorothy dealt with the issue of adequate housing for women. Like Bev Stone, who ensured that women's accommodations for the WAVES in Charleston were made private, Helen insisted that the SPAR housing was not the "open barracks" concept. In some locations across the country, the SPARs had to settle on living in old, decrepit hotels. Dorothy said, "In Atlantic City, we had a big contingent of enlisted SPARs. Even though the coast guard was very, very careful about fire, I was terrified of fire in those old buildings. I felt a very deep responsibility for the lives of the women who'd come into the service. The men's units had the good hotels. They were all taken. We had to take what we could get, and a lot of it wasn't very good."

Dorothy was promoted to captain on February 1, 1944. Mildred had been promoted to captain, as well. At that time, no more than one woman could attain the rank of captain in the navy and coast guard or the rank of colonel in the army and marines. Dorothy had a humorous experience on Pennsylvania Avenue, across from the White House. She said, "I was walking one day and this enlisted man in the navy came along. He looked at me, put his hands on his hips, and said, 'Ha, ha, ha, a captain in the Hooligan Navy,' and threw back his head and laughed. So I threw back my head and laughed, and we passed each other very pleasantly."

The enlisted man walked on without saluting Captain Stratton. Dorothy good-naturedly said that many funny incidents occurred with regards to saluting. For example, "I was down in Norfolk. I had a SPAR driver, a very good driver, who never saluted. So the officer in charge had a little chat with her, and said, 'Look, this won't do. You're supposed to salute.' She said, 'Well, I'll tell you, I just don't care very much for saluting.'"

Another story would have made good script material for an Abbott and Costello movie. Dorothy and Mildred were traveling by train to the West Coast, when they encountered a curious woman nearby staring at the two of them. Dorothy said, "The little old lady couldn't stand it any longer. Finally, she looked across, and she said, 'Excuse me, but do you mind if I ask you—are you a WAAC, a WAVE, or a SPAM?'"

15

Meanwhile, Back at the Ranch

While Dorothy and Helen were working for the coast guard and on unpaid leave from Purdue, Clare E. Coolidge was the acting dean of women, and Irene Feldt was the acting director of the Women's Residence Halls. The campus changed during the war years. Most male students were in uniform, attending classes and receiving military training through the V-12 Navy College Training Program or the Army Specialized Training Program (ASTP).

When the draft age was lowered to eighteen in 1942, the nation's colleges and universities feared economic collapse without students to fill classrooms, while the navy and army foresaw a shortage of college-educated officers. As an answer to both dilemmas, the government created the V-12. The V-12 men attended nearly 130 colleges and universities in the United States, including Purdue. African American men were allowed to enroll in the V-12 navy program nearly a year before there were any black officers in the navy. Frederick C. Branch became the first black marine corps officer in the United States after completing his V-12 training at Purdue.

The ASTP was similar to V-12, utilizing colleges and universities across the country to provide a four-year education combined with specialized army technical training. When the invasion of Normandy called for additional manpower in Europe, the army disbanded the program, and the ASTP soldiers were assigned to the infantry to fight in the European and Pacific Theaters.

Men in navy pea coats and olive drab uniforms dotted grassy Memorial Mall and the classrooms of Purdue. Fraternity houses became living quarters for military students. They also lived at Cary Quadrangle, the men's residence hall that came to be known as USS Cary. Temporary barracks were built throughout campus to house the onslaught of soldiers. Both V-12 and ASTP had a major impact on American education and produced leaders for the top echelons of business and the professions.

As universities anticipated the loss of men on their campuses, they began publishing pamphlets on careers for women, and academic departments were pushed to expand their women-oriented curriculums to woo more females to college. Throughout the United States, nearly every action and endeavor was implemented with the impetus to win the war for peace. In *Purdue News, the University Handbook,* Acting Dean of Women Coolidge wrote a page entitled "For the Women." Clare said, "Women who have the privilege of attending college today have an inescapable obligation to the nation. The resources of the University are all devoted to winning the war and the peace. You are one of our most important resources: therefore, you, too, should so devote yourselves. . . . New opportunities for women are constantly presenting themselves. It is vitally important to you and to your country that you make an intelligent choice."

There were two new groups of female Purdue students: the Curtiss-Wright Engineering Cadettes and the Radio Corporation of America (RCA) Engineering Cadettes.

The Curtiss-Wright Corporation was an aircraft manufacturer formed by the partnering of companies founded by Glenn Curtiss, the father of naval aviation, and flight's famous Wright brothers. Curtiss-Wright moved into mass production for the war and was in dire need of skilled workers, as they were in danger of defaulting on their contract to provide the navy with a new dive bomber, the Helldiver. In the fall of 1942, Curtiss-Wright contacted engineering colleges to train qualified women in an accelerated engineering curriculum. A total of seven institutions, including Purdue, trained more than 900 women as Curtiss-Wright Engineering Cadettes. They were then placed as assistants in engineering departments at the company's facilities around the country. The Curtiss-Wright recruiting booklet stated, "You as the Curtiss-Wright Cadette will be a co-worker with the Soldier, the Sailor, and the Marine, and will share with them the responsibility of the war effort. This is your opportunity to add your name to the roll of individual service, to give our valiant men the weapons to save America!"

Women were selected on the basis of academic ability, attitude, and interest, and they had to have completed two years of college. Three hundred Curtiss-Wright Engineering Cadettes trained at Purdue beginning in February 1943. The group studied forty hours a week for ten months, covering a compressed curriculum equivalent to two and a half years of the standard engineering program. The cadettes were housed separately from the traditional student population and attended classes separately. The women were considered employees of the Curtiss-Wright Corporation and were paid ten dollars a week. College credit was given, and their tuition and board were provided.

The RCA Engineering Cadettes started at Purdue in May 1943. RCA, a "heritage company" of today's Lockheed Martin, sent eighty-six women from seventeen states to Purdue for nearly a year of intense training in math, drafting, shop, electrical circuit theory, electronics, radio theory, and more. Purdue was the only school chosen for the RCA Engineering Cadette program.

According to Lockheed's website, the women donned flannel work shirts on the shop floors and toiled alongside their male counterparts. The March 1943 issue of *Purdue Engineering* mentioned the RCA Engineering Cadettes in "engineer speak": "The advent of skirts, light footfalls, and the lilt of soprano voices into the heretofore masculine environment . . . caused many a head to rotate through the angle theta and many a neck to exceed all previously known elasticity constraints."

The RCA Engineering Cadettes graduated a year after they began their education at Purdue and were immediately placed into jobs as engineering aids in one of six RCA Victor plants around the country.

The Curtiss-Wright Engineering Cadettes were hired in the airframe and propeller divisions. Amelia Earhart would have been proud of her Purdue women, yet they were underutilized. The cadettes' assignments were primarily in drafting, which included drawing, making copies, sketching changes, and checking finished sketches. In other words, they took what the men had created and handled the mundane adjustments and follow-through. Purdue cadette Jeannette Tremlin Wickes, who worked at the Columbus, Ohio, plant said, "I saw myself as an engineer in training. . . . I don't think the men felt that we were, but we felt that we were. Actually, we were probably better trained than some of the men in the department."

Many of the women felt their education had prepared them for more substantial undertakings than the low-level work they were given, and eventually they left the program because of the tedium. Curtiss-Wright claimed the cadettes did not recognize the seriousness and importance of their contributions, while the women saw "these clerical, repetitious, and unchallenging jobs" as busywork, indicating that they were not truly needed. Eventually, Curtiss-Wright conceded and declared that by 1944, "forty-three percent of the women enrolled had left the program" with the primary reason for loss of interest due to the fact the "women were overtrained and not challenged by their jobs."

The majority of women were treated kindly on the job. Some women did move up to weightier positions, like material testing or electrical design, but even those more challenging positions would abruptly end when the war was over. Dorothy Wurster Rout, another Purdue Curtiss-Wright Engineering Cadette who worked in Columbus, remembered receiving her pink slip over the airwaves: ". . . when the war was over, they announced it on the radio. 'Don't report to work,' and then the next day you were out of a job."

Rout went on to earn a degree in education and history with a minor in math. When asked decades later if she still thought of herself as an engineer, she answered in the affirmative, which is a testament to the enduring power of the cadette engineering programs, personally, if not professionally.

One would expect the cadette engineering education to have been a breakthrough for women in technical fields, and that these pioneering females would have changed employers' assumptions of women's capabilities. However, when the war ended, traditional gender roles persisted, highly touted in feel-good propaganda as the military men returned to the United States and resumed their previously held jobs. Women were shooed back home to become housewives or into conventional roles like teaching. So happy they were to have their husbands, fathers, and brothers home safely, many women were content return to these social mores as well.

Dorothy Stratton and Helen Schleman would have their work cut out for them in the next couple of decades to attempt to break women out of the traditional home economics majors and societal expectations of marriage rather than career after college.

In the fall of 1943, the Purdue *Exponent* ran a story titled, "Navy Approves Coed Canteens." The Purdue Student Senate initiated the Coed Canteen project as a morale builder to "better acquaint the service men on the campus with the coeds." The navy "urged all men to cooperate." The Coed Canteens were held on Sunday afternoons at the Women's Residence Halls, sororities, and co-op houses, with the hope that 1,000 men would attend each event.

The canteen concept was originally created by the Hollywood set as a patriotic good time for America's servicemen. The Hollywood Canteen in Los Angeles was for soldiers shipping out from the West Coast, while New York's Stage Door Canteen served men flying out from the East Coast. A uniformed man often visited the "soldier's club" on his last night stateside to kick up his heels with a pretty dance partner who could even be a famous movie star. The canteen offered platters of free sandwiches and cookies and complimentary drinks. A swing band played, and women wearing shoulder pads and swishy, printed taffeta dresses laughed and flirted with the uniformed men who were deliriously happy (at least outwardly), squelching thoughts that in mere hours the men would embark for the Pacific Theatre.

In Anne Petersen's story "The Hollywood Canteen," she writes, "What people forget about is the sexiest part of the war effort, operated entirely outside of the auspices of the war board: The Hollywood Canteen. The Canteen was the brainchild of actor John Garfield, a 'flag-waving socialist' unable to enlist because of a heart condition, and Bette Davis, the so-called 'fourth Warner Brother' and reigning queen of the studio." The two would appear in a movie by the same name in 1944.

Actresses like Lana Turner, Deanna Durbin, and Marlene Dietrich greeted the GIs at the door. Eddie Cantor sang at the Philco microphone. Hedy Lamarr handed out autographs. Red Skelton performed his sad-faced slapstick while wearing his signature fedora with the upturned brim. Jimmy Durante played the piano and cracked jokes. Dinah Shore hosted a film from the canteen and sang a song dedicated to the men serving in China, Burma, and India. She sang Indiana native Cole Porter's "Night and Day" with the lyrics rewritten for the troops: "We think of you night and day."

The Purdue Student Senate was following suit with their Coed Canteens, and Purdue's women students were the gracious hostesses in their own printed taffeta dresses.

In her annual report for 1943–1944, Acting Dean of Women Coolidge focused on what the female students did to contribute to the war effort, including the Coed Canteen. The Purdue Association of Women Students sponsored a convocation where Captain Dorothy Stratton returned to campus for a visit and spoke on "Today's Women Tomorrow." Representatives of the WACS (changed from "WAACS" in January 1943), WAVES, and U.S. Cadet Nurse Corps met with female students.

The Panhellenic Council coordinated bond selling. The War Finance Committee in the Department of the Treasury encouraged the sale of war bonds. Americans purchased securities, which allowed the federal government to finance the war. Bonds also gave civilians the feeling of being involved in the war effort.

Women Purdue students rolled bandages and knitted afghans for the Red Cross. They made scrapbooks and collected books for war prisoners, a project of the Purdue Student War Council. Many donated blood. In her annual Office of the Dean of Women report, Clare wrote about the wartime worries of the young women: "Students seek help with many questions, which reflect the impact of the war. Among these, the most common are whether to remain in college continuously until graduation, or to drop out one term each year to work in a war plant; whether to take a job for the duration; . . . worry about brothers, fiancés or husbands and fathers in the services; . . . keeping interested in school when the future is so uncertain."

Black soldiers in the V-12 or ASTP programs lived in newly built military barracks on Purdue's campus; however, no black student who was not a soldier was allowed dormitory housing. In fact, because of Jim Crow laws, no black men were allowed to live in West Lafayette, Indiana. From the 1880s into the 1960s, a majority of American states enforced segregation through these laws, named after a black minstrel show character. Many states could impose legal punishments on people for consorting with members of another race. The most common types of laws forbade intermarriage and ordered business owners and public institutions to keep black and white patrons separated.

Purdue's black male students had to live across the Wabash River in Lafayette, where two white clergymen opened the International House, a small home where African American men were allowed to live with "foreign" students.

When A. Leon Higginbotham, Jr. came to Purdue to become an engineer in 1944, there were approximately 6,500 white students and 12 black students. Higginbotham lived at the International House, where the men slept in the attic with no heat. Higginbotham met with President Elliott to ask if the students could sleep in a section of one of the heated dorms. It was said that Elliot's response was, "The law doesn't require us to put you in those dormitories. The law doesn't even require us to let you in. You take it or leave it." This incident, along with another that occurred when he traveled with the debate team and could not stay in the same hotel as the other members, influenced Higginbotham to pursue a legal career. Higginbotham said in "The World Center for Women's Archives: A Look Back at a Novel Idea," from spring 1994: "Even though I had been doing very well [at Purdue], I decided that engineering would not make any difference in America. The most . . . a black person could do as an engineer is to make a better gadget—but a gadget [that would] not significantly do anything with the oppression. So I guess on that trip back to the segregated house, International House, I decided that I wanted to go into law and to challenge the system."

Higginbotham went on to graduate from Yale Law School and became one of the United States' most prominent African American judges, as chief judge of the federal appeals court in Philadelphia. He called himself "a survivor of segregation," and in 1995 he received the country's highest civilian honor, the Presidential Medal of Freedom.

The 2009 documentary *Black Purdue* reveals discrimination African American students faced on campus throughout the decades. In the movie (which today can be found online), Reverend Nicholas Hood, Sr. said, "When I arrived at Purdue in 1942, I went through the registration line, and one of the first persons I saw was a counselor. He took one look at me, and he said, 'You don't belong at Purdue. You're not college material.' Being black at Purdue, we were just on the edge of everything. We weren't involved in any of the student organizations. The atmosphere was completely different then."

The Purdue Memorial Union had a barbershop, but black men were not allowed to obtain a haircut there. Black students had to drive an hour south to Indianapolis to find a "colored" barbershop. Hood and Higginbotham visited President Frederick Hovde (Elliott had retired by then) to protest. They told Hovde that they wanted to obtain their haircuts in West Lafayette. Hood remembered, "He listened to us very patiently, then he said, 'Well, we'll put a pair of hair clippers in the service and stores building, and you can check them out and cut your hair.' So, that was such a slap in the face that Leon Higginbotham became a federal judge, a legal scholar."

However, in direct contradiction, in *A Century and Beyond,* author Robert W. Topping wrote that Hovde initiated "an order (dated September 1, 1948) forbidding racial discrimination of any kind in the Purdue Memorial Union Barber Shop."

Housing for black female students was miles from campus in what the documentary terms "the most undesirable parts of West Lafayette." It appears that Acting Dean of Women Coolidge followed Elliott's and Hovde's misguided leads, denying black women housing.

In *Black Purdue*, Frieda Parker Jefferson discusses when she and her sister came to the University in 1946 as students and were refused accommodations. Frieda spoke of the actions of Clare Coolidge: "We received a letter from the Dean of Women, who did everything she could to discourage us from coming and living on the campus, short of telling us how much happier we would be and how the people wouldn't speak to us . . . you know, the same old thing all the time. We didn't believe them anyway."

Fred Parker, Frieda's father, sent a letter to President Hovde, seeking on-campus housing for his daughters. According to the documentary, Hovde denied their admission to the Women's Residence Hall. Parker then sought out Faburn DeFrantz, secretary of the Colored Branch of the Senate Avenue YMCA in Indianapolis. The Senate Avenue YMCA had been dedicated by Booker T. Washington in 1913, and until the 1960s, the organization held the largest membership of any African American branch in the United States. DeFrantz has been credited for the extraordinary political and social awareness and the phenomenal growth of what was called the Negro YMCA. DeFrantz believed that members of the black YMCA must "go forth into battle against the evil forces which were impeding the progress of the Kingdom of God and the Brotherhood of Man."

On behalf of the Parker sisters, DeFrantz assembled a crew of concerned citizens to pay a visit to his friend, Indiana Governor Ralph Gates. Gates, in turn, put pressure on Purdue to allow the Parker sisters access to dormitory housing with white female students in one of the newly built barracks called Bunker Hill. In the spring of 1947, black students were allowed housing at Purdue for the first time.

Decades later, Dorothy and Helen were very closemouthed about Clare and her performance as acting dean of women. To Dorothy and Helen, it was as if Clare never existed; she was an embarrassing blip in the radar of their esteemed Office of the Dean of Women. While Dorothy was away, Clare created—or was unable to thwart—incidents that Dorothy then had to attempt to correct from her post in Washington and that Helen had to "live with" for several years to come.

A talk Dorothy gave, entitled 'Women in the War," in the fall of 1943, revealed her inclusive beliefs and her watchful eye to include women in the vernacular. She said, "Recently, the *Infantry Journal* published an article containing this sentence. 'A soldier in the U.S. uniform is a solider, not a white nor a Negro, Christian or Jew, rich man or poor, but a soldier and as such is worthy of respect.' That sentence might have been expanded to read, 'A soldier in the U.S, uniform is a soldier, not a man or a woman, a white or Negro, a Christian or Jew, rich man or poor, but a soldier and as such is worthy of respect.'"

A year later a newspaper story ran a photo of Dorothy in uniform with the headline, "Leader of Spars in Chicago—Ready to Take Negro Women." Dorothy was quoted: "The Corps will make no distinction on the basis of color. All recruits will qualify on the same basis, train together, live in the same barracks and perform the same type of jobs for the Coast Guard."

16

In Sheep's Clothing

On the first anniversary of the SPARs, Dorothy spoke on two radio broadcasts, an NBC transmission and "Home Front Matinee" on CBS. She thanked the SPAR supporters, lifted up the accomplishments of the SPARs, and made reference to her visits with the women on duty in every area of the United States. She said, "Wherever I have gone, I have asked myself this question, 'What is it that makes the SPARs click? What gives them their esprit de corps?' I believe it comes first from the satisfaction of doing essential, worthwhile jobs; second, from the fact that the coast guard treats its SPARs well; and last, but most important, from sharing in a mighty effort toward a common goal."

One may venture a fourth explanation as to why the SPARs "clicked"—they had a valiant, approachable captain who led by forthright example. Dorothy said that the SPARs were no longer "an experiment," but an integral part of the coast guard and more: "The first anniversary is traditionally the paper one. This is a particularly appropriate designation for our first anniversary, since the SPARs have done a great deal of the paperwork of the coast guard during the past year. Now, however, while continuing to do the paperwork, we are doing shore jobs of almost every kind."

In celebration of their first anniversary, the Washington unit of the SPARs marched in front of the White House. Watching from the reviewing stand in her fox fur stole complete with head and paws was Eleanor Roosevelt. Next to her were Dorothy and the other heads of the women's reserves, including the WAVES' Captain Mildred McAfee.

Dorothy would have other occasions to visit Eleanor Roosevelt. She met her in the Oval Office with President Franklin D. Roosevelt. Dorothy attended Roosevelt's inauguration on January 20, 1945, as well as his memorial service four months later. She was in an elevator with Eleanor in New York City, as Dorothy said years later, "Just the two of us."

By 1945, the SPARs ventured offshore when a bill was passed authorizing women to volunteer for duty in Hawaii and Alaska. Dorothy and Helen would voyage to two exotic lands that would become states in 1959.

Dorothy flew to Hawaii by Pan Am Clipper to make arrangements for housing and to set up operations. The WAVES were already stationed there and helped the SPARs with preparations. About two hundred SPARs followed and were stationed in Honolulu.

Meanwhile, in Charleston, South Carolina, Beverley Stone, heard that the WAVES were approved to serve in Hawaii, and she wanted to go. She requested a transfer to Honolulu. Bev said, "Months went by and there was no response. The executive officer of the naval receiving station had been a regular navy warrant officer who was commissioned during the war. I had properly submitted my request through him to forward to the commanding officer. When I finally inquired whether there had been any response from my request to transfer, he said, 'No—and there wouldn't be.' He said he had refused to submit my request for transfer to the commanding officer 'because Hawaii was no place for a lady to be!'"

It would not be the last time that charming Bev would be aptly referred to as a "lady," and she would always embrace the term; however, to doubt her personal drive was a miscalculation by the navy warrant officer. In years to come, as Purdue's dean of women and dean of students, she would put her ladylike demeanor to good use. She knew how to maneuver monumental career obstacles with the best of them, for Bev was both grace and grit.

The navy warrant officer told Bev he would only forward her request for transfer within the Continental United States. She asked for an assignment to New York City. Bev received her orders to Hunter College shortly thereafter. If Bev had received orders to Hawaii, she may have bumped into Captain Stratton. Nevertheless, in due time, she would meet up with Dorothy and Helen Schleman. The three were moving in concentric circles. In the next decade they would intersect.

While Dorothy headed to a tropical island, Helen donned a fur-lined parka and trekked to Alaska. She received a special assignment to head a survey mission to study how female reservists could be used in that outpost. Her group visited various installations, observing what jobs the men performed, which could be turned over to women. Several hundred SPARs were sent to the Ketchikan, Alaska, office to work in communications and as storekeepers.

On her way to Alaska on a coast guard ship, Helen wrote letters to Dorothy in Washington each day from February 16 to 24, 1945. Helen and her shipmates were parked in a cove, unable to voyage on because of a storm and rough waters. Helen wrote:

> I just sit and wait for the weather to get better. Life is very leisurely, indeed. I just finished making a large and successful batch of fudge—the second one of the week.
>
> Yesterday and the night before were honeys—I was glad you were not aboard for there was certainly much rolling, some pitching, but we were going with the sea so it was not too bad. . . . It was raining and snowing and blowing a gale. Today we sat on deck in the sun with hardly a ripple in our beautiful little cove with pine and snow-covered mountains rearing straight up on three sides of us!
>
> We've been to a movie—*Swamp*. You probably read it. I've never seen so many movies in my life. Tonight Dorothy Lamour. Yesterday Ginger Rogers. I'll never be the same!

Swamp Water sounds like a low-budget horror film, but actually it was a movie based on the novel by Vereen Bell, initially published in serial form in the *Saturday Evening Post* in 1940. Little, Brown published the book in 1941, and it was an immediate sensation, featured on the silver screen later the same year. The story is of the exploits of a young boy, his hunting dog, and a fugitive hiding in the Okefenokee Swamp. *Swamp Water* and Bell were lauded in south Georgia for bringing recognition to the area and to the Okefenokee Swamp.

The mail from Helen's ship was censored. She said, "This censorship business cramps my style just a bit. So, I'm carefully trying not to say anything I shouldn't."

Helen wrote about the men who were her shipmates: "Apparently, the boys themselves may look as awful as they like on board—and it's only when they go ashore that they must shave, dress properly, etc. If anything can make a man look worse than a week's beard and dirty clothes, I don't know what it is!"

A personal, reflective paragraph referred to the time when Dorothy's parents died within seven months of each other, with her mother passing away in February. Helen also thought of her own parents, still living: "I've thought a lot about this time of year three years ago. Golly how it hurt to see you go through what you had to go through with—I'll never forget it. I reckon February will always bring that back to me no matter where I am. I know it does to you much more so, of course. I dread the corresponding time for myself terribly. It sort of hangs over the future somehow."

Ever the outdoorswoman, Helen wrote of the captain allowing several of the shipmates to venture over the side to go duck hunting. It was her first such experience. They saw a group of seals swimming, which reminded Helen of dogs paddling about.

She spent several paragraphs discussing books, which is a topic Dorothy always relished. Helen wrote, "I read *Green Dolphin Street* while onboard. It is beautifully written—isn't it? I keep jotting down page after page that seem to me to say particularly understanding things. Sometime I hope we'll get to talk about Beardsley Ruml's *Tomorrow's Business.* The man is really a philosopher. . . . He makes a very nice distinction between the feeling of freedom and the *fact* of freedom, which I have never heard made before but which seems to me to have merit."

Green Dolphin Street, by Elizabeth Goudge, was published in Britain in 1944. It is the story of a young man in 1800s New Zealand who sends for the woman he loves who lives in the British Isles. Inadvertently, he addresses his letter to her sister, with whom he also shares a past. The book became a top movie in 1947 staring Lana Turner, Van Heflin, and Donna Reed.

Ruml was a statistician and businessman who proposed that the U.S. Treasury collect income taxes through a withholding, pay-as-you-go system that was adopted in 1943. *Tomorrow's Business* was his first book where he unveiled a plan "aimed at something like a revolution in the way 1) many U.S. Businessmen think; 2) the U.S. thinks about business."

A note that Helen scribbled "on Washington's birthday" stated that a dispatch indicated an enemy unit had been picked up in the area where they were anchored, so their ship was in a blackout. Helen wrote in the dark, suppressing thoughts of enemy ships lurking in the murky night.

Her last entry, written in large script, was made after the ship arrived: "In Anchorage, February 28, 8:30 p.m. Three cheers—I'll call when I can."

An Anchorage newspaper ran a photo of Helen and two other SPARs in uniform standing in the Anchorage Hotel lounge with the headline, "Stares Greet Spars in Anchorage." The caption read, "Snappy salutes were the order of the day yesterday when these . . . Spars, the first ever to appear on Anchorage streets, caused a sensation in military circles. They spent the day here on an inspection trip through the Territory."

AN INCIDENT THAT OCCURRED under Acting Dean of Women Clare Coolidge almost cost Dorothy her authority over Purdue's Office of the Dean of Women and subsequent deans of women at the University. While Dorothy was on her leave of absence to lead the SPARs, George E. Davis, the director of the Office of Student Affairs, thought he would do some "rearranging."

Davis wrote a letter to President Elliott in March 1945, proposing that both the Offices of the Dean of Men and Dean of Women be placed under his jurisdiction, with his department having "final authority" over all services provided. He also proposed "the program of the Office of Student Affairs in relation to women students shall not be subject to the approval of the Dean of Women." With this proposal, Dorothy, and Clare in her absence, would report to Davis rather than directly to the president of the University.

Just prior to retiring in June, President Elliott approved Davis' proposal. Soon after, without discussing the subject with Clare, no budget was allowed for the Placement Service for Women. Dean of Engineering A. A. Potter was Purdue's interim president. On July 5, Dorothy wrote a letter to Potter:

> It seems very good to be able to address you as President Potter. The University is fortunate indeed to have you to step into Dr. Elliott's shoes.
>
> I am considerably disturbed to learn via a copy of Miss Coolidge's letter to Dr. Elliott on June 29 that the Placement Service for Women did not receive a budget. I judge from Miss Coolidge's letter that no consultation was held with her concerning this proposed change.
>
> Dr. Elliott and Dr. McHale have repeatedly said that the appointment of a Director of the Office of Student Affairs would entail no change in the women's program and would not affect the Office of the Dean of Women. The elimination of the budget for the Placement Service for Women constitutes a major change.
>
> It does seem to me that before any major changes affecting the organization of student affairs are made that those of us who are directly concerned should discuss the proposed changes thoroughly so that we all understand exactly what the plan is to be. . . . It seems to me only fair that, if changes are proposed affecting this department, there should be full and open discussion of the proposed change. . . .
>
> I believe the budget of the Placement Service for Women should remain where it is. We should not cut the dog's tail bit by bit. If changes are to be made in the area of counseling and student affairs, the full plan should be presented and discussed.
>
> I know that you have many problems on your mind but I do feel that the present confused situation regarding the supervision of student affairs on the campus should be clarified. The question of whether or not the

Director of the Office of Student Affairs has jurisdiction over the activities and the budgets now allocated to the Office of the Dean of Women should be settled soon.

Dorothy sent copies of her letter to Vice President R. B Stewart, Clare Coolidge, George Davis, and Irene Feldt, who served as interim director of the residence halls. Seven days later the only woman on Purdue's Board of Trustees, Kathryn McHale, wrote a strong and pointed letter to Potter:

> Your letter of July the tenth gave me shocking news. . . . Dr. E. C. Elliott repeatedly promised Dean Stratton and me that the Dean of Women's Office and all of its functions would never come under the Office of Student Affairs. Your reference to the May 7 memorandum of Dr. Davis, having been approved by Dr. Elliott, is the shock. It is out of order, in my estimation, for the outlines of functions for that office is a major policy that should have been decided upon by the Board of Trustees. Therefore, I think the matter should be an agenda item for the next Board meeting, which is, I have just heard, proposed for July 24. There was absolutely no reference made to these proposals at our last Board meeting, and never have we had the qualifications of Dr. Davis for the job.
>
> Purdue has had one of the finest set-ups for the care and direction of women students, with a Dean and staff who observe the professional standards set for such work. How this fact could have been ignored is incredible, to say nothing of broken promises, the embarrassment to Dean Stratton, her colleagues, and me. It is apparent that Dr. Davis and Dr. Elliott did not discuss this memorandum with their colleagues. Any one of them would know that professionally trained and nationally known women like Dean Stratton, would not work under Dr. Davis. Dr. Elliott should have at least given them an opportunity to resign before approving the functions of Dr. Davis' office, which included the counseling not only of men, but also of women. . . .
>
> I am sorry that you have inherited a "messy" situation. I shall count upon your wisdom and integrity to solve the problem.

The fear of such a "messy situation" was what may have prompted Kathryn to tell Dorothy that she "couldn't afford" to leave Purdue and enlist in the women's reserves back in 1942. Kathryn may have felt a foreboding that the Office of the Dean of Women could be swept out from Dorothy's feet. Yet Dorothy's decision to enlist was the perfect one for her. Often when one fulfills her destiny, there can be collateral damage. That's why seizing opportunities, especially for women who are nurturers and caregivers, takes courage.

In Washington, 650 miles from campus, as Dorothy worried about what was happening to her office and the jurisdiction of her Purdue women, the United States was about to make unprecedented wartime history.

On August 6, 1945, the United States dropped the atomic bomb on Hiroshima, Japan. It was said to be 2,000 times more powerful than the largest bomb ever used. President Harry S. Truman said the atomic bomb heralded the "harnessing of the basic power of the universe." It was the first nuclear weapon used in warfare.

The Hiroshima bomb made of uranium fuel was codenamed Little Boy. In essence, it *was* "little" at just ten feet in length and twenty-eight inches in diameter. It weighed 9,700 pounds.

Little Boy carried the force of 15,000 tons of TNT and devastated an area of five square miles. More than 60 percent of Hiroshima buildings were destroyed. The death toll was about 140,000, more than half of the city's population, a number that included those who died later from radiation. Thousands suffered long-term sickness, disfigurement, and disability.

Three days later, the United States launched a second, bigger atomic bomb on Nagasaki. This bomb was named Fat Man, after Winston Churchill. This plutonium bomb was about the same length as Little Boy, but it was more rotund at sixty inches in diameter. Mountains surround Nagasaki, a topography that confined the level of destruction to about two and a half miles. Nearly 74,000 were killed, and nearly that many suffered injury.

When the bombs exploded, temperatures of tens of millions of degrees were produced. The light emitted was roughly ten times the brightness of the sun. Various types of radiation, such as gamma rays and alpha and beta particles, were emitted, leaving in the bombs' wake the lasting effects of radiation sickness among Japan's people.

The same day that Fat Man was launched, Dorothy wrote a letter to Kathryn. Dorothy was planning a visit to campus to deal with the Office of Student Affairs debacle. She may not have known that the day she wrote was the day of the second atomic bomb launch, yet she discussed her deep concerns about the first bomb and her belief that peaceful cooperation would save the world. Dorothy wrote:

> If possible, I should appreciate having the opportunity to see the memorandum which President Elliott signed transferring the counseling of women to the jurisdiction of the Office of Student Affairs. It is my understanding that, while this memorandum was written on May 7, it was not signed until June 30. I am still in the dark as to the background on this whole business.
>
> Events are moving so fast these days that I feel as if I am living in an unreal world. Hardly had the shock of the news of the atomic bomb penetrated when news of Russia's declaration of war came. Surely Japan will not attempt to hold out against the present combination of forces unless her warlords are completely insane. It does not appear that, unless we can develop people who have qualities of tolerance, intelligence, and kindliness, mankind is really prepared to wipe itself out. This last invention is proof positive that science in itself is amoral and that, unless wise direction is given, scientific inventions are no solution to the problems of the human race.

Dorothy ended her letter on a happy note. Her good friend was getting married. She wrote: "I met Miss McAfee's future husband Tuesday afternoon. He is quite delightful." Captain Mildred McAfee, director of the WAVES, whose face was on the cover of the March 12, 1945 *Time* magazine, married Reverend Douglas Horton in August 1945. He was a widower with children by his first wife. Reverend Horton would become dean of the Harvard Divinity School ten years later.

Japan surrendered on August 14, and the day would become known as V-J Day: Victory in Japan Day. President Truman would not officially declare the end of the war until December 31, 1946. Dorothy started her "personal reconversion" in January. Helen Schleman was promoted to captain and would "finish up the SPARs" as the coast guard women were discharged.

Dorothy took a position in the Retraining and Reemployment Administration under the Department of Labor. She would help with demobilization and use of personnel after the war. The government was concerned with what to do with all the men and women returning home. Where would they work and live?

In a letter to President Hovde, Dorothy wrote, "I feel rather selfish about taking this job for five months as I feel I shall gain so much more from it than I can give to it. One of the special interests of the administration is the one-stop community centers for veterans in which all counseling facilities of the community are brought to bear upon veterans' problems." She said in her 1970 U.S. Naval Academy interview: "You know how anybody in the federal government loves to be coordinated? We were supposed to coordinate the activities of all of the agencies dealing with retraining and reemployment. The whole agency had just gotten out of one service or another. We didn't know as much as the people that we were trying to coordinate. There was quite a public relations program on the reemployment. Of course, the veterans had preference for jobs. We had a field service, which would go out and see how things were going."

It turned out that the reemployment problem would not be as big as had been expected. There had been such a shortage of goods and material during the war that there was a buying surge afterward and an upturn in the economy.

Upon her separation from the service, Dorothy received a Legion of Merit. Her accompanying citation read in part: "A brilliant organizer and administrator, Captain Stratton demonstrated a keen understanding of the abilities of women and of the tasks suited to their performance and, by her consummate tact in fitting women into a military organization, succeeded in directing the efforts of women of the Reserve into channels of the greatest usefulness to the Coast Guard and to the country, thereby contributing to the successful prosecution of the war."

Dorothy accepted the award and said, "I am glad that this medal is called the 'Legion of Merit,' for it is to the Legion that it is awarded, the Legion of 11,000 who volunteered to do a wartime job. As a representative of the Legion of SPARS, I am happy to accept this award and to say how much we have appreciated the opportunity to serve in the Coast Guard."

Dorothy thought she would return to Purdue after her Department of Labor position ended, but she was offered another opportunity working for the International Monetary Fund, and she decided to resign as dean of women.

Dorothy believed that the war had great implications for women. Early on, she said, "If we make good now, new avenues will open after the war." Yet there still would be much work to do to open avenues for women. It was as if women had not even been members of the service or proven themselves capable working in factories and at drafting tables. Dorothy's struggle to retain control over the Office of the Dean of Women was a hint as to what her successor, Helen Schleman, would experience while she advocated for women in the next twenty years as Purdue's second full-time dean of women.

In *The National Association for Women in Education: An Enduring Legacy* by Lynn M. Gangone, she writes of the World War II era and its effect on deans of women, particularly the threats to the position and "calls for centralization of the student personnel function, the growing prominence of the deans of men, and societal mores that placed men in superior roles."

The National Association of Deans of Women (NADW) and the American Association of University Women (AAUW) monitored the dean of women positions and advocated for females around the United States. They knew that without the personal contact with a highly qualified woman in a position of administrative significance, female students, as well as female faculty and staff, lost one of their few channels of expression of leadership and female power on campus.

An AAUW study at the time indicated that of nearly 170 colleges and universities surveyed, sixty-nine had no female administrators. This cloud would hover over Helen until her dying day. She became the watchdog for women at Purdue University, monitoring the numbers of females with positions in the administration, faculty, and staff and their pay scales (before it was public record) compared to that of the men.

In 1980, Helen, then retired and looking back, wrote of three major crises in the "women's area of Purdue" since she began her tenure there. The first was the George Davis incident. She said that the battle to preserve the Office of the Dean of Women was won but only "partially." Helen wrote: "The Office of the Dean of Women remained independent of George Davis, but President Elliott had promised him the title, and he left him with the title, but not the job—which was ridiculous. For six years, I put up with George Davis using the title of Dean of Students and acting as if he was Dean of Students unless I pointedly explained exactly what the situation was—which I had to do several times."

When President Hovde, offered Helen the position of dean of women, she accepted under two conditions: (1) the Office of the Dean of Women stayed an independent office reporting to the president of the University; and (2) the title of dean of students be corrected and changed to dean of men.

Helen said, "President Hovde agreed to both, saying he would change George's title just as soon as he could—it took six years!"

17

Barbara Ivy Wood Cook, 'Tis a Gift to Be Free

Barbara Cook could have been author Harper Lee's inspiration for her character Scout in *To Kill a Mockingbird.* As a child growing up in Memphis, Tennessee, Barbara (Barb) Ivy Wood was a tomboy, a pixie, with short hair, freckles, and a knowing gaze. She was born on December 8, 1929, putting her close to the age of six-year-old Scout in Lee's Pulitzer Prize-winning novel about judgment and justice, racism and respect, set in the early 1930s. Barb's childhood nickname was Woody, and her life would be spent eloquently proclaiming and working toward parity for all people.

Barb's father, Karl, was a pharmacist who owned an apothecary. He was a quiet, gentle, kind man—Karl was Barb's Atticus. Barb took walks in the woods with her father, a prolific and fine letter writer, and he taught her about wildflowers and birds, instilling in her a deep love of nature. He gave her a dictionary and said, "This is the most useful book you'll ever find in your whole life." When she was older, Barb's father gave her a set of Audubon fine china and a special edition of Audubon prints that she said were the finest gifts she ever received.

Barb's mother, Thelma Champaign Wood, was a homemaker who loved to garden and was liberal in her thinking. Thelma opened her daughter's eyes to those in need. She taught Barb to be a champion of the poor and underrepresented. Barb said, "I had freedom to do things, to try things, to think my own thoughts. It was something my mother valued." Thelma told her daughter, "There isn't anyone on earth who is a simple human being."

Barb's older brother, Pete, took her for walks and played board games with her at their mother's insistence. Barb said, "He was always nice to me—a good brother." Pete would follow in his father's footsteps and become a pharmacist and Harvard University's Health Services director of pharmacy.

Barb's neighborhood was filled with children. She and five of her friends created the "Penguin Club." They wrote their own chant, which Barb could repeat seven decades later. It began: "We are the Penguin Club of six, / Full of fun, good times and tricks; / First came Helen with her hair so fair; / Jeanette our big sister came home by air. . . ."

The Penguin Club ditty ended with a mention of Barb, who had a bugle she blared for her fellow Penguins: "And last came Woody with a toot, toot, toot."

Barb enjoyed the camaraderie of other girls, and she loved to spend time at Camp Kiwani, a Girl Scout camp near Memphis. She spent nine summers there, and she became a strong swimmer and an expert canoeist. In 1945, Barb kept a journal while she was a counselor for eight weeks living in tent number five with "The Thunderbirds." World War II raged in the Pacific, but Woody, age fifteen, wrote of her idyllic world of campfires, canoeing, hikes, and eating pimento cheese sandwiches and Payday candy bars. She would forever love and enjoy all of those experiences, and she served pimento cheese sandwiches throughout her lifetime, harkening back to the freedom of summers at Camp Kiwani amid the blackgum and sassafras, larkspur and Solomon's Seal, and giggles of girls.

On August 7, the day after the United States dropped the first atomic bomb on Hiroshima, Barb wrote, "Farewell banquet. Was really swell. Last campfire. . . . It was strictly a good campfire."

Barb penned her last journal entry on August 8, the day before the second atomic bomb devastated Nagasaki. Under the canopy of Tennessee trees, sheltered and safe with her fellow Girl Scouts, Barb had no idea what was happening on the other side of the world. She wrote, "This concludes one of the most wonderful years ever at Kiwani. I think there was more camp spirit in the hearts of the girls, a greater feeling of unity—more than ever before."

In years to come, Barb would hold a special fondness for the book *And Ladies of the Club* by Helen Hooven Santmyer. In the 1930s, Santmyer was a dean of women and English teacher at Cedarville University in Ohio. Originally published by the Ohio State University Press at 1,344 pages, *And Ladies of the Club* is a fictionalized story of the author's hometown in Ohio. The book unfolds as men return home from the Civil War. It follows the lives of two best friends from college until they grow very old, all set within the premise of a literary club to which they belong. The town's historically authentic political, cultural, and social changes are seen through the lives of the members of the club, which became a significant service organization for the town.

Santmyer was eighty-seven years old when *And Ladies of the Club* was first published in 1982, and few copies were sold. A year later, G. P. Putnam's Sons purchased the rights to the book, and it became a *New York Times* best seller. The Book-of-the-Month Club made *And Ladies of the Club* its main selection and sold more than 162,000 copies, and a paperback edition sold more than a million copies.

In several of her speeches given in the 1980s and 1990s, Barb recited a favorite quote from this text: "At the end, it means more than religion, to have had a happy childhood. Memory of it serves to hold off pain and fear; it is an unfailing resource . . . if one's childhood was happy, one had no reason to fear life, and those who had not feared life could face death with acceptance when they must."

Barb's childhood was happy, and it would be her fortress to ward off pain and fear. Perhaps as she aged and reflected, Barb appreciated her days of freedom as a member of the Penguin Club, as a girl named Woody who was a seasoned scout, much like the girl in Harper Lee's enduring tale. Woody would grow up to become a member of her own "ladies club"—the interwoven legacy of Purdue's dean of women and dean of students.

IN 1947, BARB ENTERED THE UNIVERSITY OF ARKANSAS. The University of Arkansas is the state's land-grant university in Fayetteville, set on picturesque acres overlooking the Ozark Mountains. The year before, Beverley Stone had accepted a position there as assistant dean of women and director of the Women's Residence Halls. After World War II ended, Bev left the WAVES to rejoin civilian life. Jeanette Scudder, the dean of women at the University of Arkansas, who was a graduate of Purdue University, hired Bev.

Jeanette sent Bev a letter describing her responsibilities. Bev would be in charge of the educational and social program of all the residence halls, for personal counseling, and for correspondence and room assignments. She would have an important voice in furnishing and equipping a new hall that was being built, including her own office and suite. Bev would be paid $2,500 plus room and board. Jeanette wrote, "We are eager to have for this position a person who will regard the residence halls as an education unit of the University and who will develop a counseling program from that viewpoint, and who will help to create their enthusiasm for gracious living."

Bev was the perfect person to fill such a position, and her future as a dean of women seemed inevitable.

Former first lady Eleanor Roosevelt visited the University of Arkansas in Fayetteville and gave a lecture entitled "Is America Facing World Leadership?" She stayed in Holcombe Hall, which was residence for freshmen women. A newspaper story about her visit and trip to the airport for her departure stated: "Always traveling as light as possible, Mrs. Roosevelt was equipped with only one piece of luggage and a large handbag. Mrs. Roosevelt was wearing a navy silk shantung costume dress and a tailored navy velour hat for travel Wednesday. The mother of six children, who made the role of first lady a precedent-shattering career, was motored to the local airport from Fayetteville by Miss Jeannette Scudder, dean of women at the state university, and Miss Beverley Stone, associate dean of women."

The newspaper failed to mention that Eleanor had inadvertently left her girdle in her room at Holcombe Hall. Bev received a letter from Eleanor requesting her girdle be mailed back to her. Bev discreetly retrieved and packaged the girdle, then mailed the parcel containing the "unmentionable" to the former first lady. The incident became a humorous story Bev would tell for years to come.

DURING THIS TIME, undergraduate Barbara Wood first met Bev. They formed a friendship that lasted more than fifty years, and both women enjoyed a lifelong friendship with Jeanette.

Barb started college majoring in prepharmacy, but she discovered she was "the world's worst scholar in science." She changed her major to history, contemplated philosophy, and attempted physical education. She landed on sociology because she was interested in racial integration and hoped someday to work with the Southern Regional Conference, a consortium of southern states concerned with this issue.

While Barb was there in 1948, the University of Arkansas admitted its first black student, Silas Herbert Hunt. His treatment and the treatment of the few other black students who soon followed in his footsteps spurred Barb's interest in working for racial integration.

Hunt was a World War II army veteran who had been stationed in Europe, where he served with construction engineers before being seriously wounded at the Battle of the Bulge. After recovering, Hunt returned to school and graduated at Arkansas Agricultural, Mechanical and Normal (AM&N), a black university. He was then admitted to Indiana University's law school, but Hunt wanted to attend the University of Arkansas because it was less expensive and closer to family and friends.

Southern colleges and universities were so rigidly segregated at the time that these states would pay the tuition for black students to attend a black college rather than admit them to white universities. Hunt applied to the University of Arkansas School of Law hoping to break the color barrier, and he did. Having witnessed the negative publicity that segregation had brought to other southern universities, University of Arkansas officials announced that they would allow qualified black students to be admitted; however, Hunt had to endure segregation within the walls of the university.

After a professor finished a class, he would teach the same subject to Hunt individually. Hunt had to go through an intermediary to borrow books from the law library and was required to use them in a separate study room rather than space within the library with the rest of the class. He was not allowed to use the student restrooms but, instead, had to ask permission of the dean's secretary to use the dean's facilities.

Hunt conformed to the segregated conditions, but by the end of his first semester, some white students who also wanted to have individualized attention from professors joined in his separate classroom. The post-World War II class was filled with returning veterans who had seen black men fighting and dying alongside white men. They did not care that they were sitting in the same room as an African American.

Sadly, in July 1948, Hunt suffered from pulmonary tuberculosis, which forced him to withdraw from school. Hunt died in a veterans' hospital in Springfield, Missouri, in April 1949, but his death did not end segregation at the University of Arkansas.

In the fall of 1948, Jackie Lamond Shropshire of Little Rock followed the trail Hunt had blazed. Since a group of white students had joined Hunt in his separate classroom the previous year, it was decided that Shropshire would share two of his classes with other students.

In the joint classroom, Shropshire was required to sit in a specific seat surrounded by a wooden railing, while other students sat wherever they wanted. The barrier was a single, horizontal wooden pole, about twelve to fifteen inches off the floor. The railing that separated Shropshire from other students apparently lasted only one day. Several faculty members demanded that the railing be removed after news of the barrier was publicized across the country. The removal of the rail was announced in a news release, but emphasized that "[t]he the Law School is continuing its segregation policy, but with a segregation system fairer to the white students," noting that 125 students were crowded into a room meant to hold 60, "while separate classes were held for one colored student."

Even after the barrier disappeared, Shropshire was required to remain in an assigned seat "in a separated section of a room, and white students [sat] in other parts of the room."

Barb watched the events surrounding Hunt and Shropshire. The humiliating treatment endured by these students—men who walked the same campus as she in the quest for an education—forever branded her social conscience. The railing that surrounded a black man for a single day remained in Barb's mind for a lifetime.

Today the University of Arkansas has a building and a Distinguished Scholar Award bearing the name of Silas Hunt. In 2007, the state legislature made February 2, the day Hunt enrolled in classes, a memorial day in his name. The next year, the University of Arkansas School of Law awarded Hunt a posthumous degree, and in 2012, a sculpture was dedicated in his honor.

Barb's calling to increase integration in the southern states led her to desire a master's degree in social work, yet her aspirations would lead her to experience her own discrimination. When she decided to further her education, Barb approached her mentor, the head of the University of Arkansas Department of Sociology, for a recommendation to graduate school. She was very close to the male professor, whose children she babysat, and as an outstanding student in sociology, she had helped him start a sociology honors society. When she asked him to write a letter of recommendation, Barb's professor said, "No, I won't. I don't think women should go to graduate school. I think women should get married and have children." In an oral history conducted in 2006 by the Purdue University Archives, Barb said, "At this point, I was stunned. I thought, 'Why have I wasted all my time here if I can't do anything with it [a degree]?' I really was saddened by that response—I didn't know what I was going to do."

Barb decided to return to her home state of Tennessee and seek a job in the public welfare department, even though her interest in the area was minimal. After waiting an entire summer to hear back from the welfare department, she returned to the University of Arkansas for a visit. Barb ran into Jeannette, who said that her office was shorthanded and asked her to work for a week. Barb recalled, "Having nothing better to do, I said yes. I packed one suitcase and left."

One suitcase was not enough, for at the end of the week, Barb was asked to stay for another month. Bev had been called back to naval duty for six weeks, and Jeannette asked Barb if she would serve as interim director of the residence halls. Barb happily accepted.

Once Bev returned to Arkansas, Jeannette wanted to take time off to study at Columbia University. Bev would act as interim dean of women in

Jeannette's absence, and Barb was asked to continue working in the residence halls. This is when Barb and Bev's friendship was solidified. The two women lived across the hall from one another in a dormitory from 1951 to 1952.

Before Jeanette left for Columbia, she asked Barb what she wanted to do with her life. Barb said she liked what she was doing, and Jeanette advised her to obtain a graduate degree. Barb entered Syracuse University in central New York to study in their two-year student dean master's degree program. Student deans were assigned as directors of resident units. Barb was assigned to supervise Blackwell Cottage, a beautiful old home transformed into a residence hall that sat across the street from a lovely park. Trees surrounded the cottage, and one day the trees called to twenty-three-year-old Barb, a woman not much older than her students. She said:

> I was looking out the back window. It was a beautiful day, and I said, "That would be a good tree to climb." Most of the students were from New York State, and they said, "Oh, we've never climbed a tree before! Let's all go climb trees!" So we did. We were all up in the tree—the whole house and me. I looked down and here came Dean Hilton, who was head of the program, with her dog. And so I said to the students, "Shh! Don't say anything!" Well, of course, that made them laugh, so they got uproarious after that. I said, "Oh, Dean Hilton, I'm sorry, none of these students had ever climbed a tree before. Will you come in the house and have a cup of tea?"—hoping she would go away. But she said, "Oh, yes." She was very nice about it. She didn't fire me. Although one of the conditions of our jobs was we had to wear hose and heels everywhere, and I was in blue jeans and tennis shoes.

While at Syracuse, Barb worked on a paper about segregation in higher education. A friend in New York sent her materials from a Communist bookstore to use for her paper. This was during the time of the Cold War and the Army-McCarthy hearings. Barb was terrified that someone would find her in possession of Communist propaganda, and she needed a hiding place for her books.

At Blackwell Cottage, the kitchen of the old house had been converted into Barb's bedroom. She had been using an old flour bin for her dirty clothes and decided it would be the perfect hiding place for her clandestine collection. In a Purdue *Exponent* interview from 1980, Barb said of the books: "I wanted to burn them, but I was afraid they [the bookstore] had my address and when they came looking for me, they would want to know what I had done with the books. It was just awful."

After determining that her friend had carefully hidden her address from any authorities, Barb anonymously donated the books to the University of Arkansas.

Barb graduated from Syracuse in 1954. Forty years later, at the age of sixty-two, she wrote her biography and included this recollection:

> I have just been looking at my Syracuse memories, which include a photograph of my brother and me after my Syracuse graduation. We were standing in front of someone else's Rolls Royce—no doubt as a hope of things to come! We both look young. We were young and thin, had hair and looked excited about the promise of world adventure. In the year 1991, about the only thing that hasn't changed about that picture is that my brother and I remain good friends and are still able to adventure together a bit in this old world of ours. Neither of us has ever owned a Rolls Royce nor ridden in one as far as I know although his first car was a white convertible!

Syracuse University Dean of Women Eunice Hilton arranged for Barb to attend the National Association of Deans of Women conference in Washington, DC, after she graduated. It was Barb's first introduction to the group she would lead decades later. Barb received two job offers after making connections at the NADW conference, one from Florida and the other from Vanderbilt, where her father had graduated. Barb liked the family link and the beautiful campus, so she interviewed at Vanderbilt. Barb recalled, "It's a lovely old campus. Good trees, good food. It made me feel like home, I guess. But the dean of students there was an elderly woman, and she kept calling me 'Darling,' and I thought, I don't think that's going to work. But the setting was gorgeous."

Jeannette came calling again and offered Barb her third job with the University of Arkansas. This time Barb would be the official director of residence halls, and she would once again work and socialize with the two women who were becoming comfortable comrades. Decades later, looking back on her life, Barb said in her slow, Tennessee drawl, "I worked with Jeannette and Beverley Stone real well—we were real good friends."

While she had been an undergraduate, Barb dated a tall, professional golfer named Salem Cook. They continued to correspond while she attended graduate school; when she returned to Arkansas, the two reunited. Soon, the romance would blossom into marriage.

Barb liked a verse from an old Shaker song, "Simple Gifts." The song was largely unknown outside Shaker communities until Aaron Copland used its melody for the score of Martha Graham's ballet *Appalachian Spring*, first performed in 1944: "'Tis the gift to be simple, 'tis the gift to be free / 'Tis the gift to come down where we ought to be, / And when we find ourselves in the place just right, / 'Twill be in the valley of love and delight."

Barb came down exactly where she ought to be. She would soon find herself "in the place just right" at Purdue University and remain there for life.

18

Bible Bequeathed

After her life-changing position heading up the SPARs during World War II, Dorothy Stratton, age forty-eight, embarked on her next chapter as the director of personnel for the International Monetary Fund, recruiting economists from around the world. She resigned her position as dean of women at Purdue University. As she cleaned out her desk in her Hovde Hall office, she came across Dean Carolyn Shoemaker's Bible. Dorothy had kept the Bible tucked away since she discovered it in 1933. She opened the book to the first page, creamy and aged with tinges of coffee brown, grabbed a blue ink pen, and wrote, "Originally owned by Carolyn Shoemaker, first Dean of Women 1913–1933 at Purdue University, then by Dorothy C. Stratton 1933–1947, Proverbs 31:10–31, then by. . . ."

After writing the inscription, including a favorite passage, Dorothy quietly bequeathed Carolyn Shoemaker's Bible to Helen. Helen signed her name: "Helen B. Schleman."

The two women's private emblem of duty was passed, and Helen became Purdue University's second full-time dean of women in 1947.

Proverbs 31:10–31 is a passage that conveys the wise teachings of a mother to her son, who would one day be king. She discusses the qualities of a great leader in previous verses, and in this passage, she paints a picture of the type of wife her son should choose, a woman with strong character, great wisdom, many skills, and abundant compassion.

The Proverbs 31 woman is an excellent wife and mother, but she also "finds wool and flax and busily spins it. She is like a merchant's ship; she brings her food from afar. She gets up before dawn to prepare breakfast. . . . She goes out to inspect a field and buys it; with her earnings she plants a vineyard." She is a manufacturer, importer, manager, realtor, farmer, seamstress, and merchant.

The passage goes on to say, "She is clothed with strength and dignity, and she laughs with no fear of the future. When she speaks, her words are wise, and kindness is the rule when she gives instructions."

The final verse suggests that a woman's character is what makes her attractive: "Charm is deceptive, and beauty does not last; but a woman who fears the Lord will be greatly praised. Reward her for all she has done. Let her deeds publicly declare her praise."

The standard set by the Proverbs 31 woman may seem terrifyingly unattainable, but each characteristic could be thought of as a pearl added at a different time in her life to eventually form a complete strand of shimmering attributes. Over a woman's lifespan, not necessarily all at the same time, there's an opportunity for education, career, friendship, marriage, motherhood, volunteerism, philanthropy, and more.

Dorothy was at the midpoint of her life when she handed Carolyn's Bible to Helen, and she already had added an extraordinary number of pearls onto her life's necklace, but she also realized she had so much more ahead. Dorothy understood that as her accomplished successor, Helen had pearls to add to her own strand.

DOROTHY PRESENTED HER FORMAL RESIGNATION as dean of women with a three-page, confidential memorandum to Purdue

President Frederick Hovde on May 27, 1946. She listed nine concerns and recommendations relating to female students and faculty, including the lack of attention to the successful liberal science curriculum for women in the School of Science and her thoughts on what the Office of the Dean of Women could become. Dorothy wrote, "Outside the School of Home Economics, the number of women who hold the rank of full professor can be numbered on one hand with fingers to spare. This situation will be remedied only by real efforts on the part of the President and by the judicious selection of some really first-rate women scientists, educators, and social scientists. I cannot overemphasize the importance of this point."

Dorothy's last directive to President Hovde was candid and straightforward. She was laying groundwork for Helen to move the Office of the Dean of Women forward. She wrote in her letter to Hovde, "The Dean of Women can be recognized as a valuable member of policy-making groups in the University or she can become a beast of burden doing the chores and the minutiae of administration. With approximately 2,000 women on the campus, it seems to me of the utmost importance that the Dean of Women be given adequate staff and secretarial assistance, opportunities for contact with interesting educators and educational projects in other institutions, and a salary which will relieve her mind of financial worry."

Dorothy presented two speeches at the 1947 annual convention of the National Association of Deans of Women that set the progressive tone of her life's work and the work of Helen Schleman. She preferred to speak extemporaneously rather than from a script, but fortunately, Dorothy did write down these presentations. Dorothy's first speech was "What the War Taught Us about the Education of High School Girls." She highlighted that women had proven themselves during the war. She also stated:

> Both boys and girls must share in the school experiences, which minimize sex differences and create a spirit of mutual respect and understanding. Teachers of home economics, industrial arts, and physical education have the opportunity to provide these experiences by expanding their programs to include activities for both sexes. If we pass up these opportunities and persist in maintaining a dichotomy of experiences for boys and girls, we can look forward to no diminution of the problems facing adult women

> in achieving equal opportunities with men to become useful and active citizens. And without the full contributions of women, we will be robbing ourselves of a large segment of our human talent.

Dorothy's second speech was "Conserving our Human Resources." Her statements were weighty and worth absorbing sentence by sentence. She said:

> The nations of the world and the peoples of the world, in truth, comprise one world. We must quickly overcome the barriers of language, race, and ideology that divide us and find a common meeting ground. . . . Appalled by the increase in tensions in our own country as well as abroad between races, religions, and ideologies, we ask ourselves what instruments we have for the promotion of understanding, for emphasis upon our likenesses, rather than our differences, for the development of the individual personality, regardless of race, creed, color, or sex.

Dorothy was a brilliant, well-read woman, and her speeches were galvanizing; however, the post-World War II 1950s were about to emerge with societal pressures for women to return to their homes after working to help the war effort. Military men needed the jobs the women had performed in their absence.

As dean of women during the next two decades, Helen had her work cut out for her. Nationwide, deans of women would strive to help females understand the importance of having an education while also becoming wives and mothers.

During this time, there was continued pressure in colleges and universities across the United States to centralize student personnel functions. The National Association of Deans of Women worked to protect the dean of women position. Despite efforts, NADW members watched as deans of men gained a distinct advantage with the population of GI Bill veterans crowding campuses.

This was during the time when Helen continually battled to hold onto the Office of the Dean of Women as an independent entity not subject to George Davis, who believed his title was dean of students with jurisdiction over Helen's domain. It seemed everywhere Helen turned, a riptide could wash away all of the advancement for female students that had been forged by Carolyn Shoemaker, Dorothy Stratton, Amelia Earhart, and Lillian Gilbreth.

Across the United States, female students (like Barbara Wood) were turned down for admission to graduate and professional schools to make way for the swell of veterans who were returning to or entering higher education.

As with most veterans, when Dorothy and Helen left the SPARs, they experienced some readjustments to civilian life. Dorothy said, "I think we were all lost when we got out. When you're in the service, everything is taken care of for you. You have your medical and dental care; you have the protection of the service. You don't have to worry about your clothes, what you're going to wear. We didn't know what kind of clothes to buy. We made mistakes. We looked stranger than other civilians did, because we hadn't bought any clothes for four years."

Because of the war's rationing and conservation efforts, and with so many Americans wearing military uniforms, apparel was hard to come by for those reentering civilian life. Dorothy wrote in a January 11, 1946 letter to Acting Dean of Women Clare Coolidge, "Washington seems to be entirely clothesless. I understand that other places are just about as bad."

One of the first things that Helen questioned as dean of women when she returned to Purdue from the SPARs was the concept of "women's hours." The women's residence halls had a set time that the doors would be locked, and the women were expected to be in for the night. At that time, women had to be in their rooms by 10:30 p.m. on weeknights and midnight on weekends. Helen had seen the coast guard women, the same ages as college students, given the freedom to manage their own lives without a curfew. Helen believed that women had good judgment and should be encouraged to use it, assuming responsibility for their own lives. In a 1985 interview, Helen said of her female students: "I wanted very much to give them keys to the residence halls so that they could come in when they got ready. This really set off quite a discussion that went on for several years."

Helen was nearly fired for suggesting that the female students be given keys to their dormitory rooms. On Purdue's campus, the ratio of men to women at the time was five to one. The running joke was that there was no need for men's closing hours because by declaring closing hours for women, men would automatically be in their living quarters at a reasonable time. Helen did not find this joke amusing. Women also had to receive special permission to be away from their living units overnight to visit parents or relatives. Helen thought these women-only rules were ridiculous, and her mantra was "stop locking the girls up!"

The Admissions Office was sure that no parent would allow his or her daughter to come to Purdue if there were no closing hours for women's residence halls. The administration and the Board of Trustees also were skeptical. It would take nearly twenty years for Helen's idea to come to pass.

In 1966, the Board of Trustees removed closing hours for sophomore, junior, and senior women, and two years later, the curfew was eliminated for freshman. Helen refused to follow suit with other universities that had set a minimum age of twenty-one for those women without closing hours. Purdue was the first Big Ten university to abolish this policy. Administrators at other universities could not believe "conservative" Purdue had taken such a "drastic" step. Numerous phone calls and irate letters from parents and alumni poured in from across the country about the decision.

In a 1966 talk given by Bev Stone, by then an assistant dean in Purdue's Office of the Dean of Women, she said:

> I spent twenty minutes at the beauty shop while my hair was being set, talking with the AWS [Association of Women Students] advisor at Michigan State. Whenever those on our staff . . . were asked to speak to Purdue alumnae groups or other groups in the state, we were bombarded with questions, apprehensions, and criticisms. Many of the sorority advisors were convinced that the academic standings of the sororities would hit rock bottom. I am certain that not one of you present really had any notion of the amount of time which our staff has spent in defending the decision and in interpreting what we considered to be the educational goal behind the "no hours" policy. Dean Schleman has probably worked longest and hardest of any one person both with students and adults, in formulating and interpreting the "no hours" policy. She . . . has unlimited confidence and faith in Purdue women.

After two decades of Helen's continual insistence that women could be responsible for their own lives, Purdue females were no longer locked up at night.

In the early 1950s, Helen lived at Ross-Ade Apartments, today named Hilltop Apartments. These residences sit on a slope next to Ross-Ade Stadium. The buildings were constructed to answer Purdue's housing needs for married students after World War II. Single Helen lived among the married students and their children. Helen had a tan cocker spaniel she named Mr. Coffee (so named before the famous Mr. Coffee percolator was popular). In the 1950 and 1952 *Debris* yearbook, she is pictured with Mr. Coffee, her companion and cohort in golf. She often took her dog with her in the golf cart as she played.

Purdue's enrollment doubled after the war, and besides student housing problems, there was a dire need for faculty housing. National Homes Corporation built small, inexpensive, prefabricated houses next to Purdue's golf course. Helen grew up next to a golf course in Valparaiso, Indiana, and she felt a house alongside Purdue's course would be ideal for her. Helen put her name on the list to purchase one of the homes with the assumption that she would have a house by the start of the 1952 fall academic year.

President Hovde notified Helen about a month before school was scheduled to start that there would not be a house available to her. The new golf course houses were specifically built for faculty members with children. Compounding her problems, Ross-Ade Apartments had instituted a new regulation prohibiting pets. Helen was sent a letter from Director of University Residences G. O. Arbuckle, notifying her that she must permanently remove Mr. Coffee from her apartment or vacate the dwelling by the end of August.

As an answer to her dilemmas, Helen built her own small house. She purchased an odd-shaped lot, nearly an obtuse triangle, which backed up to the golf course at 1807 Western Drive. Until her new home was finished, she remained in Ross-Ade Apartments and boarded Mr. Coffee with a friend. It seems that as a single woman, with a dog as her companion, she was put in a difficult position when it came to Purdue housing. On September 4, 1952, Helen wrote G. O. Arbuckle:

> If I had known I could not be assigned one of the little pre-fab houses on the golf course sooner, I should probably have been able to vacate the apartment by August 31. As it was, however, I honestly thought up until July 27 that I was on the list for one of the little houses and had been on long enough that I could expect to get one this summer. I am sorry for any inconvenience it may cause you in the reassignment of my apartment, as I know you would like to have it available at the beginning of the school year. Under the circumstances, however, I hope you understand.

Today, Helen's housing predicament might be deemed discrimination. Title VIII of the Civil Rights Act of 1968 is commonly known as the Fair Housing Act. Any person who feels that he or she has faced housing discrimination because of race, color, religion, sex, national origin, disability, or familial status can file a discrimination complaint with the Office of Fair Housing and Equal Opportunity. Because Helen was not married with a family, she was denied a house. As she rallied for freedom from "women's hours" for her female students living in Purdue's residence halls, she waged her own, quiet housing battles.

ANOTHER INITIATIVE OF HELEN'S was the freshmen conference program. The program began as an individual conference where each freshman woman was invited to the Office of the Dean of Women at the beginning of the school year for a private, informal talk with a staff member. Each freshman woman received a handwritten invitation to visit and become acquainted with the office and the staff who saw their main purpose as advocates to improve opportunities for female students. At that time, Helen had two other people in her office—a woman in charge of placement and an assistant dean of women. One of the questions posed was, "What do you think you're going to do twenty years from now when your last child is finished with school?" Usually, the student looked blank and then began to blink. She had never been asked such a question or even thought about her life in such a way.

As deans of women, Dorothy and Helen emphasized the total education of their students. With the postwar social norms encouraging women to marry and pursue homemaking, leaving the jobs open to men, the "breadwinners," Helen had a more difficult time encouraging women to plan a possible life outside of the home. Society pressured women to marry young. With the well-defined woman's role as a homemaker and mother, it wasn't deemed necessary by most for a young woman to pursue a college degree and start a career. Many women went to college to find a "good provider"—a male student to marry. The attitude of male students and faculty toward the few female students who were majoring in engineering at Purdue was unsupportive, and in some instances, downright hostile.

Society benefited economically as more couples wed, because marriages led to an increase in home construction, sale of furnishings and appliances, and production of family-related goods. Even *Seventeen* magazine featured articles and ads about purchasing wedding dresses and furniture. Teenaged girls were eager to live the fantasy of a white wedding dress, a new house, and "happily ever after." The peer pressure to conform to this fantasy was enormous, and women raced to the altar.

Premarital sex was considered taboo in the 1950s, and the birth control pill was not yet available, making relations outside of marriage a gamble most couples were not willing to take. Marriage was the only acceptable avenue for young lovers to consummate their relationships. All of these factors contributed to the unfortunate fact that nearly half of all American brides by 1959 were under the age of nineteen.

In a 1970 interview, Helen said:

> It seems to me that there's a factor in the education of women that is not present in the education of men. And that is that everybody has to keep trying to assure and reassure and impress young women that their education is important. Now boys and young men know this. They know that education is important to them. They know that they are expected to get as good an education as they can and to get as good a job as they can, so that they can make as big a contribution to society as they can. But young women do not know this. They assume, a great many of them even now, even though women's liberation is active and in spite of all of the changes that have taken place, a great many of them still assume that they will marry and live happily ever after. Period. They do not know that they are probably going to have to work outside of their homes for pay. And they don't know that they are probably going to want to work outside of their homes.

> Traditionally, young men have been long-term planners; young women have been short-term planners. They have planned only up to the time when they will marry. This is the part of it that is different. This is why somebody has to put emphasis on the importance of education to women themselves, and to society as well.

Helen and her staff were a small voice surrounded by a loud bombardment of messages that told women they would be the happiest at home with children and should not think beyond. Magazines, newspapers, radio, television, movies, and books depicted the woman at home content with striving for the whitest laundry and the tenderest of beef brisket as she created an impeccable household for her children and husband who went out into the world each day.

As the enrollment of women at Purdue increased, the freshmen conference program changed from a meeting with one student at a time, to a meeting of a small group of women students with an upper-class female student and a staff member.

The Office of the Dean of Women also held a freshmen women orientation session in the Elliott Hall of Music, Purdue's massive Art Deco theater. Helen spoke to the new students from one of the largest proscenium theater stages in the world. Of the women-only meetings, Helen said:

> The question was always, "Why in the world do you need a meeting for freshmen women, separate from freshmen men?" The reason was, of course, that someplace we or someone needed the opportunity to try to tell women students what was happening to the life pattern of women in the United States, in terms of their employment, in terms of the variety of their employment, in terms of their own outlook as to what they themselves would probably be expected to do in later life. In other words, they needed to know what the status of women was in the United States.

When there were 1,800 freshmen women at Purdue, Helen wanted the faculty to be aware of the effort of the Office of the Dean of Women regarding the program for freshmen women. She knew that counselors and professors often steered women away from the academic work they wanted if it were in "nontraditional" fields like the sciences, engineering, and agriculture, instead steering them into home economics, teaching, nursing, or other "feminine" disciplines. The all-male faculty and administration led with the underlying assumption that if a woman sought "manly" academic work, it may cost her a chance at finding a husband. To counteract this attitude, Helen sent a four-page memo to the entire faculty, describing what took place during the freshmen women's orientation.

As they sat in the steel-gray, velvet-lined seats of the Elliott Hall of Music, the female students were given a paper entitled "Your Lifeline." On the stage was a screen projecting the "Average American Woman's Lifeline." Each student was asked to think about her own lifespan. What would she want to accomplish, and when? She was asked to check and label a chart with her age, the age she planned to marry, the ages she would like to be when her children were born, and the age she would be when she anticipated that her last child would be in school. Helen's goal was to make the point graphically that even after a woman's last child was in school, she had more of her lifespan ahead of her than behind her. What would she do with the "after children" span?

Information was then presented about the tremendous need for educated, skilled workers and that "informed sources" predicted that women would work outside their homes for money for about twenty-five years of their lives. With that in mind, the point was made that a woman's education was of the utmost importance.

Helen took the opportunity in her faculty memo to address the fact that there were few female professional role models in society at that time, and that the freshmen women would have little, if any, contact at Purdue with career women unless they were in the School of Home Economics. The freshmen women's orientation was an opportunity for Helen to help her audience to see and hear about the possibility for women to be involved in professional work. It was an occasion for Helen and her female staff to be seen as role models on stage, right before the young, impressionable women.

Helen ended her memo with this plea to the predominantly male faculty: "We believe that every bit of encouragement that professors and academic counselors can give to women students to believe that their talents are needed by society and that they have a responsibility to develop and use their intellectual abilities will be useful in building aspirations to match abilities in Purdue's women students. This is why we wanted you to know what we are trying to do, with the hope that, in your own way and in your own area, you can and will help to get the message across."

For nearly two decades, Helen ran the Purdue freshmen women's conference program and orientation session like a well-oiled, woman-affirming machine. In essence, Helen told her students to be Proverbs 31 women—to be a wife, mother, and homemaker, but also to be a strong, educated, professional woman, and a compassionate, contributing citizen. Each Purdue woman was urged to take the thread of her being into her own hands and add pearls of accomplishments throughout her life.

19

Gospel of the Go-to-Hell Fund

Nearly every woman who came to know Helen Schleman was asked, "Do you have your 'Go-to-Hell Fund'?" Helen believed that every woman, married or not, needed money saved that was hers alone to control, so if life "went to hell" with a husband or a job, she could leave the unhealthy situation and not worry about finances. She preached the concept of the Go-to-Hell Fund to her students, staff, faculty, and friends.

In an era when women were looking for good providers and men were seen as the breadwinners, Helen's idea of a Go-to-Hell Fund was nearly sacrilege. Even the mere thought that women would not live happily ever after was unthinkable. But Helen was not just talking about a marriage gone bad; the unpleasant situation could be loss of a job or a boss who treated an employee poorly. Helen wanted every woman she knew to have a financial safety net, so that she could say confidently, "Go to hell."

The 1950s were a time of peaceful conformity. Purdue female students, staff, and faculty were required to wear skirts and hose. When the weather was cold—somewhere below zero degrees—female students had to receive special permission from the dean of women to wear slacks on campus. In the summer, a sign hung in the Purdue Memorial Union that declared, "By tradition, shorts are not worn in the Union."

"Hell" and "damn" were the foulest words used, and then only in situations of great stress. Helen was not afraid to raise eyebrows to prove her point and attempt to change the world with her provocatively named Go-to-Hell Fund.

Helen basically was shy, but when it came to something she believed in, or if she saw a wrong that needed to be righted, she was fearless. Helen spoke matter-of-factly, with her attention completely given to the person with whom she was in a conversation, and young women took notice. Helen was a professional, feminine role model, when few were visible; she made herself available to listen, stood her ground, and had complete confidence in the brilliance and capabilities of women.

Students and staff may have been surprised to know that a young Helen, whom Dorothy Stratton hired in the 1930s, had lacked self-confidence. Dorothy and the coast guard instilled a personal assurance in Helen that served her well as Purdue's dean of women.

Most students had never met a woman like Helen. She was a feminist decades before the term would be hurled into 1970s society like a revelation or, by some, like a misunderstood revulsion. Helen was Helen before Gloria Steinem was Gloria Steinem.

IN THE EARLY 1950s, Dorothy and Helen updated their social etiquette book *Your Best Foot Forward.* After sending out a new questionnaire to college campus leaders, they rewrote each chapter and, because people were marrying at younger ages, added a new one: "Engagements and Weddings." Dorothy and Helen were single women with no children, so they asked a married student they knew to help with the wedding section. The new chapter covered "going steady" and the question, "Is it acceptable for an engaged couple to take a weekend trip if staying at a respectable place?" The answer was "no—not by yourselves." Another question was posed: "How intimate should an engaged couple become?" They answered this from a clinical perspective: "Authorities in the marriage and family-life areas . . . advise against pre-marital sexual relationships."

The second edition of *Your Best Foot Forward*, sold for $3.50, was wrapped in a red dust jacket with a contemporary illustration of a couple, she in her bobbed hair and he in his crew cut. Dorothy was fifty-six and Helen was fifty-three when they updated their book to advise "young moderns." Their publisher, McGraw-Hill, created a news bulletin for publicity. The book was touted as a great graduation gift. Stories about *Your Best Foot Forward* appeared in Purdue's *Exponent* and other newspapers, *Ladies' Home Journal*, and the Girl Scout magazine, the *American Girl*.

By this time, Dorothy was executive director of the Girl Scouts of America, working at the headquarters in New York City. Lillian Gilbreth had been on the Girl Scouts' national Board of Directors, and she had recommended Dorothy for the position. Girl Scouts was an organization dear to Lillian's heart.

Dorothy was the ideal woman to lead the Girl Scouts, bringing her lessons learned from guiding coast guard women to thousands of girls across the United States, their troop leaders, and her staff of about nine hundred. They served under the Girl Scout oath, "to do my duty to God and my country."

Under Dorothy's direction from 1950 to 1960, membership grew from about 1,800,000 to 3,400,000. A few months after she took her place at the helm, she wrote an article that ran in the January 1951 *Girl Scout Leader* magazine, encouraging troop leaders to recruit others to head a group of Scouts. Dorothy carried her coast guard style of accessibility and authenticity into the organization, as is evident in her final paragraph. She wrote: "My own New Year's resolution is to stay as close as is humanly possible to those basic elements in Scouting—the leaders and the troops. I'll be with you in spirit when you meet with your troops, and don't be surprised if one day I'm with you in person."

During Dorothy's tenure, she marshaled the formation of the Senior Roundup, a nationwide encampment of thousands of teenage Girl Scouts. The first, in 1956, was held in Pontiac, Michigan, and the second attracted nearly 10,000 Girl Scouts to Colorado Springs, Colorado, in the summer of 1959.

Dorothy led the charge to build the organization's national headquarters, then at 830 Third Avenue in New York City. In her book *Four Walking Tours of Modern Architecture in New York City*, Ada Louise Huxtable called the thirteen-story International-style Girl Scout office building "modest but impeccable." Today, the New York Historic Districts Council website states, "In keeping with the desire of its cost conscious client, The Girl Scouts of America, the building deliberately avoided any show of extravagance. A very refined curtain wall of clear glass and white structural glass spandrel panels are crisply set in a grid of black anodized aluminum. The result, as noted in New York 1960, 'was a small building that represented a high level of design sophistication.'"

Dorothy was a streamlined, no-nonsense woman. The Girl Scouts headquarters reflected her personality: efficient, purposeful, and timeless.

Dorothy gave a speech to Girl Scout staff and leaders during this decade, entitled "Faith in Our Time." Her talk could have been given in the twenty-first century and reveals Dorothy's convictions. Dorothy, who was the daughter of a Baptist minister but who only sporadically attended church as an adult, said in part:

> Few of us, even those who were reared in homes where religion was the cornerstone of life, can say that we have come to our faith easily. Most of us have gone through considerable travail. In our scientific age it is not easy to believe in "the evidence of things not seen."
>
> Faith to me has three elements—faith in God, faith in one's fellowman, faith in one's self. Of these three, faith in God is primary, faith in one's fellowman and in one's self flows from one's belief in God.
>
> My faith in God can be stated quite simply. I believe that God who rules the vastness of the universe also watches over me. I do not understand how this can be but I have faith that it is true.

HELEN, THE FEMINIST, was a judge for the 1955 Miss America Pageant, the second in its history to be televised. Lee Meriwether, who later became an actress, was crowned Miss America the year before when Grace

Kelly was one of the judges. The pageant began in 1921 as a promotional event to keep tourists in the seaside resort of Atlantic City, New Jersey, after Labor Day.

Although the event appears counter to her personality and ambitions for women, she had her justifiable reasons for accepting the invitation made by the pageant's executive director. The previous summer, Helen had been a judge for the Miss Michigan Contest, run by the same organization. It was Helen's first knowledge of the pageant, and she found her experience to be interesting and informative in concerning what it did for young women. Helen wrote to Purdue President Frederick Hovde for his approval:

> Dear President Hovde:
>
> You are asked to give your attention to some strange and fearful projects, I am sure, but I doubt if any will have been less anticipated than this one. I have been invited to be one of the judges at Atlantic City next September for the Miss America Pageant. . . .
>
> I made up my mind I could no longer afford to be high-hat about the Miss America Pageant Program in view of the magnificent monetary scholarships that are involved for women.

Helen was impressed that the winner of the Miss Michigan contest won $3,000 worth of scholarships, and that the first prize for the Miss America Pageant was a $5,000 scholarship. She pointed out that Dr. Guy E. Snavely, executive director of the Association of American Colleges, had been an advisor to the pageant for many years. Hovde sent back a short, handwritten memo:

> My dear Dean Schleman:
>
> Congratulations! I have no objection whatsoever to mixing beauty and education. For better or for worse, the Miss American Pageant is part of the American scene—the problem is to handle it in a good way—with this you can help. Go ahead. Yours, F. L. Hovde

Helen and Hovde had an amiable working relationship. He knew she would come calling whenever she saw an inequity for one of her female students or staff member. Sometimes Hovde came to her aid to change a gender bias; sometimes he did not. Helen chose her battles carefully in a time when few women battled much of anything. Life in the 1950s hummed along complacently.

Helen received a packet of information with her itinerary and an explanation on how to judge the women in the pageant. The paper on "Method of Judging" stated:

> The modern American conception of an ideal girl minimizes the ancient classic standards of height and other physical measurements in favor of a beautiful and generally well-proportioned figure plus these other important characteristics:
>
> 1. Beauty of face.
> 2. Voice, manner of speaking, intellect, charm.
> 3. Wholesomeness, disposition, general culture.
> 4. Special talents.
> 5. Health, care of the body, dress.
> 6. Personality.
>
> In other words, you will be asked to help to select an ideal American girl, one who has beauty, intelligence, talent, culture, personality and poise.

Helen sent her requested biography to be printed in the pageant program alongside her photograph, and she included a letter to the director that gave an endorsement of her female students: "Since Purdue is so well known as an engineering school, people sometimes forget that we have women students here. We do have 2,000 women to 8,000 men students."

Helen's brother, Herbert, served as her escort. The night before the contest, the two attended a cocktail party with the other notable judges and pageant organizers. Regarding her brother, Helen said, "I am delighted to have him as we have great fun together, and I don't get very much time with him."

When Helen judged the Miss America Pageant, it was the first year that Bert Parks was the master of ceremonies. He would continue to be the fatherly, rather corny host, until he was fired in 1980 because producers wanted a younger image. Parks became an American icon with his schmaltzy tenor rendition of what became the pageant's theme song, "There She Is." Parks sang the song as the newly crowned Miss America walked the stage in her teetering crown, holding a bouquet of roses, and more often than not, sobbing with joy. Sharon Kay Ritchie, Miss Colorado, was selected Miss America for 1955.

Helen's time away to judge the Miss America Pageant was part of a leave of absence she took without pay for the 1955–1956 academic year to travel to Europe. In a letter to President Hovde, Helen wrote:

> I am requesting leave for personal reasons. A brief time away from the university I think will result in eventual good both to the university and to me. I have been on continuous appointment at the university since the summer of 1934 on a twelve-month basis. . . . As you know, I have felt for a good while that I needed a block of time to take care of some family and personal obligations. . . .
>
> I feel a distinct obligation to my parents who are both well in their eighties to make it possible for them to do some travel which they are keenly interested in doing.

Helen took her parents to Europe in the fall and then spent time on a couple of small writing projects. She hoped the year would provide her with a fresh perspective. In her absence, Doris M. Seward, who had been assistant dean, served as acting dean of women.

When Helen returned from her leave, the Office of the Dean of Women made a monumental shift. Beverley Stone and Barbara Wood Cook would make their entrances onto Purdue soil. A new synergy was on the horizon.

20

B-Squared

As if by providence, Beverley Stone and Barbara Wood Cook came to work in Purdue's Office of the Dean of Women in the same year.

Bev had a contract in hand to take the dean of women position at the University of Buffalo when her phone rang. Purdue's Dean of Women Helen Schleman was on the line. Bev remembered their conversation: "She asked me to come here [Purdue] to interview for an opening as assistant dean. I told her Purdue was wasting its money to bring me out, since I'd made my decision, but I came anyway. When I got here, I changed my mind. I just felt so at ease with the Purdue students. They were, and are, wonderful people. So I took a job for less pay and less title, but never regretted it."

It was 1956, and Bev had just earned her student dean professional diploma from Teachers College of Columbia University. When Bev left her associate dean position at the University of Arkansas, the dean of women there, Jeannette Scudder, wrote a letter of recommendation describing Bev, the genteel woman who grew up in Virginia. Jeannette stated:

> Miss Stone is a splendid executive; she does her work with dispatch and thoroughness, and organizes and delegates responsibility effectively. . . .
>
> Personally Miss Stone is lady-like and well-bred, at home in any company, with instinctive sense of the fitness of things. She has dignity and presence, and a sense of humor always near the surface. Her appearance is attractive and well-groomed. She has a beautiful speaking and singing voice, and is, incidentally, an effective public speaker. In her conversations and associations she gives the same respectful, warm attention to the humblest as to the highest, and has the capacity and restraint to suffer fools gladly.

Helen had called Jeannette asking for recommendations to fill a staff position in her office. She had known Jeannette since she was a Purdue student living in the Women's Residence Hall when Helen was the director and Dorothy Stratton was the dean of women. Jeannette had been a member of the class that named Dorothy an honorary Mortar Board member during her tenure at the University.

Bev liked the students at Purdue, but the other draw was the chance to work with Helen. Bev moved into an apartment at 524 Russell Street, just a few blocks from where she worked in Purdue's Executive Building, today named Hovde Hall. Soon the friend who had once lived across the hall from her at the University of Arkansas, Barbara Wood, would contact Bev for help. The previous summer, Bev had said good-bye to Barb, who had married and moved with her new husband to Michigan. Through the common thread of Purdue graduate and Arkansas Dean of Women Jeanette Scudder, the Purdue deans—past, present, and yet to be—Dorothy, Helen, Bev, and Barb—were about to be woven like the warp and weft of a loom.

BARB WAS WORKING AS ASSISTANT DEAN at the University of Arkansas when she and Salem Cook became engaged. Bev Stone, Barb's superior as acting dean of women at the time, wrote a letter about the engagement to the *Arkansas Gazette* society editor. It read: "I am enclosing an announcement of the engagement of Barbara Wood, the Assistant Dean of Women here, and will greatly appreciate it if you can arrange to use it on the front page of the society section in next Sunday's Arkansas Gazette. She was popular as a student and as Assistant Dean of Women has been beloved by the students and respected by their parents throughout the state."

Barb's fiancé was tall, thin, and athletic; he complemented Barb's five-foot-ten-and-a-half-inch build. The southerner and northerner looked good together. Barb and Salem corresponded about plans for the wedding and their new life together. Salem wrote letters from his home in Kalamazoo, Michigan; he missed "Woody," and the impending nuptials seemed to spin him into a dizzy frenzy. On July 7, he wrote in a four-page handwritten letter: "Woody, this has been beyond all doubt one of the strangest periods in my entire life, never before have I been quite so lost. Beginning to laugh at myself, first I turn the television on and that lasts about five minutes, then I pick up a book and that lasts just about as long. Next thing I know, I'm outside wandering around the yard and trying to figure out whether I want a cigarette or not. Can certainly tell you this Sweetie, Salem is convinced—and a lot more."

Salem mentioned looking at photos of the two of them at a dance and another of Barb at camp. He wrote of visiting a priest with his mother and needing to know from Barb the name of the priest who would marry them in her hometown of Memphis. He signed his letter, "With you more than you know, Darling, Salem."

In subsequent letters, Salem unabashedly pines for his finance: "Woody, above all else as the time grows shorter, I'm learning what it means to be lonesome. And, if it were just that, it wouldn't be so bad, but with all there is to think about—and I've argued myself blue in the face over the pros and cons of location, job, place to live, etc. . . . Guess that I've never wanted anything so much before as just having you near and being able to go over these things together as we should."

In another letter, Salem asks an important question:

> There is one small item that I need an answer from you on Woody—Mother has always wanted me to use her wedding ring, for luck if nothing else, of course she hasn't been forcible about it and believe me there is no reason why you should feel compelled in any way, just let me know what your feelings are, and I will go from there as is your wish. Ok? If you would like this, let me know the ring size. . . .

I love you more than ever—also this waiting grows progressively worse!

God bless you, and my love,
Salem

After Barb and Salem were married in August 1955 in a small ceremony in Memphis with a reception at her parents' home, they moved to Kalamazoo. Barb set out to find a job, armed with her master's degree from Syracuse and two years of professional experience. She said, "What I learned my first year back at Arkansas was nothing compared to what I learned in Kalamazoo! In 1955, if one were young and married, it was assumed that one would become pregnant and, of course, be unable to continue working. Although I interviewed for several professional jobs in education and in social services, I received no offers—just commentary that it was risky to employ married women."

In desperation, Barb took a receptionist position at Ernst & Ernst, Certified Public Accountants. She was overqualified and living in a northern state for the first time in her life. Barb said, "When I answered the phone, 'Ernst & Ernst,' with my still very pronounced southern accent, the reply from the other end was, 'Where in the hell did Ernst & Ernst find you?'"

Barb was supposed to help type tax forms when not answering the phone. Her three-finger typing was not well received by the secretarial staff. She felt underemployed although her colleagues thought she was incompetent. Barb ate lunch each day with the other women on the clerical staff. These women talked about shopping, getting dates, and the latest movies; they also gossiped about the professional male accountants. Barb said, "For the first time in my life, I spent at least eight hours a day with people who did not read books, discuss politics, or care very deeply about social issues. This was a world I had never imagined, and I didn't like it very much."

On a cold day in what Barb later termed "that Kalamazoo year," Salem and his brother went golfing. When he returned home, he looked shockingly pale. It was determined that Salem had suffered a massive heart attack. He was twenty-seven. Barb said, "I knew that my husband, who had played varsity basketball at Arkansas and who had been a professional golfer at one time, could never again do the things he loved. I was told that he would never be able to work and that his life expectancy was tenuous."

Salem was moved to a VA hospital in Ann Arbor, about one hundred miles from Kalamazoo. Barb visited him on weekends. Barb wasn't making enough money to support Salem and herself. When Salem was released from the VA hospital, he was told he probably wouldn't live long. The couple stayed with Salem's mother in Grand Rapids while Barb determined what to do. She needed to find a job located fairly close to where Salem's family lived.

Barb decided to contact the women she knew at her alma maters, Syracuse University and the University of Arkansas. She wrote Syracuse Dean of Women Eunice Hilton for help. She called her friend and former Arkansas colleague Bev Stone and told her what had happened. Bev had just accepted her position at Purdue. Bev told Barb that when she had interviewed at Purdue, she heard there was another vacancy. Bev also assured Barb that she would contact Arkansas Dean of Women Jeanette Scudder for assistance. It ended up that both Deans Hilton and Scudder readily wrote letters of recommendations for Barb.

The three influential women from different areas of the country connected to care for their former student, colleague, and friend whose life had taken an unexpected turn. Then Helen offered Barb a trial position in Purdue's Housemother Training School, the program that Dorothy Stratton had started in the 1930s to teach women how to become housemothers in residence halls, sororities, and fraternities.

All of these women—Hilton, Scudder, Stone, and Schleman—knew one another through the National Association of Deans of Women. The organization made possible a lifeline of female support, professional and personal, that snaked throughout the United States from university to university.

If she proved herself working with the Housemother Training School, Barb would be put on Helen's staff. Barb came to Purdue the summer of 1956 without Salem and stayed at the Kappa residence with the sorority's housemother. Barb was somewhat unsure of what she was to do there, but she was given the task to be a keynote speaker at the formal dinner held on the last night of the two-week training.

Lois Wark was an assistant dean in the Office of the Dean of Women, working as director of placement for women. She also helped with job placement for the women who completed the Housemother Training School. Many of the women who attended the course were widows in midlife who wanted to work but had no prior professional experience and were apprehensive about where their lives were going. Barb was twenty-seven, and she would speak to a banquet room full of women nearly twice her age. Lois and Barb struck up a friendship, and Lois remembered Barb's keynote speech:

> Barb has told me so many times over the years—she said, "Lois, you taught me everything I needed to know to make that speech." I did not remember that. I'm sure I did whatever I could to orient her, and I'm sure that Helen asked me to do that. I don't have any recollection of that, but that was her comment over and over again.
>
> She gave an absolutely right on speech [about] leadership with a goodly bit of human and personal experiences, inspirational because she was really trying to talk to these wonderful women who were out there wanting to do so many good things, but didn't know how and was really uneasy about the whole thing.
>
> That was Helen's trial of Barb, and, of course, Barb was immediately hired on staff.

When Barb gave a presentation, she drew in her listeners with her gentle Memphis intonation. She spoke honestly, with no pretense; she understood her audience. She wore her soul on her sleeve and gracefully displayed her convictions.

Lois accompanied Barb as she found a house to rent. Barb returned to Grand Rapids, packed up her belongings, and she and Salem moved to West Lafayette on July 4, 1956. Lois remembered what happened just two days later: "I got a call from her about 2:00 a.m. saying that something was wrong with Salem. I said call an ambulance. I went right over."

Salem was pronounced dead at the house. Lois immediately called Helen, who told her to bring Barb to her home on Western Drive. Helen called her staff, and each woman drove to Helen's house in the murky predawn of that hot July morning. Lois said, "Then the staff—her new family—

surrounded Barb for that night and for whatever followed the next day. There was a caring, a love, and a respect among the folks on that staff. I can't say that I've not been in other situations similar to it, but it was pretty unique."

Helen and the staff she chose were tightly knit because they shared a common purpose to help students and each other. Helen's leadership style facilitated a mutual respect and camaraderie. Lois said, "We knew we could talk about anything that was on our minds and that we would be listened to—be aided in making any decisions that needed to be made. The support was there, and I knew that somebody was there with an answer, or a hand, or something. It was a beautiful environment."

In 1991, Barb wrote these words about her husband: "One of the things that Salem used to say was the best insurance policy one could have was an educated wife. He was somewhat prophetic. . . . I've always thought that he lived long enough to make sure that I was all right, surrounded by good people in a good situation. His perceptions were accurate."

Purdue *Exponent* reporter Cindy Richards interviewed Barb in 1980. She described Barb's reaction when the two talked of Salem, the man Barb was married to for just eleven months: "Her voice still grows soft and thick as she remembers. . . . For a moment she looks at her left finger, which still bears the engagement and wedding rings she received twenty-five years ago, and then her voice clears and she continues."

Barb wore her wedding ring her entire life, yet many of her students, even those close to her, never knew she had been married.

Through a collection of coincidences, foresight, and tragedy, Bev and Barb came to Purdue within months of each other. Helen said the best thing she did as dean of women was to hire Bev and Barb, the Cook-Stone duo. Helen recalled, "Most good things that happened to me during my tenure as dean of women occurred after Bev Stone and Barb Cook came to the staff in 1956. That was when things really began to happen. They worked with students very closely, and I administered."

Bev lived in her rental on Russell Street, and she invited Barb to room with her so she wouldn't be alone as she grieved after Salem's death. The two women shared expenses. Barb's world must have felt surreal at this point, as if she moved in slow motion, quicksand underfoot. She left the house in which she and Salem lived for just two days and moved to Russell Street.

Bev, the ultrafeminine lady, wore pink suits, sling-back heels, fur coats, pearls, and her signature Shalimar perfume. Long-limbed Barb, the tomboy, disliked shopping for clothes but loved to canoe, climb trees, and dig in dirt. Bev and Barb (B-squared) were the assistant dean of women yin and yang.

Decades later, Barb said, "It was fate, I believe, that brought Beverley Stone to a job at Purdue, and that she recommended me for another opening on Helen Schleman's staff in the Dean of Women's Office."

Bev and Barb, opposite women, would continue to live under the same roof, work in the same office, and befriend Purdue students together for the next fifty years.

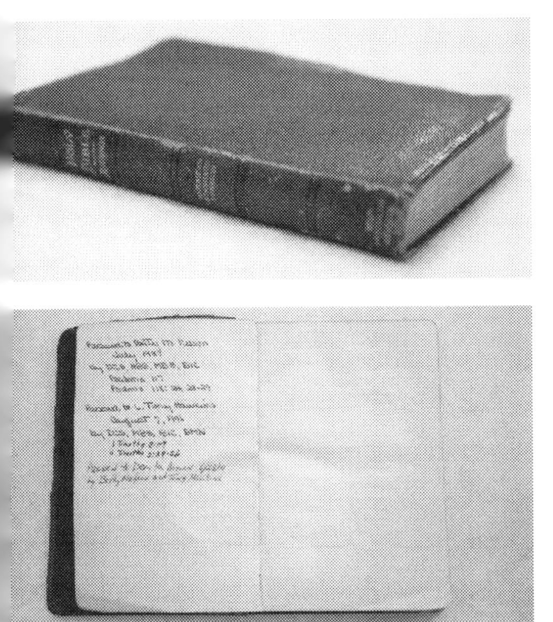

Carolyn Shoemaker earned her master's degree from Purdue University and later became an English literature instructor. She was appointed Purdue's first part-time dean of women in 1913. After she passed away in 1933, her successor, Dorothy Stratton, found Carolyn's Bible in her desk.

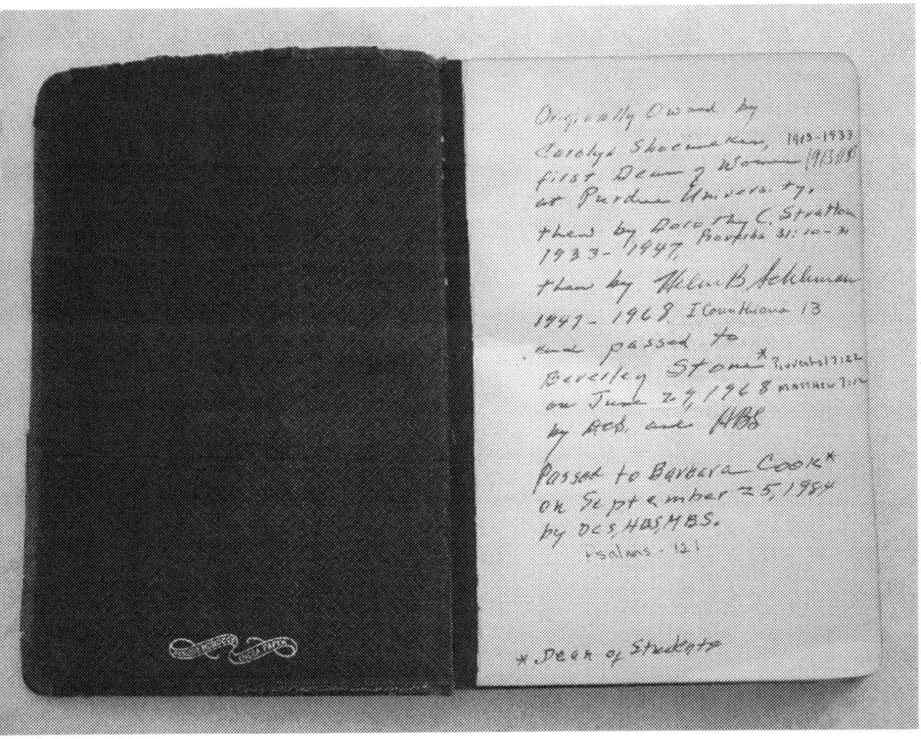

In 1947, Dorothy Stratton signed her name and marked a favorite passage in Carolyn Shoemaker's Bible, then passed the book to Helen Schleman, the second full-time dean of women at Purdue. The Bible was secretively passed to each successive dean. Photographs by Jack Klink.

Dorothy Stratton beca the first full-time dean women at Purdue Univers in 1933. Courtesy of Purd University Libraries Archives a Special Collections.

Dorothy Stratton often visited Purdue trustee and benefactor David Ross at his summer home south of campus. Today it is Ross Hills Park. Courtesy of S. Watlington.

Helen Schleman was named director of the long-awaited Women's Residence Hall in 1934. Today, Duhme is part of the complex named Windsor Halls. Amelia Earhart and Lillian Gilbreth stayed here when they resided on campus. Courtesy of Purdue University Office of the Dean of Students.

'urdue's Dean of Women)orothy Stratton, age thirty-ix, Assistant Dean of Women :lare A. Coolidge, aviatrix nd Consultant on Careers for Vomen Amelia Earhart, and 'rank C. Hockema, assistant to 'resident Edward Elliott, stand n the steps of an engineering uilding on November 8, 1935. :ourtesy of Purdue University ibraries Archives and Special :ollections.

Helen Schleman (back) a
Dorothy Stratton became go
friends when they arrived to wo
at Purdue in 1933. Courtesy of Purd
University Libraries Archives and Spec
Collections.

Dorothy Stratton and Helen Schleman board a ship in the 1930s. Helen holds a Western Union telegram that reads, "Bon Voyage." Courtesy of Purdue University Libraries Archives and Special Collections.

fter she served as Purdue's first full-time dean of women, Dorothy Stratton eft) was the founder and director of the United States Coast Guard Women's eserve, which she named SPARs. Courtesy of Purdue University Libraries Archives nd Special Collections.

Purdue President Edward Elliott supported Dean of Women Dorothy Stratton as she took an unpaid leave of absence during World War II. Director of the Women's Residence Hall Helen Schleman also took a leave of absence to become Dorothy's executive officer. Courtesy of Purdue University Libraries Archives and Special Collections.

In 1942, after then-lieutenant commander Dorothy Stratton, age forty-three, was appointed the inaugural director of the SPARs, she said, “It seems fitting for women to be connected with a unit that has as its main purpose the protection and conservation of life and property.” Courtesy of Purdue University Libraries Archives and Special Collections.

First Lady Eleanor Roosevelt and the heads of the World War II women’s reserves watch a parade on the grounds of the White House in 1943. Pictured are WAVES Captain Mildred McAfee Horton, WACS Colonel Oveta Culp Hobby, Eleanor Roosevelt, USMWR Colonel Ruth Cheney Streeter, and SPARs Lieutenant Commander Dorothy Stratton. Courtesy of S. Watlington.

Captain Dorothy Stratton, age forty-six, boards a Pan-Am clipper in San Francisco to fly to Honolulu, Hawaii, where she facilitated the assignment of the SPARs to Pearl Harbor in 1945. Courtesy of Purdue University Libraries Archives and Special Collections.

Helen Schleman headed a survey mission in Ketchikan, Alaska, in 1945 to study how the SPARs could aid the war effort there. Pictured are Commander Helen Schleman, Lieutenant Commander Teresa Crowley, Lieutenant J. P. Towey, and Lieutenant Dorothy Bevis. Courtesy of Purdue University Libraries Archives and Special Collections.

At the end of World War II in 1946, Helen Schleman was promoted to captain and would "finish up the SPARs" as the coast guard women were discharged. Courtesy of S. Watlington.

Dorothy Stratton described this 1943 photograph taken during a War Bon fund-raising drive: "Stars of stage and screen were there to help. I was ther on business for the coast guard. Ginger Rogers, Mickey Rooney, et al. wer riding in limousines and were cheered by the crowds lining the streets o St. Louis, Mo. . . . The crowds would yell, 'Hi, there, Dottie' in response to th sign on the jeep. I am trying to decide whether to try to be dignified or to re spond to the crowds. I did the latter." Courtesy of Purdue University Libraries Archive and Special Collections.

Beverley Stone is shown here in 1947, age thirty-one. Bev's favorite poem was "A Few Figs from Thistles," by Edna St. Vincent Millay. The "Second Fig" reads: "Safe upon the solid rock the ugly houses stand: Come and see my shining palace built upon the sand!" Courtesy of Betty M. Nelson.

Purdue's third full-time Dean of Women Beverley Stone enlisted in the WAVES during World War II through the influence of Director Mildred McAfee and her favorite aunt who had been a "yeomanette" in the navy during the First World War. Courtesy of Purdue University Libraries Archives and Special Collections.

Helen Schleman (right) became Purdue's second full-time dean of women i 1947, succeeding her mentor and friend, Dorothy Stratton. Helen, age fort five, sits with two students in the Office of the Dean of Women in what is tc day Hovde Hall. Courtesy of Purdue University Office of the Dean of Students.

Dorothy Stratton was executive director of the Girl Scouts of America from 195(to 1960. During her tenure, membership nearly doubled, and she marshaled th formation of the Senior Roundup, a nationwide encampment of thousands o scouts that began in 1956. Photograph by Hal Phyfe, collection of Girl Scouts of the US National Historic Preservation Center. Used by permission.

Barbara Ivy Wood, approximately age six, in Memphis, Tennessee. "Woody" was akin to author Harper Lee's character Scout in *To Kill a Mockingbird*. Her father taught her to love wildflowers and birds. Her mother opened her eyes to those in need. Courtesy of Betty M. Nelson.

Barbara Ivy Wood, age twenty-six, married Salem Cook from Kalamazoo, Michigan, in August 1955. Salem had been a professional golfer. He suffered a massive heart attack shortly after they were married during what Barb termed "that Kalamazoo year." Courtesy of Betty M. Nelson.

Barbara Cook, age twenty-nine, embarks with friend Pat Pierce on a trip to Europe in 1958. At this time, Barb was an assistant dean in Purdue's Office of the Dean of Women. Courtesy of Purdue University Libraries Archives and Special Collections.

Purdue's Dean of Women Helen Schleman holds a meeting of her staff i 1958. Left to right: Jane Van Deusen, Beverley Stone, Helen Schleman, Barbar Cook, Marguerite Albjerg, and Cecelia Zissis. Courtesy of Purdue University Librarie Archives and Special Collections.

Betty Mitchell Nelson grew up in Bluefield, West Virginia ("Nature's Air-Conditioned City"), where her father, Emory, was the city manager. He signed Betty's childhood autograph book with this advice: ". . . nothing will get you as far and cost you as little as thoughtfulness and courtesy to those with whom you come in contact each day—be they rich or poor." Courtesy of Betty M. Nelson.

n 1952, Betty Mitchell Nelson, age seventeen, was one of eight West Virginia vinners in an essay contest sponsored by the Governor's Committee for Employ the Physically Handicapped. Betty received a $25 savings bond from Governor Okey L. Patteson in the West Virginia Capitol Building. Courtesy of Betty M. Nelson.

Betty Mitchell Nelson (righ age twenty, aboard the *Queen Bermuda* with her cousin Burw Moss on June 1, 1955—a tr Betty's mother, Peg, made possib even though finances were limit after Betty's father passed aw when she was sixteen. Courtesy Betty M. Nelson.

Betty Mitchell met Richard Nelson in a class while she was in the Student Personnel Administration program at Ohio University in Athens. They married in 1959. Dick was the first PhD student for the University's Elementary Counselor Education program. Courtesy of Betty M. Nelson.

Dean of Women Helen Schleman and her staff gather at the "Cook-Stone" home at 1808 Summit Drive in West Lafayette, Indiana, in the late 1960s. Pictured are Linda Ewing, Cecelia Zissis, Helen Schleman, Betty Nelson, Beverley Stone, Barbara Cook, and Barbara Elsbury. Courtesy Betty M. Nelson.

On November 5, 1958, Helen Schleman, age fifty-six, receives a special fresh floral hat from a student wearing a green "pot," or beanie, which indicated she was a freshman. Courtesy of Purdue University Libraries Archives and Special Collections.

Beverley Stone (center) holds a Mortar Board calendar with Helen Schleman (left) and Barbara Cook (right). As advisor to Purdue's chapter of the Mortar Board National College Honor Society, Bev conceived the idea in 1958 to ask campus bookstores to sell the calendars. Today, Purdue bookstores still sell about 30,000 copies per year of the popular Mortar Board calendar. Courtesy of S. Watlington.

Helen Schleman, Barbara Cook, Jeannette Scudder, and Beverley Stone enjoyed a web of lifetime connections. Jeannette was a Purdue alumna who became dean of women at the University of Arkansas. Barb entered the Universit of Arkansas the next year and met Jeannette and Bev, who later recommende her for a position at Purdue when Helen Schleman was dean of women. Al were active in the National Association of Deans of Women (NADW). Courtesy of Purdue University Libraries Archives and Special Collections.

n the summer of 1968, Beverley Stone served as Purdue's dean of women, having ucceeded Helen Schleman (seated to her left). Foreground: Cecelia Zissis, arbara Cook, Linda Ewing, Betty Nelson, Mary Colacicco, Nancy Friedersdorf, arbara Elsbury, and Peggy Sullivan. Only Helen and Bev knew of Carolyn hoemaker's Bible tucked inside the desk drawer. Courtesy of Betty M. Nelson.

This 1989 photo was a "reenactment" of the 1968 photo above. Betty Nelson standing center) was dean of students. The difference in the photo taken twenty ears later is that Purdue's first full-time Dean of Women Dorothy Stratton stood n for Mary Colacicco, and Nancy Friedersdorf was not present as she had retired. The secret Bible was tucked inside the desk. Courtesy of Betty M. Nelson.

In May 1970, Sue Daniel Eiler presented Dean of Women Beverley Stone with the Helen B. Schleman Gold Medallion Award in Purdue's Elliott Hall of Music. Sue quoted an *Exponent* article, saying, "Bev Stone is a hip woman." Bev stepped to the microphone and said, "I *am* one hip woman," while patting herself on the hip. Courtesy of Sue Daniel Eiler.

In 1962, Dorothy Stratton (second from right) chaired the Women's Committe of President John F. Kennedy's Committee on Employment of the Handicappe The goal was to utilize the talents of women and women's organizations to carr out programs and projects to help those with disabilities obtain jobs and to gai employer acceptance of workers with handicaps. Helen Schleman, Purdue' dean of women and president-elect of the National Association of Wome Deans and Counselors, served on the committee. Courtesy of S. Watlington.

urdue Dean of Women Emerita Helen Schleman and Dean of Women .everley Stone met First Lady Pat Nixon. Helen was a consultant for President :ichard Nixon's Task Force on Women's Rights and Responsibilities. She spoke t the White House on "Women in Higher Education." The president called White House conference on women's rights and responsibilities in 1970, ne fiftieth anniversary of the suffrage amendment and establishment of the Vomen's Bureau. Courtesy of Purdue University Libraries Archives and Special Collections.

Dean of Women Helen Schleman feeds her dog Trish in her home at 1607 Western Drive in West Lafayette, Indiana, on May 11, 1968, about a month before she would retire after serving Purdue University for thirty-five years. Courtesy of Purdue University Libraries Archives and Special Collections.

Sally Watlington (far right) was like a daughter to Helen Schleman (seate
next to her). The two were avid golfers and were together in Texas when Hele
made her first hole-in-one at the age of eighty-one. Here they are at the Batt
Ground Course of the Lafayette Country Club in the late 1970s with (left
right) Shelia Shearon and Isabel Waling. Courtesy of Purdue University Librari
Archives and Special Collections.

Helen Schleman's parents owned a golf course in Valparaiso, Indiana. I
1933, she wrote *Group Golf Instruction*, a pioneering manual on the theory o
teaching the game to large groups. In later years, she took her dog Kerry to pla
on Purdue's golf course, located behind her house. Courtesy of Purdue Universit
Office of the Dean of Students.

Dean of Women Emerita Helen Schleman received an honorary degree of Doctor of Laws from Purdue University in June 1971. Helen and President Frederick L. Hovde both served Purdue for more than twenty-five years, from post-World War II to the early 1970s. Courtesy of S. Watlington.

Dean of Students Betty Nelson led the charge to make Purdue University accessible to those with disabilities. Gregg Poorman was one of the first student wheelchair-users to graduate from Purdue, and he led the initiative for student organizations to sponsor the creation of curb cuts. He is shown with his wife, Marty. Courtesy of Betty M. Nelson.

The deans gathered for the dedication of the Helen B. Schleman Hall Student Services on April 21, 1990. Helen was Purdue's dean of women fro 1947 to 1968. Front: Dorothy Stratton, age ninety-one, Helen Schleman, ag eighty-seven, Beverley Stone, age seventy-three. Back: Barbara Cook, ag sixty, and then Dean of Students Betty Nelson, age fifty-five. Courtesy of Purd University Office of the Dean of Students.

Beverley Stone and Barbara Cook join Betty Nelson at the dedication of he campus marker at the corner of Grant Street and Northwestern Avenue o October 19, 1996. Three gateway markers to Purdue University honor the Dea of Students Emeritae. Bev's marker is at the corner of Grant and State Street near the Memorial Union. Barb's marker stands at Northwestern and Stadiu Avenues near Lambert Fieldhouse. Courtesy of Betty M. Nelson.

n August 29, 1997, the "Deans' Tea" was held at Duncan Hall in afayette, Indiana, to celebrate Purdue's first part-time Dean of Women arolyn Shoemaker's "heritage of strength and warmth as a life member of e Community House Association Board." Barbara Cook, Beverley Stone, orothy Stratton, and Betty Nelson flank a portrait of Carolyn Shoemaker. ach had been a guardian of Shoemaker's Bible. Helen Schleman passed away 1992. Courtesy of Aura Lee Emsweller, executive director of Thomas Duncan Hall.

eresa Roche, vice president and chief learning officer at Agilent Technologies, new the deans beginning when she was an undergraduate student in 1974. etty Nelson, Barbara Cook, and Beverley Stone mentored Teresa, increasing er awareness of women's issues and supporting her to this day. Teresa returned o campus as an Old Master in 2005 with her daughter Kate, continuing the egacy as the deans influenced the next generation. Courtesy of Betty M. Nelson.

In 2010, First Lady Michelle Obama christened a National Security Cutter honor of Captain Dorothy Stratton, Purdue's dean of women who founded ar directed the World War II women's reserve of the United States Coast Guar It was the first time in history that a Legend-class National Security Cutt was named in honor of a woman, and the first time that a first lady sponsore a coast guard or navy ship. Official White House Photo by Samantha Appleton.

On March 31, 2012, the United States Coast Guard Cutter *Stratton* wa commissioned by First Lady Michelle Obama to head out to sea from Alamed California. Betty Nelson, Sally Watlington, and friends and family attendec including many of the SPARs from World War II who loved Dorothy Stratto as their fearless leader. Michelle Obama ordered, "Lay aboard and bring ou cutter to life!" Courtesy of U.S. Coast Guard.

21
Dean of Women Punch

Beverley Stone's first assignment from Dean of Women Helen Schleman was to work with Purdue's women's organizations, which in the beginning was a vague description. It seemed to her friend and colleague Barb Cook that "Bev advised everything." As an assistant dean of women, Bev worked with the YWCA, a Christian-based organization. Its first fall activity involved older students accompanying freshmen women to the churches of their choice on the first Sunday of the school year. Bev advised the Old Masters program, bringing distinguished alumni back to campus to speak informally with the students at their housing units and at various activities. It was a free exchange with questions and answers. Additionally, Bev served as an advisor for the Women's Panhellenic Association, which hosted a penny carnival in Purdue's Armory during "Greek Week." The 1956 *Debris* yearbook noted: "For only a nickel, we bought tickets at the Armory door. That enabled us, along with the townspeople and faculty members, to enter any of the many sideshows or try our luck at the laugh-provoking games provided by various sorority and fraternity members."

One of the ideas of Greek Week was to improve relations with the sororities, fraternities, others on campus, and the townspeople. The headline to the paragraph about the event read: "Organized Cooperation in Greek Week." A black-and-white photo taken at the event's formal masquerade dance shows female students sitting next to their tuxedoed dates looking at the camera from their half masks, the women dressed in strapless gowns with wide crinoline skirts that rustled with every move. The caption read, "Gaily decorated masks hide the identity of couples at the Greek Week Ball."

Bev worked with the Gold Peppers, the women who wore gold pots (or beanies) on their heads and cheered at pep rallies and athletic events. Many of the campus organizations had their own color of pot to wear.

All freshmen were required to wear green pots, which indicated their newbie status. Senior men wore tan corduroy pants, and senior women wore corduroy skirts that they painted with words and pictures to indicate the clubs and activities they were involved in, their major, and even their love lives. Freshmen tried to steal the seniors' cords.

Bev advised the Green Guard counseling program, a group of older students who befriended the "green" freshmen girls to help orient them to campus. Additionally, she guided Student Government and Mortar Board. About ten years earlier, the Mortar Board women had created a reminder calendar, a wire-bound schedule that also listed campus activities for the year and was about the size of a thin paperback book. Each woman was given a required number to sell.

Selling the Mortar Board calendar was a headache. Students were busy, and peddling a calendar was not something many of them enjoyed. Bev came up with a brilliant idea to increase sales and take the burden off of students. She approached the bookstores on campus, all locally owned, and asked if they would be willing to sell the Mortar Board calendar. When striking Bev came calling in her pink suit, few could refuse her. Dean of Students Emerita Betty Nelson described Bev: "She just had a lovely style about her and graciousness that made people feel really good. Without being too sweet."

Purdue campus bookstores have sold the popular Mortar Board calendar since 1958. It's a given that nearly every student owns a calendar that lists University activities and leaves plenty of space to write. The calendar can become a diary and keepsake of a student's time at Purdue. Today, the Mortar Board chapter holds a design contest for each year's cover, and the winner is recognized at the organization's annual awards program.

The Purdue Mortar Board sells about 30,000 calendars each year. Other Mortar Board chapters have attempted to imitate Purdue's method of selling calendars, but they have not met with the same level of success. But of course, other universities did not have Bev, with her Virginia accent and charisma.

Bev soon discovered that Helen was a workaholic and expected her staff to be as well. Bev's workday ran from 9 a.m. to 10 p.m., with a number of Sunday teas and pledge dances thrown in on the weekends. Decades later, Bev spoke of the early days with her colleagues in the Office of the Dean of Women: "All of us were counselors, getting to know students well, working with them. One of the most important parts of higher education should be making it human and caring."

Bev was very social and loved to entertain students in her home. She put together many dinners for fifteen to twenty students between 5:00 and 6:30 p.m., and she was known for her peach ice cream and fried chicken. In those days, no one locked their doors. Bev often came home to find notes from students or the students themselves studying or sleeping in her living room. The students were so comfortable with Bev that they would return after graduation for years to come. Bev recalled, "I've rejoiced over the number of students who have come back as alums and stayed in this house. They come, and stay . . . and eat."

Barb's first job in the Office of the Dean of Women was as a counselor and an advisor for the women's cooperative houses. Bev and Barb started working in the office at the same time, learning their way around Purdue, starting new lives in the same plane of time. Barb's grief and shock at losing her young husband of less than a year was made more bearable with Bev's friendship. Soon after, Barb worked with the Placement Service for Women, which was in the Office of the Dean of Women, helping female students find employment after they graduated. Most of the jobs for women at the time were in education, although a few employers did come to campus to interview home economics graduates for positions like demonstrating food products in test kitchens. To find jobs for the few women in science and pharmacy, Barb wrote letters to potential employers.

Bev's favorite play and Barb's favorite book had very similar central characters, even if on the surface the stories appeared completely different. In the eulogy Barb wrote for Bev's funeral when she passed away in 2003 after the two enjoyed a fifty-year friendship, she wrote: "Bev also had a great sense of the absurd, which was evident in the twinkle in her eye. Her favorite play was *Harvey*. Harvey was a six-foot, three-and-one-half-inch imaginary white rabbit kept by Elwood P. Dowd. Harvey said, 'You can be oh so smart or oh so pleasant; I recommend pleasant.' Fortunately for us all, Bev was both!"

Harvey was a Pulitzer Prize-winning Broadway play that opened in 1944. It was made into a movie starring James "Jimmy" Stewart in 1950. The story is a farce that also is an allegory about tolerance. *Harvey* celebrates the magical element of believing what one cannot see or understand and having that element help one see the good in the world. The movie represents a belief in virtue, letting life happen on its own course, staying true to one's beliefs, and ultimately being a happy, kind, and honest person.

Barb, on the other hand, loved to read biographies and historical novels. She usually read two at a time and liked to read in the bathtub. Her favorite book was Fyodor Dostoevsky's *The Idiot,* which she read four times over her lifetime. To have read the hefty tome once would be an accomplishment. In a 1998 interview, she said of *The Idiot*, "It's been a good friend of mine for many years."

At more than 650 pages, *The Idiot* portrays innocent Prince Myshkin, who is scorned by the society of St. Petersburg for his trusting nature and naiveté. Myshkin's very goodness precipitates disaster, and he finds himself a stranger in a culture obsessed with money, power, and manipulation. Dostoevsky traces the surprising effect of the "positively beautiful man" on the people around him and leads to a final scene that is said to be one of the most powerful in all of literature.

Both women's beloved stories focus on a kind, childlike man who is wiser than people believe and changes those around him by innocently and unabashedly being himself. In the decades to come, as both Bev and Barb became the dean of women and the dean of students at Purdue, they may have felt like the characters of their favored stories. Bev would become dean at the end of the turbulent 1960s, and Barb assumed the position in the legalistic 1980s. Two different, challenging campus cultures would test their resolve to be the sensitive, kind women they were, always true to their convictions—even when those convictions were thwarted—as they placed what was right for the students as top priority.

During the mid-1950s, there were about 2,000 women on campus, and each female student was personally known by at least one of the six staff members in the Office of the Dean of Women. The female students and deans developed close relationships as they were interconnected through the women's groups on campus and the approachable atmosphere of the office.

This is when Sally Watlington, a tall, confident Purdue freshman with a wide smile from Rockford, Illinois, first met Helen, Bev, and Barb. Little did Sally know, the three women would one day become like family, and Helen would eventually call Sally "the daughter I never had." Sally recalled, "Helen, Bev, and Barb were at the first picnic for all the freshmen women who lived in the women's residence halls. All the Mortar Board members marched up in their white coats and spoke. That's when I first met the deans. You felt like you knew them, of course. Every woman student coming in as a freshman was assigned to a woman in the Office of the Dean of Women. That woman would write you a note and say, "Come visit." My contact was Dr. Marguerite Albjerg, a lovely, caring woman whose husband, Dr. Victor Albjerg, would become my favorite professor."

Beginning in 1942, women who were members of Mortar Board, who exuded the values of scholarship, leadership, and service, wore white blazers with the organization's emblem on the left breast pocket depicting the mortarboard academic hat. The first blazers cost $12.95. Mortar Boards had to meet a certain grade point criteria, and it was comparable to the men's honorary society, Iron Key (Bev Stone set a precedent in 1971 when she was made a member of this society). Sally would become one of eighteen Mortar Board women during her college career, which increased her time spent with Bev and Barb as they advised the organization.

As a student, Sally looked at Helen with awe. She said, "I was scared to death of Helen Schleman. She was rather formidable. She was the dean of women! Just the title alone did it."

All three deans hosted parties in their homes. Helen often invited her staff and sometimes the staff of the Office of the Dean of Men to her house for gatherings. She also hosted faculty and administration. Helen understood that having people to her home for social potation was the great equalizer. When one got to know another person on a more personal level, the wheels of work glided a little more smoothly.

Bev and Barb hosted their famous annual Homecoming open house for former students. Through the years, the party grew to two hundred attendees. They served their special recipe for "Dean of Women Punch." The name of the beverage often led an unsuspecting guest to think the punch was some froufrou concoction of ginger ale and tea. Peering into the punch bowl, one saw floating in the amber libation an ice ring merrily dotted with cherries, as if Betty Crocker herself had formed the frozen mold and plopped it into the fine crystal punch bowl, ready to be lovingly ladled. However, once the virgin taster lifted a cup to his lips and swallowed, the juxtaposition was complete. Dean of Women Punch literally packed a punch.

DEAN OF WOMEN PUNCH

3 muscatel
1 rum
1 soda

Prepare an ice ring with cherries. Mix punch and pour over the ice ring in a bowl. Sip and savor and remember dear Purdue friends and ye ol' deans!

May 8, 2003*

*This recipe from M. Beverley Stone and Barbara I. Cook was used for years by the women for staff socials and their traditional Homecoming open house. Its origin will never be known. Bev died in the spring of 2003; at the celebration of her life, this recipe was printed on heavy stock and made available to interested friends and relatives—thus, the date listed above.

Four parts hard liquor and one part soda water, the punch tasted better with every sip. The deans also served the stiff drink at staff socials. Effectively, Dean of Women Punch was a metaphor for the deans themselves. The brew said, "Don't be fooled. Don't assume."

Helen represented Purdue at the dedication of a plaque honoring Amelia Earhart in May 1957. The plaque was placed at the Amelia Earhart Airport at Atchison, Kansas, where the aviatrix was born. Amelia would have turned sixty that year. A newspaper article titled "Helen Schleman to Participate in Earhart Rites" gave a brief history of Amelia's time as advisor to women at Purdue, her flying laboratory provided by the Purdue Research Foundation, and her ill-fated last flight. The last paragraph of the article states: "Miss Earhart lived at the women's residence halls during her frequent visits to the campus while connected with the university and was a close friend of Dean Schleman, who was then serving as director of the residence halls."

That same year, the National Panhellenic Conference (NPC) denounced Dorothy Stratton's successful establishment of deferred rush for sororities at Purdue, which gave young women a chance to become acquainted with campus, make friends, and get to know themselves before deciding that membership in a sorority was something they really wanted.

Helen received a letter from the NPC regarding the annual Fraternity Month Award. The letter had been mailed to all college sororities and deans of women in the United States who had entered the contest. The letter announced that the Panhellenic Council of the University of North Dakota had won the award and commended two other universities. Purdue University, however, was given a public slap on the hand and deemed ineligible. The letter read: "Purdue University Panhellenic was complimented by the Committee for achievements as portrayed in its carefully prepared application. The Purdue Panhellenic, however, was ineligible for the award because its practice of deferred rushing is not consistent with NPC policy."

Helen was livid. She wrote a letter to the president of the National Association of Women Deans and Counselors, saying that the Panhellenic letter

> . . . has caused a mild furor of indignation here at Purdue. So far as I know, this is one of the most conspicuous attempts of NPC to determine operational policy on a given campus. Moreover, this letter I assume has

> gone to all college fraternities and deans of women in the country who entered the contest. This means, in effect, that a great many college Panhellenic groups are being warned not to step out of line and Purdue is used as the example of what happens if one does.
>
> Needless to say, I have been encouraging myself to cool off a bit about the whole matter before I protest as widely and as loudly as I am inclined to. . . . While I am indignant for the Purdue students involved in the particular instance, I am a whole lot more concerned about the general principle of NPC's continually working against the best judgment of college administrators on certain campuses, as far as their own campuses are concerned.

While deferred rush continued at Purdue until the early 2000s, the incident exhibits Helen's tenacity and is one more example of the varied fires she squelched. For decades, Dorothy and Helen's good works for women were targets for many with differing views and goals.

In 1958, Carol Ecker was a student who wanted to become a veterinarian. Purdue had just broken ground for its new School of Veterinary Medicine in February, and the building would be completed the next year. Carol met the admission requirements for Purdue's veterinary school, and she had been accepted for admission at two out-of-state institutions on the basis of her academic record, but she was told point-blank by Purdue that she would not be admitted because she was a woman. Carol told Helen about the denial, and Helen promptly set up an appointment with President Hovde and the first Dean of the School of Veterinary Medicine L. M. Hutchings. Carol recalled, "I'll never forget the image of Helen standing toe to toe with President Hovde. 'With respect,' she asked him, 'Why can't women become veterinarians at Purdue?'"

Sally Watlington further described Helen's conversation with Hovde: "Helen marched across Fred Hovde's desk. She said, 'Why did Edward C. Elliot bring Earhart to campus? Why did Elliott bring Stratton to campus? Why did he bring Dr. Gilbreth to campus? It was to expand opportunities for women.' She said this is unacceptable, and Hovde agreed."

Carol was admitted and became one of the first two female graduates in the school in 1964. She went on to own Clayview Animal Clinic in

South Bend, Indiana, and became the first female president of the Indiana Veterinary Medical Association. From 1988 to 1997, Carol served as a member of Purdue's Board of Trustees.

With Helen's help, Carol and a few other female students made hairline cracks in the barriers for women in Purdue's School of Veterinary Medicine. For many years after, there was a quota of just five women allowed into the school for each entering class. The grade requirement was higher for women than for men. On Purdue's six-point grading scale, the grade point prerequisite for women entering the school was 5.75, while the grade point prerequisite for men was 5.5. Dean Hutchings died in July 1959. When Dr. J. J. Stockton became dean of the school, he was willing to eliminate the quotas for women.

Decades later, Carol said of Helen, "She picked her battles and fought them with dignity and respect. She was Purdue's great lady."

Throughout her twenty-year tenure, Helen came to the rescue of hundreds of female students who were told they could not be, do, or have what they wanted during their college education because they were women who did not fit a set of standards or rules.

Linda Rieger wrote a letter in the *Washington Post* in 2013, remembering when Helen came to her aid in the 1960s. She wrote, "In my junior year at Purdue University, I got married. When my marriage was discovered, I had a scholarship withdrawn. I set up an appointment to find out why, since I had a [perfect] grade point average. I was told that now that I was married I could drop out and support my husband, who also was a student at Purdue. I went to the dean of women, who was active in the National Organization for Women. I had my scholarship back in twenty minutes."

Sally Downham Miller wrote of Helen in her book *Mourning and Dancing*. Sally lost her twenty-four-year-old husband unexpectedly, leaving her with two children under the age of four. Sally returned to school after her husband's death in the late 1960s and wanted to obtain an apartment in Purdue's affordable married student housing. One parent in the family had to be a full-time student to qualify.

When Sally applied for the apartment, Purdue's director of housing said, "I'm afraid you don't qualify for married student housing because, uh . . . well, you aren't married."

The young widow was devastated, for she still *felt* married and was trying to make a better life for her children by returning to college. Sally pulled herself together and called Helen for an appointment. Sally wrote, "I decided to wear a suit and my white gloves to meet Dean Schleman. She politely ushered me into her office, and I sat in a chair across from her desk. She asked what brought me there. I firmly patted my gloved hand on her desk, and said I was being discriminated against in a situation entirely beyond my control."

Sally told her story, saying that her application was denied because her husband was not only *not* a student, but he was dead. Sally wrote of Helen's reaction: "The shock registered on her face, and she told me how sorry she was. Dean Schleman leaned back in her chair and folded her hands in front of her and waited what seemed an age before she spoke. 'No, Sally, it doesn't seem fair to me either.'"

Helen promised to check into the matter, told Sally she was brave, and wished her luck. The next day, Helen called Sally to tell her she had an apartment in married student housing. Sally asked her how she had accomplished this, and Helen said, "Sometimes policies that no longer are working need to be changed. The measuring stick I use for making a decision always is, 'What's best for the student?'"

22

At the Service of the President

WHILE BEGINNING HER WORK as the director of Girl Scouts of America, Dorothy Stratton also was a charter member of the Defense Advisory Committee on Women in the Services (DACOWITS). It is a committee of high honor that looks out for women in the military still today.

Established in 1951 by Secretary of Defense George C. Marshall, the committee is composed of civilian women and men who provide advice and recommendations on the recruitment, treatment, employment, and well-being of professional women in the armed forces. Members are selected based on their experience with the military or with women's workforce issues. Dorothy was a perfect choice, as was her good friend Helen Schleman.

Helen was appointed to DACOWITS in 1957. The committee of about fifty people had two functions: to encourage public acceptance of military service for women and to advise the assistant secretary of defense and military departments on matters relating to women in the service. Helen was chairwoman of the Professional Education Subcommittee and made it possible for the directors of each of the women's services to be accepted as members of the National Association of Women Deans and Counselors (NAWDC). In 1956, the organization had added the word "counselors" to its name.

The NAWDC was broadened and strengthened when the directors of the women's military services became members. That strength would flow down to influence thousands of college women across America.

Helen served on the committee for two years, and upon completion of her DACOWITS service, she was awarded the U.S. Army's Patriotic Civilian Service Award in 1960, with a ceremony in Purdue's Armory. President Frederick L. Hovde and Vice President and Executive Dean Donald R. Mallett were in the reviewing stand. The citation read in part: "She has generated in her staff at Purdue University an intense desire to assist the women's services and provided many opportunities for servicewomen to inform both faculty and student body of the opportunities available to women and to explain their place in the military picture."

Helen had collected many weighty, inspiring accomplishments as director of a residence hall where she befriended Amelia Earhart and Lillian Gilbreth, as captain of the SPARs, as dean of women, and as a DACOWITS member. Because of her numerous endeavors, it is understandable that she would feel frustrated when dealing with the chilly climate of a college campus that in so many ways indicated it did not place a high value on education and careers for women, but instead believed females were there to find a husband. Yet Helen was always tactful and never strident as she led the charge for her female students.

Many of the female students did not know Helen had been in the coast guard. Purdue senior Sally Watlington was unaware until she was invited to Helen's little prefab home on Western Drive for a gathering of Mortar Board women—a get-together that would change Sally's life. Sally said, "Helen entertained Mortar Boards in her home. . . . She had written an article for the *Mortar Board Quarterly,* which was a publication of our national Mortar Board organization, and it was about women in the armed forces. She wanted to test it with our Mortar Board chapter. Did it resonate? Was she writing about the right kinds of things that young people might want to know about being in the military?"

Helen's article resonated profoundly with Sally, even though she didn't act on it immediately.

Sally's major was education. In her senior year, she completed her student teaching at West Lafayette High School, which proved to be a challenge. One student set off a cherry bomb in her classroom. Another student she taught was Charlie Brown. Not the *Peanuts* Charlie Brown, but the son of Purdue's Herbert C. Brown, who was bestowed the Nobel Prize for his work with boron compounds that revolutionized synthetic organic chemistry. The Charlie Brown in Sally's class was brilliant and bored, so Sally gave him a special project about the navy and the sailing ships of old to keep him engaged during her short stint as a student teacher. Her experience was enough to convince her that she did not want to be a schoolteacher. Given the project she assigned to Charlie, perhaps in the recesses of her mind, Sally was subconsciously thinking about the navy for herself.

In Helen's *Mortar Board Quarterly* article that ran in January 1960, "Women in the Armed Forces," she stated:

> Women officers are currently performing responsible administrative and technical duties in finance, transportation, personnel public relations communications, intelligence, nursing, law, dietetics, and education. They are engaged in scientific research of many kinds. Furthermore, these women officers, most of whom are college graduates, find themselves working side by side with men officers of comparable background. Their rank, pay and benefits are the same as for their brother workers. Vocational opportunities in this quantity in this variety, and in this setting of equality, are well worth adding to the choices of college women.

For the baby boom era, Helen's words were remarkable. She talked of women in scientific research and women working alongside men, receiving equal pay. These were "unthinkable thoughts"—the very kind Amelia Earhart had dared to voice on Purdue's campus twenty years before. In military service, some of the unthinkable thoughts had actually come to pass and were reality.

Through Helen's influence and that of Beverley Stone, who had been a WAVE in World War II and on active duty during the Korean conflict, Sally joined the navy and spent more than twenty-three years in the service. Her father was supportive of his only child joining the military, but her mother, a high school typing teacher, was not enthusiastic. Sally said, "When I went home and told my parents that I wasn't going to teach school, but that I was joining the navy instead, I thought my mother was going to lose it. But my father thought it was pretty neat."

Sally first became aware of Dorothy Stratton (who would eventually also encourage her military involvement) during Purdue's Old Masters program held the previous year. Sally was the news editor for the Purdue *Exponent*, and Bev, who was the advisor for Old Masters, talked to Sally about a story featuring the distinguished professional men and women who would be on campus to speak to students about their roads to success. Dorothy was one of the Old Masters who spoke during the three-day event. In the *Exponent* photo, Dorothy is wearing her Girl Scout uniform. Sally would one day get to know Dorothy well, and nearly forty years later she would become Dorothy's chauffer and "head gopher" during her golden years. Sally would follow in Dorothy and Helen's footsteps and be the navy representative to DACOWITS in 1982. The life stories of Dorothy, Helen, Bev, Barb, and Sally interweave in numerous ways.

Bev Stone was the advisor for Old Masters for years, and alumni remember a dish she served at their gatherings—tomato aspic. In the 1950s, meat or vegetable aspics were popular. An aspic is a gelatin "salad." Tomato aspic is made with tomato juice, gelatin, onion, and spices, poured into a ring mold, and then put into the refrigerator to congeal. Once the contents are a solid mass, the mold is turned upside down on a plate of lettuce leaves, and the aspic releases from the sides of the container to glisten in all its crimson glory as a perfectly shaped ring.

To be polite, the students choked down the aspic as best they could, but one young man carried the charade too far and told Bev he *liked* tomato aspic. At every Old Masters gathering henceforth, Bev served the red, shimmering, congealed salad that looked like an anemic kidney.

DOROTHY LEFT HER POSITION AS EXECUTIVE DIRECTOR of the Girl Scouts of America in 1960 and went on to represent the International Federation of University Women (IFUW) at the United Nations for six years. Dorothy attended sessions connected to the United Nations that included the Commission on the Status of Women, the Commission for Social Development, and the Commission on Human Rights. She then reported back to each IFUW branch on what was asked of the women to further the goals of the United Nations.

The IFUW had branches in fifty-two countries, so Dorothy traveled extensively, taking the United Nations objectives to women worldwide. In 1964, Dorothy wrote an article for the *American Association of University Women Journal,* entitled "Women on Women," where she covered highlights of the eighteenth session of the United Nations Commission on the Status of Women, which met in Tehran. Queen of Iran Farah Pahlavī opened the session. The queen had some commonalities with Dorothy—in her youth she had been a Girl Scout and was an excellent basketball player, and she eventually would influence her country with regard to women's rights. Yet her mark on United States history came to a negative crescendo in the late 1970s.

The queen married Mohammad Rezā Shāh Pahlavī in 1959 at age twenty-one, and her wedding garnered worldwide press. The shah of Iran had been married twice before and had one daughter, but no male heir to inherit his throne. He had divorced his second wife because she was infertile. The pressure for the new young queen to bear a son was intense. Queen Farah gave birth to a boy ten months after her wedding. After she bore three more children, the queen eventually became active in government affairs and influenced her husband to focus attention on social causes, particularly in the areas of women's rights and cultural development.

The shah and queen were in exile when they came to live in the United States and seek medical treatment for the shah's non-Hodgkin's lymphoma in the late 1970s. His stay became the tipping point for renewed hostilities between the United States and Iran, and ultimately led to the attack and takeover of the American embassy in Tehran from 1979 to 1981, in what became known as the Iran hostage crisis. The shah died in 1980. After President Ronald Reagan declared that she was welcome in the United States, the queen eventually settled in the country, where she still lives part-time today.

The opening paragraph of Dorothy's 1964 article about the U.N. session provides a glimpse into the status of women in the world at the time:

"The majority of the illiterates in the world are women. . . . As of September 1964, six countries were limiting the right of women to vote, and in nine women still had no voting rights and were not eligible for election to office. In most countries, progress toward equal pay for equal work remains disappointingly slow; in some countries, the situation is worsening."

The agenda for the session included political rights of women, preparation of a Draft Declaration on the Elimination of Discrimination against Women, the status of women in private law, equal pay for equal work, part-time work, and access to education—all challenges that still weigh on our world today.

Now in her sixties, Dorothy was living a well-traveled, eye-opening, cultured life that few women or men experienced at that time—and even today. Dorothy was the incarnate of her "favorite theory" written in Purdue's 1941 *Debris* yearbook, "to be interesting, do interesting things."

As if her work with the United Nations wasn't enough to keep her busy, Dorothy also was a charter member of the President's Committee on Employment of the Physically Handicapped. Beginning in 1962, Dorothy chaired the Women's Committee, which served all people with disabilities—not just women. The goal of the thirty-one-member committee was to utilize the talents of women and women's organizations to carry out programs and projects that helped those with disabilities to obtain jobs and to gain employer cooperation with accessibility needs. Dorothy's good friend and mentor Lillian Gilbreth was a member of the Women's Committee as well.

Lillian and her husband, Frank, had been inspired by disabled World War I veterans to perform the couple's first motion studies on behalf of disabled workers. The polio epidemic of the 1950s drew attention to the needs of disabled homemakers, and Lillian designed kitchens for women with challenges, as well as simplified methods of performing housework and childcare. Lillian was a natural to be selected for the President's Committee on Employment of the Physically Handicapped.

As president-elect of the NAWDC, Helen Schleman also was a member of the Women's Committee, which met at the Department of Health, Education, and Welfare in Washington. Another member was Assistant Secretary of Labor Esther Peterson. Peterson served in the administrations of Kennedy, Johnson, and Carter, and she was a tenacious consumer advocate. Among her accomplishments was the labeling of foods with their nutritional value.

The group decided to promote the removal of architectural barriers, which barred people with disabilities from entering and using buildings to work or transact business. Deputy Executive Secretary K. Vernon Banta spoke to the committee and listed architectural obstacles he called "barriers of thoughtlessness": "Imposing flights of steps, which persons with braces or a heart condition or in a wheelchair cannot climb; restrooms and phone booths unsuited for wheelchair occupants, phones without amplifying devices, and hazardous doorways leading to boiler rooms, incinerators, or the like, with no sense of touch markings for the blind."

In a time when the term "crippled" was still acceptable, the committee's cosponsor was the National Society for Crippled Children and Adults, and Banta said that together the two groups would like to see barriers eliminated through widespread adoption of the criteria approved by the American Standards Association. "Popular demand is the only way to bring this about," he said.

The United States was just beginning to recognize that there were people hidden from society, banished to their homes or bleak institutions, isolated from eyes that saw them as outcasts and imbeciles because they could not walk, ambled in leg braces, were hearing impaired, or suffered a speech impediment.

Major General Melvin J. Maas, chairman of the President's Committee on Employment of the Physically Handicapped spoke to the Women's Committee, emphasizing the value of women in molding public opinion. He said, "Women united in America can change not only America, but the world."

He also told the group that the most difficult part of their job would be "to overcome attitudes ingrained by myths and fairytales over the centuries. For centuries children have grown up hearing about one-eyed ogres, evil giants, little humpbacked men, and peg-legged sailors—always with physical imperfections equated with evil. This residual feeling must be wiped out. We have got to reeducate the people, and show them that the handicapped are ordinary people."

In 1961, a set of building standards for handicapped user-friendliness had been developed through the combined efforts of the President's Committee on Employment of the Physically Handicapped, the National Society for Crippled Children and Adults, and the American Standards Association. The goal was to make public buildings, other structures, and facilities accessible to the physically challenged.

Interest had begun in 1957 when wheelchair user Hugo Deffner was selected as "Handicapped American of the Year," an "honor" that sounds impertinent today. Embarrassingly, Deffner was unable to enter the Departmental Auditorium in Washington, DC, to accept his trophy from Eisenhower because of the steps surrounding the building. Two husky marines carried Deffner up the steps.

Deffner's humiliating plight led to the creation of standards for building entrances and equipment, which would permit people with disabilities to enter all buildings to work, conduct business, vote, play, or pray. Of course, the next difficult step to overcome was to convince institutions, architects, and the public that adoption of the standards was of the utmost importance.

In a 1961, Maas sent out a press release announcing the development of the building standards that were outlined in a newly created brochure. He knew that just writing down the standards was not going to ensure implementation. He wrote, "The task really belongs to the many voluntary groups over the country. If you folks will spread the word, watch the planning work, keep an eye on builders, alert the building committees, and let the architects know why building entrances should be street level or ramped, your influence will be felt. The blueprint has been made. You are no longer selling an abstract idea. The future of architectural barriers is largely in your hands."

In his release, Maas thanked Tim Nugent of the University of Illinois for his help in developing the standards. Nugent had been working for more than ten years refitting the premises of the school so that students with disabilities, many of them World War II veterans, could obtain admission and pursue their studies. In 1948, Nugent founded the first comprehensive program of higher education for people with disabilities. He founded the National Wheelchair Basketball Association the following year.

In the “Architectural Barriers and the Handicapped” brochure, the “Handicapped American of the Year” for 1960, Charles E. Caniff, was quoted: “To fulfill our responsibilities as citizens, we often must circumvent these barriers by entering through the rear door, where freight is hauled in and garbage hauled out, and make our way through coal bins, storerooms, and boiler rooms to reach a freight elevator, which can accommodate our wheelchairs. Architectural barriers have made us ‘back door’ citizens.”

The word “physically” was dropped from the title of the President’s Committee on Employment of the Physically Handicapped in 1962, when President John F. Kennedy expanded the committee’s charge to develop employment opportunities for both the physically and mentally challenged. Kennedy’s sister, Rosemary, sixteen months his junior, was born with mental disabilities. Kennedy made cognitive handicaps, such as intellectual disabilities, a priority for his administration. Few scientists at the time were researching the causes and few doctors were trained to support people with these incapacities. At age twenty-three, Rosemary Kennedy was given a prefrontal lobotomy that left her in an infant-like state; she required institutional care for the rest of her life. John Kennedy and his sister, Eunice Kennedy Shriver, brought intellectual disabilities out of the shadows and into public light. Shriver founded the Special Olympics in Rosemary’s honor.

Also in 1962, Edward V. Roberts, a quadriplegic who had polio as a teenager, became the first severely disabled student at the University of California at Berkeley after he sued the school to gain admission. “We’ve tried cripples before, and it didn’t work,” said a university dean. Roberts had experienced rejection the year before when the state vocational rehabilitation agency had refused to serve him because the agency considered him too severely disabled and labeled him unemployable. The decision was later overturned. One of the many ironies of Roberts’ life was that fourteen years later, Governor Jerry Brown appointed him as state director of the same agency that deemed him too severely disabled to ever work.

When Roberts first attended the University of California at Berkeley, he was housed in the campus hospital, where he used his iron lung at night. During the day a respirator was attached to his wheelchair. Other disabled students enrolled in the university, and together they formed the

Rolling Quads to advocate for greater access on campus and started the independent living and disability rights movement. Roberts proposed that the struggle for independence was not a medical or functional issue, but rather a sociological, political, and civil rights struggle. He earned a bachelor's and a master's degree, and went on to teach political science at the university for six years.

Roberts died in 1995 and is known as the father of the Independent Living Movement. He cofounded the World Institute on Disability. Thanks to Roberts' initial strides to make the campus accessible to the physically and mentally challenged, the University of California (along with the University of Illinois) was decades ahead of most of America's institutions of higher learning in making the educational environment open to all—including Purdue.

The Women's Committee implemented a campaign to educate the public. As chairwoman, Dorothy wrote a memorandum in February 1963 to the committee about a concept spawned from member Mary Lou Simon:

> Like most good ideas, this one is simple in conception. All of us have been seeking some way in which our Committee can move the objective of the President's Committee forward. Mary Lou's suggestion is that all the organizations represented on our Committee . . . print at least one article on employment of the handicapped in the issue of the magazine or journal that reaches the membership in September 1963. This timing is suggested so that the full impact of the concerted effort may be felt just prior to National Employ the Handicapped Week, October 6 to 12. We believe that the effect of all member organizations joining in a common effort at the same time will be immeasurably greater than under the one, plus one, plus one approach. We can get off the ground with jet propulsion.
>
> If we receive a generally favorable response, we plan to request President Kennedy to give us a statement for use in connection with the articles.

Dorothy readily gave credit where credit was due and was quick to act on a good idea that could move a concept into action "with jet propulsion." Yet the propulsion would lose steam when President Kennedy was assassinated a little more than a month after the 1963 National Employ the Handicapped Week of which Dorothy referred.

Dorothy Stratton, Lillian Gilbreth, and Helen Schleman worked toward accessibility decades before it would become a common, everyday part of America's vernacular and landscape. Dorothy was awarded the Distinguished Service Award from the President's Committee on Employment of the Handicapped in 1967.

As an assistant dean of women hired by Helen in the late 1960s, Betty Nelson would lead the charge in making Purdue University physically accessible after the Rehabilitation Act of 1973 was passed, which prohibited discrimination on the basis of disability at any federally funded institution. This is when curb cuts, entrance ramps, and accessible parking and bathrooms would begin to emerge, albeit very slowly, on college campuses. Dorothy and Helen's work with disability awareness would echo in the good deeds of Betty, who would follow in their footsteps and one day be the keeper of Carolyn Shoemaker's Bible when she was named dean of students in 1987.

23

Mixed Messages

A Western Union telegram came click, click, clicking over the telegraph in 1962, delivering a message from Eleanor Roosevelt to Helen Schleman:

> WOULD APPRECIATE YOUR SERVING AS MEMBER OF EDUCATION COMMITTEE OF PRESIDENT'S COMMISSION ON STATUS OF WOMEN. YOUR EXPERIENCE WOULD BE INVALUABLE IN ANALYSIS OF PROBLEMS AND PREPARATION OF RECOMMENDATIONS. DR. MARY BUNTING, COMMITTEE CHAIRMAN, WILL NOTIFY YOU OF FIRST MEETING. PLEASE WIRE MRS. ESTHER PETERSON, ASSISTANT SECRETARY OF LABOR, OR CALL COLLECT FOR DETAILS AND YOUR REPLY WASHINGTON 961-2056.

Eleanor Roosevelt was chairman of the President's Commission on the Status of Women, established by President John F. Kennedy in

December 1961. The commission's task was "to set forth before the world the story of women's progress in a free, democratic society, to review recent accomplishments, and to acknowledge frankly the further steps that must be taken."

For Kennedy, the committee was a compromise. He was trying to advance the equality of women's workplace opportunities without losing the support of organized labor. Until the 1970s, organized labor opposed the Equal Rights Amendment (which would have prevented laws that held different standards for men and women), believing that female workers deserved or needed protective legislation as opposed to equal rights.

Workplace regulations for females had taken the form of protective legislation because it was believed that women's biological differences needed to be accommodated to help them avoid injury and exploitation. However, oftentimes the protective legislation provided employers justification to avoid hiring women. If women supposedly needed special treatment at work, it was easier and cheaper to hire only men.

The commission fostered major progress for women's rights and was one of the principal events that would spark the "second wave" of feminism later in the decade.

Helen received a sixteen-page memorandum from Assistant Secretary of Labor Esther Peterson, giving basic background about the President's Commission on the Status of Women. She encouraged the members to help make known the real need for the commission and what they hope to accomplish. She anticipated that the members would give speeches, write articles, and discuss the goals of the group. The memorandum included a quote from Kennedy, who voiced his belief in utilizing women's potential but also strongly conveyed what he believed to be women's central duty: "We want to be sure that women are used as effectively as they can be to provide a better life for our people—in addition to meeting their primary responsibility, which is in the home."

A quote from Eleanor Roosevelt (the video of which can be found online) spoke more to how women felt in the United States: "The President's Commission was established to examine the needs and rights of American women today and to make recommendations for the elimination of barriers that result in waste, injustice and frustration."

Peterson's memorandum indicated some of the inequities of that time. Women were not eligible to serve on juries in Mississippi, Alabama, and South Carolina. In Texas, a married woman could not go into business for herself without permission of a court. In four states, a man had complete control over his wife's earnings. The commission's Committee on Civil and Political Rights was exploring all avenues for tackling those problems.

Helen served on the Committee on Education, which explored the educational needs of women at different stages in their lives, from elementary school through college.

Peterson said that the question heard most often was, "Is the commission trying to encourage women to work outside their homes?" Sometimes the question was posed another way: "Does the commission have ideas as to what women ought to do? Is it trying to push them out of their homes?" Peterson's answer on page 13 of the memorandum remains relevant in the twenty-first century:

> In this Twentieth Century women are extremely fortunate. They have many avenues through which they can contribute their talents to the world around them. One woman may prefer to concentrate all her energies on her family and home. Another may volunteer to help with community work. Another may want and need a paying job. In the course of her life, a woman may shift from one kind of contribution to another. Or she may combine all three. . . . The average woman can look forward to about thirty useful, productive years after her youngest child enters school and her daily home responsibilities lessen somewhat. What she does with her time is a question *she* must decide.
>
> The Commission is interested in two phases of her decision: first, we would like her to be free to make her own choice; and, second, we'd like to be sure that our society does not limit what she can do, solely on the grounds that she is a woman.

Peterson's words would be carried forth by Helen to female students at Purdue University and every woman she met through her speeches, journal articles, and conversations. Helen ballyhooed life planning for women. She attempted to stir women to make choices and design a blueprint—to think beyond a wedding and children to the numerous opportunities available for their lives.

Yet, as Peterson stated in her 1962 memorandum to the commission, there were large numbers of women in the United States who had no choice but to work for a paycheck. She stated that one-tenth of the twenty-four million women who worked were the sole breadwinners.

Many people worried that women would take men's jobs. Peterson explained that the jobs women held were not positions for which men prepared or sought. Seven million women were clerical workers; more than one million were teachers; half a million were nurses; more than three million were factory workers; and more than three million were service workers, which included waitresses, cooks, hospital attendants, and beauty operators.

The majority of jobs held by women did not require a college degree. Peterson summed up her paragraph on women's work by saying, "If women withdrew from the labor force, not only would fewer goods and services be produced, but the standard of living for the population as a whole would go down." By performing much of the menial work in society, women made possible the comfortable standard of living of the white middle and upper class.

Helen worked closely with Technical Secretary for the Committee on Education Antonia Chayes. In a speech given in 1978, Helen said:

> As a measure of the conservative national climate in 1963, I often think of how hard Tony Chayes and I worked to get a recommendation into the report on the need for sex education for young women. We failed. One didn't talk about such things in 1963.
>
> Just as a bit of what the New Yorker would call "incidental intelligence"—and as an example of some of the interesting things that women are doing today that they were not doing fifteen years ago. I'll just mention that Tony Chayes is currently Assistant Secretary of the U.S. Air Force. I think Amelia Earhart would have liked this!

At the outset of her service for the commission, Helen experienced an incident on Purdue's campus that heightened her verve for seeing more women on the faculty and in administration. In 1980, Helen wrote of her "top three crises" as dean of women. Her number one crisis was George Davis becoming dean of students, and her number two crisis was the naming of a man as dean of the School of Home Economics. She would monitor the number of female faculty and administration members at Purdue until her death in 1992.

In a letter to Dr. Mary I. Bunting, chairman of the Committee on Education and president of Radcliffe College, dated June 7, 1962, Helen explained the incident:

> Our Dean of Home Economics retires June 30. A few months ago our Vice President in Charge of Academic Affairs started looking for a replacement. Two women candidates were brought to the campus but for one reason or another neither was appointed to the deanship. Without discussion with the present Dean of Home economics or with me as Dean of Women, and with only sketchy conversation with women department heads in Home Economics, the President's Office named as new dean the man who is head of the department of Child Development and Family Life in the School of Home Economics.
>
> No public announcement of this appointment was made since the Trustees had not as yet confirmed it. However, the appointment was firm enough that the new appointee called on the present dean and explained that he had been appointed and wished to talk about future plans with her. Since this was the first she had heard of the appointment of a man, she called me at once to see if I had had any notion this was to be done.

Dean of Home Economics Beulah V. Gillespie was the only female dean on Purdue's faculty. William Martin was the head of the Department of Child Development and Family Life in the School of Home Economics. President Hovde, an engineer, once admitted that he failed to achieve significant change in the School of Home Economics, and he said, "It was the one academic area at Purdue that stumped me."

After hearing that a man was to be named dean, Helen did some investigative work. She talked to the female department heads in home economics, some of the faculty men in other schools on campus, female students, and members of the Committee on Education. She then wrote a four-page letter to Hovde. She began her letter: "I believe strongly that the appointment of a man to the deanship of Home Economics will have detrimental effects in areas in which I am vitally interested and for which I carry some measure of responsibility."

Helen indicated that for the past fifteen years, those interested in women's education had been aware of special problems that had been discussed in national meetings. She listed the national associations of which she was a part, including the National Association of Women Deans and Counselors (NAWDC), DACOWITS, and the President's Commission on the Status of Women. She recognized that Purdue made it possible for her to participate in these meetings.

Helen discussed the lack of motivation among young women to pursue education. Then she penned the kicker: "If young women are to be inspired or persuaded to exert themselves intellectually to achieve as they can (and should), they have got to see, with their own eyes, that they have a chance to work at top level if they will prepare themselves to do so. They must see examples of women who are playing a significant part in the intellectual life of our society at a demanding, prestige level and earning the approval of men by so doing."

Helen was deflated. She felt like a "second-class dean." She continued:

> In the past several years, the Dean of Women has had increasingly fewer and fewer opportunities to participate directly in any top-level University policy discussion. When the decision was made not to include the Dean of Men and Dean of Women in the deliberations of the academic deans that deal with University-wide matters, this automatically made them second-class deans and closed an important channel of communication between the academic and non-academic segments of the University. . . . This decision also effectively removed the possibility of all but one woman's voice in top-level administrative policy-making. The appointment of a man as Dean of Home economics eliminates that voice.

The world was giving sixty-year-old Helen mixed messages. She was valued for her knowledge and actions to improve educational and military opportunities for women on a national level, but as the years rolled on, at her workplace she was given less of a voice. She watched as around her other women's voices on campus were suppressed. She began to question herself. Helen ended her letter:

> The only possible question I can ask myself is, "What is wrong *with me* in the Purdue situation?" For the appointment of a man as Dean of

> Home Economics to have been discussed widely (with 70 to 80 other women) but not to have been discussed with me in terms of the impact on Purdue women students and women staff is indeed troubling to me. Ten years ago, President Hovde, before Dean Gillespie was appointed, you did ask my opinion on this matter. I can only ask myself why my opinion has become less valuable after ten years. If I am discouraged personally, that, too, would be understandable.

In *Traces of CDFS: A Partial History of the Department of Child Development and Family Studies, Purdue University*, Richard K. Kerckhoff wrote of Hovde's final action:

> Gender became one of the major issues in the appointment of a new dean for the School, with the retirement of Dean Gillespie in 1962, University President Frederick L. Hovde finally decided that his plan to appoint Martin as dean would not be accepted by various members of the School faculty, the Office of the Dean of Women, and alumnae, and so he moved the Department of Child Development and Family Life from the School of Home Economics into the newly organized School of Humanities, Social Science and Education in 1963. Martin remained as head.

Gladys E. Vail, head of the Department of Foods and Nutrition and acting dean of the School of Home Economics, became dean in 1963. Helen's earnest letter to Hovde had been effective. She won the battle for Purdue women and faculty.

To answer the question she posed to Hovde and to herself, there was nothing "wrong" with Helen Schleman "in the Purdue situation."

HELEN WAS INVITED TO THE WHITE HOUSE on several occasions. Shortly after dealing with the School of Home Economics crisis at Purdue, she attended the Women's Conference on Civil Rights on July 9, 1963, representing the NAWDC with about three hundred other women representing other major women's organizations in the United States. The administration had sponsored a series of citizen conferences for the purpose of presenting the civil rights issues in proposed legislation and to enlist support. Previous conferences had consisted almost entirely of men.

The attendees of the Women's Conference on Civil Rights gathered in the East Room of the White House. In her NAWDC annual report, Helen described the events: "President Kennedy himself spoke first to the group, followed by Attorney General Robert Kennedy, Vice President Johnson and Assistant Attorney General Marshall in charge of Civil Rights work. President Kennedy then answered questions from the audience informally. It was an unforgettable experience. President Kennedy left no doubt about where he stood. For him, this matter of civil rights for all citizens was a fundamental moral issue."

Helen also shared a charming sidebar to Robert Kennedy's speech:

> There was one amusing incident that endeared Mr. Robert Kennedy to this group of women, which I can't resist sharing with you. Everyone was listening to the Attorney General intently, and I think every woman in the room must have been scribbling notes on a note pad as fast as she could so as not to lose a point. The Attorney General stopped short in the middle of a sentence, grinned, looked all around the room, and said, "This conference is different. I've attended all of the others. At those, the men sat absolutely poker-faced and stared straight ahead. They took no notes. You are obviously going to do something about it."

Helen was invited to the White House again on October 11 for a ceremony presenting the final report of the President's Commission on the Status of Women to Kennedy. The event was held on the birthday of the late Chairman of the Commission Eleanor Roosevelt, who had passed away the previous November. The report was entitled *American Women.*

American Women was a groundbreaking report that documented workplace discrimination and recommended affordable childcare, equal employment opportunities for women, and paid maternity leave; however, it did not mention the Equal Rights Amendment. The report focused national attention on issues of women's equality and is said to have represented a sea change in the way policymakers and the Unites States talked about women's contributions. The Equal Pay Act of 1963 grew out of the recommendations of the commission.

Peterson spoke about the report in numerous public arenas, including the *Today Show.* Newspapers ran a series of articles from the Associated Press about the commission's findings. The resulting awareness of women's discrimination led to a domino effect with many states, universities, and organizations establishing their own Commission on the Status of Women. The President's Commission mailed a copy of *American Women* to every member of NAWDC.

In her 1964 annual report as president of NAWDC, Helen clarified intentions: ". . . any improvements in the status of women sought by the Commission are sought in the context of a richer, fuller life for *all* citizens. The Commission says specifically that the adoption of their proposals would benefit men directly as well as women. This is important; special privilege is not sought."

American Women was published when the civil rights movement was nearing crescendo in the United States. The March on Washington for Jobs and Freedom, where Martin Luther King, Jr. gave his "I have a dream" speech, had occurred in August, less than two months before the commission's report was presented on the discrimination of women. The irony is that women were nearly left off the official program for the historic march. A story for the *Washington Post* written by Krissah Thompson for the fiftieth anniversary of the march stated: "The list of female pioneers in the movement was long, but men ran the show. Scratch that: Women ran the show, too, but mostly out of public view. Few women were in pulpits, although church ladies kept the houses of worship in order. Next to no women were leading labor unions, even as increasing numbers of them joined the workforce. And the largest civil rights groups were run by men, although plenty of the organizers, thinkers, and volunteers were women."

After women heard they were left off the event's agenda, some protested and "A Tribute to Negro Women Fighters for Freedom" was added to the program, but it consisted of flowery words and little substance. No black woman was slated to give full remarks on the need for freedom and jobs. The "tribute" was to be delivered by a man, March on Washington Chairman A. Philip Randolph, but after further protest, a woman named Daisy Bates was scheduled to give the speech.

Daisy spoke 142 words. She had advised the Little Rock Nine when they attempted to integrate the city's high school. Her slim speech packed power. Bates said in part: "We will join hands with you. We will kneel in; we will sit in until we can eat in any corner in the United States. We will walk until we are free, until we can walk to any school and take our children to any school in the United States. And we will sit in and we will kneel in and we will lie in if necessary until every Negro in America can vote. This we pledge to the women of America."

Another snub occurred when the female activists, many of whom had jeopardized their lives for freedom, were assigned to walk with the wives of civil rights leaders rather than with their fellow male activists. That included Dorothy Height, president of the National Council of Negro Women, and Rosa Parks, the seamstress who began the bus boycott in Montgomery, Alabama, in 1955. Parks had been involved in the fight against Jim Crow laws longer than many of the men who gave speeches at the march.

The exclusion only served to galvanize the women who met the day after the march to band together to ensure that in the future women would be represented.

One of Martin Luther King, Jr.'s children, Bernice, spoke at a gathering of women in 2013 commemorating the March on Washington. She reminded her audience that the Montgomery bus boycott would not have happened without women and that the protest in Alabama prepared the country for the event. She said, "We must ensure that the story of women in the movement is told and the record is accurate. Oftentimes it's in the periphery, in the backroom, somewhere on the fringes where the story of women is told."

As is indicative of like minds bringing forth an idea in the same synergistic timeframe, 1963 was also the publication year of Betty Friedan's game-changing, best-selling book *The Feminine Mystique.* The book launched the second wave of the feminist movement. In a speech years later, Helen said, "As far as I know, it was sheer coincidence that *American Women,* an official, fact-filled, forward-looking government document, and Betty Friedan's *The Feminine Mystique* both appeared in 1963. They complemented each other perfectly. Thousands of women, housewives, and professional women alike read *The Feminine Mystique* and identified with many of the frustrations that Betty Freidan described so well. And many professional women found support for their goals and efforts in *American Women.*"

In *The Feminine Mystique,* Freidan dared to name and dissect "the problem with no name"—and the problem had a great deal to do with how America viewed the education of women in the 1950s. The problem was that after women had all that society told them would make them happy, they were left feeling empty. They were placed in a jewelry box, of sorts, the ornaments of the perfect household, and they didn't talk about their feelings of dissatisfaction for fear of being seen as ungrateful. To many women who ran the household and made their husband and children's lives a priority, life became fraught with sameness. Friedan named that empty feeling—that sensation of discontent resulting from living a woman's traditional 1950s life—the feminine mystique.

Freidan questioned the barrage of images, words, rules, assumptions, and disregard that told American women what they needed and wanted after World War II, the "great divide." She centered her questioning on education.

After the war, women were told by magazine articles, ads, television shows, books, and movies that happiness and fulfillment were found in a husband with a good job, five healthy children, a lovely home in the suburbs, a patio, and a barbecue. It was said that this idealized life was envied by women all over the world, so those who experienced this as reality should be grateful. By science and labor-saving appliances, those women had been freed from drudgery, dangers of childbirth, and the illnesses of their grandmothers. Of course, Freidan was focusing on middle-class white women.

In 1957, Freidan came to realize that something was very wrong with the way American women were trying to live their lives. She sensed it first in her own life. She was a wife, mother of three, and "half-guiltily, and therefore half-heartedly, almost in spite of myself, using my abilities and education in work that took me away from home."

Freidan held a degree in psychology from Smith College and worked as a reporter before she married. She returned to work after her first child was born, but she lost her job when she became pregnant with her second child. Freidan stayed home to care for her family, but she grew restless as a homemaker and began to wonder if other women felt as she did.

To answer her own personal quandary, Freidan gave a questionnaire to two hundred of her college classmates, fifteen years after their graduation. The survey asked intimate, open-ended questions. She found that these educated women were living disjointed lives. Most weren't using their education in work that was just theirs. Instead, they were doing what they were "supposed to," taking care of others. Society's message was that suburban housewives should be happy; after all, they "didn't have to work!" She used the results of her research to write *The Feminine Mystique*. Freidan wrote:

> Sometimes a woman would say . . . "I feel as if I don't exist." Sometimes she blotted out the feeling with a tranquilizer. Sometimes she thought the problem was with her husband or her children, or that what she really needed was to redecorate her house, or move to a better neighborhood, or have an affair, or another baby. Sometimes, she went to a doctor with symptoms she could hardly describe: "A tired feeling . . . I feel like crying without any reason." (A Cleveland doctor called it "the housewife's syndrome.")

Housewife unhappiness began to be reported in 1960 media outlets. However, nearly all the stories were summed up with a glib rationale to dismiss the unhappiness—"incompetent appliance repairmen (*New York Times*), the distances children must be chauffeured in the suburbs (*Time*), or too much PTA (*Redbook*)." The most shocking scapegoat by today's standards, and by Helen Schleman standards, was "the old problem—education: more and more women had education, which naturally made them unhappy in their role as housewives." Freidan continued, "A number of educators suggested seriously that women no longer be admitted to the four-year colleges and universities: in the growing college crisis, the education which girls could not use as housewives was more urgently needed than ever by boys to do the work of the atomic age."

The Feminine Mystique must have seemed like an answer to prayer for Helen. The book spoke her language. Friedan saw the big, skewed picture for women, a disheartening image that Helen had been dealing with since she left the SPARs to become Purdue's dean of women. Fewer and fewer college women were preparing for a profession. Two out of three women who entered college dropped out before they finished. Friedan said, "Some women's colleges went out of business; some professors at coeducational universities, said one out of three college places should no longer be wasted on women; the president of Sarah Lawrence, a women's college with high intellectual values, spoke of opening [to men]; the president of Vassar predicted the end of all the Great American Women's colleges which pioneered higher education for women."

Friedan's chapter "A New Life Plan for Women" aligned deeply with Helen's goals for her female students and the recommendations made in *American Women*. Friedan wrote, "When society asks so little of women, every woman has to listen to her own inner voice to find her identity in this changing world. She must create, out of her own needs and abilities, a new life plan, fitting in the love and children and home that have defined femininity in the past with the work toward a greater purpose that shapes the future."

Helen with her staff of Bev Stone, Barb Cook, and other dedicated assistants would talk about life planning to female students into the 1970s, and Bev and Barb spread the message of *The Feminine Mystique* in their speeches. Bev spoke at the Association of Women Students State Day at Valparaiso University on November 2, 1963—twenty-one days before America was blindsided by Kennedy's assassination. Helen was in the audience. Bev talked of Friedan's book and also spoke words that resound today:

> To you able young women I should like to talk briefly about a subject for which I have a very strong conviction—the role of the educated woman in the community, or to use a quotation from one of my favorite professors at Columbia, "At last it's respectable to be responsible." . . . It takes only a superficial grasp of the situation to realize that the attitudes and talents women have—aesthetic sensitivity, communication skills, and concern for human beings—could go far in meeting some of these problems of our society as well as of the world at large. . . . Somehow ideally and we hope realistically, women with her needs and society with its needs must be brought into a complementary and mutually enhancing relationship.

On her typed speech, Bev scrolled this note in pencil:

> Just prior to my coming in the building, Dean Schleman handed me a slip of paper with the following quote:

> In 1962 there was an article in the *Saturday Evening Post*, which contained the following quote: "We have in the American woman one of the nation's great neglected resources. We have always admired her, pursued, her, whistled at her—even enshrined her. Now we need to use her. Not just at the jobs men don't want to do. Not grudgingly because we want to shut her up. Not slyly because we think she's cute, but thankfully—because she has brains, time, knowledge, courage, sensitivity, and dedication that are needed in our struggle for survival."

Friedan was a force for change, and Helen was her disciple. In 1962–1963, Helen was president of NAWDC. She urged its program committee to invite Friedan to speak at its annual convention before Friedan's name became well known. Friedan spoke on "The Crisis in Women's Identity: A Challenge to Education" at the 1964 meeting in Portland, Oregon. She gave every woman in attendance a free paperback copy of her book. In a speech in 2002, Barbara Cook said, "Not all the women deans at that time thought Betty Friedan's writing was appropriate, and some thought it was pretty radical, but Helen Schleman knew the deans needed to read this book, and she was certainly right as usual. Betty Friedan's book sparked the 'feminine revolution' in the twentieth century."

The Civil Rights Act of 1964 also helped to launch the "feminine revolution." Considered the crowning legislation achievement in United States history, the Civil Rights Act ended segregation in public places and banned employment discrimination on the basis of race, color, religion, sex, or national origin. First proposed by President John F. Kennedy, it was signed into law by his successor, Lyndon B. Johnson.

Representative Howard W. Smith added the word "sex" to the language of the Civil Rights Act at the last moment. His critics argued that Smith, a conservative southern opponent of federal civil rights, did so to kill the entire bill. Smith, however, argued that he had amended the bill in keeping with his support of Alice Paul and the National Women's Party, with whom he had been working. Martha W. Griffiths led the effort to keep the word "sex" in the bill.

Griffiths had been a lawyer and judge before she became a member of the United States House of Representatives from 1955 to 1974. The first woman to serve on the powerful House Committee on Ways and Means,

Griffiths also resurrected and sponsored the Equal Rights Amendment, one of only a few proposed amendments to pass in Congress and be sent to the states for ratification, originally drafted by suffragist Alice Paul in 1923.

The Civil Rights Act was later expanded to include disabled Americans, the elderly, and women in collegiate athletics. It also set the course for the Voting Rights Act of 1965, which prohibited literacy tests and other discriminatory voting practices, and the Fair Housing Act of 1968, which banned discrimination in the sale, rental, and financing of property.

Marylu McEwen was a Purdue freshman in 1964. The summer before school started she received a letter from Helen welcoming her to Purdue and inviting her to come to the Office of the Dean of Women for the traditional, informal conversation conducted with all freshmen. The Civil Rights Act had just been enacted in July, but most female students probably had no idea about the significance of the legislation to their future lives. Helen also suggested that Marylu read a new book that had just been published, *The Feminine Mystique.* Fifty years later, Marylu recalled:

> I wasn't about to read it or pick it up. I didn't know what it was. I wonder how many women, if any, did read it. I did come in for my freshmen conference with a staff member, a Mortar Board member, and a few other students. We went over life planning. We were asked, "What are you planning for your future?" Most everybody said, "I will finish college, get married, have kids." Then they said, "Even if you have children, look at this life plan."

Marylu would eventually work in Purdue's Office of the Dean of Women and become an associate professor in counseling and personnel services at the University of Maryland College Park. Evidently, the life-planning nudge took hold.

It's unknown how many Purdue women read *The Feminine Mystique* at Helen's suggestion the summer of 1964—the same summer it became illegal for an employer to discriminate in hiring on the basis of gender. But there is no doubt that every woman was asked, "What is your life plan? What are you planning for the future?"

24

Winter's Death Rattle

Helen Schleman built a "Robert J. Smith House" in 1963. It was a memorable home filled with distinctive modern architectural details that few houses in the Midwest had at the time. Those who visited Helen never forgot her house. Former students and colleagues remember 1607 Western Drive and say, with awe, "the house."

Robert Smith, a professor of architecture at the University of Illinois at Urbana-Champaign, was commissioned to design twenty homes in West Lafayette, Indiana, between 1955 and 1972. These homes featured Smith's signature style—the melding of house and nature. Expansive glass walls create a symbiotic relationship with indoors and outdoors. Smith's homes have post-and-beam construction, flat roofs, natural materials, and louvered openings to boost ventilation. Today, the Smith design is referred to as mid-century modern.

Helen knew exactly how she wanted her new home to look and feel at 1607 Western Drive, just down the street from the small National Home she had built at 1807. She would move two blocks south to live in her newly built house with its clean, geometric lines. Smith homes had a California feel. Helen added her own panache.

Helen's new house sat on the fringe of Purdue's North Golf Course like her postwar home up the street. Floor-to-ceiling windows on the west wall gave an expansive view of the course, Helen's preferred place to perfect her favorite pastime and walk her dog. Golf was a natural extension of Helen ever since she grew up living next to a golf course in Valparaiso, taught golf to high school girls, and wrote the book *Group Golf Instruction* in 1933, a pioneer text in the theory of teaching golf to large groups.

Helen played Purdue's North Golf Course for nearly sixty years and lived next to the course for forty of those years. Helen also played other golf courses around Lafayette and West Lafayette, and as she aged, she carried a one-legged chair that was actually a cane with a seat, which she could unfold to sit and rest as she played. Today, the Purdue North Golf Course is named Kampen Course "in honor of Emerson Kampen and his support of Purdue Athletics," states the course website. A statue of Kampen overlooks the first tee.

The entryway of Helen's home set the design tone. The front of the house was a solid brick wall with no windows, but it included an opening that one walked through to the actual front door. A miniature courtyard flanked the walkway between the opening and the entrance door.

Once inside, an indoor pond with fish and water lilies welcomed visitors. A skylight shed sun onto the pond where a cement statue resided. The statue depicted a stout woman squatting in her dress, elbows on knees, with her hands cupped around a bowl held to her mouth; water flowed from her mouth, over the bowl and into the pond.

Hand-finished to resemble weathered bronze, the statue was an Isabel Bloom handcrafted sculpture. Bloom was an artist who grew up in Davenport, Iowa, where artists still carry on her work creating figurines from locally available materials of concrete and river stone found along the Mississippi River. In the 1930s, Bloom spent two summers at the Stone City Art Colony in Iowa, carving limestone under the tutelage of Grant Wood.

The water flowing from the statue into the pond presented a calming, almost Zen-like, atmosphere. The gentle sound of flowing water was an ever-present backdrop during hundreds of gatherings that Helen hosted, including student group meetings, staff parties, and intimate dinners. The sound of the moving water also provided white noise so a conversation held nearby could be carried on with confidence.

An article published by the Purdue University News Service in 1966 described Helen's entryway: "Like a prologue to a book, it is the portent of things to come. For just beyond is a magnificent view—a house designed for the twenty-first century. Within its subterranean walls, the pool's tranquil waters mirror a warm picture. Friendly, colorful surroundings and rooms often filled with young Purdue women. Exotic? Perhaps, but for down-to-earth hardworking Helen Schleman, it's really quite practical. 'A quiet poolside chat with one's self can do wonders for smoothing out the kinks in one's armor,' she says."

Helen's white pedestal kitchen table flanked her windows that looked out on the golf course. Eero Saarinen originally created the table and matching tulip chair design in 1955 for the Knoll Company of New York City. His tulip table and chair were made with experimental materials for the time and are considered classics of industrial design. Sally Watlington said of Helen's kitchen setting, "Many a really good bridge game took place in that kitchen location watching the birds, and in the dead of winter, watching snow coming in across the Purdue North Golf Course."

Helen's conference table in the Office of the Dean of Women also was a round, white pedestal with matching swivel tulip chairs. She often sat at the conference table when meeting with someone, rather than sitting behind her desk. Dean Emerita Betty Nelson, who was hired by Helen in 1967, recalled, "The round table and swivel chairs made for a comfortable place to gather to talk through the issues of the day, hold a staff meeting, or research a project with lots of documents spread around."

Coincidentally, Betty and her husband, Dick, purchased a similar table and chairs when they moved to Lafayette in the mid-1960s, and they still enjoy the set. Betty said, "At our house, we spend a great deal of time at the tulip table—any committee that meets here automatically gravitates to the kitchen table. There is something very special about a round table beyond whether that is a good shape for the space it fills. I think it reflects an attitude, and Helen knew that, consciously or unconsciously."

Helen had a housekeeper named Mrs. Carlyle, whom she referred to as her "house manager." Betty said, "Mrs. Carlyle was a very substantial woman, and she and Helen worked together extremely well. Mrs. Carlyle's husband was the caretaker of Ross Hills Camp." Ross Hills was the hands-on summer camp for Purdue's Civil Engineering students.

By this time, Bev Stone and Barb Cook had moved to 1808 Summit Drive, which was in the same neighborhood where Helen lived. Bev's initial invitation for Barb to move into her place (while she grieved her husband's death back in 1956) had worked out so well that the two friends and colleagues remained living under the same roof.

On Summit Drive, Barb had her private space in the basement, where she created her study and kept her clothes and belongings, but she slept upstairs in the second bedroom on the first floor. Bev had the other bedroom in the house, and her belongings were on the main floor. Bev was neat and tidy, and Barb's domain was a bit messy. The two deans continued to invite students to their home and host their Homecoming parties in the shady neighborhood filled with towering trees, including prolific cherry-bearing trees in their backyard.

Helen's cocker spaniel, Mr. Coffee, was well known around the Purdue North Golf Course for his ability to hunt golf balls. Helen gathered Mr. Coffee's finds and often shared them. Purdue students Teresa Roche and Jody Fisher met Helen for the first time in her home in the 1970s. To many students, Helen was a legend in her own time. In 2013, Teresa said, "I remember [Helen] sits down, and she was just very joyous to meet us. She said, 'I'd like to give you some golf balls.' Jody and I said, 'Okay.' It was like getting manna from the heavens. She brings this box out filled with golf balls that she and her dog snagged on the golf course. Jody and I were sitting there, and I just remember thinking, 'I'm going to keep these all my life.' I still have them."

Helen's annual staff Christmas party at her house was notoriously festive. Often, if the weather cooperated, guests peered out the windows and watched the glittering, falling snow. The staff attire was formal, with the women in long dresses and furs. Bev wore her champagne-hued mink jacket. Her name was embroidered inside in ecru thread in lovely script on satin lining.

The dean of women staff drew names for a gift exchange. The names were kept secret, and each person wrote a poem about the recipient of her gift. She then read her poem at the party for others to guess the name of her giftee. Betty said, "It was absolutely the world's worst poetry. I mean terrible."

In the front yard there was a perfect evergreen that Helen strung with Christmas lights to welcome her visitors. One year while the party was in full swing, some cheeky students chopped down the six-foot tree and carried it away, lights and all. Betty was there that night and recalled, "How bold can you be? Go to the dean's house and chop down a Christmas tree while she had a party going on? She did not take to that kind of thing very well. 'You don't take other people's things. You take care of your own.' But you can't be mad all Christmas."

Bad poetry was recited, women in evening dresses guessed names, tittered, and sipped Dean of Women Punch. Meanwhile, unbeknownst to them, a tree was whack, whack, whacked to the ground and carried off by a Purdue grinch, never to be identified.

THE SCHLEMAN FAMILY OWNED a home on Lake Michigan a couple of hours north of Purdue in Beverly Shores, Indiana. The house was Helen's respite for natural splendor and serenity. Helen's beach house occupied a peninsula-like jetty just big enough to hold it, surrounded by massive boulders to keep the water at bay. A long room with window seats faced the azure lake that is ocean-like with an ebb and flow of the tides. Her indoor pond and fountain on Western Drive may have been her idea of a little bit of Lake Michigan tranquility in West Lafayette.

Helen hosted parties at her Lake Michigan home. Summer picnics with the dean of women staff were popular, but she also liked to go as winter arrived. Helen invited her staff, friends, and family to come watch as the temperature fell and the ice formed across the lake. Some of the waves solidified, locked in massive frozen blocks that piled upon the sandy shore. One could walk along the shoreline in January and climb upon shards of Lake Michigan.

In 1973, during a freak St. Patrick's Day snowstorm, winter arrived wearing a death mask for Helen's cottage. Nearly four inches of snow fell, and then winds with gusts up to sixty miles per hour triggered nine-to-twelve-foot waves on Lake Michigan that caused destructive erosion. The National Guard and volunteers attempted to bolster levees in an effort to stop encroaching waves. Several homes along the Beverly Shores beachfront had to be evacuated, including Helen's. Sections of Lake Front Road were washed away. Helen's house became the poster child for the devastation. Photos of her cottage appeared on the front page of several newspapers, including the *Chicago Sun-Times.*

The photo in the *Sun-Times* was taken from the air. It showed Helen's house jutting into the water, lonely and mangled. The caption read, "Abandoned to Lake Michigan's fury." A photo in the *South Bend Tribune* showed Helen's house looking like a cake that had fallen, deflated and iced with white frosting, icicles dripping from the eaves and deck banisters. More than likely, she and her brother, Herb, entered the home together to survey the damage and salvage what they could. The *Tribune* also included interior photos of the house, in which one can see windows with the lake waves lurking close. The furniture is disheveled, as if Mother Nature herself had entered the cottage and decided to do some rearranging. Helen scribbled at the top of the clipping: "February 12, 1973—This is what we saw when we walked inside the living room!"

The other interior newspaper photograph was of the basement. Cement blocks and broken pieces of basement floor were buckled against the brick walls. Icicles hung from water pipes that had broken when the house shifted as it was hit by waves. Helen wrote at the top of this image, "And this is what we found in the basement!"

The *Sun-Times* story read:

> Homeowners on Lake Michigan were envied once for the good life they led on the lakeshore, for the seagull's view they had from their perches on the Indiana dunes and Michigan bluffs. For many of them, however, this is no longer so. Envy is turning to public sympathy. . . .
>
> During the St. Patrick's Day storm . . . oceanic waves rendered eight Beverly Shores homes uninhabitable and destroyed the town's lakefront road. Isolating an additional 12 homes. Other storms have made tremendous inroads up the shore, toppling pine trees, gobbling up lawns and patios, half-devouring a tennis court and undermining houses until they collapse into the lake.

Helen circled the paragraph in the story that revealed the true reason why the shoreline was unable to hold up under the snowstorm and winds. The article read:

> What infuriates property-owners is that the Army engineers unwittingly accelerated the erosion and now they lack the congressional authority to do anything about it. The corps acknowledges that the jetties it built years ago to guard the harbor mouths at Michigan City and St. Joseph, Michigan are speeding up down shore erosion.
>
> These structures extend out into shore current and intercept the sand being carried along. As a result, there's no sand to replenish what is being eroded from the sandbars and beaches. This leaves the shoreline vulnerable to the lake's fury.

One of the color photographs taken of Helen's dilapidated beach house showed Michigan City's harbor in the background. The city's smokestacks and industrial complex a few miles away flanked the shoreline where the jetties stood, the true culprits of the 1973 St. Patrick's Day destruction.

The day after the storm, the *Post-Tribune*, which covered three northern Indiana towns, including Helen's hometown of Valparaiso, ran an above-the-fold front-page photo of her home, the waves hurtling against the deck and the roof sagging. The caption read, "Going, going . . . High seas mercilessly pound away at the home of Helen Schleman, one of several abandoned along Beverly Shores beachfront, when high waves crashed over a protecting seawall yesterday." Helen had underlined her name on the clipping she kept.

On March 21, the *Logansport Pharos-Tribune and Press* printed a photo of Helen's house crumpling into the lake with a "Road Closed" sign in the foreground and this ominous prediction, "At least 30 homes are expected to be washed away before the current winter is over."

Helen kept all of the tragic newspaper accounts and accompanying photographs about the demise of her beach house like obituary clippings of a loved one. The final blow came in April. The *Michigan City News Dispatch* ran a photo of Helen's house on fire. The flames roared into the spring sky while Lake Michigan languished below. The caption read: "Landmark burns—A much-photographed lakefront cottage in Beverly Shores was burned last night by the Beverly Shores fire department. Formerly owned by the retired Dean of Women at Purdue University, West Lafayette, Helen Schleman, the structure had been sold to the Indiana Dunes National Lakeshore, which had it burned."

Today, the land where Helen's summer home once stood simply does not exist, for it was washed away, but the nearby area is part of the Indiana Dunes National Lakeshore.

In her 1987 Christmas letter to former students and staff, friends, and family, Helen, age eighty-five, wrote about a summer drive to Beverly Shores she had taken that year with friends "who love Lake Michigan as much as I do." She wrote:

> Some of you will remember that the Schleman family used to have a "beach house" on the water side of the beach road about three miles out of Michigan City, in what is now the Indiana Dunes State Park. Thanks (?) to the long breakwaters and piers that have been built at Michigan City; practically the whole Beverly Shore beach has been washed away. There is no sign that there ever was a semi-circular steel breakwater, on the water side of the road, with the Schleman Beach House sitting on it.
>
> I remember when the beach extended over a long block out from the road and the beach house had lots of front yard. I often say that losing the beach house, and the lovely sand beach, is the only physical thing that I ever grieved over losing. It is hard to accept the fact that the beautiful sand beach has disappeared into the water and that the beach road has had to be shored up with huge chunks of rock. I don't usually grieve over losing physical things—most can be replaced—but this is different, and I still miss it.

TEN YEARS BEFORE THE DEVASTATING St. Patrick's Day snowstorm, winter beckoned like a death rattle across campus on November 22, 1963. Barb Cook, age thirty-four, was director of Placement Service for Women in the Office of the Dean of Women, and she had just begun to work on her PhD in counseling and personnel services. Barb liked to write and kept a journal expressing her feelings eloquently and honestly. She wrote about the day President John F. Kennedy was assassinated. The handwritten account stands on its own and begins with Barb in psychology class:

Bev [Stone] had dropped me off at my 1:30 class a few minutes early, as was often our custom. . . . The atmosphere in the class was light and gay even though this was a general period of examinations. Two young men in the class wanted a date with one of the young women graduate students and had asked me to find out her name. . . .

As we left the class lightly smiling, I was immediately aware that something was not right. Students and faculty were packed in the hallways wearing expressions I had never seen before in a college environment. The atmosphere was tense and tragic even at that moment. I walked up to a young man who said, "They've been shot—Kennedy, the Vice President, Governor Connolly—in Texas!

"How badly?" I asked.

"I don't know," was the reply.

"You're not kidding? You're sure?"

I pushed through the crowd and out the building. Students were gathered in small groups. Many were holding transistors to their ears as they walked along. It all seemed to me strangely unreal—a sensation that was to become familiar to all of us. . . .

I walked quickly then to the office, silently willing him to live and praying vehemently to God not to let this happen.

It was quite natural that everyone would be in Helen's office. Somehow there were two radios. I wondered where they had come from. No one said anything when I came in. Room was made at the table, and I sat down. I lit a cigarette someone offered.

She loved Kennedy. She had worked on committees in Washington and had visited the White House several times in the past months—once for civil rights and once in connection with his commission on the American woman. She often told of his quick warmth and concern mixed with a quick wit. We had laughed together over her autographed copy of his inaugural address, which she had received for contributing to his campaign. The joke was that I had also donated but did not get one. I was furious with the omission. Kennedy was a subject of many office jokes. Helen and I were well known for our dedication to him and to the Democrats. We supported him uncritically and totally.

Whenever a staff member happened to be in Washington, a Kennedy postcard was always sent to the office, and there were several scotch taped around. . . .

We were greatly satisfied over his election and were probably his first supporters of the Peace Corps—an idea which was looked upon with some distrust by many of our colleagues and more particularly, by Helen's immediate boss. . . .

Our belief that he would save the country and the world was strengthened by the signing of the Nuclear Test ban treaty. We were proud and perhaps somewhat smug over our continuous support for him.

The big issue he faced now was a domestic one—civil rights, and Helen had urged all members of NAWDC to support the organizations resolution by writing to their congressmen in Washington. . . .

It was 2:30 p.m. I was told Johnson had not been shot. The reports on the radio were strangely inadequate and inaccurate. All of the staff were there, along with those staff from the Dean of Men's Office. No one said much, only occasionally commenting on newscasts.

The report came that NBC had talked with two priests who had been with Kennedy at the hospital. The report said, "Two priests report that President Kennedy is dead. Kennedy is dead is the report just made by two priests who have just left Parkview Memorial Hospital. They report the President was dead when they arrived."

Helen left the room.

Most of us just sat—waiting for some miracle to come from that box saying that none of this had happened. That it was all a bad Texas joke. Bev looked at me from across the table. Tears were running down her cheeks.

25

Betty Mitchell Nelson, Message in the Hollow Oak

Bluefield, West Virginia, was named for the meadows of blue chicory that once waved in its summer breeze tinged with coal dust. Betty Rebecca Mitchell was born on St. Patrick's Day in 1935 in Bluefield, which teeters on the Virginia state line at the foot of East River Mountain. Many prospered from the coal dug from the town's underbelly. The Norfolk and Western Railway transported the fossilized carbon from the area's coal mines through the United States to provide warmth and light while generating jobs in Bluefield.

The gritty mines amid the magnificent Appalachian Mountains created a socioeconomic divide, a disparity of scenery and of spirit. Decades later, Betty remembered what her school's blend of classmates taught her. She said, "I pull out the picture of my sixth grade class, and we are the scrappiest—we are the tackiest looking group. There are two who are cross-eyed; I kid you not. Over the hill from where I lived was a little area called

Grassy Branch. There was a little stream, and the little houses there were unfinished boards and really poor, poor housing."

A particular student from Grassy Branch came to mind. Betty continued: "Arthur was just not very good at attending school, and I thought, 'How can you be a good student if you're not attending school?' I learned later that Arthur came to school when it was his turn to wear the shoes. I was so fortunate to go to a school with that kind of mix. It's easy and fun and exciting to be where everybody is kind of alike and has enough. I learned a lot about the whole continuum of economic plenty and excess. Then here is Arthur who has a turn at wearing the shoes."

Betty's father, Emory P. Mitchell, became Bluefield city manager in 1937. Prior to that appointment, he had been city treasurer. Bluefield is the most elevated town in West Virginia, giving it pleasant summer temperatures that inspired the nickname "Nature's Air-Conditioned City." It was so rare for the temperature to rise above ninety degrees, that the Chamber of Commerce vowed to serve free glasses of lemonade when the thermometer peaked. The first ninety-degree day occurred in 1941, and citizens lined up for free lemonade poured by a "lemonade lassie," a teenage girl with a bow in her hair and a metal pitcher of thirst-quenching juice. The program was suspended during World War II because of sugar rationing, but by 2010, the Chamber of Commerce had served free lemonade a total of two hundred days over the past seventy years.

Betty's father often took her with him on Saturdays to visit city departments. "I felt really special riding along with him in that Pontiac coupe," she said. When she asked him to sign her childhood autograph book, he wrote, "Remember all through life that nothing will get you as far and cost you as little as thoughtfulness and courtesy to those with whom you come in contact each day—be they rich or poor."

Every action Emory performed carried out the philosophy written in his daughter's autograph book. When he had a task for one of his employees, he did not ask them, point blank, to perform the job. Instead, he said, "There is a memo on my desk for this to be done. Would you take care of it?"

Nothing Emory did was performed halfway or half-heartedly. In college, Betty wrote, "Thus, everything that Emory undertook was done in his most proficient manner. The garden was planted exactly by schedule; he left for work each morning at the same time, and he kept the church records with precise detail."

Betty inherited her father's bent for organization and meticulous follow-through. She described herself as a finisher. When Betty started a project, she saw it to completion, no matter the obstacle thrown her way. Her birth order may have contributed to this characteristic.

Betty was born ten years after her brother, Lewis, known as "Bud." Betty's father was fifty when she was born, and her mother Margaret, known as "Peg," was thirty-five. Both were from Radford, about sixty miles from Bluefield. The vast age differences between Betty's parents, and that between her and her brother, created an atypical family dynamic. Betty was a "functional first." She explained: "If there is five or more years of age separation between children, the family has its feet on the ground again before that next one comes along; so that next one can be treated like the first. The family's resources can again be focused on that one child, so I am a functional first."

Betty was independent, setting goals, vowing never to be married, and forgoing children, even though she came of age during the 1950s when many young women placed a premium on a wedding and offspring. It was as if Helen Schleman asked Betty, "What are your plans for the future?" And Betty answered with a nonconforming life plan.

In 1957, Betty graduated from Radford College, and her friend Mary Sutton wrote a letter of farewell in Betty's yearbook remarking on their "different" plans after graduation. Mary was going to marry Dick Skutt. Betty was going on to graduate school. Mary, nicknamed "Sut," wrote: "I do hope that everything turns out as you want it to—you can go so far and be such a big success. We're so different—*my* only aspiration is to be the mother of four little Skutts and a good wife to the most wonderful husband."

Looking back decades later, Betty said, "[Sut] was correct that what we wanted in life was very different, but I doubt I ever articulated that—just a bit too avant-garde. I was the only one among my friends who went immediately to graduate school, and I was the last to marry."

Betty grew up in a white colonial on Heatherwood Road with two towering pin oak trees in the front yard. Pin oaks do not shed their leaves in the fall, but hold tight to their brown fronds throughout the winter. As a child, Betty heard the tree's branches rustle against her second-story bedroom window. She was probably nestled in bed reading a Nancy Drew book. The fictional Nancy Drew was one of Betty's heroes.

Nancy Drew Mystery Stories was a series published between 1930 and 2003, with such titles as, "The Hidden Staircase," "The Bungalow Mystery," and the one published the year Betty was born, "The Message in the Hollow Oak."

The early Nancy Drew was smart, adventurous, flippant, and daring. She had blond hair and "drove a smart blue roadster," not unlike Amelia Earhart's roadster of the era. Betty was born the year Amelia was hired as an advisor to women at Purdue University. Amelia and the fictitious Nancy were like-minded women. Betty said of Nancy Drew: "I didn't know many women who didn't have traditional roles. Nancy was different. She was an independent thinker, good at analyzing situations, willing to step beyond some of those boundaries most women were afraid to approach. She didn't wait around for Ned [Nancy's special friend] to do something."

Petite, bespectacled Betty would become a Nancy Drew (or Amelia Earhart) kind of woman and take her independent thinking, fearless boundary breaking, and astute powers of analysis into her deanship at Purdue University. Betty's Nancy Drew-esque personality was most effective because it was tempered with a soft-spoken, West Virginia-tinged accent and a heavy dollop of courtesy, humor, and impartiality. Yet when she was crossed or presented with an inequity, Betty's backbone was as hard as the coal pick-axed from the depths of Bluefield. She would not bend to wrongdoing, unjust practices, or campus politics that did not work toward the good of students and the law of the land.

Margaret, Betty's mother, was a homemaker. Betty believes that lifestyle was somewhat difficult for her. Margaret graduated from Radford Normal, a teacher education institution. When Betty graduated from the same college, it had become the Women's Division of Virginia Polytechnic Institute. After Betty graduated, it separated, becoming its own institution, Radford University.

Betty said of her mother, who taught school before she married: "Terrific manager. She could have had another life had she chosen to do that. At the Methodist church we were involved in, my father was a treasurer for years. Mother was responsible for the meals for groups at the church. That's how her circle made their money to do mission work. It was always homemade yeast rolls. People knew my mother was in charge, and they'd come fill the fellowship hall once a week at least."

Betty often described stay-at-home mothers as "good managers," a respectful and apropos title considering what women did to raise children and run a household.

Margaret developed some health issues when she was pregnant with Betty, so the family hired someone to help—Edna Perry, a black woman. Edna assisted with Betty when she was a baby and then stayed to care for the house. As a "functional first" growing up alone, Betty, became close to Edna. Betty said: "Edna was my buddy. She would have Wednesday afternoon off. I can remember just bawling, because Edna got an afternoon off and I didn't. Here I am, at three and four years old, and I thought I ought to be going with Edna."

Betty's mother had some quirky and telling expressions, like "pretty as red shoes," "handy as a pocket in a shirt," and "all that glitters isn't." Yet with all her offbeat words of wisdom, there was a question from Betty to which Margaret had no answer. Betty said, "Why did I fret as an elementary schoolchild because my mother packed my brother's lunch but made me pack mine? When I asked her why, she could not answer the question. I knew somehow at that moment that males and females were valued differently in our society, and I didn't think that was rational."

Several events in Betty's life led her to value independence, and in essence, she created a Go-to-Hell Fund before she had ever heard of Helen Schleman. When she was in junior high, Betty read *Gone with the Wind*, Margaret Mitchell's Pulitzer Prize-winning 1936 novel. The film was released three years later. The main character, Scarlett, was a strong-willed woman who took life into her own hands. She fearlessly did what she had to do to survive. Betty said, "Reading *Gone with the Wind* in junior high school, I learned emphatically that women better be able to take care of themselves by themselves, and I was on my way to being a feminist and didn't even know the terminology."

Betty's Aunt Pearl taught her to sew, spent hours reading with her, and told her niece stories about her career as a nurse. Aunt Pearl also, unwittingly, taught her to value self-sufficiency. Her aunt was a widow with no home, so she lived with the Mitchell family part of the year. Betty said, "I learned from observing her status and fragile economic circumstances that women can be abandoned one way or another and treated like wounded puppies."

When Betty was sixteen, her father died. Margaret became another woman in Betty's life who was wounded and frightened, at least temporarily. Betty's mother knew nothing about the financial workings of their family, including how to write a check. She was a quick study and did well, but it was a steep learning curve for a woman in her mid-fifties. Betty said, "I saw the impact on my mother, her concern about how the family would keep body and soul together, her lack of experience in business affairs. I decided I wanted to be able to take care of myself. I wanted to feel I could manage, I could cope. I didn't want that kind of surprise."

Years later, Betty was an assistant dean in Purdue's Office of the Dean of Women when she first heard Helen Schleman urge her staff to have a Go-to-Hell Fund. Betty had watched two women she loved struggle without the security of their own money, so she understood Helen's directive perfectly. Betty had decided years before that she would never be left like a "wounded puppy."

A newspaper writer paid tribute to Betty's father upon his passing: "Always he was thinking about and talking about something that was good for the general community and for the welfare of its citizens. . . . Bluefield owes much to Emory Mitchell. The things he did for the good of the town and the services he rendered will have their effect for years to come. His name should always be remembered as that of a man who was a great city manager . . . and a real Bluefielder."

Across the street from the Mitchell home was a gorgeous house with columns where Mr. James T. Frazier resided. He was president of a coal mine supply firm. Betty worked at Kroger Grocery in the summers. Soon after Betty's father passed away, Frazier came into the store. Betty said:

> I was working at the cash register in Kroger, and Mr. Frazier was in a dress suit and tie. He recognized me as he went through, and he turned to his friend who was with him and said, "Oh, this is so sad."

> I finally figured out that he thought because my father had died the family finances were so bleak that I had been put out to work at Kroger's. The finances probably were kind of bleak, but I didn't see it that way. I was out there earning my money.
>
> That was my first clue that people were looking at me and making some judgments about if we were making it or not. I didn't like that. I didn't like people making assumptions about what was going on in our family. I would have been working anyway. I liked earning money.

During Betty's junior year, the class play was *Ah! Men!: A Satirical Comedy in Three Acts.* A page of photos ran in the *Bluefield Daily Telegraph* with a description of this "futuristic" production: "This play, a three-act satirical comedy, takes place in the year of 2050 with the women in power of the world."

The young women in the play were dressed in men's suits and ties. Some of the young men had on scarves tied at the neck, as was a popular fashion for women in the 1950s. The costumes suggested that if women were in power of the world in 2050, it would mean dressing in the clothing of the opposite sex. The play foreshadowed the 1970s, when women began to join the workforce and wear "power suits" that included the once-forbidden workplace attire—pants. The student director for the 1952 Valentine's Day production of *Ah! Men!* was Betty Mitchell.

That same year, Betty was selected to attend the Know Your State Day in Charleston. Participants were chosen for leadership and character. Betty participated in the panel discussion called "Citizenship in Action."

Also that year, Betty was one of eight state winners in an essay contest sponsored by the Governor's Committee for Employ the Physically Handicapped. The essay topic was "Employ the Handicapped for National Security." Betty won fourth prize and received a $25 savings bond from Governor Okey L. Patteson in the West Virginia Capitol Building.

Each winner was presented an Award of Merit, from the President's Committee on National Employ the Physically Handicapped Week. Sixteen-year-old Betty had no way of knowing that decades later, she would lead the charge to make the Purdue University campus accessible to people with disabilities and work to change the perceptions of faculty toward students with limitations. Betty's essay was entitled "The Physically Handicapped—A National Asset."

The following May, Betty won the National Forensic League's first place trophy for girls' extemporaneous speaking. Betty's topic was "What Can Schools and Colleges Do to Ameliorate Corruption in Government?"

Soon after, Betty was selected as Bluefield's representative at the annual Girls State. Sponsored by the American Legion Auxiliary, Girls State gave young women experience in how their state and local government worked. They held a mock democratic convention and cast ballots for their favorite candidates.

Despite losing her father her freshman year, Betty participated fully in the things she loved, excelling in writing, speaking, and leadership. One would think she was a confident teenager, but Betty said, "Forensics and thespians were the important social groups for me in high school—good covers for a shy, hesitant adolescent. The bits and pieces of my life [from high school] are painful reminders of the struggles of growing up—keeping a shaky faith that one will move from ugly duckling to something better—trying hard to believe that success will not be defined forever by whether one is the cute, popular cheerleader with the effervescent personality."

AT RADFORD UNIVERSITY, Betty majored in psychology with a minor in sociology. Her senior year she was editor of the yearbook, the *Bee Hive*, which was said to deviate "from previous annuals in layout, photography, and copy." The most unconventional aspect of Betty's version of the *Bee Hive* was that the text was written completely in lowercase letters. There was not a capitalized character to be seen.

"I think what I ended up doing as a career was simply an extension of what I enjoyed in college," Betty said. She was not afraid to draw outside the lines. She also liked going to a women's school. Betty explained:

> I hadn't been away from home very much, and boys kind of scared me to death. I'd done a fair amount of dating one fellow more than others. I just don't think I knew enough to think I could compete with males on a campus in student activities. A women's college was the perfect place for me. I gained lots of confidence and figured how I could do things. I was

> still deferring to boys. If they had their hands up then they must know the answer, and I would sit back and see. I just don't think I would have been this assertive about making opportunities for myself.

When Betty was home for the summer after her freshman year, she overheard a conversation between the next-door-neighbor, Mrs. "Mint" Robbins and her mother. Mrs. Robbins said, "Oh, Margaret, Betty certainly has changed."

Margaret replied, "I'm really pleased. That's what she went to college to do."

"My mother wasn't one to be generous with praise," Betty said. "So to hear her say something like that, I thought, 'Hooray!'"

Betty was published in the *Radford Review.* She was a fine writer, and her piece, printed in 1954, was entitled "Life As Art: A Challenge." She was published again the next year with "A Pen Portrait of Emory," a poignant essay describing her late father. Amid controversy a few months before, the Bluefield football stadium had been named after her father.

Emory was skilled and frugal with money. He worked to receive additional Works Progress Administration (WPA) funding for Bluefield and encouraged construction of a city park, pool, auditorium, baseball field, tennis courts, and football field. Not being an elected official meant he was unconcerned with political agendas. Betty recalled, "He stayed somehow removed from the political fray and as a result was able to get a lot done. He had a good relationship with the newspaper. They got pretty aggravated with him, but also expressed some great admiration for somebody who functioned with obvious integrity."

The Bluefield football stadium was special to Emory. When it was built during the Great Depression in 1935, the year Betty was born and the year Emory served as the city treasurer, government money was allocated to build the stadium with the provision that the city match the funds. Bluefield nearly lost the grant because the city did not have the equivalent dollars. Emory and members of his family signed a personal note enabling the city to borrow the necessary money to equal the government grant.

On October 23, 1954, Governor William Marland dedicated the Bluefield stadium as Mitchell Stadium during the fourth annual Coal Bowl, featuring West Virginia and Virginia Military Institute. Emory had passed away three years earlier. The football program for the day featured a tribute and photo of a balding Emory in his round spectacles and amiable smile. Betty and Lewis were at the dedication and appear in a photo accompanying a *Bluefield Daily Telegraph* article. Noticeably missing from the photo is Betty's mother. Betty said, "My mother chose not to attend. There was some political quarrel about the stadium naming among a few of my father's adversaries, and Mother wanted no part of it. It has been said regarding characteristics of a great university president, 'If you need to be loved, get a dog.' Perhaps the same is true of a progressive city manager; my father was not a 'do nothing' city manager."

Before the dedication, the arena had been unofficially called "Mitchell Stadium" by newspapers and citizens. When the city proposed to make the name official, there was opposition by the American Legion, the members of which wanted the name "Bluefield Memorial Stadium" in memory of war casualties. Even after the venue was named in honor of Emory, the American Legion continued to rally for a name change, and the controversy streaked across the pages of the *Bluefield Daily Telegraph.*

In years to come, Betty would hold fast to decisions that benefited all students of Purdue University, even when others in higher positions pressured for special exceptions for a particular group. Betty was her father's daughter.

Betty's sketch of her father in the *Radford Review* eloquently described the essence of what she had learned from the man she knew for a mere sixteen years. Her written memory was about an ordinary day that had nothing—yet everything—to do with taxpayers, funding, and political posturing. Betty, age twenty, wrote: "I can see him yet as he stood in the garden one afternoon as the sun was going down. He had just finished hoeing a row of potatoes and was leaning on his hoe watching the everyday miracle of a sunset. He said not a word, but it seemed that as I stood there so close to him I could almost understand his thoughts—that this truly was one of the real and beautiful things of life."

26

'Twas Ever Thus

After she graduated from Radford University in 1957, Betty Mitchell entered the Student Personnel Administration program at Ohio University in Athens. Betty had never been to Ohio, but she headed there to work as a graduate assistant for the newly built Georgian-style Jefferson residence hall. The hall manager became the first of several female mentors who influenced Betty's trajectory. Betty said, "At the age of sixty, Mrs. Moll had just completed her undergraduate degree. She raised her family and then decided she wanted a degree. She was mellow and practical. Just so balanced, and we had a lovely relationship. I had a grand time being at a coed university as a graduate student. I'd be on duty until 11:00, and then I'd have a date. If I wasn't on duty, I might have two dates in one night."

Betty left her shy, hesitant adolescent struggles in West Virginia. She was evolving, as she said, "from ugly duckling to something better." Betty recalled, "I had a very good time and did well academically. I ramped up my social skills, and I found I could have a good time on dates."

Betty met Richard "Dick" Nelson in a class the second year she was at Ohio University. Dick was the first PhD student for the university's Elementary Counselor Education program. Betty said, "Dick was accepted at Harvard, and then he asked to marry me. He said, 'If you'll marry me, I'll stay here; otherwise, I think I'll go to Harvard.' I told him he needed to do whatever he thought was best for him. He decided to stay."

Nepotism rules were prevalent in universities at this time. Spouses were not allowed to both be employed in the same institution. With this in mind, after Betty married Dick, she began to think ahead, to revise her life plan. Betty said, "It seemed clear that if he was going to be a faculty member somewhere, I wouldn't be able to be employed at that university, so I better get myself organized so that I could be employed. I took courses in counseling practicum and counseling theory so that I could be certified as a school counselor."

The couple moved to Baltimore, where Dick would have access to a large population for his dissertation research. Betty became a counselor at a junior/senior high school north of the city. It was a beautiful part of the country, with rolling land, grazing horses, and abundant wealth, but the area also had pockets of very poor families who had escaped from the inner city. Betty said, "There were the students in wool plaid, pleated skirts and blazers, and then some of the kids were dressed in clothes from Goodwill. I had a very interesting client collection, and I enjoyed them. A little guy brought me a possum tail because his mother left home, and he wanted his dad to marry me."

An uncomfortable Baltimore experience stuck with Betty and "enlightened" her, as rough as it was. Today the occurrence would be termed sexual harassment, though that term did not exist at the time. Betty said, "I didn't have a car, so I rode with two men who were teachers at the school. I paid them for transportation each week. The two fellows had been in the navy. I don't know what their agenda was, but they thought I was naïve, which I was. They would tell dirty stories—while I'm trapped in the car. Today, I would handle the situation so differently. It was their mission to embarrass me as effectively as they could. I just hated that experience."

Carpooling with the two offensive former navy men was so difficult that Betty would begin on Friday evening to worry that the weekend would end and her reprieve from the two would be over on Monday. What did Dick say about his wife's treatment? Betty said, "He was a good listener, but that was something I needed to figure out on my own, as hard as it was. I learned a lot about that. I tolerated it, and I should not have. I thought it was what I had to work with."

In the *Mad Men* era, women often had no choice but to tolerate sexual remarks made by males. There were no workplace laws to protect women from lascivious banter. The only option a woman had was to quit her job.

Waiting at the end of each daily, demeaning road trip to work was Betty's saving grace, Anna Meeks, the director of guidance for Baltimore county schools who treated Betty like her protégé. She gave Betty career-building speaking opportunities on radio, television, and at conferences. Betty said, "Here I am, a super young professional. Anna was really good to me. There was this really good thing—Anna—that helped balance out these crazy men with whom I was riding. I thought many times, 'What did their wives put up with? What was life like for them?' It must have been worse, if this is what they would do in a public venue with a woman."

Another incident Betty encountered spoke to how mainstream society saw a woman's role, again, á la *Mad Men*, and how a physician, the authoritative omniscient, perpetuated those stereotypical responsibilities. Betty said:

> There was a period where I had severe headaches. My mother had migraine-type headaches. I think I was predisposed. I went to see a doctor. I needed to know that everything was okay. His response was that I just needed to quit my job and start having children. I never went back to see him again. He was a good Catholic doctor, and that was his answer to whatever ails you at my age at the time. I was in my late twenties, and I "just needed to get on with it, go have some babies." Life would be just perfect after that. Little did he know.

This was 1960, the year John F. Kennedy ran for president. A life-altering jolt occurred for Betty when she and Dick attended a Methodist church in the Baltimore area. Betty had grown up attending Bland Methodist Church in Bluefield, where her parents had been pillars of the congregation. As a teen, she was a member of the Methodist Youth

Fellowship. Remembering the Baltimore Methodist church, Betty said, "It was a big church—Georgian-style, with huge columns. The preacher wore a white robe. It looked good. One Sunday before the election, this minister instructed the congregation that we should not vote for Jack Kennedy because he was a Catholic. I couldn't believe that from the pulpit I was hearing this political admonition. I thought it was so inappropriate, so offensive. It had a huge impact on me then, and has for much of my life. I didn't go to church for the next twenty years."

Betty and Dick lived in Baltimore for only a couple of years, but the soul-crushing carpool, the doctor who turned a deaf ear to her pain, and the bigoted church sermon left a gritty residue on Betty's memory.

This was the year that the first birth control pill was approved by the U.S. Food and Drug Administration. The pill changed women's lives. They could plan more reliably when to have (or not have) their children. It put the power to prevent pregnancy entirely in women's hands. Some thought that the birth control pill would lead to loose morals. By 1967, the pill was *Time* magazine's cover story. *Time* asked, "Does the convenient contraceptive promote promiscuity? In some cases, no doubt it does—as did the automobile, the drive-in movie and the motel. But the consensus among both physicians and sociologists is that a girl who is promiscuous on the pill would have been promiscuous without it." Nothing was written about a *boy's* promiscuous behavior. It was as if a *girl* was promiscuous all by her lonesome.

After Dick finished his dissertation research, he found a one-year appointment at Ohio State University in Columbus. Betty did not have a job that year. She said, "That was one of the worst years I've ever had. I moved the furniture around. I won't lie to you; it was terrible."

The couple then moved to Muncie, Indiana, where Dick worked as director of guidance at Burris Laboratory School at Ball State University, and Betty was an assistant in the personnel office. Had they stayed, Betty would have started a PhD there. After two years, Dick was offered a position as a faculty member in counselor education at Purdue. Betty said of her role:

> I was a trailing spouse, because I thought that was what one was supposed to do. I had no idea of a position at Purdue. Somebody told me that there was a placement service in the Dean of Women's Office. I

> didn't know it was just for Purdue students, so I made an appointment and talked to Donita Stobaugh, who was the successor of Barb Cook as director of women's placement.
>
> Donita very graciously explained to me that this service was for Purdue students—women students or graduates—not for miscellaneous women who wanted employment. I must have looked so forlorn that she gave me a few clues, including the fact that she thought there was a position open in psychology for a psychometrist.

Betty was hired immediately in the Department of Psychological Sciences, where she conducted paper and pencil testing, like personality tests and medical school testing. She was responsible for the area and had oversight of all testing. A handful of graduate students worked with her, and it was a close group.

In the fall of 1965, Barb Cook, assistant dean of women, made a panel presentation during an orientation for graduate students in counseling and personnel services. Barb was working toward her PhD. Her thesis was entitled "Role Aspiration as Evidenced in Senior Women." Betty was in the audience, and Barb's speech made a marked impression on her. Betty said:

> She mentioned to the group that it's really hard to be a student as a woman. As a graduate student, a man has a wife who generally does all kinds of helpful things, such as fixing meals and doing laundry and keeping the house tidy. Barb said, "I don't have anybody who does all that for me."
>
> I thought, "Wow! She is saying it the way it is, and her adviser (a man) is out here part of this crowd!" There was no way anyone could say she's not right. It was like a beacon. Here's this light around Barb. She is speaking the truth. It was a profound moment for me.

The testing center where Betty worked was in the basement of the old, crumbling Education Building on the site where Beering Hall stands today. It was in this building that Betty encountered Barb for the second time. Barb met regularly with her PhD advisor, whose office was on the same floor where Betty worked. They encountered one another in the stairwell. The two spoke, and then soon after Bev Stone, assistant dean in the Office of the Dean of Women, called Betty. Betty remembered:

> There was a position open in the Office of the Dean of Women, and Bev called. The only way she would have known about me was from my little conversations with Barb. Bev asked if I would be interested in a position as Junior Panhellenic Advisor. I was enjoying what I was doing and the people I worked with. I knew I wouldn't be as enthusiastic about Panhellenic activity as they probably expected and needed. It wasn't a good match for me, and I said no. I told one of the graduate students who worked for me about declining Bev's job offer, and he thought I'd lost my mind. He thought I was in a dead-end job.

A week later, Bev called Betty again. They had reconfigured the position to focus more on counseling, and she thought Betty might be more interested. Betty interviewed with Bev and then with Dean of Women Helen Schleman. Betty, age thirty-two, accepted the position.

When Betty began working in the Office of the Dean of Women in 1967, the staff included a remarkable group of women who became her mentors: Helen Schleman as dean, and Bev Stone, Barb Cook, and Cecelia "Celie" Zissis as associate deans. Linda Hurd Ewing also was on the roster.

Celie Zissis had a personality that matched her Greek name. She buzzed around the office, constantly moving. She was a voracious reader, and she adopted an old English expression and made it contemporary. When a situation occurred that presented a conundrum and seemed all too familiar, Celie would say, "'Twas ever thus," meaning, things never change. Charles Dickens wrote the phrase as part of a poem in *The Old Curiosity Shop*: "'Twas ever thus—from childhood's hour I've seen my fondest hopes decay."

All of the women in the office had wonderful working relationships. Betty and Linda became close. Linda was the wife of Ken Ewing, pastor at the University Church at Purdue. Betty said, "Linda was a wonderful friend and superb professional associate. We enjoyed lots of funny experiences and our share of sad times. My first office in the Office of the Dean of Women was adjacent to Linda's—I was in a fine neighborhood. Soon we could finish each other's sentences."

Linda was another woman in Purdue's history to have served as a member of the Defense Advisory Committee on Women in the Services (DACOWITS). Betty recalled, "Linda took her work with DACOWITS seriously. In addition to the regularly scheduled meetings, Linda made a series of visits to military bases where she interviewed servicewomen who wanted to talk with a representative of the group about matters of concern."

The women in the office were part of a symbiotic support system. Looking back, Betty said, "When I came to Purdue, I fell into a whole network of mentors. There are advantages to group mentoring because there's somebody to lead, while the group supports each individual. What we had in the Dean of Women's Office was group mentoring. Helen Schleman was the lead mentor and was practicing mentoring long before that was a term that everybody used. She was doing it because that's what you do to take care of your colleagues, and your friends, and the emerging generation of new professionals."

The annual conference of the National Association of Women Deans and Counselors (NAWDC) was the pinnacle of women mentoring one another. Betty remembered, "We had a significant Purdue group that always went to the national conferences, and Helen was mama hen—she introduced us to the old guard in the association, and she saw to it that we attended the business meetings because that's where the action was. She checked to make sure we were there. She was enormously generous in coaching us and in applauding all we did."

When a staff member had a function with one of the campus groups she advised, others in the office attended to show support. Betty said, "I can't remember a student program with a Purdue group that I advised—a program of any significance—that one of the staff did not come. The students and I were honored to see Helen or Bev or Celie. The practice was that you supported your colleagues and applauded their efforts. That was the culture of our office."

Betty began working in the office at the time that Helen Schleman was making headway in eliminating the restrictive women's hours in residence halls. Betty remembered a shocking question Helen asked her:

> I was walking by her office, and she called me in. I couldn't believe she wondered what I thought about something. I went in and sat down, and we chatted about changing hours in the residence halls and how that made sense. We chatted on, and she said that she would never think

about marrying somebody without living with him for a couple of years. She wondered what I thought.

This woman I was still calling "Dean Schleman" asked me what I thought about a woman living with a man before marriage! And this was the 1960s! My mother would never have said that. I told Helen, "I need to think about this."

27
The Quiet Crisis

The "lady deans" were famous on the Purdue campus and throughout their community. Helen, Bev, and Barb, in their sherbet-hued suits, were seen around town as examples of refined women. Because female faculty and staff were not allowed to wear pants, the deans wore their hose and skirts at all times—even to pick asparagus. Susan Gunderson's father, Daniel Grier, was an assistant dean of men. As a little girl, Susan revered the deans. She said, "They came to our house a lot because my dad gardened. He had a huge asparagus patch, and Helen loved asparagus. I used to go up and down the rows with her, and she'd eat it raw. They were always dressed up. They would come to pick a tomato or two, and Bev would be dressed in powder blue or pink, always with hose. I was in awe of them. When I think about them collectively, they were models for what I could become. For me, those ladies were a powerhouse."

Hair was an issue with the deans. It was the 1960s, when bouffant hairstyles were the rage, and teased, backcombed, voluminous hair took work. Their friend Sally Watlington said:

> None of those women knew how to deal with their hair. They would have weekly hair appointments. They would put little curlers in their hair in between times and sleep on satin pillowcases, anything to protect that hairdo. Helen would come back from the beauty shop, and she'd look just stunning. If I wanted a picture for some reason, I had to get it right then, because within two hours she looked like a disaster.
>
> Of course, she'd jam a hat down over it to take the dog for a walk; well, that certainly ruins a hairdo. If it took going to the beauty parlor three days a week, that's what these women did.

Barb, the tomboy, put pin curls in her hair every night for most of her life, even on a Colorado River rafting trip. On one occasion, Barb tinted her chestnut locks a different color. Betty Nelson, who served as assistant dean at the time, said, "Barb returned to the office from the hairdresser one day, and her hair had been dyed rather pink. It did not turn out well. I was coming through the office, and she bolted. Everyone she saw had a quip to make about her hair. Never did she have it colored after that. I'm guessing Bev persuaded her to do it."

As friend, colleague, and housemate, ultrafeminine Bev often gave Barb advice about her personal grooming habits, suggesting when she needed to purchase new clothes, for example. While Bev adored the latest fashions, Barb had no interest.

New-dean-on-the-block Betty met Dorothy Stratton when she visited Helen. Sometimes when Dorothy was in town, Helen would invite her to staff meetings. Dorothy, Helen, Bev, Barb, and Betty gathered around Helen's white tulip table in her office. As the "youngster," Betty had no idea the deep connection she would begin to form with the other four women, and by this point in time, only two of the women knew about a certain Bible waiting in Helen's desk.

Dorothy, age sixty-eight, made an impression with her understated confidence and grace. Betty recalled, "Dorothy wore these beautiful Forstmann suits. They were top-of-the-line and the loveliest wool—really soft. Often, her suits were in a very subtle plaid with a little collar. And the plaids always matched. I was just beginning to tailor clothes, so I knew it was special to see the plaid in perfect alignment at the seams. There was no 'frou-frou' about Dorothy. She was beautifully put together with a style that was very appropriate and attractive for her."

Helen generously shared her visiting friends. She invited her staff to luncheons or end-of-the-workday wine and cheese parties at her home so they could meet her remarkable guests. Lillian Gilbreth was one of the famed callers. Betty said, "It was a wonderful luncheon with Lillian in the [Purdue Memorial] Union. I remember some of the staff brought their copies of *Cheaper by the Dozen* and asked for autographs. She was older by this time, and she was not a big chatterer. Helen would invite her into the conversation. For us to see somebody like Lillian was remarkable. I never dreamed I would have opportunities like that."

In 1967, Barb completed her thesis for her PhD in counseling and personnel services. She determined that for college women the senior year becomes one of the most crucial for decision making and conflict. In her first chapter, Barb stated:

> The role expectation for an educated woman is loosely defined: she finds herself in a situation where, on the one hand, being only a wife is to reject academic and professional commitments, and, on the other hand, where choosing a career seriously is to reject her natural propensities as a wife and mother. The area between these two extremes is seen, therefore, to be the most acceptable ground for most educated women. . . .
>
> The difficulty of the middle choice is that it offers the woman no total commitment to either extreme and must in fact compromise her loyalties both to professional work and to homemaking.

If one substitutes "motherhood" for "homemaking" in the last sentence, Barb's statement still speaks to a woman's dilemma in the twenty-first century. The constant tug between work and children has not been alleviated. The difference today is that perhaps men feel the tug a bit themselves as they attempt to coparent on an equal level with their wives more than men of previous generations.

Barb described what having a PhD means in a note of congratulations to student Marylu McEwen when Marylu earned her own doctorate. Barb was famous for her eloquent, honest notes, and many who knew her saved her correspondence as a cherished memento. Barb wrote, "Having a PhD means and doesn't mean many things. It doesn't necessarily indicate brilliance. (In your case it probably does—of course!) It certainly means endurance and persistence and a will to accomplish no small feats in themselves. . . . But most of all what it really means is what is important to you and what you make it mean. My guess would be that for you it will mean considerable. . . . More than anything else the attainment of a PhD means giving more of yourself than ever before."

HELEN ENTITLED HER 1966–1967 ANNUAL REPORT for the Office of the Dean of Women "The Old Grey Mare Ain't What She Used to Be." The gist of the report was that the function of her office had changed because the country had changed. Helen wrote:

> Student life is not the same. . . . Student organization programs, which were focused previously on campus issues, are today focused on the broader social issues that the country as a whole is grappling with. . . .
>
> The questions of whether a woman student who married secretly or otherwise should be permitted to remain in school long since has been supplanted by questions of what course the University should follow in respect to unwed pregnant women students or unwed mothers with children. Who needs an education more than a young woman with a fatherless child to rear?
>
> The job of counseling and advising students is no routine job for the weak in mind or heart. Nor is it second in importance to business management or academic teaching.

One of the change agents for the country was the Vietnam War. Conflict in southeast Asia had been going on since the 1950s. In 1964, Congress authorized President Lyndon Johnson to take "all necessary measures" to protect American soldiers from the Communist Viet Cong. Within days, the draft began. The war dragged on and divided the nation. Young people began protesting on college campuses.

The Purdue administration watched nervously as other campuses erupted with student sit-ins, protests, and violence. The Free Speech Movement of 1964 began at the University of California at Berkeley, where students protested limitations on their political activities on campus. Inspired by the civil rights movement, students asserted, as part of their constitutional right to free speech, that they should be able to use campus facilities for political discussion and the dissemination of political literature.

More than eight hundred students were arrested during a sit-in, and soon after, Berkeley faculty voted to drop campus restrictions on students' political activities. Berkeley's well publicized student protests played a key role in Ronald Reagan's 1966 election as California governor, on a campaign promise to "clean up" the student unrest at Berkeley.

Students on Purdue campus felt uneasy during these turbulent times. At the end of the academic year, Purdue's Board of Trustees announced that tuition would be raised beginning in the fall of 1968 because of budget cuts made by the Indiana General Assembly. The new tuition for in-state students would be $400 per year, up from $330. While today those numbers appear shockingly low, the tuition upturn was a significant 20 percent increase.

In the spring prior to the tuition hike, students would push back. A combination of events stirred their ire. An unpopular war, the lack of a voice in campus decisions, belief that the "establishment" was not listening to their needs, and the increase in tuition were all factors in mounting student dissent.

It was as if Helen was looking through her crystal ball when she delivered her 1966–1967 annual report. She wrote, "In view of the widespread unrest among students on many campuses, partially, at least, because they feel that they do not have enough personal contact with faculty, the University should make every effort to continue to provide students with as much personal contact in the future as it has been able to give in the past."

On March 1, 1967, one student had given a public warning of things to come, but few paid much attention to his cautionary tale. Student editor Joe Bankoff wrote a prophetic series of articles in the *Exponent,* entitled "The Quiet Crisis." Bankoff said in part:

> I am a Purdue student. I am proud to be one. I am proud of her heritage; but I fear for her future.
>
> I have heard her Director of Libraries say that because of the inadequacies of her library there is no reason for a serious student of philosophy to study here. . . .
>
> I have heard her President tell students that they have no voice in academics or degree requirements. . . .
>
> I have heard of fellowship candidates refused an interview simply because of their Purdue degree in the humanities.
>
> I have seen the Political Science department torn asunder by petty professors who "can't do." And I have watched the deans sit passively by and observe.
>
> I have been told that each year Purdue receives a brighter, better, equipped group of freshmen. And every year I have watched the spark being ground out of them.
>
> I have seen signs, "Staff and Faculty ONLY" in the Memorial Union . . . a place for the faculty and the faculty in its place . . . students are students and faculty are faculty and never the twain shall meet.
>
> I have been told that at a campus of 22,000 students we have an enrollment of 132 American Negroes, fewer than some foreign countries represented on campus.

Bankoff's observations eventually would gather steam and roar to a boil in 1968. Helen retired that year, and Bev succeeded her. Bev moved into her new position as dean of women, not knowing that even for the campus nestled in cornfields and conservatism, Bob Dylan sang the truth—"times they are a-changin."

28

Uncharted Waters

Helen Schleman, age sixty-six, retired as Purdue's second full-time dean of women in June 1968. She wrote her official letter of resignation to Purdue President Frederick Hovde in January. The two had worked together for more than two decades and had enjoyed each other's company during countless golf games. Hovde's reply gave a glimpse into their relationship and the man:

> How fortunate Purdue has been to have thirty-five years of your professional life and I twenty-two years. This place we work in has something about it that captures both the minds and hearts of its people.
>
> While you will soon shed your administrative burden, I am happy to know that you will remain on the staff in a part-time capacity to undertake some more interesting jobs with real challenges, particularly that of continuing education of women. When we see each other again, I will talk with you about some thoughts I have along this line. Your help will be greatly appreciated.

> I hope you are recovering satisfactorily from your latest foot surgery, because you still have a lot of "running around" to do for Purdue.

Helen battled podiatric issues for most of her life. That's why she wore orthopedic shoes. One never saw Helen in high heels.

The part-time work to which Hovde referred was a new initiative Helen created. She named it "Span Plan." Helen worked out the idea on an unassuming sheet of lined yellow notebook paper that could easily have been tossed, but Helen was a saver. Today the scrap is preserved with her other documents in the Purdue University Libraries Archives and Special Collections. She scribbled: "Work on this—Women's Center for Information and Life-Span Planning. 'Span-Plan' Office. How would you like that for a name for the 'Purdue Program under the sponsorship of Office of the Dean of Women'?"

Helen created Span Plan to offer much-needed educational counseling for female graduate students, wives of married students, and mature women who returned to college later in life. Many of the women who did not finish their college degrees in the 1950s, but instead left early to marry, were finding themselves in need of their educations (as Helen had predicted) after their children were in school or their marriages had gone bad.

When Helen's retirement was announced in the spring, the Purdue News Bureau released a press release that stated, "Miss Helen B. Schleman will shuck her administrative duties July 1 to concentrate on her favorite mission—keeping women from going to seed intellectually."

Helen saw the statistics, and they weren't pretty: The number of students attending college was at an all-time high, yet the percentage of women attending college had plummeted. Moreover, nearly 50 percent of the women who attended college did not graduate. Helen also saw that the education level of husbands and wives needed to be similar. If the husband was better educated than the wife, the marriage often ended in divorce, for the two were intellectually incompatible.

Other universities had made notable progress in meeting the needs of the "mature" woman (likely in her thirties). For example, the University of Minnesota created the "Minnesota Plan." Women were returning to school after awakening to the "feminine mystique" and asking, "Is that all there is?"

Helen was concerned about the wives of male students. She addressed the National Association of Women Deans and Counselors at the 1969 annual convention and said of married students:

> We all know why most of the wives are not enrolled in classes: They are secretaries in our offices, or they do our hair in the local beauty shops, or they check us out at the grocery check-out counter, or they are at home in the married student compound looking after their own youngsters and probably those of their women neighbors. . . .
>
> These young women are absorbed in getting their husbands through school. I always remember the young man who was pleading his case before the readmissions committee. When asked why he thought he would succeed the next semester when he didn't the last . . . he replied, "Oh I'll never be able to thank my wife enough for what she is going to do for me next semester."
>
> Meanwhile, June after June, husbands are awarded bachelor's or master's or professional degrees of some kind. There is banter among the husbands and their professors about the P. H. T. degree that is awarded to the wife.

P. H. T. stood for "Putting Husband Through." The "joke" of the P. H. T. degree was so prevalent that it was even used in a newspaper ad. State Farm Insurance ran an ad in the *Exponent* with a photo of a young woman in her bouffant hair sitting with a man in a suit as if in an interview. The copy read: "Welcome Student Wives. Full Time Employment Opportunities. Earn your P. H. T. (Putting Husband Through) at State Farm Insurance Companies. Office positions available include filing, typing, keypunch, and clerical. No experience necessary."

At the bottom of the ad were these words: "An Equal Opportunity Employer."

Helen and Celie Zissis were the principals in the Span Plan office, and they encouraged wives with financial assistance and moral support; however, Helen met resistance to her "wives program." Some of the men in Purdue's administration were worried that if the wives also attended classes, there would not be enough women to fill the low-paying secretarial positions on campus. Wives, themselves, needed convincing. In a speech titled "Educational Planning for Wives of Men Students," which Helen gave on April 11, 1969 at the NAWDC annual conference, she said, "Young women . . . say without a shred of question in their voices, 'Oh, my husband wants me to get my education. He says he's awfully glad I can take a course if it doesn't interfere with his schedule. Of course, his education has to come first. He studies very hard, and he doesn't have much time. . . . I do not think that it ought to be so unimportant to him that he is enthusiastic only if it does not inconvenience him.'"

The "student wife grant" provided tuition and books, and was the first of its kind at a major university. Helen retired fully in 1970, having groomed Celie to be the second director. Span Plan grew exponentially with Celie's effervescence. She created the noncredit course "Educational Planning for Women." It was filled to capacity for years and was designed for women to examine goals and personal motivations for returning to school. The *New York Times* ran a story in 1971 referring to Purdue's Span Plan as an "advocate for women's adult education." In the late 1970s, the "Span Plan Program" became a regular series on Purdue's access channel.

When Helen passed away in 1992, she left her home to the Purdue Research Foundation. The endowed money from the sale of 1607 Western Drive continues to support Span Plan grants for adult nontraditional students.

Scholarship presentations take place annually on a date close to Helen's June 21 birthday and near her portrait in Purdue's Schleman Hall. Barb Cook and Betty Nelson have made the grant presentations to the Schleman scholars.

At the June 16, 2006 event (the video of which can be found in the Purdue Archives), Barb spoke about Helen, giving the audience a glimmer of the woman behind Span Plan. Betty introduced the scholarship recipients and told the stories of their exceptional paths to begin an education at Purdue, saying:

> Our sense was that this group of individuals had so seldom been recognized and applauded that this was an opportunity for them to have a little light shone on them.

> They were women who were in their forties who had dropped out of school, those who had taken care of their younger siblings because dad died, or their mother had an illness. The recipients had made sacrifices for their families. They now had time to go to school.
>
> We gave them the gift of a marble clock, a token to put on their desks as a reminder that they were Schleman scholars.

After she announced her retirement, Helen received many letters of congratulations and thanks for her service to the University. Dean Emeritus of Purdue's School of Agriculture Earl Butz sent one of his infamous notes. His salty jokes were notorious. Butz had been an assistant secretary of agriculture in the Eisenhower administration. He later served under Presidents Richard Nixon and Gerald R. Ford, but he came to be remembered for a vulgar racial comment that brought about his resignation during the 1976 presidential election race. His "barnyard humor" got him in trouble several times, yet he was admired by many for his amiable personality.

Speaking before members of a farm credit association in Champaign, Illinois, in 1973, Butz said that if housewives did not have "such a low level of economic intelligence," they would understand that the price of everything had gone up and "you can't get more by paying less."

Butz often chided Helen for her "feminist ways," yet she took it in stride. Upon her retirement, he sent her a letter welcoming her into the "ranks of the old deans" and kindly remarked of their shared Purdue experiences. Butz was seeking the Republican nomination for governor of Indiana that year, and he had just been named dean of continuing education and vice president of Purdue Research Foundation. Helen took the opportunity to write a two-page return letter to Butz, outlining her goals for educating more women and seeing more females elected to important governmental positions. She wrote in part:

> It is only because of my deep interest in your future and my sincere appreciation of your abilities that I would like to be serious with you for a few minutes. You are the greatest "kidder" that I know, but I also know that you are very serious about education. Here goes.

> We both know, for instance, that there is literally no woman's voice at the policy making level in higher education in the state of Indiana. This is true, in spite of the fact that there are over 50,000 under graduate women in our colleges and universities and over 10,000 graduate women.

Helen described specific Indiana agencies in charge of higher education as almost completely masculine. She penned a comment about the discrepancy of women's salaries to men's in higher education, and then concluded: "If all this makes me a feminist of the first order, I guess it will just have to be that way, but I have found it very hard to try to inspire women students to have high ambition and great aspirations when they see so little around them that makes them think they have any possibility of achieving anything very great. I'd just like a little real help on the job!"

PURDUE'S MORTAR BOARD CHAPTER, headed by student Marylu McEwen (who would intertwine with the deans' lives in years to come), spearheaded the assembly of six women's organizations to present Helen with a gold medallion at the annual University Sing (or U-Sing). An all-campus performance competition, the first U-Sing was held around Mother's Day in 1913, the year Carolyn Shoemaker became Purdue's first part-time dean of women.

The Helen B. Schleman Gold Medallion Award would be presented annually to a female faculty member or administrator in recognition of her contributions in areas related to Helen's career—encouragement of women in academic and professional areas, leadership and service within the University, and scholarship and character displayed.

Helen made an endowment gift to Purdue so future recipients also would receive a monetary gift. Through the years, Bev Stone, Barb Cook, and Betty Nelson received the Schleman Award.

The medallion is inscribed with an apt description of Helen: "Woman of protean talents—author, teacher, captain of the SPARS, adviser to presidents and dean of women at Purdue—she has with imagination, judgment, courage and good humor shown women of all ages, creeds, races and social stations their rights and responsibilities to bring about a better world, an enterprise in which men have too often failed. Serene voyager in uncharted waters, she is unrivaled in her dedication to young women and their happiness in proud and creative living."

IN MARCH 1968, a student at Barnard College, a private women's institution affiliated with Columbia University in New York, became the spark for a national discussion on women's hours and regulations in college residence halls and the taboo of cohabitating with the opposite sex.

Barnard's in loco parentis policy (akin to Purdue's) held that the college assumed a parental role and could set limits on student freedoms. Students were required to live on campus unless they lived with their parents or had a live-in caretaker job off-campus. Barnard student Linda LeClair had taken a leave of absence due to illness and didn't want to return to campus housing. She lied on her housing form by saying that she had a job as a live-in caretaker, and she moved into her boyfriend's apartment.

The *New York Times* interviewed Linda for an article on unmarried students living together. She requested anonymity, but after the story was published, Barnard officials identified her. Uproar ensued, and Linda was issued a slap on the wrist; she was banned from campus dining facilities. The incident came to be known as the "LeClair Affair."

While Linda's story became titillating national fodder, she had not been the first woman to challenge housing polices. Former Barnard student Estelle Freedman said in an April 27 *Columbia Daily Spectator* article, "We all resented the rules of having to sign out of the dorms at night, meet curfews, and limit male visitors to certain hours. When men were in Barnard dorms, you had to keep your door open the width of a book, hence the ubiquity of a matchbook."

A confident, well-spoken brunette, Linda saw the incident for what it really was. She continued in the *Columbia Daily Spectator* article, "Barnard students had to live at the dormitories, and there were some stringent curfews, and Columbia students could do whatever they wanted to. The media coverage made it into a story about sex . . . but really what it was about was power and equality."

The scarlet letter that was placed on Linda was deeply rooted in the sexual mores of the era, in which abortion and even birth control for unmarried women were illegal. Linda was astute and saw that she was disregarded and marginalized. She said that throughout history there had been tendencies to trivialize actions women had taken against sexism and its various manifestations.

In a *Time* magazine letter to the editor, reader Harriette Wagner wrote, "I don't know what kind of student Linda LeClair is or what kind of a mistress she makes, but judging from the picture of her apartment, she makes one lousy housekeeper. Doesn't Barnard College have a Home Economics department?"

Ultimately, Linda's fearlessness in dealing with the incident that seems inconsequential today helped bring sexual double standards and women's rights to the forefront, which actually translated into students' rights. Students were really saying, "We're adults, and we should be trusted to have our own freedoms."

Coinciding with the LeClair Affair in April, students at Columbia University began a nonviolent occupation of their campus buildings that lasted nearly a week and grabbed the nation's attention. Students and community supporters called for the university to cut its ties to research for the Vietnam War and to end construction on a gym that offered limited back entrance access to residents of nearby Harlem.

After negotiations failed, the administration sent in the police, who beat many of the demonstrators, bystanders, and faculty members; more than seven hundred were arrested. The building occupation ended, but the outrage escalated. Thousands of students and faculty went on strike, and Columbia University was shut down for the remainder of the semester. In the wake of Columbia's violence, campuses around the country exploded with student unrest.

In an *Exponent* interview, Helen talked about the Columbia uprising and future problems Purdue could face. She said that the same "sort of thing" could happen at Purdue. She commented on racial discrimination: "Open housing is not open enough here; it is too difficult for a Negro family or single student to find proper accommodations."

Helen encouraged more interactions between the races. Using verbiage of the day, she said, "There are not enough Negroes participating in 'bull sessions' with whites." Helen warned that white students had better open up leadership to blacks before "black militants" demanded action.

The 1968 National Association of Women Deans and Counselors annual convention was held at the Conrad Hilton Hotel in Chicago on April 3–7. Martin Luther King, Jr. was assassinated in Memphis, Tennessee, on April 4.

Marylu McEwen was a senior at Purdue planning on continuing her education in student affairs. Helen and Bev made it possible for her and another student to attend the NAWDC convention. Marylu said, "We were wowed at being at the national conference, because the women deans group was big then. During the time of the conference was when Martin Luther King, Jr. was assassinated. The women deans group had a lot of black members as well as white members. We saw both black women and white women so upset with the absolute horror that this had happened to this leader. They wondered what it would do to the civil rights agenda."

While Helen, Bev, and Barb were at the NAWDC convention in Chicago, Assistant Dean Betty Nelson was at the American Counseling and Personnel Association Convention in Detroit. Both cities exploded with the King assassination riots, also known as the Holy Week Uprising. Easter Sunday was April 14. The *Chicago Tribune* described the days following King's assassination as "hellish." National Guard troops were called to back up police who dealt with fires, shootings, and lootings. Soldiers with machine guns secured the overpasses along Eisenhower Expressway.

In Detroit, there was a dusk-to-dawn curfew. Betty remembered, "It was a scary place to be. From our hotel room window that night I could see only armored personnel carriers rumbling down the street and no normal traffic. The city was under a curfew, and it had the appearance of a scene from *On the Beach* [a 1959 postapocalyptic film based on a novel by Nevil Shute, set in the then-future 1964 in the months following World War III]. We, like so many others, had no idea what the next hour would bring and how long it might be before we could leave town."

Robert F. Kennedy was in Indianapolis and was about to speak to a crowd in the heart of an African American ghetto when he received word that King had been gunned down. Kennedy's impromptu speech on the flatbed of a truck was credited with preventing riots there. He said:

> For those of you who are black and are tempted to . . . be filled with hatred and mistrust of the injustice of such an act, against all white people, I would only say that I can also feel in my own heart the same kind of feeling. I had a member of my family killed, but he was killed by a white man.
>
> What we need in the United States is not division; what we need in the United States is not hatred; what we need in the United States is not violence and lawlessness, but is love, and wisdom, and compassion toward one another, and a feeling of justice toward those who still suffer within our country, whether they be white or whether they be black.

From the White House, Vice President Hubert Humphrey made a statement to the country: "This nation of law and order, which has its presidents shot down in cold murder, its spiritual leaders assassinated, and has those who walk and speak and work for human rights beaten and killed—my fellow Americans, every one of us must resolve that we will never, never, never let it happen again."

Since 1950, the NAWDC had created resolutions to support civil rights and human dignity. Bolstered by shock, sorrow, passion, and anger, the NAWDC presented a special resolution at the conference the day after King died stating that they would carry King's mission forward.

Less than a month later, on May 1, 1968, Senator Robert Kennedy landed at the Purdue airport on his presidential campaign trail. He addressed a rally there, and then his motorcade toured Lafayette before he gave an address at the Elliott Hall of Music.

A few days later, Helen was asked to speak at the Purdue Student Government annual banquet. There was a cloud of division in the air. The group was working on the Bill of Student Rights, and they wanted a voice in Purdue's decision making. They wanted to be treated as adults—no more "in loco parentis."

Helen's talk was printed in *Vital Speeches of the Day*, a magazine that featured "the best thought of the best minds on current national questions." In the June 15 issue, other speeches alongside Helen's were "The Need for Disarmament" by President Lyndon B. Johnson and "Communications in a University" by William S. Paley, chairman of CBS. Also in the issue was Robert Kennedy's speech given to the Cleveland City Club the day after Martin Luther King, Jr. was assassinated, entitled "Violence in the United States."

Helen's speech was titled "Human Trust." She said:

> If there is any lesson for Purdue from Berkeley or Barnard or Columbia or any of the other seventy plus colleges and universities that have suffered disruption to their normal constructive, productive educational processes in the past few years, it is this: Indulgence in force, physical violence, and material destruction results in sickening damage to the spirit of the campus, in damage to the confidence and belief of people in each other. . . .
>
> We must work together toward preserving and strengthening Purdue's climate of human trust and confidence. We dare not let it disintegrate if we care about the essential human qualities of ourselves as persons.

Two months after he gave his speech about forgiveness on a flatbed truck in Indianapolis and his oration on violence in the United States in Cleveland, and one month after he visited Purdue University, Robert F. Kennedy was assassinated at the Ambassador Hotel in Los Angeles following a victory speech for the California Presidential Primary. Five other people were wounded. As he lay on the floor of the hotel kitchen, Kennedy's last words were, "Is everybody all right?"

29

Peace, Love, and a Bible Passage

In the mid-1960s, Purdue's student population was about 20,000. That number included a smattering of black students. Marion Williamson Blalock, a black student, said: "Back then we were called Negroes, or coloreds, or the other famous n-word. I was about one of twenty female African Americans out of . . . about one hundred African Americans on campus at that time. Most of which were football or basketball players or majoring in engineering or pharmacy."

Marion was a founding member of Purdue's chapter of Delta Sigma Theta, the black women's sorority founded by Howard University. The organization's first public act was marching in the 1913 suffrage parade in Washington for women's right to vote. Although she had heard there were about twenty black females on campus, Marion only knew of ten. Marion was a minority within a minority.

Black students at this time followed the lead of Martin Luther King, Jr. who said: "The new Negro is a person with a new sense of dignity and destiny, with a new self-respect. Along with that is the black fear, which once characterized the Negro, this willingness to stand up courageously."

In the film *Black Purdue* (the video of which can be found online), Marion was interviewed about her memories of the Purdue campus. She said, "There was a Vietnam War going on, and the news was constantly reporting . . . casualties, and it began to report the unrest by the population, perpetually younger people, folks who started to call themselves, 'hippies.' Other universities started to have demonstrations, some violent, some nonviolent. Purdue was probably the last to show any level of unrest by any student."

Electrifying black leaders spoke at Purdue, including Jesse Jackson, activist and comedian Dick Gregory, and a member of the Indianapolis chapter of the Black Panther Party. African American students listened intently, and then they looked around at the inequities of the Purdue environment. To discuss their frustrations, black Purdue students organized the Negro History Study Group, which later became the Black Student Union. Marion said, "We had a number of meetings . . . to discuss demands that we had as black students. About that time we started calling ourselves 'black,' as opposed to 'Negro' . . . we weren't tolerating that [reference]."

One month after the assassination of Martin Luther King, Jr., black students developed a plan. During the noon hour of May 15, 1968, 129 black students armed with nine demands stoically marched in a straight line to the steps of the Executive Building (today's Hovde Hall) where the offices of the president, the dean of men, and the dean of women were housed. Each student held a brown paper bag. Marion said:

> The day of the march, we had been told that we needed to get a brown paper bag and find a red brick. Purdue had red brick buildings everywhere. We each got our brick, put it in our little paper bag. We assembled in Stewart Center, and we got in a single line. . . .
>
> We walked single-file, quietly, with many people wearing black sunglasses—that was real cool back then—to Hovde Hall, and one by one, we . . . took our red bricks out of our brown paper bags, and . . . we walked up the steps and each put a brick on the steps.

Office workers and administration members peered out of every window of the Executive Building, watching the silent black men and women as they symbolically placed bricks, one by one, on the cement steps. The bricks lay beneath a tall white sign that spanned the top of the sweeping steps. The sign read: ". . . OR THE FIRE NEXT TIME." Assistant Dean of Women Betty Nelson was inside looking out. She remembered:

> I was in the foyer. The president was not present. John Hicks was there, and he volunteered to be the spokesperson. John went outside, and I was just dumbstruck by the whole thing. I was fearful.
>
> I didn't know what all this meant, and what were the options, and where do we go from here—whether John would incite a riot or whether he would diffuse the situation. I learned quickly that he was a very good diffuser.
>
> John was very willing to say, "We'll set up a time, and we'll be glad to talk this through to identify issues and what our options are."

John Hicks was executive assistant to President Frederick Hovde. The demonstration ran forty-five minutes, and nearly five hundred bewildered, silent spectators gathered to watch. One of the organizers, Homer LaRue, suggested that the sign, ". . . OR THE FIRE NEXT TIME," meant that Purdue could be turned into "another Columbia or Northwestern," two universities that had been taken over by angry students in the weeks before.

In a talk given by Dean of Women Bev Stone on October 7, 1969, entitled "Women's Role in Campus Unrest," she said:

> Seven students were scheduled for a meeting with Dean Schleman, Dean Roberts, Dean Scott, and me when we received word that sizeable crowd of black students was marching toward the Executive Building with bricks in hand. None of us had any notion of the potential outcome. We had met with the seven students a week earlier and asked that they return with a list of established priorities of things they felt were critical for black students. In this group there were four women and three men students. . . . The women had up to this point been more militant and articulate than the men. Also, the advisor for black students had been away . . . and a rather militant black woman who was on the campus temporarily had encouraged the march on the Executive Building, and I would guess had supported the seven students in their decision to present "demands" rather than list priorities of changes, which seemed critical.

The demands of the black students included: more recruitment of black professors; integration of Purdue's "segregated, bigoted, and insulting" United States history courses; integration of all student activities; addition of courses dealing with black arts and culture; and a compilation of a list of discriminatory off-campus housing. At the end of the list of demands were the same words on the banner that blared from the steps of the administration building: ". . . OR THE FIRE NEXT TIME."

The Fire Next Time is a 1963 book created from a letter and an essay by James Baldwin as the civil rights movement was gaining momentum. It became a national best seller, and Baldwin was featured on the cover of *Time* magazine.

Baldwin's book is filled with significant quotes that give society its comeuppance still today: "The impossible is the least that one can demand"; "Whoever debases others is debasing himself"; and "Do I really want to be integrated into a burning house?"

The book's title is taken from a biblical prophecy that was articulated in a black slave song: "God gave Noah the rainbow sign, / No more water, the fire next time!"

In 2 Peter 3:6–7, the Bible states: "Then he used the water to destroy the world with a mighty flood. And God has also commanded that the heavens and the earth will be consumed by fire on the Day of Judgment, when ungodly people will perish." To paraphrase, in Noah's day, God destroyed the earth by water; the next time, at the Second Coming, it will be destroyed with fire. The rainbow that appeared to Noah when the water receded was God's sign of his assurance that there would never again be a flood to destroy all life. Whenever Noah saw a rainbow, he was to be reminded of God's promise.

President Hovde agreed that Purdue had to work aggressively to end all bigotry. He assigned the task to the same faculty committee that was studying the proposed Bill of Student Rights. Hovde immediately wrote a reply, responding positively to the black students' demands, ending his note with: "God gave Noah the rainbow sign."

Helen was instrumental in urging the administration to hire Beverley Stone to be her successor. President Hovde asked Helen if Bev was tough enough for the job. Perhaps Bev looked like she would be more at home on a veranda sipping a mint julep, but Helen recognized that Bev was equipped for the task; however, none of them knew then what the next year would hold.

Helen cleaned out her desk and revealed Carolyn Shoemaker's Bible. Dorothy Stratton joined her in presenting their secret emblem of deanship to the Purdue's fourth dean of women. Helen opened the nubby cover to the inside page where she and Dorothy had signed more than twenty years before, and under her name, she wrote the years of her tenure and a chosen passage. Then Bev signed her name, and Dorothy and Helen engraved their initials: "1947–1968 1 Corinthians 13 / and passed to / Beverley Stone / on June 29, 1968 / by DCS and HBS."

1 Corinthians 13 has been called the "love chapter." The apostle Paul saw that some members of the Corinthian church were seeking spiritual gifts with the wrong motive—to gain superior status. Verses 4–6 of the New American Standard Version read: "Love is patient, love is kind and is not jealous; love does not brag and is not arrogant, does not act unbecomingly; it does not seek its own, is not provoked, does not take into account a wrong suffered, does not rejoice in unrighteousness, but rejoices with the truth; bears all things, believes all things, hopes all things, endures all things."

The Message, a paraphrased translation of the Bible, states in verse two: "if I have faith that says to a mountain, 'Jump,' and it jumps, but I don't love, I'm nothing."

Patience, humility, truth, belief, hope, endurance, and love—are all essential characteristics of an effective dean of women. Helen Schleman walked out of her office. Beverley Stone walked in. The love chapter's message of unity lingered in the air.

30

Off Guard

Dorothy Stratton wrote Bev Stone a note welcoming her "to the goodly life in the Dean's office." It had been thirty-five years since Dorothy was appointed the first full-time dean of women at Purdue. She wrote, "I've always loved Purdue and still get nostalgic. I hope with all my heart that you will like Purdue and the job. . . . There were always some 'greats' at Purdue. After you've had awhile here I'd like to talk about Dave Ross, Mrs. Meredith, Kathryn McHale, Dr. Elliott, Dean Potter and Dean Shoemaker, et al. . . . Helen is happy to have you. She says you can do anything. . . . Good luck! Will be thinking of you."

On Saturday, September 14, 1968, the Green Guard counselors—upper-class women who fostered the freshmen—hosted an ice cream social at Slayter Center. Slayter was Purdue's outdoor amphitheater, built four years earlier at the foot of a grassy knoll with a design inspired by England's Stonehenge.

The freshmen women sat on the lawn in their starched cotton dresses—waiting to hear about the exciting ways they could be involved in student life at Purdue. A number of female faculty were present, and in front, sitting primly on chairs, were all the sorority and cooperative housemothers and the Office of the Dean of Women staff, including semi-retired Helen Schleman, age sixty-six. It was a bright, clear Indiana day. The Association of Women Students chairwoman had invited the newly appointed *Purdue Exponent* student editor Bill Smoot to speak. Smoot, a philosophy major, approached the podium. He opened his mouth, and what came out made scandalous Purdue history. Bev said, "He spoke of his expectations for women students. The title of the speech was 'Emancipation of Students from Purdue.' He discussed some startling taboo topics of the time—'beer and beds, open dorms, diaphragms and pills, and the planned overthrow of the establishment.' He advocated free love, rejection of parental standards and values, and defying the University establishment."

Bev and Helen were furious with Smoot, but Bev, the shiny new dean of women, was unsure of what action to take. The young woman who had invited Smoot to speak was frantic. When Smoot finished his tirade peppered with four-letter words—at the time, words only heard in locker rooms and at stag parties—Helen walked up to him and said, "I insist on having a copy of your remarks."

Smoot claimed that he had spoken only from notes. This was not the first speech given by Smoot that had incited gasps, giving notice to the community that he did not share their conservative nature. In July, he had spoken to the local Rotary Club, painting a "derogatory" picture of what student life was like at Purdue.

Smoot published his speech in the *Purdue Exponent*, although Bev said it "was the most watered-down version imaginable—even so, it was still pretty bad." In part, the *Purdue Exponent* version read: "Specifically, let's consider sex. I choose sex for two reasons. One, I am convinced that the essence of human existence is emotional, and therefore, at least in Freudian terms, sexual. The other reason is that sex is more fun to talk about than all those other things. Right now I can sense a feeling of shock in the crowd. Many are thinking, 'Oh no, he's not going to talk about THAT!' But why not? Aren't we all big boys and girls now? Why shouldn't we?"

Smoot continued, discussing sex before marriage and saying that technology made possible the liberty to separate lovemaking from baby-making. He touched on religion and the idea that sexual relations were the girl's decision. He said, "It is never the boy's decision—he just naturally wants to." He talked of the "double standard" for unwed women who were pregnant—"It's all her fault. He was just doing what he's expected to do. How can you stand a society that puts all the blame and responsibility on the woman?"

Smoot quoted Robert Kennedy, who wrote that the main concern of youth then was the dignity of the individual. He mentioned the 1967 movie *The Graduate*. Smoot said, "I think the best commentary ever I've seen on our American society was when the boozed-up, fat, old man put his arms around Dustin Hoffman and said, 'One word—PLASTICS.' So everyone is concerned about the meaning in a man's life, but what of a woman's? Women, too, have the potential to become persons, and just as often as not, they fall short."

Smoot ended his speech by quoting Purdue Professor William Gass, a man he described as a philosopher, artist, human being, and a treasured friend: "For I am not persuaded that if you regiment a man, constrain his choices, drive all feeling from his mind, all imagination from sensation, ridicule his thirsts, insult his stomach, and put a padlock on his penis, you will have helped in any way to make a man of him. And alas, is such a situation, also for the education of women."

After Smoot's speech was published, an onslaught of letters to the editor followed. A letter by H. Richard Rasmusson, minister at the University Church, stated:

> I read Smoot's address and found it mild, certainly not advocating free love, per se. . . . I support free speech even to using the quote "padlocked penis." Are we too immature to allow the expression? . . .
>
> It was an attempt at shock therapy, and it evidently worked. . . . Then Friday, September 18, I read Mr. Foley's letter urging the dismissal of Mr. Smoot from Purdue. The inquisition is on. No free speech for the thought I hate. Off with his head.

> I fear more such mentalities as Mr. Foley's than anything I know. We are in less danger from pornography, nudity, open sex, even free love, than from those who would "padlock the mouth."

Karen Kirincic gave a woman's viewpoint in her letter, titled "We're All Big Girls Now." She wrote:

> A big boy would, hopefully, be mature and perceptive enough to realize there is a certain time and place for certain topics of discussion. Basically, the content of the speech was good since it posed a challenge to women to live their life to their fullest extent and derive as much fulfillment as possible. . . .
>
> Sex, Mr. Smoot, is a private matter. Frankly, the freshmen women do not need to be told that "technology has liberated us . . . and we can now separate lovemaking from babymaking." We're big girls, after all!! . . . .
>
> Mr. Smoot appeared not unlike a child who has first learned his first profane word and cannot wait to show it off like a "big boy."
>
> Unfortunately, the reaction was not shock, but mainly disgust at the lack of discretion shown in Mr. Smoot's word choice. . . .

Irreverent, four-letter words and cocky delivery aside, Smoot's speech at the Green Guard ice cream social actually exhibited many of the feminist ideals of the deans who sat in the audience. Helen, Bev, Barb, and Betty fought double standards for women every day. If only Smoot had spoken with decorum and eloquence, rather than following the lead of his "treasured friend" Professor Gass, who spoke in the vernacular of the restroom wall; then his words actually may have made a difference. His speech, in essence, encouraged women to own their bodies and their lives. Delivered with panache, his remarks may have been lifted up today as an extraordinary, revolutionary moment in Purdue history.

Throughout the fall, Smoot published more provocative content in the *Purdue Exponent*, including a column written by a couple in graduate school that defiled President Hovde in four-letter-word fashion. The Board of Trustees was outraged and demanded that Hovde remove Smoot from his position, which he did. They also wanted him to shut down the newspaper, but this did not fall under Hovde's purview because Smoot was a student and the *Purdue Exponent* was a student club activity, independent of the administration.

The student staff of the *Purdue Exponent* printed a proclamation of Smoot's removal by the Board of Trustees and President Hovde. Alongside the piece, they printed a photo of bearded, forlorn Smoot sitting in his desk chair, head tilted down, fingers interlaced.

However, through legal counsel it was determined that the University was the owner (and thus, the publisher) of the *Purdue Exponent.* Additionally, just days after he removed Smoot, Hovde decided to let the student remain as editor while the president formed a committee to study the *Purdue Exponent* and its relationship to the University. John Osmun, head of the Department of Entomology, was made chairman of the committee that was comprised of ten people—half students and half faculty members. Osmun said, "The difficulty was that Fred Hovde, feeling that the president of the university should take action, had bypassed due process. He didn't mean to, but he did. Even though it was determined eventually that the *Purdue Exponent* was owned by the University, as a student organization it was something that he just couldn't close down."

The following February, the "Osmun Report" was completed with the recommendation that the *Purdue Exponent* become a "nonprofit, nonstock corporation." The report stated that the paper's coverage had become "issue-oriented rather than event-oriented." The administration saw the *Purdue Exponent* as a publication to highlight campus activities, as it had in the past, not to rouse questions and debate.

The *Purdue Exponent* offices were housed in the basement of the Memorial Union. The "Osmun Report" recommended that the location be retained, but with a rental fee paid. The *Purdue Exponent* would remain a student activity, while it became an autonomous body, removed from the direct responsibility of the University. It was suggested that the name of the newspaper be changed from the *Purdue Exponent* to simply the *Exponent.*

Today, the *Exponent* is an independent newspaper published by the Purdue Student Publishing Foundation and is Indiana's largest collegiate daily newspaper, housed in its own building on Purdue's campus.

Student newspaper editors from around the country faced opposition for editorial pieces they published during Smoot's time. The "problem of obscenities" had occurred at several Big Ten University newspapers. Many students who would become famous for their involvement in the 1960s student movement used their campus newspaper as a means to lead, mobilize their peers, and share ideologies. Even though some became edgy diatribes, the student newspaper was a key avenue for the younger generation to voice antiestablishment views. This was the era when students were demanding a say in their university experience.

Osmun took leave as department head for a year, while he chaired the *Exponent* review board. He said:

> I almost lived the life of a student at the time. I'd stay up all night with the *Exponent* staff who took over in Smoot's absence because he didn't come back. He could have been reinstated, but . . . he wasn't really reinstated. It was a challenge, and it gave me an insight as to why the students protested. They protested status quo. It was a new era. The Vietnam War had completely changed the attitude of people in the United States, and the University was thought of as simply an organization run by the president and his executive group, and the students didn't like it. So they rebelled.

An optimistic student rally took place on Purdue's Memorial Mall to hear speakers analyze the *Exponent* issue. More than five hundred gathered in thirty-five-degree weather to hear students, faculty members, an Old Master named John W. Blanton, a manager for General Electric Corporation, and folk singer Guy Brubaker. The *Exponent* debacle was touted as a beginning that opened the way for real dialogue with the administration. The "Osmun Report" had been created through student input, as well as input from faculty. Dr. C. E. Eisinger of the Department of English spoke: "As a member of the faculty, I will ask for your support when the faculty wants a share [in the decision-making process], and we will support you when you want a share. We look to youth of the country to show us with two cars and a cocktail before dinner a better way."

THE INFAMOUS GREEN GUARD ice cream social was the launching point for an unprecedented academic year for the Office of the Dean of Women. Bev said, "When I became dean of women, I didn't know I had an ounce of aggression in me, but the campus turmoil of the late 1960s brought out qualities I didn't know I had."

In the 1950s, *Time* magazine deemed Purdue University a "hot bed of *rest*." By the end of the next decade, students were insulted by the University's perceived low-key persona and out to prove that axiom wrong; however, Bev Stone always had a high regard for Purdue's young people. She said, "There was a group of very left-wing students . . . they were bright, articulate, persuasive, and moving. They convinced large numbers of students that if they would protest and create havoc, student fees wouldn't go up, the war in Vietnam would be solved, Cambodia would no longer be a problem, and the draft would become extinct."

For about three years, Assistant Dean of Women Barb Cook had the daily job of "rally watcher." Activists demonstrated on Purdue's Memorial Mall, steps away from the grave of the University's founder, John Purdue. Barb and a member of the Office of the Dean of Men kept an eye out for disruption. Barb said, "We were there to make sure there wasn't a lot of serious trouble, and we also didn't want the police to be manhandling our students. We were there to observe."

Because Barb always attended the rallies, even those that occurred off-campus, she wondered if some of the students thought she was one of the "gang leaders." On occasion, there were threats made. Barb continued, "I can remember walking to the courthouse with the students, and walking to the airport about some rally that was going on. And we had a little destruction out of that. Oh, you'd walk into your office and there would be a note under your door saying, 'We know how to get in here, and we know where your furnace is in this building.' But that never happened. They were just threats. But they kept you off balance."

A two-volume collection of material assembled by Barb, now housed in Purdue University Libraries Archives and Special Collections, documents student protests and campus mayhem during 1968–1969. Two black binders are filled with clippings from the *Exponent* and other newspapers, memos, student-generated flyers, and Barb's analysis of the issues. She compiled a table of contents and an index, and she titled the papers "Year of Confrontations."

Sue Daniel Eiler was a freshman that year. She said, "I'm sure Barb and Bev lost sleep over some of those incidents, but they were eternally calm about it. They were not judgmental. They were never the kind of women to say, 'Oh, those people,' or 'I can't believe what they did.' Instead, you would hear them worrying about students, wondering of the impact."

While Barb "rally watched," she stood back, considered, and preserved the paper trail of significant social changes and events that formed a volatile slice of Purdue history. There seemed to be a new development of unrest on campus each day, and one may wonder how President Hovde was able to sleep at night, fearing what would greet him the next morning after he climbed the steps to his office.

31

Sit in, Stand Out

At the Homecoming football game in November 1968, cheerleader Pamela Tyson King displayed the black power salute during the playing of the national anthem, modeled after the gesture made by two African American runners at the summer Olympics four months earlier. In her white sweater with a block "P" and megaphone image on the front, pleated, white skirt, bobby socks, and tennis shoes, King stood at attention with her right arm extended into the air, her hand holding a black pom-pom.

The gesture received little publicity and was not noticed by many, although a few days later, the *Exponent* ran a full-page story about the black salute and its meaning. King displayed the salute again during the first home basketball game. This time the administration, athletic department, and cheerleaders received critical comments, including demands for banning the black salute and for taking disciplinary action against King.

Many felt that the salute was an act of disrespect to the flag or, at best, a gesture of poor taste.

The cheerleading squad was given the task to create a code of conduct. When they did not complete the code by their last scheduled appearance at an Ohio University game, Purdue Athletic Director Guy "Red" Mackey, for whom the arena would one day be named, barred the cheerleading squad from the floor during the playing of the national anthem. King entered the arena with the other cheerleaders after the song ended, and the group performed during the first half of the game; however, during halftime, King turned in her uniform and left the squad. A photo of King wearing her cheerleader uniform and demonstrating the black salute appeared in the *Exponent* with the caption, "Cheerleader Quits."

This prompted Purdue's Student Senate to draw a resolution stating that there were no state or federal laws banning the salute and: "Be it resolved that the Student Senate, noting the right of the individual to salute the flag in any manner he deems fit, condemn the racism explicit in the Head of the Athletic Department's decision."

King wrote to the dean of women and the dean of men, stating that the order for the creation of a cheerleader's code of ethics—coupled with the demand that the cheerleaders not enter the basketball arena until after the national anthem—was a subtle way to "prohibit the Black Man's Salute permanently" and was "racially discriminatory." She recommended that the cheerleading squad lose its status as a recognized organization on the grounds of racial discrimination.

Dean of Women Bev Stone explained that the incident was out of her jurisdiction because the cheerleaders were not an official student organization. They were under the auspices of the Purdue Athletic Department. The black salute controversy rolled into 1969, and a committee reviewed the incident. Barb Cook kept every clipping, resolution, and memorandum related to the event, even writing a paper entitled, "Chronological Account of the Black Salute at Purdue."

It was found that the black salute was not a violation of either civil law or University regulations, and that a University policy regarding the salute would "be considered either as an arbitrary infringement of individual freedom or as a discriminatory regulation." King vowed to continue pursuing what she believed. She quoted civil rights leader Jesse Jackson: "To stop my communication via the Black Salute would further break down communication at a time when Blacks have 'quit laughing when they aren't tickled and scratching when they don't itch.'"

As the Black Salute controversy faded away, Helen was waging a battle she later deemed her third major Purdue crisis. The first crisis had been when George Davis was made dean of students and misguidedly lauded his title over the Office of the Dean of Women. The second crisis was when a man was to be named Dean of the School of Home Economics, potentially leaving no female deans on the faculty. The third crisis occurred with the consolidation of men's and women's residential systems.

The men's and women's halls had separate leadership until 1969. Betty Arnsman, the women's hall director, helped lead the consolidation of the residence halls for men and women. Yet Robert L. Page, the men's hall director, a man who always wore a brown suit, western-style shirt, cowboy boots, bolo tie, and wide belt with a hefty silver buckle, was appointed vice president for Housing and Food Services. Arnsman was appointed "second fiddle" to Page. Helen, semi-retired, wrote a letter to President Frederick Hovde on February 6, 1969:

> I cannot . . . observe the reorganization of residence halls management without going on record in protest of the downgrading of professional women in overall Purdue management policymaking. . . . [Women students] are not unaware of the implications of a top-policy move that promotes men rather than women to positions of authority over competent professional women, even in matters relating *directly* to women. They can only interpret such a move as implying that women are not considered by Purdue's top policymakers (all men) competent to do managerial jobs.
>
> It is quite possible, too, it seems to me, that men students are getting poor education on this score. They are learning that women aren't supposed to be included at top-level policymaking.

Helen did not win the battle of her "third crisis." Betty Nelson, then assistant dean of women, remembered: "There was great unhappiness in some quarters about that change in the organization and the choice of leadership. Considering the institutional leadership at that time, there was *no* possibility of a woman being appointed to the number-one position for the residence halls. I don't think the wound inflicted by that appointment ever healed."

In 2008, the dining room for Windsor Halls was named for the late Arnsman.

STUDENTS ACROSS THE UNITED STATES PROTESTED when Dow Chemical Company came to their university campuses to recruit graduates. Dow Chemical made napalm, an acronym derived from naphthenic and palmitic acids. Like a jellied gasoline, napalm was used in bombs during the Vietnam War. Many Americans protested its use on the grounds that it was a cruel and barbaric weapon. Napalm stuck to practically anything and burned up to ten minutes. The effect of napalm on a person's body was excruciating and nearly always caused death.

Dow Chemical, the CIA, and the FBI came to Purdue to recruit in 1968, and the Student Peace Union demonstrated in the University Placement Center, sitting on desks, filing cabinets, and the floor. The Peace Union was a nationwide student organization on college campuses that protested the Vietnam War, nuclear weapons, racial segregation, and more.

Vice President and former Dean of Men Donald Mallett promised the students that the three entities would not be allowed to recruit until the trustees could discuss the matter; however, this was not Mallett's bailiwick, and he spoke out of turn. President Hovde was forced to backpedal and go on public record "reversing" Mallett's ad-libbed, unauthorized guarantee. The false promise was like sandpaper on the students' trust of the administration, and good faith fell away. A story was printed in the *Exponent* that stated, "We've been had!"

A year later, after a tuition fee increase was announced, students staged a ten-day sit-in at the Purdue Memorial Union. They trooped into the sprawling redbrick building with its interior stone arches, terrazzo tile floors, stained glass windows, and regal woodwork, plopping on couches, chairs, floors, hallways, and stairs. They brought sleeping bags, pillows, record players, and guitars. The sit-in was a theatrical illustration of students demanding a voice in their education, in the Vietnam War, and in the countless dreams that languished after the assassination of Martin Luther King, Jr. and Robert Kennedy.

Representatives from the Office of the Dean of Women and the Office of the Dean of Men were assigned as a pair to remain in the Union twenty-four hours a day. The duo walked the halls, talking to the students in the party atmosphere. Then Assistant Dean of Women Betty Nelson, age thirty-four, was assigned sit-in duty. Always up for the next adventure and making valuable connections with students, she remembered, "One night the lounge just east of the Great Hall was filled with students who were playing guitars. They were all over the floor, and they were having a good time. They were not being ugly or abusive of the place, but there were a lot of bodies there, and folks didn't quite know what to do about that."

The sit-in occurred during Alumni Gala Week, a time set aside for class reunions. Dean of Women Bev Stone said, "Alums had come back. Many walked into the Union, looked around, saw the chaos, and vowed never to take out their checkbooks again. . . . Some turned around and went back home."

During one of the nights of the sit-in, the Purdue Women's Club held their annual trustees formal dinner dance in the Union ballroom. Betty was on duty with dean of men representative Eldridge "El" Roark when attendees clad in tuxedos narrowly missed seeing students clad in *nothing*. Betty said:

> The last group of men in tuxedos was walking and talking their way toward the South Ballroom when we heard the sound of runners coming toward us. I looked around . . . my goodness, two full-sized, naked runners were flying down the corridor. They appeared to have no awareness that all the important people of Purdue were gathered just around the corner in the ballrooms.
>
> El and I looked at each other in amazement at how close we had come to a career-ending event—if our assignment was to keep activities under control at the Union, we surely would have been shot at dawn for allowing streakers to join the tuxedo-attired leaders of Purdue!

Betty and El followed the streakers outside, where students were gathered with a few police officers. Betty continued, "To our amazement, a couple of horses were coming toward us with bareback riders—not only were they riding bareback, the riders on the horses were bare! And a couple of streakers came toward us on roller skates!"

The police wisely let the streaking incident play out, and it was over in a flash.

After students lounged in the Union for ten days, action was taken. The announcement was made through a bullhorn that students had to vacate the Union by a specified time, and if they did not, they would be arrested. Bev said, "Much against the wishes of some of us, the police were called in, and 229 students were arrested. The trustees mandated that any student involved in disruption would have to be suspended, and the dean of men and the dean of women staff had the responsibility of handling this."

Bill Smoot, the infamous *Exponent* editor who had exhibited gutsy tactlessness the previous year, was one of five leaders of the sit-in. The leaders had predetermined an escape route for themselves. Upon hearing the evacuation decree, Smoot and the other rabble-rousers deserted their minions and hightailed it out of the Union through a basement window. Afterward, the leaders lost all credibility with students.

During the summer of 1969, the Office of the Dean of Women saw each of the fifty-eight women who were arrested. In a speech decades later, Bev said, "We had no choice but to suspend them. Almost every student had a good enough relationship with a member of the dean of women staff that through the summer they made contact. They asked for recommendations. . . . The alums that I still know the best and love the best are former student leaders . . . and students that I got acquainted with in discipline situations. I think you can combine [discipline and counseling] if there is compassion . . . if there is genuine concern for the individual."

If a demonstrator was from outside Indiana, he or she was referred to as an "out-of-state agitator." It was as if Purdue thought no one from the Hoosier state would cause such an antiestablishment ruckus. One so-called out-of-state agitator was a female student who looked like a militant in high boots, grubby jeans, and army green. She had been arrested in the Union sit-in. When she was about to graduate, she told Bev and Barb that she had a job interview. A fellow student named Nancy Norton Nargi remembered, "She had been a thorn in their side, but they took her under their wing and said, "Now, when you go for an interview, you can't wear that. We need to get you some professional clothes so you have a shot at getting the job."

Bev and Barb obtained money to buy the student an interview suit. She went on to receive a fellowship to study with the French feminist Simone de Beauvoir. Beauvoir was an author and philosopher known for writing *The Second Sex*, a 1949 treatise about women's oppression.

The out-of-state agitator was invited to give a guest lecture at Purdue in the 1980s. Bev entered the lecture late, and when her former student saw her, she stopped mid-sentence, ran to give her a hug, and said, "Oh, Dean Stone, where would I be today if you hadn't been so nice?"

Anthropologist Margaret Mead had a theory about why there was an uprising of students in the United States. She believed the students were breaking out of a cocoon, woven for them and accepted in times past, but no longer useful. She compared the students' revolt to that of the suffragettes who fought for the right to vote. In an October 16, 1968 article in the Lafayette *Journal and Courier*, she said the women "resorted to similar types of behavior—marches, hunger strikes, throwing themselves in the path of mounted police. Whenever a group that has been required to be docile, segregated, submissive, undemanding, and unparticipating, glimpses the possibility of wider participation in the society, we may expect phenomena like these."

The twitchy turmoil of 1968–1969 caused the general programs of the Office of the Dean of Women to take a backseat to the campus stress du jour. There were bomb threats, sit-ins in the Executive Building with the summoning of the state police, discriminatory issues with black athletes, and an underground obscene publication called *Bauls*, which published nude photos, including the famous John Lennon and Yoko Ono snapshot.

Some student demands were legitimate needs and delivered positive outcomes—for example, it was made compulsory that a student representative be appointed to serve on the Board of Trustees. The Student Bill of Rights was created, which recommended for the first time behavior appropriate to the University and covered a wide range of areas that protected the students from arbitrary and capricious treatment. Bev said, "No single event accomplished more changes on the Purdue campus than the adoption of this document."

During this time, alumna Marylu McEwen returned to campus for a visit with Bev, who had been her most significant mentor as an undergrad. Bev said she was really busy but could spare about thirty minutes. Marylu remembered:

> She said, "Well, I'll pick you up. Let's just ride around for thirty minutes." . . . She had a blue Buick. . . . She talked and talked and talked. This was new to me because she had been the mentor asking me how things were going. But here she was talking about how upsetting the student unrest was for her. She was sharing with me and talking very personally. The roles were reversed. Here I was listening to her. She talked and talked, and then before long she was sobbing. I felt so bad for her, but I also treasure that time now. She talked about all the different forces and how she wanted to do what was right, but she wasn't always sure what was right.
>
> This was a profound moment for me. I don't think she and I ever talked about it later. I'm sorry we didn't because it stood out to me, and I expect it did for her. She probably said, "I feel so bad. I shouldn't have burdened you with all this."

Bev, age fifty-two, became ill during her first year as dean of women. It is hard to say which came first: her new position during one of the tensest years in campus history, or her illness. Betty Nelson remembered:

> It was clearly very, very stressful for her. She had a health problem, and she was away from the office for a period of time. I remember the day she returned. She was moving from one piece of furniture to another to hold herself up. She was wearing a navy dress she had never worn before. It had a square neck and a white collar. Here she was looking peaked as she could be and had on a dress that was as unbecoming as could be, and she had something draped around her shoulders, which made her look like Methuselah's wife. It was the most pathetic scene. It was a long time before she was up to speed again.

However, Bev put on a smiling face and a neutral countenance when she answered to the news media and others regarding campus activities.

Her favored reply to questions that were not to her liking was, "I am not prepared to respond to that." It was an all-purpose reaction that Bev used in many situations throughout her career. Said with a charming smile, the words were received in a most benign, nonthreatening manner.

Associate Dean of Women Barb Cook handled Bev's responsibilities when Bev was ill and away from the office. Years later, Barb saw the campus turmoil in a positive light. She said, "It was a difficult time. I think the University learned a lot from that . . . instead of being so rigid and thinking that only faculty or administrators could make rules. The dean of women staff and dean of men staff did a good job in this period. We probably understood the students better than most of the administration and a good many of the faculty, although some of the faculty were instigating the riots."

Sue Daniel Eiler, a student during this time, saw the deans as highly successful in handling the anarchy. She said, "Bev and Barb had a wonderful role in calming the environment. It wasn't their job to calm it, but just being the people they were, they helped bridge that chasm that was growing between administration and students."

Even though Bev was sick and highly strained, she proved her grit. She said, "The thing I learned when I became dean of women was that if you have responsibility for other people, you have to fight for them in some situations, particularly when you are in the minority situation. You had to do some things politically."

Bev dreaded seeing the renowned jokester Earl Butz on campus, the former dean of the School of Agriculture. Whenever he saw Bev, Butz teased, "The reason for student unrest is the new dean of women. We never had these problems when Dean Schleman was here."

Bev recalled, "There were times when I thought perhaps he was right."

32

In Walks the Pantsuit

Purdue graduate Neil A. Armstrong was the first man to walk on the moon on July 20, 1969. A few weeks later, an article in the Lafayette *Journal and Courier* bore this headline: "Dean Stone predicts Purdue Coed Will Be First Woman Astronaut." Bev Stone repeated the prediction during the Freshmen Women's Convocation that fall, the beginning of Purdue's one hundredth year. Bev said, "You are the centennial class—in this unforgettable year—1969—the year when the first man to put his foot on the moon was a Purdue graduate—with a Purdue wife—the year of the immortal statement, 'One small step for man, one giant leap for mankind.' Those of us here feel confident that following in Neil Armstrong's footsteps will be a female astronaut who undoubtedly will be a Purdue woman. Perhaps even one of you!"

The previous year had brought transformation wrought by tragedy for the United States. On that summer day, when Americans watched the grainy, shadowy images of Neil Armstrong and Buzz Aldrin planting an American flag on the moon, John F. Kennedy's space-race optimism flickered from millions of Zenith televisions. Hopefulness was restored; possibilities for the country once again seemed infinite; and because Armstrong was a Purdue graduate, the potential for the University also appeared boundless.

Bev was certain that Purdue women would be part of the space program. She reminded her staff that Armstrong's wife, Janet Shearon, was in Purdue's class of 1956. Shearon majored in home economics but did not graduate. She married instead. The dean of women staff wondered, "Did we prepare her well for her role in the space age?"

The *Journal and Courier* article continued:

> Thus, 1970 will find Purdue gearing its womanpower to a new kind of society. That is, women students will have to be educated in the art of science of maintaining equal status in a highly computerized "astronomical" age. . . .
>
> Meanwhile, any young woman whose ultimate objective is to work directly in the U.S. space program will find no better place to start than at Purdue University.
>
> No one can predict where her adventures will lead, but the university's astronautical engineers and scientists will readily comprehend and encourage her interplanetary dreams.

The story's final paragraphs are the most telling about Janet Shearon Armstrong and her role in the space age: "And about Mrs. Armstrong . . . reportedly, she is the only wife of the Apollo crew who reads all of the technical transcripts of the space flights released by NASA. During the moon shot, the story is told of a missing page in a transcript she was reading. She inquired about this and was told by NASA that a page was, indeed, missing from her report. They were amazed that anyone but those closely involved in the technical aspects of the flight would have noticed such an omission."

NASA screened a couple of female pilots in 1959 and 1960 for possible astronaut training, but the organization later decided to restrict astronaut qualifications to men. Russia was the first country to put a woman in space in 1963, when cosmonaut Valentina Tereshkova spent seventy-one hours in orbit—more time in the space than all United States astronauts combined to that date.

Stanford University graduate Sally Ride was America's first female astronaut, joining NASA in 1978. She served as mission specialist on the space shuttle *Challenger* in 1983.

Purdue's first female astronaut was Janice E. Voss, who graduated in 1975 with a bachelor's degree in engineering science. She was just sixteen years old and a freshman at the University when she first worked for NASA as an intern at the Johnson Space Center. Voss's love of science began when she was six and read a library book—Madeleine L'Engle's *A Wrinkle in Time*—with a main character as a scientist who happens to be a woman.

Forty-five years after Bev's optimistic, convincing speech predicting that a Purdue woman would be the first female astronaut, only one woman other than Voss is included on the list of Purdue's twenty-two astronauts—Mary E. Weber, class of 1984.

HELEN SCHLEMAN HAD AN EAGLE EYE for newspaper and magazine stories that pertained to women's accomplishments, the pursuit of equality, and struggles against discrimination. As the 1970s exploded with women's liberation, her file cabinet bulged with clippings.

A 1969 *Indianapolis Star* headline read, "Engineer Very Much a Girl." It was about Lynnda McGinty, who had majored in math and electronics at Purdue. She was the first woman to be appointed as sales engineer for Westinghouse. Often the only woman in her Purdue classes, McGinty said, "The guys were real nice about it, although sometimes the professors grumbled I was taking the place of a deserving male."

Bev talked of a senior female student in engineering who she met on a flight to a Purdue football game in 1975. Bev asked the woman who gave her encouragement to enter a nontraditional field—did she get this from her high school counselor? The woman student smiled and said "no"—in fact, her high school counselor had told her that although she had the ability, she'd never make it. When she came to Purdue, she tested out of an advanced course and was the only woman placed in a high-level session. At the end of the first session, the professor called her aside and told her she would never be able to pass the courses. She stayed and became the first woman in Purdue's engineering coop program in engine design at General Motors. The men with whom she worked assumed she was a new secretary.

In fall of 1972, a Lafayette *Journal and Courier* story headline read, "87 Women Study Engineering Here." There were nearly 4,300 engineering undergraduates, and of those, eighty-seven were women—one in fifty. This was ballyhooed as a "significant increase," because in 1968 there had been forty-six women in engineering.

Forty years later, in fall 2013, Purdue had 7,743 undergraduates in engineering, and of those, 1,742 were women—approximately one in five.

HELEN WAS ASKED TO BE A CONSULTANT for Richard Nixon's Presidential Task Force on Women's Rights and Responsibilities. She traveled to the White House and spoke before the group about her concerns for the future of women, presenting a paper on "Women in Higher Education."

Released in 1970, the task force report, "A Matter of Simple Justice," recommended a national commitment to basic changes to "bring women into the mainstream of American life." It stated, "So widespread and pervasive are discriminatory practices against women they have come to be regarded . . . as normal." The task force recommended "the President call a White House conference on women's rights and responsibilities in 1970, the fiftieth anniversary of the ratification of the suffrage amendment and establishment of the Women's Bureau."

On Purdue's campus, a women's liberation movement had formed. The most controversial of all women's rights issues was birth control and abortion. The campus group started a campaign to give out information and to "push the Health Center to give birth control pills to anyone, if it is physically alright for that person." However, Laurie Hunt, the group's leader, warned, "Being sexually liberated only opens the woman to more degradation, gaining status through the men she sleeps with."

Bev Stone talked of the topic in her speech to a Presbyterian Church, entitled "Women and Civil Rights." She said:

> Congresswoman Shirley Chisholm of New York stands squarely for this being a matter over which the individual woman must have control. So do the more militant women's groups. On the other hand are the long-standing religious scruples of millions of our people, both men and women. I won't even venture a personal comment on this subject except to say that the individual woman's stake in this matter exceeds that of any bystander. If we really mean that individuals, women individuals in this case, have the right to control their own lives, then the least society can do is to equip them as adequately as possible for the task.

After President Frederick Hovde announced that he would retire in June 1971, a Committee for the Selection of the President was formed. Helen received a request to nominate candidates, and she took issue with the wording on the form. Faculty and administrators were urged to nominate someone who they believed "would make a fine president." The form read, "You may hesitate to suggest a nominee because he is not perfect in all respects." It was the word "he" that angered Helen.

Helen promptly obtained ten nomination forms and officially nominated ten women to become president of Purdue University.

Accompanying her nominations was a lengthy explanation of the reasons for her action. She wrote that the most compelling reason was that of fairness to the people served by Purdue: the Indiana women citizen-taxpayers, the many girls graduating from Indiana high schools (and the nation), and the ever-increasing number of female Purdue students. Helen said, "'Male sex' is no longer accepted as a valid occupational qualification for the job of presidency of the University by a great many constituents."

Helen also sent her nominations and explanation to the *Exponent* and to Mary Anne Butters, a reporter for the *Indianapolis Star.* Butters wrote a story entitled, "Can Woman Become President of Purdue?" The pictures and biographies of Helen's nominees appeared in both newspapers. Among Helen's nominees were Katharine Graham, publisher of the *Washington Post* and *Newsweek*, and Barbara W. Newell, acting vice-president for student affairs and associate professor of economics at the University of Michigan. Upon hearing of her nomination, Newell wrote Helen a note:

"Dear Suffragette: It's fun to see such demonstrations of spunk, and I am highly honored to be included in your list of ten. Thank you."

Helen also nominated the only woman on Purdue's Board of Trustees, Margaret White, who sent her a thank-you note.

Helen said, "There are two hundred to three hundred vacancies nationwide for college presidents, but nobody offers them to women. I could have nominated twenty . . . thirty women."

Arthur G. Hansen was named president of Purdue University in 1971. Purdue's first female president was France A. Córdova, who served from 2007 to 2012.

HELEN RETIRED COMPLETELY IN 1970. In February, the same month Helen had nominated ten women as candidates for Purdue president, former Dean of Agriculture Earl Butz sent a memo to Vice President George A. Hawkins, Vice President for Student Services Donald R. Mallett, Dean Bev Stone, and "Dean Emerit-? Helen Schleman." It concerned a ballot to recommend the emeritus ranking for retiring faculty members. The memo was in regard to "Emeritus vs. Emerita." He wrote:

> A question is raised regarding the recommended rank for our good friend and long-time Purdue servant, Helen Schleman.
>
> I am amazed that a persistent crusader for "equality between the sexes" and "obliteration of all professional boundary lines between the sexes" should now be recommended for a rank in retirement that is "distinctly female."
>
> Am I to interpret this to mean that the persistent drive of this great crusader, as we approach the finish line, is something less than complete and final?
>
> Seriously, doesn't the word "Emeritus," an adjective, modify Dean rather than Women? If this be so, and the word "Emeritus" is used rather than "Emerita," then Helen's final title from Purdue University would carry no evidence of sexual discrimination.
>
> Even so, the word "Women" would be left in the title. I see no biologically acceptable way to erase that last shred of evidence.

By the summer, Helen was formally an "emerita." Earl Butz wrote her a letter:

> Now that the title "Emerit*a*" is official, even though it does denote discrimination and perhaps inequality between the sexes, we'll knuckle under and use it from now on.
>
> Seriously Helen, whether it's *a* or *us,* we are all extremely grateful for the wonderful job you have done through the years as a member of the Purdue team.
>
> I have always felt comfortable having a bona fide farmer in the office of the Dean of Women. One who sprang from the soil as you did, was nurtured in it, and was fully imbued with the philosophy of production, hard work, integrity, and responsibility associated with that background, could never have done otherwise than have a no nonsense attitude in student administration and in faculty relations.
>
> I am confident that the "Schleman Era" in student administration at Purdue University will long be remembered as one characterized by firmness, fairness, and an always present objective of developing young men and young women into responsible leaders and citizens.

Edmund Brucker, instructor at the Herron School of Art and Design in Indianapolis, created a portrait of Helen upon her retirement. She wore a soft blue suit and pearls for the sitting. Helen thought the colors in the rendering were lovely.

On behalf of the staff of the Office of the Dean of Women, Bev nominated Helen for an honorary degree of Doctor of Laws, which she was awarded at the June 13, 1971, Purdue commencement.

Mallett wrote Helen a warm letter on the last official day of her Purdue employment:

> Your finishing your span of work at Purdue leaves a vacancy at the very heart of the University, which cannot be filled. At the same time it creates a sense of true loss to many of us who are still on the job, of whom I am one. In the field of student personnel I do not know how one can measure what a person has done or what trails he has left behind in the sands of time. . . .

> I have never worked with anyone, male or female, who was as basically honest as you. There was never a time when there was any doubt about what you thought, what you believed, and what contribution you felt you could make to the problem at hand.
>
> And so you become Dean Emerita. This need not in any way diminish the sparkle of your eye, the warm handclasp, the understanding heart. All I ask is that we do have a chance to visit once in a while to reminisce, to argue, and to plan.

Mallett died the next year. He need not to have worried. Helen was in no way finished with the University. During the next two decades, she would continue to argue and plan for Purdue.

With the fiftieth anniversary of the suffrage amendment and women receiving the right to vote, the 1970s were deemed the "decade of women." In 1970, the Equal Rights Amendment was introduced into Congress. Bev spoke to the Purdue Women's Interhall Council in the fall and said, "Those of you here—student leaders at Purdue—are undoubtedly aware that you are in the midst of a revolution."

Bev was quoted in the *Exponent*: "One of my special concerns is with the Equal Rights Amendment, which the House has passed but which is stymied in the Senate. This is long overdue. We've been pushing for it for over 50 years."

Bev gave a talk in the Memorial Union entitled, "Is a Woman a Person?" She offered the reason why women have been pushing for the ERA for decades. She said "the Supreme Court has interpreted the word 'persons' to mean males—white and black, but not women." She added, "The only right granted women under the Constitution is the right to vote."

In February of the next year, Bev wrote a letter to Purdue female students. By this time, Purdue was the only school in the Big Ten to still have an Office of the Dean of Women. Others had created an Office of the Dean of Students to serve both men and women. She began her letter with "Focus on Women!" Then she harkened back to the story that had perpetuated through the ages at Purdue about the first part-time Dean of

Women Carolyn Shoemaker—the original keeper of the now-secretive deans' Bible, waiting like a talisman inside the desk of Dean of Women Bev Stone. Bev wrote:

> Back in 1913, Miss Carolyn Shoemaker was named Purdue's first Dean of Women. She expressed to Dr. W. E. Stone, then President of Purdue, that she was awed by his offer of this important post, to which he replied, "Be a man, Miss Shoemaker, be a man! Do not let this or any other task worry you."
>
> Now in the decade of the 70s, which is being called the decade of women, I doubt that any university president anywhere would have the temerity to make such a comment.

Bev ended her two-page letter with this: "And so I say to you, do not let any task you are a capable of handling worry you. 'Be a woman . . . be a 1971 woman!'"

Through the tumultuous late 1960s, Bev Stone demonstrated her capabilities as a sensitive, fair, yet firm leader. No one needed to tell Bev to "be a woman." There would be more for her to handle in the 1970s, but Bev was a woman for all decades.

In 1970, CBS experienced a "pants-in." Helen kept a clipping from the *New York Times* with the headline, "Pants-Ban Tempest at C.B.S." The pants-in demonstration was the result of a memorandum tacked to CBS bulletin boards that stated: "Please be advised that it is not Company Policy nor the discretion of the immediate supervisor for female employees to wear slacks during the course of their normal working hours. Slacks may be worn going to and from the Broadcast Center in the morning and evening; and/or on a lunch hour, business or personal errand."

A "manifesto" was circulated to women at the New York office that read: "Urgent Notice. Anti-CBS Policy, Girls Fight For Your Rights, Wear Pants Tomorrow, Tuesday, January 20, 1970."

About thirty women participated in the CBS pants protest by wearing fashionable slacks to work. The *New York Times* reporter described the ensembles: "Mike Wallace's secretary, Merri Lieberthal (in grey knit),

Harry Reasoner's secretary, Jean Dudasik (in tweed bell bottoms), and Earl Ubell's secretary, Mara Posner (in beige cuffed trousers), had chosen pants to show female solidarity."

The story stated that *Time* magazine employees had received a memo poo-pooing pants with selectivity: "Pants may be 'desirable' when interviewing Katharine Hepburn; "Inappropriate" for questioning Wall Street bankers."

In Purdue's Executive Building, female staff members were not allowed to wear pants above the first floor where the provost and president's offices were located, as well as the Office of the Dean of Women. Dresses and skirts were required apparel for women who worked on the second floor and above.

In 1973, Assistant Dean of Women Betty Nelson read etiquette expert Amy Vanderbilt's opinion on pants in the *Indianapolis Star*. The story stated:

> As for pants, she's [Vanderbilt's] researched the subject of where they can and cannot be worn and comes up with this: "They have no objection to them at the White House. At St. Patrick's (the 5th Ave. cathedral) they pointed out that some brides wear evening pants. Even in the Vatican you can wear a pantsuit.
>
> The only place I know of right now where you wouldn't wear pants is Buckingham Palace. I was there not too long ago in the courtyard to watch the Queen leave for Parliament.

Betty, age thirty-eight, had seen some attractive and stylish pantsuits in the stores. She thought the Amy Vanderbilt story might sway her boss to allow the Office of the Dean of Women staff to wear slacks. Betty said, "So, I thought, 'Hot dog!' We certainly ought to be able to wear pants. I thought I'd give this article to Bev with a diplomatic note. We have nailed this."

Betty's note to Bev—the pinnacle of feminine etiquette—accompanying the Vanderbilt declaration that pants can be worn anywhere but Buckingham Palace read: "This article suggests that you and Queen Elizabeth have some similar status. Is DOW office the Buckingham Palace Annex? In case this might influence you, I want to send it for your review."

In understated, imperial fashion, Bev replied: "Bev's Buckingham-on-the-Wabash may not have royalty—but we all do seem to have royal tastes!"

33
Hip Women

Into the 1970s, Dean of Women Bev Stone attended Board of Trustees meetings as the students' interpreter. Her magnetism and polish bridged the social gap between students and the board. Bev understood the students' quest for freedom and autonomy, and also realized the University's need to place boundaries.

Marylu McEwen, doctoral intern in the Office of the Dean of Women, asked Bev if she could shadow her at a Board of Trustees meeting. The meetings were closed, but there was a window of time where she could attend before the "real" gathering. Marylu described Bev as she appeared before the trustees:

> She wore peep-toe shoes that were slingbacks, except the slingback would always be dropping off her heel. It looked and sounded like her shoes were about to flop off. She was always impeccably dressed. She loved clothes, and she loved to have her nails done.

> She was wearing a suit with her short fur over her shoulders. She wouldn't actually put her arms through it. She would wear sweaters and jackets just perched on her shoulders.
>
> The meeting was in a big conference room, and of course, it was all men in there. Executive Vice President John Hicks was there. He loved her. She walked in this room, with the fur on her shoulder and her shoes flopping, but looking perfectly put together, and smiled and the men just swooned over her. She wasn't playing up; really, that was her identity. It was just who she was. Of course, some of the men didn't know underneath it all was this tough cookie.

Bev was fun, good company, and attractive. She liked attention from men, and she had a number of suitors. One gentleman caller was a doctor she met periodically for dinner. She had opportunities for serious relationships, but she chose not to become tied to another person.

Purdue graduate Teresa Roche came to know and love all of the deans. Today, Roche is vice president and chief learning officer at Agilent Technologies and is married with one daughter. She said:

> Bev never married. Neither did Dorothy or Helen. Barb had married, but her husband died very tragically. Many times I thought about the era in which they were born, the choices that they had to make consciously or unconsciously. What choices did some of them have? They gave so selflessly to so many other women and other students; we were their family. I know that as a mother, and as a working person, I've never tried to have it all, not all at once.
>
> Honestly, I don't know what men would have been strong enough to hold the container of some of these remarkable women.

IN 1969, Associate Dean of Women Barb Cook wrote a paper predicting what the twenty-first century would hold for families, quoting from books and studies. She talked of banks of deep-frozen reproductive cells, both male and female, maintained so that what we thought to be a female function—the bearing and raising of children—would become less so by the twenty-first century. Barb wrote:

> By the year 2000, the family meals will be handled by a computer. . . . Food will come out of the freezer and move into a microwave oven where it will be cooked in a matter of seconds. Meals will be served on plastic plates; when dirty, they will be placed in a special machine, which will re-melt the plastic, clean, it, and reform new plastic plates again. By the year 2000, a robot maid, called . . . a "Uni-mate," which is already being worked on, will be in existence. Costing around the amount of a small car, each household will have one to do routine household tasks.

Barb went on to wonder about the effects of such a society on women. She quoted Professor Wallace Denton of Purdue's Department of Family Life, who said, "This is the thing about which we are most anxious. A woman risks losing her sense of significance or worthwhileness in such a home."

Although some of Barb's predictions did not come to pass exactly as she thought, women were spared the worry that those conveniences would take away their "sense of significance." Instead, women were sold the unattainable scenario of "having it all."

Barb wrote another paper that appeared in the fall 1970 *Journal of the National Association of Women Deans and Counselors,* entitled "Woman's Search for 'A Way of Becoming.'" Barb said to her fellow deans of women and counselors:

> We need . . . to listen very closely to what women are trying to tell us, and even to the way they say it. . . .
>
> A significant number of those who come to a counselor show a kind of workless discontent with the housewife role, but they try to suppress this in the belief that by showing it, they could be disloyal to their loved ones. . . .
>
> Women quite easily deplore some of the concrete tasks with which they fill their days—the washing, cleaning, cooking, sewing so powerfully supported by business and industry trying to sell their products. But the intangible tasks—the loving and caring, the deep sharing of life experiences with husband and children, the ministering to the emotional needs of the family—they often experience these as too little supported, understood, or valued. . . .

Barb ended her piece with words that are still apropos for today and tell of her openness to helping other women: "Women desperately need encouragement and support; surely they ought to be supporting each other. Pioneers travel in groups, and women ought to move in groups as well as individually. In this way each could definitely ease the path for the other, sharing experiences and learning from failures."

Barb was named the 1971 Woman of the Year by Purdue's student chapter of Theta Sigma Phi, a professional organization for women in communications. Stephanie Salter, a former *Exponent* editor, made the presentation. Stephanie said:

> Since my first spring at Purdue, I've wanted to officially praise someone who has made it a habit to do everything she can for the betterment of women. She has encouraged me, personally, and she has always made a good case for picking yourself up and getting back into the fight.
>
> I once used a term in an editorial to describe one of her associates. It's a term I save for outstanding women I meet—those who know what they want and get it. The term is "tough lady" and if I ever met a 100 percent tough lady, it's Mrs. Cook.

Dean of Women Bev Stone was the second woman to receive the Helen B. Schleman Gold Medallion Award in May 1970. As a Mortar Board member, student Sue Daniel Eiler made the presentation on the stage of Purdue's Elliott Hall of Music with six thousand people in attendance. Sue said:

> I highlighted that Bev Stone was universally valued across campus. One of the Students for Democratic Society (SDS), which were the Vietnam War protestors who were about as far left-wing as possible, had said, "You can't trust the administration. Burn Hovde Hall." That was the rhetoric.
>
> A young woman who was an active part of that group was quoted in the *Exponent* as saying, "Bev Stone is a hip woman." I used that quote at the end of my presentation. When Bev heard that, she smiled, stepped to the microphone and said, "Yes, I am one hip woman." And she dramatically patted herself on the hip.

THIS WAS THE SPRING THAT BARB COOK, age forty-one, took the close-knit Mortar Board women on a harrowing canoe trip down Sugar Creek, about thirty miles south of Purdue, near Crawfordsville, Indiana. Barb loved canoeing—it reminded her of her childhood summers spent at Camp Kiwani near Memphis. Bev, on the other hand, didn't want the women to go, for she felt someone could be hurt. Sue Daniel Eiler remembered: "The water was high and none of us except Barb really knew how to canoe. I'm sure Barb almost had a heart attack a few times that day, feeling responsible for these young women on the water who were tipping their canoes. I fell out at one point. You'd hit rock, and there were lots of roots."

One of the women on the trip was Kris LaMar, who had been named Miss Purdue that year. The Miss Purdue Scholarship Pageant is the preliminary to the Miss Indiana and Miss America programs. Often the chance at winning scholarships is the draw that attracts women to beauty pageants—just the reason that Helen Schleman had swallowed her feminist pride and judged the 1955 Miss America Pageant. Women still "endure" a swimsuit competition for monetary gain.

Sue continued: "Back then the Miss Purdue Pageant was a big deal. Kris needed some financial aid and saw it as a way to get scholarships. I think she won for her accomplishments. So she is with us on this canoe trip. We're getting out of the creek, and we all looked like drowned rats. We're walking up hill carrying the canoes, and we're muddy. Some people walked past us, and one of them said, 'Isn't that Miss Purdue?' We thought that was hilarious."

BARB'S CONTRIBUTION TO THE SPRING 1971 *Journal of the National Association of Women Dean and Counselors* was "Roles, Labels, Stereotypes: A Counselor's Challenge." She talked of Bev Stone's strategy for guarding against the elimination of the Office of the Dean of Women. Barb wrote:

> In our office we also make a point of demanding equal representation in every area with the Dean of Men's staff. . . . As the only Dean of Women's Office left in the Big 10, we feel we have a real obligation to hold on.

> My boss, a woman, exploits greatly the communications media open to her so that when any member of her staff does anything, or any woman student does anything, that might be considered slightly newsworthy, she makes a point of providing full publicity. This, at least, calls attention to the fact that there are living, breathing, and functioning women somewhere. . . .

> We must learn to speak out. As women we are accustomed to sit back and not demand the floor. We must learn to speak out before we are asked to react.

Barb and Bev cowrote *Counseling Women* as part of a Guidance Monograph Series, published in 1973 by Houghton Mifflin. The editors summarized the monograph: "Ms. Stone and Cook eloquently and persuasively describe the current situation of the American female both from the vantage point of history and women's contemporary situation. . . . There is little doubt that major forces are operating to change the position of women in society and that even greater alterations will be forthcoming. . . . The authors are to be commended for making available a very readable and thorough treatment of material about which every educator and counselor should be knowledgeable."

In their preface, Bev and Barb thanked Dean of Women Emerita Helen Schleman for reading and editing their manuscript and discussing concepts and issues. One can imagine the three deans sitting in Helen's living room near her Zen-like fountain that flowed into a goldfish pond, sipping wine and discussing the feminist movement.

JUST AS COLLEGE CAMPUSES ERUPTED with student revolts in the late 1960s, women began to rise up in the 1970s like a collective phoenix from the ashes. Sometime those ashes were veiled in seductive false intentions. Virginia Slims cigarettes made by Philip Morris were launched in 1968 with an advertising campaign that became part of American pop culture. "You've come a long way, baby" was the tagline for a new, thinner cigarette marketed to women, banking on the emerging new female who was independent, self-sufficient, and confident, while looking fabulous in a miniskirt and wedge heels.

The ads showed the "old days" in jumpy, black-and-white "footage" of women hiding in chicken coops or attics to smoke until their husbands discovered them and sent them to their rooms. Images of suffragettes marching for the vote appeared, and a male announcer said, "In 1920, women won their rights."

The ad did a *Wizard of Oz* color morphing into the 1970s and showed a modern woman smoking a cigarette as the jingle played, "You've come a long way, baby, to get where you've got to today!" A guttural female voice said: "This is the slim cigarette made just for women. Tailored for the feminine hand. Slimmer than the fat cigarettes men smoke. With rich Virginia flavor women like. In the striped purse pack. You've got your own cigarette now, baby. You've come a long, long way!"

The American Lung Association determined that six years after the introduction of Virginia Slims, the rate of smoking initiated by twelve-year-old girls had increased 110 percent.

To further their "alliance" with women, the cigarette brand sponsored the 1970 Virginia Slims American Women's Opinion Poll, conducted by Louis Harris and Associates. Helen Schleman kept a copy in her files. It was "an in-depth survey on the attitudes of women—America's significant, relatively silent majority."

The eighty-page report covered "Is Protest 'Unladylike'?," "Women's Place in the Home," "Working in a Man's World," "Women on Sex: No Bed of Roses," "Dissatisfactions," "Women Versus the Fashion Industry," "Coping with a Man's World," and "Women as Citizens." Evidently, there were no questions on women's health.

In 1980, Virginia Slims conducted its fourth poll out of the eight they would eventually sponsor, and the report included a letter from Shepard P. Pollack, president of the U.S. branch of Philip Morris. Pollack wrote:

> To Our Friends:
>
> Since the introduction of Virginia Slims in 1968, the brand has always maintained a sense of responsibility to the American woman. It was for this reason that we commissioned the 1970 Virginia Slims American Women's Opinion Poll specifically designed to survey the attitudes of women. . . .

> The 1970s, more than any other decade, has witnessed the greatest change in the status of the American women. We felt it would be both useful and important to update the findings of the previous Virginia Slims Opinion Polls.

Gloria Steinem wrote "Sex, Lies and Advertising" in the first ad-free issue of *Ms. Magazine* in 1990. As the founding editor in 1971, she addressed the missions of the magazine and the financial pressures to run cigarette ads. She wrote:

> When *Ms.* begins, the staff decides not to accept ads for feminine hygiene sprays or cigarettes: they are damaging and carry no appropriate health warnings. . . . the Virginia Slims theme, "You've come a long way, baby," has more than a "baby" problem. It makes smoking a symbol of progress for women. . . .
>
> We agreed to publish an ad for a Virginia Slims calendar as a test. The letters from readers are critical—and smart. For instance: Would you show a black man picking cotton, the same man in a Cardin suit, and symbolize the antislavery and civil rights movements by smoking?"

Findings from the Virginia Slims American Women's Opinion Polls have been quoted in numerous books and papers over the years; however, the accuracy of such a poll is in question when we know the sponsor's intention was to sell more cigarettes as they touted their "sense of responsibility to the American woman."

"You've come a long way, baby" was so pervasive that an *Exponent* story about Bev appeared with that headline in 1973. The accompanying photo of Bev shows her looking tired, wrinkles furrowing her brow. She had been ill and out of the office that fall, and she was given radioactive iodine in the hopes she would feel better. The story was about the change in women's opportunities compared to a decade before. Bev said, "Women no longer believe they cannot succeed—that there's nothing important on this planet for them to do." The story describes the bustling activity in the Office of the Dean of Women: "Each of the deans and counselors is a crusader for women's rights. They can, in fact, hardly remember the days when they had time or regular meals, family activities and a full night's sleep. But their round-the-clock efforts to educate parents, high school counselors, employers and community organizations have paid off."

Both Barb and Helen kept magazine and newspaper clippings about the women's movement in their "speech file." Meanwhile, Dorothy Stratton, age seventy-two, was living in New York City and clipping stories from the *New York Times* and other publications to send to Helen.

In 1971, Dorothy attended the Madison Avenue Presbyterian Church. She sent Helen the worship bulletin from the service, highlighting the minister's sermon, "Adam's Rib and Woman's Lib," based on Genesis 1:27: "So God created man in his own image, in the image of God he created him; male and female he created them."

The minister was Scottish preacher David Read. An author of thirty books, Read had served as the chaplain of the University of Edinburgh and chaplain to Queen Elizabeth II when she was in Scotland.

Dorothy wrote to Helen: "Wish you had been with me yesterday to hear Dr. Read on Adam's Rib and Women's Lib. Will tell you all when I see you. Dr. Gambrell, President of Hunter for a short while and a long-time professor there, sat by me by accident. I thought Dr. Read was pretty good, everything considered. Dr. Gambrell said, 'They are all alike. When it comes right down to the point—equality, I think she meant—they can't face it.'"

Mary Latimer Gambrell was the president of Hunter College in New York, in 1967. She was instrumental in helping Hunter adjust to the admission of male students to the previously all-female college. Dorothy continued:

> I think she may have referred to Dr. Read's emphasis on complementary roles. . . . [He said] "Of course this doesn't mean that women are going to take over 50 percent of the positions held by men or that they are going to be doing the same things as men in the same way." Now you can read that, as you will. I thought he meant that women weren't going to occupy pulpits, be presidents of boards of deacons, etc., but I may have misread him. He didn't elaborate. I think he is as confused as the rest of us. He didn't go into the changes in family life. He quoted from Kate Millett. Obviously has been doing some homework.

Kate Millett was a feminist who wrote *Sexual Politics,* published by the University of Illinois Press in 1970. *Sexual Politics* explored the treatment of women in art and literature, confronting and analyzing revered authors. It was a landmark book, praised and criticized. Millett has been described as one of the most influential Americans of the twentieth century. *Sexual Politics* fueled feminism's second wave. A portrait of Millett by the great American painter Alice Neel appeared on a cover of *Time* magazine in 1970.

Betty Nelson remembered when Millett visited Purdue. Betty said: "In the 1970s, when Kate Millett was a speaker at Purdue on sexual politics, Helen had a reception for her at her house following the lecture. Helen captured the moment, and created a more intimate experience for women on the Dean of Women staff. It was quite an event with Kate addressing issues in a totally avant-garde fashion. She was dressed in a long white caftan with colorful embroidery . . . and looked more like a mystic than anyone I had ever seen before."

34

Entitled to Title IX

On June 23, 1972, President Richard Nixon signed into law an amendment to the Civil Rights Act of 1964, and thirty-seven words changed American women's lives forever. Title IX of the Education Act reads: "No person in the United States shall, on the basis of sex, be excluded from participation in, be denied the benefits of, or be subjected to discrimination under any education program or activity receiving federal financial assistance."

Women stood poised at starting gates all over the United States, and when the Title IX pistol fired, they rode change into every academic and athletic area in the country.

A wave of girls and women poured onto athletic fields and into nontraditional occupations. Title IX helped create numerous social and professional opportunities for women. It has been deemed one of the most successful pieces of civil rights legislation ever passed. But change didn't happen quickly. Title IX—or what a magazine titled *Hoosier Schoolmaster* labeled "The Ladies' Bill of Rights"—forced educational initiatives, from kindergarten to doctoral programs, to scrutinize their conduct for discriminatory practices.

Title IX was the brainchild of U.S. Representative Patsy Mink, an Asian American who was the first woman of color elected to Congress. In the 1960s, her daughter, Gwendolyn, was elected president of the school class, but her teacher forced her to relinquish the title because she felt that a girl should be only vice president. A few years later, Gwendolyn was denied admission to Stanford on the grounds that the university had filled its quota of women. After seeing her daughter's treatment and drawing on her own experiences of bias as an Asian American woman, Patsy Mink coauthored Title IX with Representative Edith Louise Starrett Green.

Title IX originally was created to focus on equity in education, not on athletic programs. But after the law passed, the National Collegiate Athletic Association (NCAA) and the male athletic establishment lobbied to attain an exemption for intercollegiate athletic departments, not wanting to funnel money away from men's athletics. Thus, Mink became fully engaged in the struggle to ensure that athletics were not carved out as an exception. Gwendolyn said, "She knew that exceptions would swallow the rule."

The NCAA's effort to undermine Title IX failed, as did several later attempts. A month after Patsy Mink's death in 2002, Congress renamed the still-intact law the Patsy T. Mink Equal Opportunity in Education Act.

The understanding and ramifications of how to implement Title IX took several years to sort out. What did Title IX mean to organizations that were all-female or all-male, such as national organizations like Girl Scouts, Boy Scouts, YWCA, and YMCA, or on Purdue's campus, the men's society of Iron Key and the women's Mortar Board chapter? Where did the National Association for Women Deans, Administrators, and Counselors (NAWDAC) stand as an organization solely for women? (By 1973, the name of the association had changed to include administrators, a name it would maintain until 1991.)

Barb Cook gave a keynote speech at the 1979 Mortar Board National Conference, and she spoke of Title IX. At first, Barb believed that some groups on campus, particularly Mortar Board, should remain segregated by sex, and she had written a position paper on the subject. Barb said:

> The arguments used in that paper were that groups were necessary to continue affirmative action efforts for women. Historically on American campuses, men have held leadership positions. Society operated to separate women from other women, and that this wasn't the time to abolish the few organizations that served to bring women together. . . .
>
> As one studies Title IX, one begins to realize that one-sex organizations and even athletics are not the important parts of that document. The really significant parts of Title IX deal with equal access to opportunity not based on sex in educational curricula, to professional and graduate schools.

As president of NAWDAC and consultant to Mortar Board when Title IX was implemented, Barb Cook guided these two entities as they eventually welcomed men. As a graduate student, Jane Hamblin, who is now executive director of Mortar Board National College Senior Honor Society, visited Barb in her office. Jane remembered, "There were immense books of regulations piled and strewn everywhere as she was charged with the implementation of many aspects of Title IX on campus. It was natural that Barb would be assigned to establish a process for Mortar Board to decide whether or not to admit men. . . . She had to have broad shoulders to hold the weight of bringing Mortar Board to that decision."

The magnitude of the responsibility was evident in Barb's honest keynote. Fear spurred her to learn as much about Title IX as she could. Barb said:

> As different groups reflecting their own vested interests began to pick at the parts of Title IX that were distasteful to them, I began to think we might lose it all, and I found myself becoming a spokesperson for the legislation. I know it is a burden on institutions—it takes time—it costs money but equality is somewhat finite. It either exists or it doesn't exist. It took me a full year with a great deal of soul searching to reach this conclusion by the fall of 1975.
>
> In this spirit, I helped participate in opening membership to men in the two organizations in which I was involved. One can think, as I sometimes do, that the risk of opening women's groups to men is greater than opening men's groups to women.

In autumn 1975, NAWDAC, under Barb's leadership, removed requirements that excluded male membership. Also that fall, with Barb's consultation, the Mortar Board National College Senior Honor Society opened membership to all qualified students and affirmed a commitment to promote equal opportunity among all people, while also acknowledging the historic and still significant principle to advance the status of women.

Barb was hopeful in her speech to her audience of Mortar Board members who came from campuses across the country:

> I remember leaving that conference in 1975, thinking that if it is ever possible for men and women to enter into a full partnership where there is equal respect for what our society deems masculine qualities and feminine qualities, Mortar Board is surely the place where this can happen. . . . We have always known that it takes strong women to work in a man's world. It also takes strong and understanding men to work in a woman's world.
>
> Perhaps this association together in such a group of equal peers may help us all learn to work someday in a human world where talent, ability, responsible behavior, and creativity are the only required prerequisites for opportunity.

IN 1973, BILLIE JEAN KING and Bobby Riggs played their history-making tennis match, which was about much more than tennis. The deans watched the media hype and clipped stories for their files as the King/Riggs frenzy played out.

The Women's Tennis Association had formed that year and began the worldwide professional tennis tour for women. The predecessor of this tour was the Virginia Slims Circuit, formed in 1970 after nine courageous players, led by King, signed one-dollar contracts with *World Tennis* magazine. The women went against the United States Tennis Association and formed their own tour. Philip Morris cigarettes provided financial backing. The women put their careers at risk to put an end to the inequities of tennis prize money between male and female players. The daring women are known today as the Original 9.

The King/Riggs bout in September was touted as the "Battle of the Sexes" or "Battle of Lib vs. Lip," and it added fuel to the fire of women's liberation and what it meant to be a male chauvinist.

King, age twenty-nine, had won that summer's Wimbledon. In a time when a woman could not obtain a credit card without a man's signature, King had a lot riding on her muscular shoulders: brand spankin' new Title IX, the validity of women's sports, and the very visual example of a female taken seriously for her expertise when pitted against a man. King took the match seriously, training heavily beforehand.

Riggs, age fifty-five, a gambler and long-ago tennis champ, came off as a publicity-seeking buffoon. He granted interviews where he strutted and proudly claimed to be a male chauvinist, denouncing women's liberation. He was so sure he would win that he didn't train.

Nora Ephron wrote a story about Riggs for *Time* magazine. A caricature of Riggs appeared on the cover with the phrase "The Happy Hustler." Ephron quoted Riggs:

> I wish the women would stay in the home and do the work and take care of the babies and compete in the areas they can compete in, because it's a big mistake for them to get mixed up in mixed-sex matches like this. We're going to put those women right back where they belong like they used to be when we had the slippers and the pipe, . . . and they were around the house, and they didn't try to get out and get the man's job away from him. They can't even do it half as good, and they still want the same kind of money. That's why I got involved in this thing in the first place.

The match was played before thirty thousand people in the Houston Astrodome, and it remains on the record books as the largest crowd to watch tennis in the United States. Fifty million Americans viewed the match on television. Riggs entered on a gilded rickshaw and was a walking advertisement as he was paid to wear a canary yellow "Sugar Daddy" (candy) jacket. The jacket was one of his downfalls as he became overheated during the match. King wore a blue-and-white sequined tennis dress and sat like Cleopatra on her own chariot.

King handily won the match against Riggs. A pre-win photo of her waving from her chariot ran in the *Indianapolis Star* with the caption,

"Male chauvinism takes one giant step BACKWARDS . . . [King's] victory . . . is a symbolic one for all women who want to reach their goals, be the goals in athletics or other forms of endeavor."

About his defeat before the whole world, Riggs said, "This was the worst thing in the world I've ever done."

Women's tennis had found a new place in the sun. Barb Cook was watching. In a July 1974 letter to a fellow member of NAWDAC, Barb wrote, "This summer is wild. I am going to leave for a week in August—can't wait. . . . Bad news—Billie Jean King will be playing a tournament the week of our Conference, Damn!"

As women's groups accepted men and male organizations incorporated women, it was only natural that the last Big Ten university in the country to meld the Office of the Dean of Women and the Office of the Dean of Men into one gender-neutral entity would have to face the change. In a 1985 interview, Bev Stone said:

> The Dean of women's position and the Dean of men's position disappeared in 1974 when the two offices were merged into the Dean of Students Office. Many of us had fought such a consolidation for many years. We had seen this happen in lots of other institutions and in almost every instance, a male had been designated as Dean of Students, and the Dean of Women was subordinated to Associate Dean of Students, even though her qualifications were stronger than the Dean of Men's.
>
> The humanistic kinds of things which had been accomplished in many Dean of Women's Offices where on large university campuses the numbers of women were smaller than [the numbers of] men disappeared when offices were merged.
>
> We did not want the personalization that Dorothy [Stratton] had started and we all built upon to disappear.

Bev was offered the position of Dean of Students, which came as an overwhelming surprise to her; however, Bev didn't really want the job of "deaning" 22,000 students. She liked advocating for women and giving them a special place in the University where they knew they would be heard, heralded, and nurtured in an all-female environment. Bev said, "When I was offered the job, I much preferred to keep the situation as it was and to remain as dean of women. When it was evident that it was going to be consolidated, I almost left the University."

It was a difficult decision for Bev to accept the job. She had another offer at Agnes Scott, a private liberal arts women's college. She wrote a note to Helen Schleman saying, "Life at Agnes Scott would be much easier—much less pressure, and I could tackle it with confidence, which I don't have at the moment."

The pressure to take the Purdue position was immense. Female students intently watched Dean Bev Stone, their role model. The few female faculty members were waiting to hear what Bev would decide. Other universities observed the situation to see who would become Purdue's first dean of students. So much was riding on Bev's shoulders, covered by cardigan twinset and a fur coat.

In the end, Bev accepted the position because she loved Purdue students. Prior to taking on her new role in July 1974, Bev was on a flight to Denver and wrote a note on Continental Airlines stationery to Helen: "Thank you for your loving and supportive note last night and one again this morning. I know I must have been a difficult person for everyone to be around these past few weeks of indecision. I was torn between Buffalo and Purdue in 1956, and that was the most difficult decision professionally I had ever made. This one was even more difficult for a number of reasons. I hope several years hence I will be as sure I made the right one as I am about the earlier one."

Purdue physics professor Anna Akeley happened to be on the leg of the flight to Chicago, and the two talked in the airplane of Bev's new position. In her thick Austrian accent, Anna said, "You could not have let the women at Purdue down. The men would have said, 'See, we give women a chance and they won't take it!' Helen Schleman will help you. She knows everything about organization of such a program."

This was the year Bill Moreau began a lifelong friendship with Barb and "her sidekick" Bev. Bill was editor of the *Exponent*. He remembered:

> This was the Watergate era, when every student journalist aspired to root out scandal, topple administrations, and be the Woodward/Bernstein of our campus. I unleashed . . . *Exponent* reporters to scrutinize every action of the Purdue administration, with the going-in assumption that someone must be lying. The biggest cheerleaders on campus for a vibrant, relevant *Exponent* were Barb and Bev.
>
> We all awoke one day to learn the VP for Student Services Bill Fischang had decided to merge the offices of the dean of men and dean of women into a single dean of students and had appointed Bev to the position. No prior notice, no study committee, no search committee—"poof." We ran a story blasting the process—while carefully applauding the outcome. Our cartoonist, however, thought this was a dandy time to create a picture of Bill Fischang displayed as the Fairy Godmother turning Bev, as Cinderella, into the princess with a wave of his wand.

When the paper appeared, Bill felt guilty. He was too apprehensive to call Bev directly, so he phoned Barb for a reaction. Barb could barely suppress her delight. She and Bev agreed completely with the article and loved the cartoon. Bev gathered every copy she could find. It turned out that Bev and Barb had fought with the administration for a public process and a search committee.

The cartoon prompted the deans to create a "poofer." They obtained an eight-inch stick, attached a cardboard star covered in aluminum foil, and added a white bow made from fuzzy yarn. The poofer was waved whenever something fortuitous occurred or over someone's head when good fortune came their way. Betty Nelson kept the poofer in her desk drawer until her retirement in the 1990s. She said, "One thing always led to another for us."

Bev wrote her last annual report from the Office of the Dean of Women, and she titled it "The End of an Era." She began the report by retelling the legendary story of Carolyn Shoemaker and the "Be a man" adage from President Winthrop Stone. Bev said, "Today, I doubt that any male administrator would offer the charge 'Be a man' to any woman administrator, even in jest." Bev's very presence and professional tact was evidence enough that she did not need to act like a man to be a leader.

Barb Cook was chairman of the consolidation committee to bring the offices together, which had differing methods of paperwork, protocol, and goals for students. Betty Nelson was a member of the committee. The group that felt the most apprehensive about the reorganization was the clerical staff for the Office of the Dean of Men, particularly the office manager. In the beginning, this was not known by Bev and the committee. Barb said, "It took us a little while to be sensitive to the secretarial concerns. We finally picked up on that and involved every one of them on committees." Betty said, "I think they felt like the least powerful entity in the whole reorganization."

One may wonder if Bev and Barb "talked shop" while living in the house they shared on Summit Drive. Close friend Sally Watlington said, "I think they tried not to talk about work a lot. That would have really made them crazy."

In staff meetings, Bev and Barb balanced each other. Sandy Monroe worked in the dean's office as a counselor. She said, "We would be in a staff meeting, and Bev would be telling us something about a new policy or something that's up and coming, and then Barb would say, 'Bev, I just think that's stupid' or 'that's ridiculous.' She'd mumble something under her breath. Bev would smile and go on. Bev may have felt the same way, but she was never going to say it."

Bev's promise to students was that the Office of the Dean of Students would provide the kind of personal attention that was available at smaller institutions. When Bev retired in 1980, Assistant Dean for Administration Dick Walbaum wrote her a letter about what he thought when she was named dean of students. He also summed up Bev's career, accomplishments, and personality:

> I must admit to skepticism when you were chosen as the first Dean of Students. The job of uniting two offices and altering our sexist preferences for separatism was gigantic. Yet you handled the challenges with ease and, in so doing, gained the respect of the entire University community. You simply allowed no room for negative sentiment.
>
> Even more remarkable, the improvements made in the office were accomplished without upsetting the system. Sometimes you received

> support from the upper echelon and sometimes you just ventured forward on your own, but the result was the same: you demonstrated that Purdue could have a single office that was effective in dealing with both men and women. You further disproved the myth that Purdue could only be managed by men. . . .
>
> Since you handled the responsibilities without being branded as a "crusader" or a "pioneer," you accomplished the ultimate—doing something without people even knowing what was being done, let alone believing that there were any other alternatives.
>
> Still your greatest asset is your way with people. You have a kind word for everyone; you care and you listen. You are infectiously fun and people always enjoy being with you. If there is a selfish bone in your body, it's never been found.

It took Bev several years after she accepted the position of dean of students to admit that it was a good move for the University and for herself. She described her leadership style: "When you are responsible for a staff in our society, not only do you need to be aggressive, but also you need to walk a tight rope, and particularly as a woman, you do need tact. You have to be political if you want to accomplish some of your goals. You have to be careful that you don't go out like a firefighter swinging an ax or you won't accomplish what you hope to accomplish."

35

The Hand That Rocks the Cradle Can Rock the Boat

Through the 1970s to 1980s, the deans became salary watchdogs for female faculty at Purdue. Retired Helen Schleman led the way from her home on Western Drive. She asked her friend, John Hicks, executive assistant to then Purdue President Arthur Hansen for the "black book."

The black book was a computer-generated listing of all Purdue salaries. The book was actually sheets of the old-style "tractor-feed" computer paper. Sally Watlington helped Helen with the numbers in the late 1970s, although Helen had begun her investigative work of Purdue women's salaries and ranks a decade before. Sally said, "When Helen was doing the study on salaries, I was doing the math. She had this IBM computer printout, and I'm taking a ruler going down through the list, giving her the numbers and the names. She finally got that thing finished in 1980 or 1981. Boy was she irritated. She had completed the salary tabulations multiple times with several iterations—all handwritten. She didn't type because she never wanted to be assigned to be the secretary of anything."

This was a time before the Access to Public Records Act (APRA) was in place, and people were not yet allowed to openly access government documents. Today, several of Helen's hand-scrawled tables of statistics on salaries and faculty positions of Purdue women compared to that of Purdue men are housed with her papers in the Purdue Libraries Archives and Special Collections.

Cindy Metzler, the president of the Association of Women Students (AWS), presented a speech to the Purdue Women's Club in 1970, entitled "The Status of Women at Purdue University." She used Helen's data in her presentation, and her speech set off a string of unexpected events that began slowly to turn the tide of discrimination for female faculty and staff at Purdue. Metzler wrote:

> The actual breakdown of the figures can be rather revealing as to what the women employed by the University are actually doing. In the supervisory category there were 527 men classified as administrators and 215 women. But most of the women in the category are almost completely lacking in any sort of real administrative authority. Of these 215 women in the administrative category, 43 are classified as administrative officers and the remaining 172 as administrative assistants. The majority of the 43 administrative officers can be found in the residence hall kitchens. As if this was not enough to indicate that the women do not hold the most visible decision-making positions! . . .
>
> There do not seem to be many visible role models for the women students in decision-making roles.

Next, a bold move by a young woman furthered publicity of the inequality. A graduate student who was a women's liberation proponent obtained a copy of Metzler's speech and sent it to the Women's Equity Action League (WEAL), which was founded in Cleveland, Ohio, in 1968 to promote economic equality for women by focusing on educational, legal, and tax issues that impacted women. The organization is best known for its initiatives to reduce sexism in American colleges and universities.

After receiving a copy of Metzler's speech, WEAL filed a complaint with the Department of Health, Education, and Welfare (HEW), charging Purdue University with sex discrimination. A sex discrimination suit also had been filed against the University of Maryland and the University of Michigan that year.

After the dean of women staff and Metzler made speeches using Helen's faculty ranking data and the University was buzzing with rumors of their eye-opening exposés, John Hicks invited Bev to meet with fellow deans and vice presidents in November 1970 to discuss the situation.

Once Bev met with the group, the Office of the Dean of Women urged Hicks to create a Committee on the Status of Women, which the president did in May 1971, naming Bev as chairman. The committee was comprised of fifteen female members of Purdue's faculty and administration. Helen handed her salary and ranking tabulations to Bev for use in her committee's findings.

Barb Cook used the same data in her own talk given to the Indiana University at Kokomo College Colloquium in January 1971. She pointed out Purdue's lack of role models for female students: "We have six department heads who are women—all in the fields of home economics, physical education for women, and nursing. In our school of humanities, in which 75 percent of our students are women, there is no woman department head. There are no women academic deans or assistant deans except again in our school of home economics. There is certainly no woman president or women vice presidents. There is one woman on our Board of Trustees, and she is there because state law requires at least one woman."

Barb continued with questions that, today, show how far women have come, though more work still needs to be done. Many twenty-first-century women have broken through glass ceilings, but they float above the shattered glass all alone—single females among clouds of men. Barb said, "How many of you sitting here this afternoon know a woman judge, a woman high school principal, have you ever heard of a woman surgeon, or a woman astronaut? Most of you, I would wager, don't even think that these are appropriate roles for women, and they aren't—not yet—not in our society. We have historically and carefully prescribed roles for both men and women in our society, and this cultural prescription by sex is the enemy, which the women's liberation movement is trying to dispel."

By 1973, Helen had moved on to monitoring retirement benefits for Purdue's female faculty and administrators. The Purdue Women's Caucus, consisting of Helen and twenty Purdue women who were full professors, filed a charge of discrimination against Teachers Insurance and Annuity Association-College Retirement Equities Fund (TIAA-CREF) and Purdue University. The group claimed that women were paid lower pension benefits than men, even though equal contributions were made to the pension program. The complaint said, "We feel that the decision to use sex as the sole criterion for differentiation of payments than to include other factors . . . is . . . discriminatory."

TIAA-CREF is the retirement plan founded by philanthropist Andrew Carnegie. The historical irony here was that Purdue's first "unofficial" Dean of Women Emma McRae had been the first female faculty member to receive a Carnegie Foundation grant after her retirement in 1912.

TIAA claimed that because women in the general population lived longer, female faculty should receive lower periodic benefits. However, the only variable that TIAA used in determining benefits was gender, ignoring the different life expectancies, for instance, of smokers and nonsmokers, blacks and whites, and those with hazardous jobs. The difference in benefits was substantial; retired female faculty members received about 15 percent less than men with similar service at Purdue. In one case, the discrepancy amounted to $90 per month.

Five years later, the Equal Employment Opportunity Commission (EEOC) announced a decision on the complaint made by the Purdue Women's Caucus, saying, "the use of sex-segregated actuarial tables to determine unequal employment benefits violates Title VII." Title VII of the Civil Rights Act of 1964 protects individuals against employment discrimination on the basis of race and color, as well as national origin, sex, and religion. TIAA and Purdue were found to be discriminating against female retirees. The EEOC urged all parties to negotiate. The Purdue Women's Caucus agreed. TIAA and Purdue refused.

The Purdue Women's Caucus wrote President Arthur Hansen a letter, which read: "We would welcome the opportunity to meet with you or your representative to discuss the case and explain the position of the AAUP [American Association of University Professors] and the Purdue Women's Caucus on the matter. Given Purdue's commitment to affirmative action under guidelines from HEW, it seems to us that the University would want to go on record as supporting the rights of women employees to equal retirement benefits."

Hansen wrote a return letter: "I appreciate your letter of February 19 and the statement of your 'equal in-equal out' retirement benefits from TIAA-CREF. The position of the University currently is to await the outcome of several Department of Justice lawsuits pending against TIAA and various universities. This issue is fraught with complexity, as readings of the appellate courts to date have clearly indicated. Without a clear signal from the courts I think the University is not in a position to decree on what is 'fair.'"

TIAA had announced that it would begin to use unisex insurance tables on July 1, 1980, but would only pay equal benefits from contributions made after that date. Helen wrote in a memorandum to the Purdue Women's Caucus members: "What does this mean? Women will not receive benefits equal to men of the same age and service until 2020 when a woman who begins employment at age thirty in 1980 retires. Surely this is not the equality envisioned in Title VII of the Civil Rights Act of 1964. Forty years is too long to wait!"

Helen was seventy-eight when she decided enough was enough. She had been fighting for women's rights since she stepped on Purdue soil in 1933. It had been nearly fifty years, and she was still willing to stand up for what was right, no matter the cost.

In 1980, a committee of Purdue women filed a class action suit in U.S. District Court on behalf of the Women's Caucus alleging that Purdue and its retirement programs violated the Civil Rights Act of 1964. The suit demanded full equalization of benefits, plus back pay to past female retirees. Helen was quoted in an *Exponent* story about the suit: "Women have traditionally been at the bottom of the pay scale. Unequal retirement benefit scales add up to a sizeable disadvantage. After all, retirement pay isn't a gift. It is earned. It's only a form of delayed compensation."

The judgment was handed down on March 27, 1987, and each member of the class with an annuity issued prior to March 24, 1972, was awarded an equal division of a $20,000 payment. TIAA and CREF also were ordered to match annuity benefits for those women in the class action suit issued from that date to May 1, 1980. Expenses and attorneys fees were to be paid by Purdue University, TIAA, and CREF. As a result of the seven-year lawsuit, Purdue was ordered not to contribute to any employee retirement benefit plans unless the benefits derived were calculated without regard to gender. Purdue women won the battle for equalization of benefits, plus back pay to past female retirees.

In 1981, Helen again tabulated the latest salaries of men and women at Purdue and sent her list to President Hansen. She then set up a meeting with Hansen and asked for a computer printout of the University's data on salaries. After her meeting, Helen was despondent and wrote:

> I had just come from a one-hour "appointment" with President Hansen (I thought). It turned out to be Provost Haas *and* President Hansen. I think this made a change in the conversation somewhat. I was totally surprised by having V.P. Haas there. They had both obviously "studied" the salaries as I had listed them.
>
> I asked right away whether a computer printout had been requested. I said I thought it was very important that the people who had to deal with the material have complete confidence in their data. I doubt if they will ask for one. At the end, President Hansen said it was an "embarrassing" report. My guess is that they don't want to give it the dignity of the legitimacy of an "official" report.

Hansen's position was that Purdue paid what the marketplace dictated. Helen countered:

> I thought somebody had to take leadership in rearranging the values of the market place.... I was very specific that I thought ... Purdue ... had a responsibility to help teach women how to be university presidents, deans, etc., that the reason they couldn't find women "qualified' in the way they wanted them qualified was because they hadn't taken them as assistants to learn the game....
>
> The conversation was pleasant, but I came away feeling that I had disturbed them, but probably hadn't done any good. The president did say, "Someone had to speak up." I said I had done it because anyone employed really didn't dare to and that I had nothing to lose.

In 1972, Bev gave a talk to the Purdue Women's Club, explaining the function and timeline of her Committee on the Status of Women. She began with a quote from *Children's Letters to God:*

> Dear God,
>
> Are boys better than girls? I know you are one, but please try and be fair.
>
> Love, Sylvia

36

Easier to Move a Cemetery

Periodically, the staff in the Office of the Dean of Women traded responsibilities to keep a fresh view. As Betty Nelson said, "It was a great way to change jobs without having to pack up all your belongings in a Mayflower van."

In the mid-1970s, Celie Zissis was responsible for providing support for students with disabilities. She was ready to change hats and move that role to someone else. That someone was Betty. As she passed the hat, Celie said, "There's not much to do in this area." Betty thought that was good because she had no training in providing support to disabled students. At that time, there were two students at Purdue who were visually impaired. The Purdue campus was so challenging, architecturally and programmatically, that people with disabilities did not enroll.

Then came the Rehabilitation Act of 1973. Betty said, "Celie got out of Dodge just in time."

A printed copy of the legislation and a cover letter arrived on Betty's desk. The terms were printed in tiny type on thin newsprint. Betty said, "At first, I didn't understand all of the ramifications." She soon learned that it was "the third leg on the civil rights stool."

Legislation had passed to ensure that minorities received their rights to access; women had pressed for legislation in an attempt to pass the Equal Rights Amendment; and now the disabled wanted a user-friendly environment in the third effort of the civil rights movement. Betty recalled, "I quickly learned this would not be an easy assignment. Our Purdue history caught up with us. We had an old campus with old buildings constructed in the traditional style with steps and more steps."

Purdue's buildings were a product of a timeworn Indiana regulation that required every classroom to have natural ventilation, before the advent of air-conditioning. Purdue's structures were built with the bottom floor half underground so that the window ledges are at street level, allowing windows to be opened to the breeze. Betty said, "That was a practical way for meeting the requirements for natural ventilation, but it was terrible for people with mobility limitations to get into a building. They would approach the front of the building and have outside steps to climb, walk inside to a vestibule, and immediately have to go down a half-flight or up a half-flight."

Representatives from Indiana's state universities formed a group to study how to implement the requirements of the Rehabilitation Act on individual campuses. Implementation was required by 1976. This group was the nucleus that formed the Indiana Higher Education Committee on Disabled Students (Indiana AHEAD). Betty said, "We needed to determine what it all meant. How would we make the changes? How would we convince institutional leaders what we had to do? After a couple of meetings, I began to take someone from Purdue's physical facilities and the University architect with me to get some other people on board."

At a conference in Washington, DC, regarding the implementation of the Rehabilitation Act, an attendee who was a faculty member at another university made a statement that stuck with Betty. He said, "You will find that it's easier to move a cemetery than to change your academic institution when it comes to accessibility."

There were no appropriations to accompany the legislation that demanded a college campus to be accessible to all people, which translated to the addition of lifts, elevators, automatic doors, curb cuts, ramps, left-handed desks, handicapped-accessible restrooms, and parking for *every* building. Betty said, "Businesspeople at Purdue were not thrilled about giving up a lot of money to make very expensive changes in the institution. Clearly, we were going to be in legal difficulty if we didn't begin to show faith that we were moving in the direction of making the campus accessible. It was similar to implementing Title IX—opening the door of opportunity wider so women could participate was as unpopular to some as creating an accessible environment for those with disabilities."

It was helpful when a faculty member, a department head, or a member of the advisory committee had a family member with a disability. They understood that students with disabilities had a right to a Purdue education as much as the "temporarily able-bodied." This was a term that Betty and the committee coined to drive home the fact that one in four people will have a temporary or long-term disability before age fifty. Accessibility should be the concern of all.

To handle the monumental task of transforming a university founded in 1869 into a twentieth-century institution accessible by all, for three years Betty worked part-time in the Office of the Dean of Students and part-time in the Office of the President; however, for hardworking Betty, it was like having two full-time positions. She said, "Half-time here and half-time there never adds up to one." So much for Celie's reassurance that "There's not much to do in this area."

Betty reported to laid-back Vice President John Hicks. She wanted to make the changes as quickly as possible, but Hicks knew the modifications would be rolled out in due time, and he helped Betty keep on an even keel.

There was work to do in every corner of the campus, and just conducting an inventory of needs was a major undertaking. Chris Berg was a student in a landscape architecture course, and she needed a project. She inventoried the campus for accessibility and created a map. The document was an unrefined inventory, but it served as an essential component to moving awareness and action forward.

A year after the first crude but crucial map was made, Purdue's Tomahawk Service and Leadership Honor Society took on the responsibility of taking an accessibility inventory of the campus as a service project. The students visited buildings and asked questions like, "What does it mean to have an accessible entrance?" and "How should ramps be fashioned?" Because of Berg's and Tomahawk's work, the University decided to produce an official accessibility map.

The first lift—a small, open elevator that one can roll onto and move up or down a half-flight—in Indiana was installed in Hovde Hall. Because the lift was such a new piece of equipment, state elevator inspectors came en masse to meet with Purdue's physical plant staff to inspect the contraption. Betty said:

> We had to learn what was necessary to pass inspection so we could put lifts in a number of our buildings.
>
> We had much to learn because we had so many impediments to disabled students. Some of the public spaces were especially sensitive—the Hall of Music, Mackey Arena, and Ross-Ade Stadium were not constructed to accommodate people with mobility limitations. Parking was a huge conundrum. Stewart Center was a challenge to ramp, and the ramp at the north door is one of the longest you will find anywhere.

A group of students with disabilities was enlisted as consultants to make suggestions and critique changes. These students had been accepted as Purdue University students, but they could not access classroom space because of physical barriers. Betty said, "We became a working group, and they were wonderful. They'd get a little crabby about all of the things we didn't have, but for the most part the focus was always on, 'How do we make things better?'"

The more the student consultants interacted with Purdue's personnel, the more committed the staff was to helping. The effort took on a human element once employees had faces and names to match the students in need. Two of those students were sisters, Sharon Arvin Byrkett and Janie Arvin. Both wheelchair users, Sharon and Janie were born with muscular dystrophy. Sharon led the movement on campus to create physical access and awareness. As a result of what she and the group fostered, Sharon was able to attend a Purdue Christmas Show in Elliott Hall of Music, enter Stewart Center to attend meetings, and park reasonably close to her classes. Sharon went on to become a state leader in the promotion of services for people with disabilities.

In the late 1970s, the group of student consultants planned "Handicap Awareness Week" with "Awareness Day" being a powerful experience for the brave individuals who consented to participate. The group asked twenty people from administration, faculty, and staff to be assigned a disability for one day. Purdue's chief of police became a wheelchair user. A disabled student in a wheelchair accompanied him. Participants were given an itinerary that instructed them where to go on campus and what to accomplish. Betty said:

> They started at about 9:30 in the morning when they received their assignment in Stewart Center. Getting out of Stewart Center was a major accomplishment. "Which doors can I use? Where is the elevator? I need to go to the bathroom before I go." All those ordinary things became very good learning opportunities. After they'd gone through their scavenger hunt for the day, they returned at about 3:00 p.m.
>
> They would be exhausted. We would have a "talk back," asking questions such as, "What was your experience like? What did you learn? What do we need to do? What are the priorities?"

Some administrators declined when asked to participate. Candidly, one said, "It reminds me too much of how vulnerable I am."

One of the assignments for the chief of police was to go to the Engineering Administration Building where the police department was housed and obtain a parking permit. There were railroad tracks near the building. Betty said:

> As soon as his wheels hit that rail, they turned so he was stuck on the railroad track. His helper, also in a wheelchair, couldn't help him. He had to wait for a student who was strong enough to help him over the track. When he got to the police department, he realized that there were steps outside to get into that space. Of course, he couldn't do it. There

> was no ramp. He started throwing rocks at the window. The glass was opaque, so whoever was on the other side couldn't see that their chief was outside throwing rocks at the window. It was a long time before he was able to get any help.
>
> After he got somebody's attention, they had to bring a clipboard out to him so he could fill out the form to apply for a parking permit. He was asked on the form to indicate that he had a disability and provide documentation to prove it.

By the beginning of the next semester, a wheelchair-accessible ramp had been installed outside the front door of the police station.

Barb Cook participated in Awareness Day and became blind for one day. She was blindfolded and provided with a cane and an assistant as she walked the campus. Betty said, "It was traumatic for Barb. She burst into tears at the end. It had been so disconcerting to be in this world, which she really knew, but was disoriented the whole day and feeling very, very vulnerable."

Betty's charge to implement the Rehabilitation Act of 1973 was reminiscent of the President's Committee on Employment of the Physically Handicapped, of which Dorothy Stratton was a charter member in 1962, chairing the Women's Committee with Helen Schleman as a participant. Their work to remove architectural barriers, which barred people with disabilities from places of employment, began a decade before Betty's enterprise.

In 1978, Dorothy, age seventy-nine, was retired and living in a beautiful colonial on Poverty Hollow Road in Newtown, Connecticut. She continued to volunteer as chairman of the President's Committee on Employment of the Physically Handicapped. By this time, twenty-eight women's organizations, along with individual members, comprised the Women's Committee.

Dorothy was interviewed for the *Newtown Bee* about her life, emphasizing her public service. The reporter asked Dorothy about the status of women and the disabled, and wrote: "Miss Stratton thinks that while opportunities for women have improved, so have they also for the handicapped. 'There's definitely a big change among the handicapped,' she said. 'And they themselves have done a great deal. I certainly hope the President's Committee helped with this.'"

As the chairman of the Women's Committee, Dorothy had spearheaded the push for legislation that mandated the provision of accessible facilities in federally funded buildings, like universities. Dorothy said, "The big push is to get handicapped persons educated with so-called 'normal' people. There's all the talk now about human rights. Well, living a full life is a human right, and I think we have come to feel that way about the handicapped."

Betty and others from Purdue visited the University of Illinois, which had been architecturally accessible since the end of World War II thanks to Tim Nugent, professor of rehabilitation education and director of the Rehabilitation Education Center. He had refitted the Illinois campus to accommodate veterans with physical disabilities. In the 1960s, Nugent advised in the creation of building standards that were developed by the President's Committee on Employment of the Physically Handicapped. His was a name that Dorothy and Helen knew well. Betty said:

> A group of us from Purdue spent an entire day going through the University of Illinois campus seeing what they were doing for students with disabilities. We must have seemed liked toddlers learning from our big brother. It was easy to be envious of Tim and the remarkable environment he spearheaded at Illinois—not only the bricks and mortar work, but also the attitude of people on campus who welcomed students with disabilities. On the other hand, by coming to the party late, we could learn from Illinois and try to avoid some of the pitfalls they had encountered.

Some Purdue administrators suggested that one university in the region be designated for disabled students, and Purdue would support that initiative financially. To that idea Betty said, "Well, that isn't what the law says we are to do."

While it was a challenge to alter the campus landscape to become accessible, the architectural changes were easy compared to changing the perceptions of faculty, particularly when a student had an invisible challenge, such as hearing loss or a learning disability. Betty said, "The faculty had come through schools where there was this separation of people with disabilities. They were not comfortable . . . especially if they couldn't see the disability. So that was hard."

Budgeting ahead of time for needs, such as expensive sign language interpreters, was difficult. Betty said:

> I felt like I was in hot water all of the time because I was supposed to be able to estimate what this budget would be and then not use as much as I asked for. I would receive complaints, "This is really expensive. Can't you make it a little less?" I started working more closely with Ken Burns, who was executive vice president and treasurer. Physical facilities reported to Ken, and our needs fell under that department. He understood why we could not create a budget for the next year. It was just pick a number, whatever you want, put it in. We just can't estimate.
>
> Ken was wonderful. He understood the conundrum that we had. He had a nice attitude. If you have money you can make available, that is as good as it gets.

Friend Sally Watlington described Betty's tenacity during this time: "Had she not been very persistent—like a baby bulldog—providing assistance to those with disabilities would have bogged down into nothing. There were those on campus who held the funds and weren't very pleased about having to pay for the changes needed. Attempted road blocks simply didn't work with Miss Betty M. on duty!"

The cost of creating curb cuts in sidewalks was funded through a project initiated by students Gregg Poorman and David Huxhold. In 1977, Purdue needed approximately three hundred curb cuts to make the entire campus sidewalk accessible. A six-to-eight-inch curb is impossible for a wheelchair to climb. Up until then most of the curb cuts had been created on the basis of individual student needs.

Poorman had been active in Purdue intramural sports and was a wide receiver on the varsity football team. He was an aspiring airline pilot in basic training with the marines, where he was to learn to fly. The summer between his sophomore and junior years, he worked at a day camp for underprivileged children. One day, a girl's sock was thrown into a pine tree, and Poorman climbed the tree to retrieve it.

As Poorman reached for the sock, the top of the tree snapped off and he fell thirty-five feet to the ground. Poorman said, "I missed boot camp by three days and thirty-five feet."

Poorman eventually returned to Purdue as a paraplegic who used a wheelchair, and although the campus was not accessible, provisions were made for him to attend classes. In December 1976, Poorman and an agriculture economics major were the first student wheelchair-users to graduate from Purdue.

As a grad student, Poorman evaluated the campus and said in an October 18, 1977 *Exponent* article, "You can't get from one side of this campus to the other and the reason is there are not enough ramps and curb cuts to do so." Poorman and his friend proposed that student organizations sponsor the creation of curb cuts. The name of the sponsoring group was pressed into the fresh cement of the curb cut, which would cost $250 each. If the cost was more because of location needs, the physical plant would make up the difference. Betty was quoted: "When the recent federal legislation was passed requiring universities to make facilities accessible to the disabled, Purdue requested $750,000 from the Indiana State Legislature for architectural modification. The Commission on Higher Education and the legislature turned down this request."

From a campus map showing the most critical locations, organizations were able to choose which curb they wanted to cut. Betty said, "It became a hot ticket to have your group's name on the sidewalk."

Looking back on her duty to make Purdue accessible to all, Betty said, "The staff who worked with me was wonderful. We had a mission, and we knew we were right and the institution needed to change. It made a difference; you could see the difference it made for people."

Yet unlike her fellow deans, Helen, Barb, and Bev, whose former students returned to campus year after year and visited them in their homes over Homecoming Dean of Women Punch, many of Betty's students did not live long enough to make the pilgrimage back. She said, "Gregg Poorman, who was instrumental in getting the curb cut program going, was swimming one day and experienced cramps. He came up from the water too fast and died. Sharon and Janie Arvin, who both had muscular dystrophy, are deceased. I'm realizing what a fragile group that was. At least three other members of that first consulting group died within a few years: Sandy Jones, Mark Hahn, and Francis Pearl."

However, the legacy of the students who led the movement for change on Purdue's campus remains. Today, ramps, lifts, automatic doors, curb cuts, handicapped-accessible restrooms, handicapped-accessible parking, and sign language interpreters are a natural part of Purdue's everyday panorama.

Once the Office of the Dean of Students established support for students with learning disabilities through the Adaptive Learner Program, the number served increased dramatically. In the 1982 school year, the number of students with documented learning disabilities on campus was just 24, and by 1994, Purdue welcomed 530 such students. The "invisible" disabilities were addressed, and Purdue welcomed those with special needs.

About the shift in culture Betty stated, "It's exciting to be around when a change as dramatic as that takes place. That's a piece of the link back to Dorothy, who was on the president's commission on the handicapped a zillion years ago. That's how long it takes. Even though it's as hard to change an institution as it is to move a cemetery, Purdue moved—with reluctance—but it moved."

37

And She Did It!

Near a corner of Bev Stone's tastefully decorated office hung a hand-embroidered sampler that read, "People are lonely because they build walls instead of bridges."

Bev was the consummate bridge builder, even when it may have put her life in danger. Bev picked up hitchhikers. While driving to work in her mammoth blue Buick, she would stop in the middle of the road if she saw a hitchhiker she presumed was a Purdue student—*her* student. Despite her colleagues' reprimands and warnings of the dangers of picking up strangers, Bev continued her taxi service.

In January 1978, Bev, age sixty-one, saw graduate student Bill Riesser walking in the Ross-Ade Stadium parking lot. She stopped her car and offered him a ride. The meeting ended up becoming a topic of a letter Riesser submitted to the *Exponent*. Riesser wrote, "Although I didn't have far to go, I accepted, as it was sort of cold. An elderly lady was driving and introduced herself as Beverley Stone, Dean of Students."

Helen Schleman kept the newspaper clipping. She underlined the words "an elderly lady."

Riesser asked Bev what she was doing picking up strangers with all the concern on campus about safety. Bev said, "I've been around here long enough that I know a student when I see one. I like to help students when I can."

Bev had picked up a disgruntled student. The gist of Riesser's letter was to vent about an incident a few years prior when a friend of his had accused a teaching assistant of rape. According to Riesser, Bev had been in charge of the hearing and she said, "The coed was not the sort of person who could profit from attending Purdue." Riesser accused the administration of blaming the victim and admonished them for not giving Bev guidance in the matter.

On the *Exponent* clipping, Helen wrote, "Bev never turned a hair about this letter. She has taken much ribbing on this, needless to say. She has had dozens of telephone calls from faculty and students all indignant at the 'attack' on her—also follow-up letters to the *Exponent* to her. She says she has never had better publicity in her life—with more positive support."

One letter of support was from Bill England, who knew both Riesser and Bev and arranged a meeting. England said, "I felt somewhat as if my own mother or grandmother had been slandered, and I could not let that letter go unanswered. I arranged a meeting between Dean Stone, Bill, and myself, and through Dean Stone's wisdom and understanding of people and students, Bill and I both profited from that experience."

Another incident occurred that proved Bev's bravery and caring for all students. A student had threatened the Office of the Dean of Students staff and had been placed in a local mental health facility. The next week he was apprehended on suspicion of several felonies and incarcerated. Bev knew that being confined in jail could aggravate this student's mental state, and she tried to convince the police to readmit him for observation at the mental health facility. After her efforts to obtain his transfer to the facility failed, Bev wrote a personal check to cover bail and took custody of him so she could find an appropriate place to help her student.

In 1975, Student Body President Mark Lubbers was to speak at the freshmen welcoming convocation. Mark had just met Bev, who he said was "gentle and gracious" with "the finest manners north of the old Confederacy."

On that hot August day, five thousand students waited in the Elliott Hall of Music. Mark was to speak after President Arthur Hansen and before Bev, who stood behind him offstage. Mark remembered: "The Glee Club was finishing its last number, and we were signaled—fifteen seconds. We waited quietly in between . . . gigantic stage curtains. I was nervous. Then, like a shot, I felt a sharp poke in my back and an equally sharp command: 'Get rid of that gum!' I didn't dare turn around. The gum was swallowed."

Over the course of that year, Bev and Mark shared many projects. Mark said, "I learned very quickly that she was incredibly smart and worked unbelievably hard. She appreciated dissent and sought it out. Consoling me one day after a disagreement I was having with a colleague, she reminded me, 'If two people agree on everything, one of them is superfluous.' I learned a lot from my year with the dean—a lot about myself and a lot about life. And we came to love each other in a very special way."

When Mark and his wife, Teresa, who became an Indiana State Representative, had their first daughter in 1984, they gave Bev a namesake, Elizabeth Stone Lubbers. By happenstance, Bev was in Indianapolis the day after "Betsy" was born, and she was able to hold the baby. "Auntie Bev" bestowed her wisdom on the girl in the years to come. When Betsy was seven, Bev taught her a rhyme:

> Somebody said it couldn't be done,
> but she with a chuckle replied:
>
> That maybe it couldn't, but she'd be the one
> Who wouldn't say so 'til she tried.
>
> So she buckled right in,
> with a bit of a grin on her face.
> If she worried she hid it.
>
> She started to sing,
> as she tackled the thing that couldn't be done.
>
> And she did it!

BEV RETIRED IN 1980. The *Exponent* described Bev's position with this headline: "Dean of students plays ringmaster to circus." The numbers alone sounded like a three-ring spectacle: the previous year, nearly 62,000 persons visited the Office of the Dean of Students, 32,000 appointments were scheduled, and 49,000 telephone calls were made. The home phone numbers of all twenty-one staff members were listed in the Purdue faculty-student directory, and students were encouraged to call day or night. Bev said she was especially proud of recent efforts to help Purdue's 1,260 minority students. A new offering was the Motel Outreach Program, designed to serve students living in motels during Purdue's housing shortage. Even with mountains of bureaucratic form filing, Bev set her priorities as "people first, paper second."

In another *Exponent* article, Bev recapped the changes she had seen in the nearly twenty-five years she had been at Purdue. She described the previous ten years as "the decade for women," with all Purdue curricula now open to females. Bev said, "Twenty-three years ago women had to sign out of residence halls if they were going to be gone for the night; if a woman spent the night at a male's apartment, disciplinary action would be taken."

However, the situation for female students had advanced much more rapidly than for Purdue faculty. Bev said, "In 1971, there were six women academic heads. Presently, there are two."

Upon hearing of Bev's retirement plans, former President Frederick Hovde sent her a congratulatory letter that touched Bev like no other. She replied, "Thank you for you beautiful letter about my retirement. It is one, which I shall always cherish and preserve and one of the very few which has moved me to tears. Your letter contained just the words I had been groping for in an attempt to respond to the question, 'What are you going to do after retirement?' Your mention that I could now be a 'free spirit' has provided me with an answer. . . . I intend to be a 'free spirit.'"

That year, Bev won the first Distinguished Purdue Woman Award during the annual Day for Women on campus. During the thirtieth Old Masters program, she received an honor that had never been given before—a Distinguished Old Master citation. The M. Beverley Stone Award was established in her honor to be presented annually to an individual who exhibits the same personal concern, gives unselfishly of time, and shares as much love through outstanding service in counseling Purdue students as Dean Stone did during her years of work. A plaque with Bev's photo and nameplates indicating winners hangs in the Purdue Memorial Union. The inscription below the photo contains her quote: "People are lonely because they build walls instead of bridges. We all must work together to close gaps, whether these be generational or communicational—we must work together to build bridges."

Bev was retiring on a high note, and she wanted a big bash shared with all of the students, staff, faculty, friends, and alumni she loved. A dinner was held in the ballrooms of the Purdue Memorial Union on Saturday, May 10, 1980. Letters of invitation were sent by Barb Cook asking for notes, cards, and photos to be bound and presented to Bev. Betty Nelson was a member of the planning committee. A coffee hosted by Helen Schleman and Sally Watlington was held the next day at Helen's house. Dorothy Stratton was unable to travel from Connecticut because her friend and housemate, Jinny, was very ill and Dorothy was tending to her.

Bev's retirement soirée was called "Three Decades with the Dean." Bev sat on the stage with the selected speakers, including Helen Schleman, Barb Cook, Betty Nelson, President Arthur Hansen, and President Emeritus Frederick Hovde. A backdrop was created in Bev's signature color of pink with the event title in swirly script. More than four hundred people attended from around the country. Bev wore a long pink chiffon evening gown, pearl earrings, and flowers in her hair. She was the belle of the ball, greeting those who meant so much in her life. Betty remembered, "That's when you knew Bev might not have a crown, but she was royalty. We maxed out the ballroom. She played it to the hilt, and it worked. It was perfect for her."

Bev also wore a gold Purdue pendant watch made by Bulova Watch Company, which had been given to her by Helen Schleman. An image of Purdue's oldest building, University Hall, graced the face of the watch with the words, "Purdue University, Founded 1869." Eventually, Helen and Barb would own similar Purdue watches on gold chains. The deans can be seen wearing their commemorative timepieces in numerous photographs taken throughout their golden years.

Vice President of Student Services Bill Fischang generated laughter during his speech when he said the only thing he refused to do for Bev was to get Purdue's colors of gold and black changed to pink and pink.

Betty gave a speech on behalf of the Office of the Dean of Students staff. Later, she received numerous letters touting her tribute as the best speech of the night. Retired Purdue Vice President and Treasurer Lytle J. Freehafer wrote, "It showed excellent preparation, much polish, and great perception. The delivery was superior. You outperformed a dean, a vice president, and two presidents!"

Betty thought about her presentation three months prior to Bev's party, remembering that she once read the definitions of charm and class given by advice columnist Ann Landers. Betty wrote a letter requesting a copy of the definitions, and she received a reply from Landers.

Betty wore a bright orange and fuchsia dress as she stood at the podium in front of the rosy backdrop and delivered her homage. She compared Bev to the stuffed bunny in the children's book *The Velveteen Rabbit.* The rabbit talks to the Skin Horse about the difference between "only toys" and those that are *real.*

Real isn't how you are made but is something that you become—it is something that happens to you. Betty said, "When a child loves you for a long, long time, not just to play with, but *really* loves you, then you become *real.* That's why it doesn't often happen to toys that break easily, or have sharp edges, or that have to be carefully kept."

Bev had become *real.* She did not break easily or have sharp edges. She may have looked like she needed to be "carefully kept," but that was an illusion. Betty ended her tribute: "Ann Landers must have met you. She wrote in a recent newspaper column about charm. . . . 'Charm has that magical quality that defrosts, disarms, delights, and fascinates. It is not a sudden gush of sweetness that can be turned off and on like a faucet. It is woven subtly into the fabric of the personality like a golden thread. It glistens. It shines, and it wears well. For months. For years. Forever.'"

BEV WROTE A PAPER ON "RETIREMENT ADJUSTMENTS." She said that her most difficult change was the absence of a secretary. She did not miss being on call twenty-four hours a day, but she did feel it was necessary to have something significant to do every week. Bev wasted little time finding that significant something. She ran for political office.

Bev never had political aspirations until Major Sonya Margerum asked her to run for West Lafayette City Council. Politics appealed to Bev's free spirit.

Sonya Margerum knew Helen, Bev, and Barb, and she looked to them for advice when she was the first woman to run for mayor in West Lafayette. Helen was on Sonya's campaign committee. Sonya called the women "the Lady Deans" because "they were always ladies and yet firm and not wimpy." Bev had encouraged Sonya to obtain her master's degree in political science. Sonya remembered asking Bev to run for office: "It was one of those things where you say, 'Who should we get to run? Bev Stone could win. Well, let's just ask her.'"

Sonya paid Bev and Barb a visit at their home and asked Bev if she would consider running. Immediately, Barb said, "Of course, you should." Bev was not expected to walk door-to-door canvassing neighborhoods—that would not be ladylike. Sonya and her political team suggested that Bev attend coffee klatches and write notes to her friends. Note writing! Now that was "Bev-like."

Bev purchased pink stationary, gathered friends, and they set to work on handwritten notes for the November 8, 1983 election. When alumni returned to campus for Homecoming and attended Bev and Barb's annual party, they learned their former dean was running for office. Doting alumni gathered up stacks of pink, hand-scrawled "Bev-Stone-for-office" notes and pink brochures, combing neighborhoods and distributing the sweetest political propaganda this side of the Mason-Dixon Line. Bev handily won her race to become a city council member.

Bev cheered for Sonya as the first female mayor of the city, reminding her to fight for a salary that compensated her fairly for the work she was performing. Sonya was trying to save the city much-needed funds. Bev said, "I know you don't need the money. That isn't the question. The question is, 'What is that job worth?' You should do it for the women who come after you."

Bev was a proponent of women helping each other. She said, "The worst obstacles are the women at the top who have the attitude of 'I made it, you'll get there.' Women leaders must help other women."

Sonya remembered stopping by Bev and Barb's house during campaign season. She said, "They were always so encouraging. If things weren't going well and there was some terrible thing that was happening, they'd say, 'You're doing fine, now you just keep going.'"

38

Deanie Weenies

Barbara Ivy Wood Cook became Purdue's second dean of students in 1980, succeeding her colleague, sister-friend, and housemate Bev Stone. A Lafayette *Journal and Courier* article announced the change: "It's always tough to follow a legend. But Purdue's Beverley Stone did it in 1968 when she replaced retiring Dean of Women Helen B. Schleman, a thirty-four-year West Lafayette campus administrator. And Barbara I. Cook will do it July 1 when she succeeds the retiring Stone."

When Barb became dean, 45 percent of students lived off-campus because there was a residence hall shortage. There were nearly 32,000 students enrolled. Barb said, "It used to be that off-campus students lived that way by choice. But now, it's not by choice. Many are lonely, not a part of the campus environment, and have no one to relate to."

Barb suggested that Purdue appoint a housing specialist to help students find accommodations in the community. She said that when beginning freshmen visited during "Day-on-Campus," the lobby of the Office of the Dean of Students was filled with frantic people looking for housing.

Barb was willing to speak up when institutional policy affected students adversely, and she and her staff had the ability to cut red tape. She said, "We need to be as verbal as we can. We're not always listened to, but we still need to speak up. . . . We try to never be so inflexible that we can't accommodate someone with a legitimate problem. To treat people as individuals, you have to be willing to bend regulations and make exceptions when they're needed."

As Purdue's enrollment grew, the campus became more legalistic. Barb's willingness to speak out for what was right and hold her ground would bring her great challenges as dean of students. Barb was perhaps the most sensitive of all the deans.

The early 1980s were very busy years for "the Lady Deans." Perhaps this is the reason that Carolyn Shoemaker's Bible was not officially passed to Barb Cook until 1984, even though she had become dean of students four years prior. Looking back, the delay seems like an omen, foretelling the challenges headed Barb's way.

An event in the lives of the deans in October 1980 was the Helen B. Schleman Symposium. Sponsored in part by the National Association for Women Deans, Administrators, and Counselors, the symposium topic was "Promoting the Development of College Students." It was held at Purdue's Stewart Center and coordinated by Marylu McEwen, Purdue graduate and former staff member of the Office of the Dean of Women. Marylu was a professor at Auburn University at the time.

The family of Purdue deans participated in the event. Bev gave a tribute to Helen. Barb gave a greeting, was a panelist, and presided over a dinner. Betty Nelson sat on a panel discussing "Development of Special Groups of Students." The four deans had the symposium flanked on all sides. Whenever they appeared together, fellow administrators took notice.

ON THE DOMESTIC FRONT, Barb and Bev were busy building a new house. Even though their home on Summit Drive was "comfortable and cheerful," it was small, with Barb's living quarters housed in the basement. The deans each needed and deserved better individual space to call their own, yet after twenty-five years of friendship and sharing expenses, they did not want to live apart. A year after she became head dean, Barb wrote a letter to her long list of alumni and friends detailing the experience. The six-page note reveals her sense of humor. Barb wrote, "We are often asked, 'Why did we decide to build a house?' I am still not sure of the answer to that question. . . . Bev replies that she doesn't think a dean of students should live in the basement. (There are probably a few people who think that such locale is not really down far enough.)"

The two women found a house they liked, but Helen Schleman and friend Sally Watlington, who suggested that they build, nixed it. Barb continued: "Then Helen Schleman offered a lot on the golf course. It is so typical of Helen just to have an extra lot lying around. We began to get carried away—we were in the proper mood. 'Why not? Why not build a house just like we want!'"

Helen's lot was the skinny, obtuse triangle of land where she had built her National Home when she was denied Purdue-backed housing after World War II. (Helen gave the little home to a dear friend in Purdue's English department, who moved the house to the outskirts of West Lafayette.) The lot Helen offered Barb and Bev was at 1807 Western Drive, two blocks from Helen's famous contemporary at 1607. She sold the lot to her friends for the amount she paid—$7,000.

The land was situated between the seventeenth green and the eighteenth tee of Purdue's golf course. Barb said, "One really has to be erratic to hit our house with a golf ball." The odd shape of the land posed unusual building demands, and when one sees the configuration of the two-story, narrow, white colonial with two garages jutting out perpendicular to one another on the front lawn, it seems miraculous that a house was even built there. Barb described it as "an Indiana farmhouse on the edge of the prairie (and that's not bad for two southerners!)."

Actually, their house encroached upon land owned by the golf course; however, no one at Purdue, in West Lafayette zoning, or in local government was going to tell sweet Bev Stone she couldn't build a house where she wanted.

In her letter, Barb drew a rough layout of the three-cornered lot and house that looks like a high school geometry problem. The women had their own living areas. Barb was on the second floor and Bev on the first. During her first year as dean of students, Barb drove by the construction on her way to and from work in the morning and at lunch. She continued, "A gem is our breakfast nook on the first floor, which extends to the second floor and makes this wonderful, rather small but comfortable area with a cathedral ceiling . . . such a delightful room. . . . The view from there is really marvelous."

The two conferred on selections of carpet, tile, lighting fixtures, and kitchen cabinets, but as the retired person with free time, Bev made the initial screening. Barb said, "Amazingly, we haven't disagreed on many things, although I am glad her pink carpet is restricted to her bedroom and study!"

Barb gave a nod to Purdue and female workers in her letter: "Our carpenters are both Purdue graduates (shows you what a Purdue degree is worth). They are really fine young men who have taken a real interest in the house. This week we had four lady roofers! One of them has her master's in physical education from Purdue—a good major if one is going to crawl around a roof."

Barb loved to garden, and she planned the patio and landscape to have a southern feel with azaleas, rhododendrons, and a weeping cherry tree. She closed with an invitation: "Gosh, it's fun, and I wish you were here to see it every day grow into something kind of marvelous. We are scheduled to be ready to move by August 15—34,000 students arrive August 21. As I said earlier, it's just good timing!"

Barb ended the letter with her customary sign-off to personal friends—a doodle of a smiling face with two strands of "hair" shooting out at each temple.

Throughout the following decades, Barb would spend many hours at the table in her breakfast nook, writing affable notes in front of the window as she watched birds and the shifting seasons playing out between the seventeenth green and the eighteenth tee.

The first Schleman-Hovde Golf Classic was held on Purdue's South Golf Course in 1978 to benefit women's athletic scholarships at Purdue. It was sponsored by the Executive Council of the Purdue Sportswomen Society and featured alumni golf celebrities and Purdue leaders. The following year it was deemed a "jubilee." The printed program included caricatures by Keith Butz of Helen in a Purdue sun visor holding a golf club and Hovde wearing plaid golf pants as he leaned on a club.

The jubilee included a dinner at the Lafayette Country Club, where Helen hosted many dinners with friends and staff over the years. Her favorite table was next to the windows that looked out over the club's swimming pool. Former Agriculture Secretary and Purdue Dean Earl Butz (no relation to Keith Butz) paid tribute to Helen and Hovde at the jubilee dinner.

The annual tournament was especially poignant in 1983, as it was dedicated to the memory of President Emeritus Frederick Hovde, who had passed away earlier that year.

Helen played a lot of golf during her retirement years, often with friend Sally Watlington. Sally took Helen to Texas for a vacation in March 1984. While there, Helen made her first hole-in-one at the Harlingen Country Club. She was eighty-one.

The "ageless" Helen, as she came to be called, did not want the world to pass her by. Helen wrote in her 1983 Christmas letter: "Too many people know too many things that I don't know anything about. I had a strong feeling I better get 'organized.' I had in mind relatively simple things like CPR training, microwave cooking, and computers. . . . My 'purposefulness' persisted through the CPR and as far as defrosting pot roast quickly—but computers remain a total mystery. 1984 maybe?"

During this time, Dorothy Stratton and Helen were contacted by Frank Gilbreth, son of Lillian Gilbreth, asking if they would write to the United States Postmaster General endorsing a proposal to create a postage stamp commemorating his mother. Lillian had passed away in 1972 at age ninety-three, and Dorothy attended the memorial service in Montclair, New Jersey, of the woman who had been her friend and one of her greatest influences. Lillian's ashes were strewn in the Atlantic, as were her husband's decades before.

Helen and Bev were on the committee that wrote a Purdue "Memorial Resolution in Appreciation of the Life and Career of Lillian Moller Gilbreth." Upon her death, Lillian left her papers to Purdue, and they are housed in the Frank and Lillian Gilbreth Library of Management. They also have a permanent collection in the Smithsonian National Museum of American History, where Lillian's portrait hangs in the National Portrait Gallery.

Dorothy and Helen wrote their letters of endorsement to see "Dr. G." on a postage stamp. In 1984, Lillian Gilbreth's portrait appeared on a forty-cent stamp as part of the Great American Series. "America's first lady engineer" was also the first psychologist to be commemorated on a United States postage stamp.

By winter of 1983, after twenty-three years in the navy, Captain Sally Watlington retired and moved to West Lafayette. In the late 1970s she had returned to Purdue, becoming the navy's first female officer appointed to the role of executive officer of a Naval Reserve Officers Training Corps (NROTC) program. She moved permanently to her Purdue stomping grounds to become a full-time community volunteer, helping extensively with the Lafayette YWCA Women's Shelter.

Bev Stone and Barb Cook flew to Washington, DC, to drive one of Sally's two vehicles to Indiana. The two, along with Helen Schleman, found Sally a house to buy, the same home she lives in today. Prior to moving into her home nestled on a couple of rolling acres south of Purdue's campus, Sally lived in Helen's basement for five months.

Sally first knew Helen, Bev, and Barb when she was a student. She had always referred to Helen as "Dean Schleman." As the years marched forward, Sally had stayed in close contact with the three women. They were all friends. They were like sisters. Helen was like a mother. They had influenced her decision to join the navy. Sally coined a term of endearment for the women; she began calling Dorothy, Helen, Bev, Barb—and ultimately Betty Nelson, their "junior partner"— the "Deanie Weenies."

The year after Sally moved to West Lafayette, the woman with whom Dorothy Stratton shared a home in Connecticut, Jinny, had died. Dorothy, age eighty-four, was living alone. Helen invited her to return to West Lafayette and be a part of all the fun the Deanie Weenies were having. Sally remembered Helen on the phone with Dorothy:

I was sitting at Helen's kitchen table reading the newspaper, minding my own business or at least trying, when I heard Helen say, "I will send Sally out to pick you up, and she will bring you here." I looked at Helen, looked at my newspaper, and thought, "Whoa boy, where am I going now?"

She got off the phone and said, "You will, won't you?"

I said, "I will what?"

"You'll go get Dorothy."

I said, "Of course, I'll go get Dorothy."

Spending two days in a car with Dorothy Stratton meant that Sally had to bone up on the *New York Times*, the *Wall Street Journal*, "and fourteen other magazines" in order to be up on world events to converse intelligently. Sally said, "People would ask me, 'What did you and Dorothy talk about?' I fell back on her old phrase, 'of cabbages and kings,' because I wasn't going to tell anybody."

When Barb heard that Dorothy was going to live down the street from her, she said, "That will change all of our lives. We will have to read the *New York Times* every day and know a lot more about what is going on or we'll never be able to keep up." When the deans ate together, with Sally Watlington included, Dorothy would produce one of her infamous index cards containing topics she wanted to discuss during dinner. Barb invariably would be the one to debate Dorothy, take the opposing side, and egg her on. Helen and Sally would leave the table and busy themselves in the kitchen to avoid the heated discussion and rising voices.

Once all four women were settled on Western Drive, they enjoyed time together playing golf, attending Purdue athletic events, especially women's basketball, and a plethora of other campus activities. They vacationed together and attended the annual deans' conferences. Sally became the willing chauffer and gofer. When Bev and Barb visited Helen and Dorothy, or vice versa, the deans did not walk the two blocks but, instead, drove their car. They didn't want the weather to mess up their hair. Helen wrote in her 1986 Christmas letter: "This year Purdue had four consecutive deans in its contingent who had a spot on the [NAWDAC] program to talk about 50 years of personnel deaning at Purdue. We had fun reminiscing . . . and we all four live within two blocks of each other here on Western Drive along the Purdue North Golf Course. The neighbors have dubbed our street 'Deans' Row.'"

39

Bible Holding Pattern

Once a house was built, a political campaign was won, a friend was moved to town, and the first years of Barbara Cook's reign as dean of students had occurred, the four deans gathered to pass down Carolyn Shoemaker's Bible.

In the fall of 1984, Dorothy Stratton opened the Bible to the yellowed page bearing the names of Purdue's women deans and their chosen passages. By now the list of deans was nearing the end of the paper. An asterisk was placed next to the name of Beverley Stone. At the bottom of the page, in Dorothy's handwriting, a corresponding asterisk was scrawled next to the words "Dean of Students." The deans wanted to acknowledge the change from dean of women to dean of students.

Bev wrote down two favorite passages. The first was Proverbs 17:22. The New American Standard version reads: "A joyful heart is good medicine, / but a broken spirit dries up the bones."

A Life Application Study Bible translates the verse to this: "A cheerful heart is good medicine, / but a broken spirit saps a person's strength."

The verse is accompanied by this explanation: "To be cheerful is to be ready to greet others with a welcome, a word of encouragement, an enthusiasm for the task at hand, and a positive outlook on the future. Such people are as welcome as pain-relieving medicine."

One can see Bev greeting a student in her office in Hovde Hall, warmly shaking a hand, and building a bridge. Bev was pain-relieving medicine. Her other selected passage was Matthew 7:12. It is commonly referred to as "the Golden Rule." The New American Standard version reads: "In everything, therefore, treat people the same way you want them to treat you, for this is the Law and the Prophets."

Dorothy, age eighty-three, wrote in Carolyn Shoemaker's Bible: "Passed to Barbara Cook* / on September 25, 1984 / by DCS, HBS, MBS."

"THINGS ARE 'COOKIN'" read the photo caption in the *Exponent* when Barb Cook became dean of students. Bev Stone gave words of wisdom for her successor, "My philosophy . . . is keep a sense of humor and perspective, and when you encounter frustrations, go out and garden or play golf."

Barb jotted notes to herself on a paper that she titled "Problems/ Strategies of Advancement" and addressed her new position: "I was in the office for twenty-four years before being named dean. Maybe I outlived my competition. Not sure I really wanted to be dean, but I didn't want anyone else to either."

The *Exponent* article touched on Barb's long-awaited trip on the Colorado River rapids. Each time she talked about the expedition, someone volunteered to go along but invariably backed out. Finally, she found a friend with her same sense of adventure—Sally Watlington. Sally said, "Barb is a very dear friend. We golf and garden together. In 1978, we spent a vacation shooting the Colorado River Rapids. She loves to be outdoors and enjoy nature."

Those on the river tour with Barb and Sally drew straws to see who would sit in the front of the raft when they plummeted down the most difficult fall. Barb, age forty-nine, and Sally, age forty, chose the second-most daring plunge on the trip. They sat together on the first row of seats when the raft dropped three hundred feet in five seconds.

Barb's office was painted in pastel shades of blue and green for a soothing environment. Barb said, "I wanted it to be a nice place for students to come if they have a problem and needed to talk." Stacks of files and papers crowded her desk and couch. Student Kevin Eikenberry described meeting with Barb: "I've never walked into Dean Cook's office without being offered a gumdrop. And when we sit down to talk, we always sit at a small round table. It's just her way of placing you on the same level."

Two years into Barb's deanship, Associate Dean Betty Nelson hosted a luncheon for retirees of the Office of the Dean of Women/Students. Bev Stone wrote a thank-you note expressing how the five women deans looked out for one another. Bev, age sixty-six, wrote: "I am so glad that Barb has you. In many ways you are fulfilling the same function for her in the office that Barb filled for me and that I think I filled for Helen. The DOS job is a *very* stressful one—even more so now than two years ago—and to have someone whose judgment and confidence you can trust completely is almost essential if one is to keep any semblance of mental health."

In 1988, all five deans participated in a panel discussion for a Mortar Board Leadership Conference. Betty Nelson was the moderator. Fifty years of Purdue women deans appeared on the stage to tell the young female and male students in the audience what it was like during each of their tenures. The Lady Deans were the perfect women to speak at a conference on leadership. Barb stepped to the podium as the other deans sat at a table onstage. She said:

> All of my predecessors were tough ladies who could battle when necessary, although their individual techniques varied a lot, who were always compassionate, warm, and understanding toward the individual and his or her problems. There was never any doubt that they were people you could count on to be honest, professional, and visionary.
>
> My job was always defined for me by the kind of people my predecessors were and are, and by the very strong beliefs they held so dearly. My best qualifications for dean came not so much from degrees and experience, but rather from the opportunity to learn and to attempt, often

> inadequately, to emulate the leadership roles they defined so well. So I thank them for that.

In the second year of Barb's stint as dean, her office mailed letters to more than six thousand students who lived in neighborhoods near campus, urging them to be "responsible citizens" of West Lafayette and make contact with the Office of the Dean of Students if they had problems. Barb's goal was to connect with as many off-campus students as possible to prevent troubles down the road.

At the Mortar Board Leadership Conference, Barb talked of the new set of problems brought on by the shift "from essentially a residential campus to one of forty-six percent of our students living off-campus." She said:

> It was necessary to make new relationships with the community, mayors, police, and community development. I've often yearned for the time . . . when [we] sat around Dean Schleman's table and discussed problems with the clear understanding of individual roles. By 1987, the Dean of Students staff had grown to twenty-seven professionals and eighteen clerical. We were located on two floors of a building and two other separate buildings.
>
> We had to learn to deal with new problems—eating disorders, dyslexic students, stress, academic pressures, bureaucracy management, crisis intervention, alcohol concerns, crowd control, AIDS, harassment, and student safety.

Barb had many challenges during her time as dean. Her office had four major moves, and she served three different presidents. When Barb started working in in 1956, many of the student issues of the 1980s did not even exist, or if they did, the issues were unrecognized or hidden from mainstream society. In the 1986 *Debris* yearbook, a page was devoted to "A Look Back: Tragedies" with a photo of actor Rock Hudson and this paragraph: "Actor Rock Hudson was the first public figure to announce that he had Acquired Immune Deficiency Syndrome, or AIDS. His words caused an avalanche, thrusting the disease into the media limelight with a realization of the threat to national health. Hudson died ten weeks after his announcement, at age 59."

A totally unexpected event for Barb brought back memories of the University of Arkansas African American student Jackie Lamond

Shropshire, who was required to sit behind a railing that segregated him from his white classmates. In an article clipping titled "To Build Bridges," Barb said: "The things that happened last year [1980] that were concerns to me . . . were the cross burnings. I don't know if that was a serious attempt at intimidation or somebody's idea of a sick joke. There's no doubt that we live in a society that's racist in lots of ways. That was the one thing that happened last year that had never happened on this campus."

Student alcohol abuse was a major concern during Barb's deanship. In 1982, she said that one of her most significant accomplishments had been the adoption of an alcohol policy. The point of the policy was to try to eliminate large open group parties. Yet the problem escalated. In a January 1984 speech to the Purdue Interfraternity Council, Barb said, "Alcohol abuse is our number one student problem on this campus. It is responsible for shattered lives, for untimely student deaths, for theft and vandalism, and assault. I think it threatens our whole campus environment."

This was the same year that Helen Schleman nominated Barb for the Lafayette-area annual YWCA Salute to Women in Education Award. In her nomination letter, Helen wrote of the varied student hardships and tragedies that Barb addressed:

> What do you say to a young man who has just been dropped from engineering because of poor grades, when his father and his grandfather are both Purdue engineer graduates, holding significant positions in industry? How do you respond to 500 plus teenagers chanting noisily, "Hell no, we won't go!" as they lock arms and march across campus? How do you comfort parents who are grieving over the loss of a daughter [and] the coroner's verdict is suicide? What do you say to a senior woman whose fiancé told her the night before he has changed his mind? How do you handle a group of shattered young men who have just lost two of their best friends in a drunken driving accident?
>
> I don't know what you say or how in the world you do it, but Barb Cook does. She has been teaching understanding to individuals and groups for years by identifying with them. What else is education all about?

By that fall, what Barb called "our worst experience to date" occurred on a Friday evening prior to the Purdue-Ohio State football game. An outdoor movie was shown on the lawn near the Memorial Union, which brought a mass of students. A pep rally had been scheduled to follow the movie, but was cancelled at the last minute. Students were milling around looking for something to do, and there was an outdoor party in progress a few blocks away. The crowd migrated to the party, and the number of students in attendance grew to about four thousand.

The West Lafayette police called in the state police for assistance. The crowd was not aggressive—until the police showed force. They began to use tear gas. Fortunately, the state police captain, Purdue's head of safety and security, and the dean of student staff present convinced the police to cease the use of tear gas. After a few arrests, the crowd dispersed.

The incident frightened the community, the Purdue administration, and most certainly, Dean of Students Barb Cook. A task force was created to examine problems and solutions and to encourage events that would attract both students and citizens. They asked landlords to discourage open parties. Students were encouraged to join neighborhood associations. Purdue began to impose discipline on students arrested for public intoxication and DWI offenses.

Barb talked to Mayor Sonya Margerum at least once a week to monitor the situation. Bev was a city council member, so as former dean, she had a view into the Purdue student/community relationship from both perspectives.

Barb and Sonya sent a letter to all students living in West Lafayette, reminding them of their citizenship responsibilities and encouraging them to meet their neighbors and be a part of the neighborhood. The letter was an expensive endeavor, but Barb and Sonya would try anything to help preserve the neighborhoods. Purdue did not want "student ghettos" any more than did the citizens of West Lafayette.

In notes she titled "Lafayette Street Party Zone," Barb wrote, "*But still* the situation is volatile and when the weather is warm, I pray every weekend for a hard rain. My prayers are not always effective, unfortunately, but bad weather is our best allay."

An eyebrow-raising event during Barb's time was the Nude Olympics, a tradition of a secret committee of the Cary Quadrangle residence hall. They would determine when the coldest day of the year would be and call local radio stations to announce the event. Around the Cary Quadrangle courtyard, students ran laps buck naked, except for a pair of sneakers and perhaps a brown paper bag over their heads. By the mid-1980s, the event made national news. In 1986, President Steven Beering decided to shut down the event.

The student body resented the ban on the Nude Olympics. The Cary Quadrangle committee announced the event anyway, and it drew a crowd. Starting at 11 p.m. on the coldest day of the year, about two to three hundred students gathered to watch the spectacle. Student George Avery was there. He remembered:

> The campus police chief came out on a balcony overlooking the courtyard and told students to go home, and was greeted by flung toilet paper rolls. As the runners . . . started their laps, the campus police . . . tried to corral the runners. At least one officer tripped a runner, who decked the chief with flailing arms as he fell. Things started getting uglier, with a few empty beverage cans joining the toilet paper. At this point, Dean Cook came out on the balcony and asked everyone to calm down, which actually did have that effect. After the last runners escaped into the Quad's units, the crowd dispersed.

Helen, former director of the Women's Residence Hall, did not approve of the Nude Olympics, and she wrote a letter to the Lafayette *Journal and Courier*: "The Cary Quadrangle Nude Olympics certainly deserves the title 'Crass Act.' . . . University officials . . . must act positively, and soon, if they expect to repair the damage that this activity does every year to the reputation of the whole residence halls system. Besides this activity is dangerous, as well as crass, and it damages the whole Purdue reputation."

The worst time for Barb was when she closed Purdue's outdoor amphitheater, Slayter Center, for one year. Pep rallies, pre-football game shows, and rock concerts took place at Slayter. In May, festivities around Purdue's go-cart race, the Grand Prix, were also held on "Slayter Hill." Back in 1968, it was where Bill Smoot gave his raunchy speech to female students, faculty, and deans at the Green Guard ice cream social. Nearly twenty years later, the dirty word on Slayter Hill was "alcohol." Betty Nelson remembered: "The closing of Slayter Center was the most significant event of Barb's tenure. Alcohol had become a huge issue, and behavior at Slayter was out of control. We knew from what had happened on other campuses that it didn't take much to end up with a lot of student deaths—alcohol poisoning, vehicular accidents. We had some students who came close to extinction. It was an especially bad year in the spring of 1985."

The Office of the Dean of Students closed Slayter in May while the Purdue Alcohol Task Force conducted an investigation and presented a report to President Beering. Betty said, "It was a very sensitive report, and the president had endorsed the plan. Somewhere along the line, he got the impression that the decision to close Slayter came down too hard on students. He thought that our office was too restrictive—not being student-focused—to close something they loved."

During this time, President Beering spoke to a fraternity about the Slayter closing issue and allegedly made disparaging statements about the Office of the Dean of Students. The president's words got back to Barb and the others in the office from two sources who had attended the fraternity meeting. Reportedly, the gist of the words used to describe the Office of the Dean of Students and its relationship with students were "oppressive" and that "the Dean of Students Office hold themselves well above the students and a happy medium needed to be achieved." Betty said of Barb:

> For her, it pulled the plug. It was the turning point. Barb was perceived by the administration as being too hard on students, which is the strangest thing in the world. It's just not her. She was a very sensitive person, so she felt the impact.
>
> The president may have received some criticism, and instead of saying, "You know this is what we need to do to prevent student deaths on our campus," he waffled and said, "I'll take care of that," which is what we were told he said at the fraternity meeting.

Slayter Center reopened on a trial basis in the spring of 1986. When she retired the next year, Barb said, "The hardest, most unpopular decision I had to make was to close down Slayter Center. . . . But it was a good decision. I think all of the problems have been ironed out."

While the Slayter closing year was a rough one, there was a spunky incident that offset the turmoil. It was unacceptable by the dean of students staff to refer to college women as "girls." They also frowned upon student organizations that played on female stereotypes. The annual Grand Prix go-kart race featured a group called the "Grand Prix Girls," which held events related to the competition: Grand Prix Girls' fashion show, queen contest, and Les Filles Prix bed race. Betty said, "There was a movement on campus to persuade Grand Prix that the term 'Grand Prix Girls' was not an acceptable name for a group of women students—the men's group was not called 'Grand Prix Boys.' If it is good for one, it should be appropriate for the other. That was a bone of contention for a number of years."

In 1985, the Grand Prix named their group of male student supporters "ambassadors." The dean of students staff thought it was the perfect opportunity to include men and women under the same moniker, but to their surprise, the Grand Prix Committee continued to call females the "Grand Prix Girls."

Unbeknownst to others in the office, including Barb, the dean of students staff advisor for the Mortar Board calendar wiped out all references to the Grand Prix Girls events in the 1986–1987 datebook. The Grand Prix Girls held many events throughout the year, but not one appeared on the Purdue calendar. Barb knew nothing of the sneaky omission until the day the Grand Prix advisor stormed into her office, furious. Betty said, "I suspect she promised to investigate, find out how the problem had come about, and assured him the information would be handled ever so carefully in the future. Barb was very, very good at diffusing explosives."

During this time, Bev Stone received the University's highest honor: the degree of Doctor of Humane Letters. Bev and her family of deans were thrilled. Barb wrote Bev a note for her special day: "As a former student, I thank you Bev. As my best friend, I love you very much and always will for who you are—a wonderful human being. What better reason for rewarding an honorary degree? I think it may be Purdue's finest hour!"

THE MOST PUBLIC AND CONTROVERSIAL EPISODE of Barb's tenure was the readmission of an expelled football player. At various times over the years, all of the deans served the Committee on Scholastic Delinquencies and Readmissions (CSDR). Betty said, "I served on [CSDR] for a long, long time. We would occasionally have a new faculty member who would be appointed, and I think they may have anticipated that it was not going to be very demanding of time and energy, and that it was just kind of interesting. There was no committee out of University Senate that required as much time as [CSDR]."

Oftentimes, the academically dropped student had to appear before the committee and plead his or her case. Betty said, "They represented just about every emotion. Sometimes they were goofy and silly. Some were nervous. Some were so blasé about the whole thing that they did not serve themselves well."

There were a number of politically sensitive readmission cases. Betty had an experience that proved the administration could back a decision. She said:

> I had a call from a man who was a large donor to Purdue. He thought his offspring should be readmitted. I told him that was not how it worked, and his child would not be treated differently. He announced that he would withdraw his money from Purdue and give it to another Big Ten institution. I said, "I'm really sorry, but that is your decision," and I hung up. I went to Barb and told her of the conversation.
>
> Barb made an appointment with Phil Haas, who was provost. We went upstairs and told him what happened, and Phil, bless his heart, was very supportive. He said, "You did the right thing. I'm glad you made that decision. Thank you for letting me know." I thought that was a refreshing response, and I appreciated it so much.

During the 1986–1987 school year, Barb dealt with what she termed, "the worst experience I ever had at Purdue. I thought I may be fired—but the faculty supported the [CSDR]." On four occasions, a Purdue football player who had been placed on scholastic probation after flunking out of school had been denied readmission to the University. Despite the committee's four-time denial of readmission for the athlete, the administration overruled the CSDR and admitted the linebacker.

Members of the CSDR were seasoned, having served ten or more years. The administration's extraordinary actions shocked them. They drafted a letter to President Beering on September 8, 1986: "In the past the [CSDR] has attempted to respond sensitively to individual situations, which have been brought to its attention by the President's Office as well as other areas on campus; to our knowledge, your action in overruling the [CSDR] was unprecedented at Purdue."

The letter continued, highlighting the CSDR's careful thought and time spent on the decision, and their sincere attempt to be fair and consistent "so that expectations about readmission will be clear to faculty, students, and counselors." They conveyed that the overruling made them question their role regarding the process. The letter asked: "What do we say to the 47 students who applied for readmissions for summer or fall and who were denied but whose records are better than that of [the football player]? What kind of future support can we expect from the Purdue administration in permitting the [CSDR] to make educational decisions without undue pressure from vested interests within and outside the University?"

Barb presented the letter to President Beering in a private conference, and then she wrote a letter to the members of the CSDR:

> He asked that I convey the following to the Committee. President Beering wishes the Committee members to clearly understand that no one from the athletic department ever contacted him directly about [the football player]. The contact regarding an exception for [the football player] came to the President via Vice President Hicks from the Associate Dean of the School of HSSE [Humanities, Social Science, and Education]. The Associate Dean requested the exception and said he would personally work with [the football player]; that he believed [the football player] could succeed in HSSE. . . .
>
> The President agreed with the Committee that [the football player] never should have been admitted to Purdue in the first place, but he felt, in view of this academic support, that compassion could be shown to [the football player] at this time.
>
> The President also wanted the Committee to know that all committees are advisory committees. There will be occasions when he will act according to his knowledge and judgment.

The newspaper stories rolled out in the Lafayette *Journal and Courier* and the *Exponent*. The September 22, 1986, the *Journal and Courier* said:

> A Purdue University readmissions committee considered resigning when its decision not to readmit a football player was overturned by the university administration, a committee member said.
>
> Purdue President Steven C. Beering said he unofficially agreed to readmit the student, but he said that the final decisions had emerged from discussions between his office and the Dean of Students Office. Beering would not identify the Dean of Students official involved in the decision.
>
> Barbara Cook, Purdue's Dean of Students, refused Sunday to comment on the case. . . .
>
> [Beering] said Sunday, however, that the recommendation was not an official ruling. He said the case was never officially brought to him on appeal by either the student or the athletic department.
>
> Beering said he has the authority to readmit students on appeal but that he didn't use it in this case.

The Athletic Department was silent about the readmission, but the next day the *Exponent* ran a story with this quote from Athletic Academic Advisor Bob King: "Sure there are charges of favoritism of athletes. I'm not saying it doesn't happen sometimes. The requirements of the athlete are much stricter. They must maintain progress semester-by-semester. The average student doesn't have to."

The *Exponent* followed up with an editorial entitled "Favoritism," saying, "What's the point of a committee if the administration is going to do as it pleases, anyway? The whole situation reeks of policy cover-ups."

That summer, before the final decision on the football player was declared and the student was readmitted, Barb took a much-needed vacation. While Barb was out of town, Associate Dean Betty Nelson received a phone call at home on a Sunday night from a Purdue football coach. She said, "He started calling me 'honey,' and I knew this was not going to go well. That's always a red flag that somebody wants something exceptional. He kept calling me 'honey.' I encouraged him not to do that. I told him people do not call me that. He went on to tell me about this football player, and he would like a reconsideration of the case. He thought that was what it took to get things turned around—call me at home and call me 'honey.' That's not useful."

40

Chicken Salad Reprise

Barb Cook clipped and saved a magazine article, which was entitled "Ten Ways to Fall Back in Love With Your Job—Your job, once a light of your life, now seems lackluster. Here's how to renew the old flame."

Barb was battered and bruised, and after seven years as Purdue's dean of students, she was ready to retire. The stress may have made her forgetful. In December 1986, she wrote to Helen Schleman: "I want to thank you for your note on the event of my absent-mindedness several weeks ago when I forgot to give a presentation. The last two years have been very difficult ones in a professional sense, and I have become, I fear, preoccupied with worrying about things I cannot change. I'm afraid I dumped on you on Monday evening and I should not have done that. I have always appreciated your wisdom and good sense and what you think is important to me."

Barb kept a file of *Exponent* cartoons. She wrote on a piece of attached notepaper, "Several years of cartoons—most are fun!" The newspaper selected favorite cartoons of the year and ran them in December, calling them "Purdue Christmas cartoons." The introductory article by Mike Caughill must have deeply hurt Barb, yet she kept it in her file. It stated: "The first Purdue Christmas cartoon to air this year is a stunning tribute to our beloved Dean of Students Office entitled 'The DOS that Stole Christmas' . . . the DOS sneaks around prohibiting concerts at Slayter hill, shutting down the nude Olympics and accusing everyone of drinking too much. At the end of the cartoon the Dean of Students' heart grows three times, but since three times zero is still zero, they don't change their mind."

However, in 1986, there was an *Exponent* comic strip that vindicated Barb, "Emancipation" by Will Holland. In each of four panels, Holland drew the back of an office chair at a desk. A bald head with a few sprigs of hair peeked from the top of the chair. The rounded pencil mark depicting bare scalp was enough to make the man in the chair resemble President Steven Beering. An office intercom rested on the desk. One of the cartoons read:

> Click
> Yes, sir.
> Barb, get me a cup of coffee.
> Click
> Yes, sir.
> Barb, will you sharpen this pencil?
> Barbara . . .
> Hold on Mr. Beering, when did I become your errand boy?
> That's errand Girl, Barb.
> Errand Girl.
> Click

Helen Schleman, Dorothy Stratton, Bev Stone, and Sally Watlington hosted a retirement party for Barb on May 13, 1987 at the Lafayette Country Club. It was an intimate gathering compared to Bev's ballroom bash in 1980.

When Barb retired, Mortar Board honored her national service to the organization and her thirty-three years as adviser by naming the University's chapter the Barbara Cook Chapter of Mortar Board at Purdue.

Also upon retirement, Barb declared that she was changing her birthday from December 8 to July 4. For several years thereafter, the family of deans and friends gathered with balloons and cake to mark Barb's new star-spangled birthday and celebrate her independence from Purdue.

Betty Mitchell Nelson was named Purdue's third dean of students in the summer of 1987. With two weeks of experience under her belt, she was invited to lunch at Bev and Barb's home on Western Drive. Helen and Dorothy drove a car the two blocks on "Deans' Row" from their home at 1607 to 1807. Their hair needed to look good for a photograph.

The women gathered around the table in the breakfast nook. Celestial Chicken Salad was served.

Betty sat unaware that history was about to be made over Key lime pie. Barb pulled out Carolyn Shoemaker's Bible, and the deans proceeded to tell the story of their historic hand-me-down. Years later, Betty said, "My mouth just fell open. I was speechless about the whole thing. To think this had been going on for years, and I didn't know about it."

The honor of writing in the Bible was given to Betty. The list of women deans' names had grown so long that the original signature page was turned, and Betty wrote on a fresh, blank page. In her precise, tight cursive that slants ever so slightly to the left, she wrote: "Passed to Betty M. Nelson / July 1987 / by DCS, HBS, MBS, BIC / Psalms 117 / Psalms 118:24, 28–29."

The New American Standard version of Barb's chosen passage, Psalms 117, reads: "Praise the Lord, all nations; Laud Him, all peoples! For His loving kindness is great toward us, And the truth of the Lord is everlasting. Praise the Lord!"

Psalm 117 is the shortest chapter in the Bible and also the middle chapter. The passage declares that God's salvation is for *all* people.

Barb's selection, Psalms 118:24, reads: "This is the day, which the Lord has made; Let us rejoice and be glad in it."

In the Life Application Study Bible, Psalms 118:24 is explained, and Barb's tough tenure as dean of students floats among the words: "There are days when the last thing we want to do is rejoice. Our mood is down, our situation is out of hand, and our sorrow or guilt is overwhelming. We can relate to the writers of the Psalms who often felt this way. But no matter how low the psalmists felt, they were always honest with God. And as they talked to God their prayers ended in praise."

Barb's final chosen passages, Psalms 118:28–29, reads: "You are my God and I give thanks to You; You are my God, I extol You. Give thanks to the Lord, for He is good; For His loving kindness is everlasting."

The Life Application Study Bible explains the theme of the passages: "God's word is true and wonderful. Stay true to God and His word no matter how bad the world becomes."

Purdue University photographer Dave Umberger arrived to snap a photograph of the historic moment with five Purdue women deans. He suggested that they walk outside to the golf course. Dave lined up the women in front of a backdrop of lush trees and told the deans to smile and walk toward him. In some of Dave's shots, the deans held hands. In others, their hands were at their sides, their shoulders touching. Barb was the tallest and Helen the shortest, Dorothy was the oldest and Betty the youngest. Bev was the one wearing faux pearl earrings.

In years to come, the most requested photograph taken by Dave Umberger was the black-and-white picture of "Five Deans Walking."

41

The Main Thing

Betty Nelson was described as an iron fist in a velvet glove. Her soft-spoken West Virginia lilt and her small stature may have caused some to assume she was a pushover. Brilliant, intuitive Betty used that miscalculation on the parts of others—particularly men—to her advantage. As Betty said, "It's okay to be a sleeper."

On August 16, 1987, Betty wrote in a journal the night before she officially began as dean: "Real 'deaning' begins tomorrow with the residence hall counselors' orientation program—my first intro to a group as dean. Prepared but anxious. . . . I try to think about this job a piece at a time rather than a whole new role. I'm ready for tomorrow's piece."

Betty's office was spruced up during the summer with fresh paint, waxed floors, and the delivery of new name badges. She continued writing in her journal in the third person: "Betty is struggling with the calendar—hard for her to say 'no' to anyone. Have told her to be more assertive, otherwise I won't survive."

She ended her journal entry with this honest reflection: "After feeling terrified for two months, I'm just scared now—that's progress."

Betty moved into the Office of the Dean of Students after waves of angst had washed across the campus, from street party mobs to the closing of Slayter Center and the contentious readmission of a football player. People asked Betty if she was going to move to "Deans' Row" on Western Drive. Independent Betty did not care for the question. She and her husband, Dick, remained on Hideaway Lane. Betty said:

> Barb's tenure affected my administration significantly because of the misperception that she strived for control. Provost Vero Tyler was the one who told me that I had been hired for the position of dean of students. He followed it up by saying, "You know, I think Barb's problem was that she just listened to too much advice from the people on Western Drive. I think you do not want to follow that pattern."
>
> I said, "Well, you know I am accepting advice from anybody who wants to give it to me, but understand that it is up to me to make the decision about what advice I am going to listen to."
>
> I was so stunned that anybody would say something negative about these people who I thought walked on water.
>
> People misread me. And that is not a good thing to do.

Betty learned early on to prepare herself for each day of "dean-dom" by stopping to pick up an *Exponent* before she headed into the office. She would check the newspaper to see if anything had happened overnight that would greet her when she arrived at her office door. If there was a student arrest, a policy change being considered, an editorial regarding changes in fees, tuition, policies, deactivation of a student organization, or other more serious events like an assault or death, she would have a heads-up on what the day would bring. Her proclivity for preparation was the backbone of her leadership style of tact and grace, even under fire. When there was a problem or project to be tackled, it was time "to get organized."

Betty implemented more structure into the Office of the Dean of Students with specific job descriptions and performance reviews for the staff.

Before the advent of e-mail, Betty devised her own system of communicating in snippets at nearly all hours of the day by leaving memos on her staff members' desks. Associate Dean of Students Sandy Monroe said:

> Betty expected a lot of her staff because she expected a lot of herself. She would work until 10:30 at night. She would use a scrap piece of paper—half of an 8.5 by 11, and you would get this sheet of paper with red ink listing the things she would like for you to work on or that she wanted to talk to you about the next day.
>
> She was great to work for. She was someone I was also very proud to be associated with because people held her in such high regard. The way she did her work, you could always count on her. She had integrity and was confident. All of the deans had high integrity and were very confident.
>
> I wanted to please these women. I wanted to make them proud of me. I wanted to do the work in the way they expected it and in a way that honored them.

Betty could see at the outset of her time as dean of students that others perceived her as pliable, an easy target to get what they wanted. Because she was mild-natured, they assumed they could push or intimidate her to help them game the system. Betty spoke softly, but she carried a big stick—engraved with the word "integrity." She said, "There were points of friction all along the way where I would be put in the position where somebody wanted me to do something that I felt was lacking in integrity. It was the wrong thing to do. I wasn't going to do it, and I have a 'Go-to-Hell Fund.'"

Helen Schleman had taught Betty well. As the dean of women and Betty's former boss, Helen had set the example of confidently standing up for what was right, and if she needed to tell the job to "go to hell," she had the financial security to back up that decision.

As Bluefield City Manager, Betty's father had instilled a strong sense of justice in his daughter as well. Emory Mitchell did not kowtow to politics, and neither did his daughter. Little did the Purdue administration know that Betty Nelson was a Nancy Drew/Scarlett O'Hara kind of woman.

Betty learned a great deal from her vice president about a more typical work environment. These new experiences gave her an appreciation for the working conditions of many other colleagues. She realized how blessed she had been up until that point to have outstanding bosses and mentors. When she became dean of students in 1987, Betty, age fifty-two, was thrown farther into a typical man's world than she had ever been before. She said:

> The language was so different for me. I would sit in staff meetings and make hash marks for all the words that were bellicose or war terms, like "I need plenty of ammunition. This will be decided in the war room. Let's bring out the big guns." This was a different way of communicating. It was male language. My dog is bigger than yours. My gun is bigger than yours. They thought competition was the way to accomplish something, even though we talked about working in teams. It was good to be older because I had an understanding of the game and how to try to make it fit my style.

A dean of students deals with people from nearly all aspects of a University—the students, their parents, their teachers, and administration. So many people want a piece of the dean. Betty said, "You better know who you are."

Administrative headaches aside, Betty loved her job because she relished creating services to support Purdue students. Betty gave hundreds of speeches to numerous Purdue and community organizations. On a couple of occasions, she spoke on "A Day in the Life of a Dean." She said the essentials for surviving a day included support from colleagues, the ability to laugh, and the acceptance that everything can't be fixed immediately. Leading the Office of the Dean of Students was like owning your own business; the job was part of one's comings and goings and was never finished. Betty said, "Most days I believe I have the best job in town, and I know I work with the best staff in the country. Our goal is to make a difference. I believe we do."

Betty touched on the joys and the sorrows of deaning. She knew the great sadness of a mother whose son died in a car accident and needed his clothes from his residence hall for his funeral viewing. She knew the confusion of a student who wanted to talk about a date rape experience, and the vulnerability of another whose teaching assistant made suggestive sexual remarks.

On the other hand, Betty knew happy times—the joy of seeing a shy student blossom into leadership roles, celebrating three blind students as they graduated in engineering, watching the progress of a student graduate who was raised in foster homes, and receiving a bear hug during commencement from a student who had been a runner in the Nude Olympics.

Betty quoted Lee Iacocca, who was president of Chrysler Corporation at the time: "The main thing is to keep the main thing the main thing." She said, "The main thing for the Office of the Dean of Students is the intellectual development of students, including their development beyond the classroom of autonomy, identity, relationships, and integrity."

Betty kept many plates spinning as she kept the main thing the main thing.

One of the highlights of Betty's speaking life was her introduction to columnist Ellen Goodman. Goodman gave a guest lecture at Purdue on April 4, 1990, on "Making Sense of Social Change in the '90s." Goodman was a Pulitzer Prize-winning columnist and associate editor of the *Boston Globe*, and her column ran in four hundred newspapers. She had been awarded the Hubert H. Humphrey Civil Rights Award for her dedication to equality. The lecture was funded through the Flora Roberts Endowment. Roberts was a member of the Purdue class of 1887, a woman far ahead of her time.

A dinner was held before the event for a small group of women. Betty said there was no way she could eat before, but she was ecstatic to attend. She and Goodman left early for the drive to campus. When they arrived outside of the Loeb Playhouse, they saw a throng of people waiting to enter. Betty said, "I rejoiced to know there were so many concerned about the equality of women's lives. It was apparent we were in a period of cultural shift, and it felt wonderful! Goodman was a wonderfully gifted writer and pioneer who stayed on the front line promoting equal rights for women."

A story about Goodman's lecture appeared in the Lafayette *Journal and Courier* with the headline, "Goodman: Let's adopt the values of women." The story read: "Despite the seriousness of her topic—making sense of social change—Goodman cracked up the 1,000 people at Loeb Hall. . . . 'The women are supposed to have it all by doing it all,' Goodman said. . . . Goodman also lamented the social changes that have left men confused about their dual roles of father and worker. 'Men are supposed to be the superdad of the '90s, required to leap tall emotional buildings in a single bound while becoming the president of General Motors.'"

Goodman noticed numerous changes in her twenty-five years of social observation. For example, the woman who labored to rid her husband's shirt of ring-around-the-collar in television commercials had disappeared. She said, "I always wondered why she didn't tell him to wash his neck."

Betty's introduction received many accolades. Dorothy Stratton, age eighty-nine, had been in the audience and phoned Betty the next day at the office. Betty was out, so Dorothy left a message that the secretary wrote on a memo pad. To have Captain Stratton, the prolific consumer of the *New York Times* and the *Wall Street Journal,* sing one's praises meant the world to Betty. Dorothy said, "You did a beautiful job of introducing Ellen Goodman last night."

Betty clipped and saved many of Goodman's columns over the years. She used one of her articles to make a point. Betty said:

> When I wrote to a Virginia bank officer years ago and observed there were no women on the board, and, as a stockholder, I didn't like that, he wrote back saying, "We've been looking for a qualified woman for some time."
>
> My response was to express my dismay that in *all* the state of Virginia, with its fine colleges and universities and industries, there was *no* qualified woman or two or three who could bring an important perspective to that board? I also included with my letter a copy of an Ellen Goodman column titled, "We're still looking for a qualified woman."

The two women connected again when Goodman spoke at the 1991 National Association for Women Deans, Administrators, and Counselors conference in Boston, which Betty chaired.

IN THE SPRING OF 1988, Betty was working around 9 p.m. on a Friday evening in quiet, vacated Hovde Hall. Her radio was tuned to classical music on WBAA. Betty's spacious office was on the northwest corner of Hovde, with views of the Elliott Hall of Music and the Armory parking lot. She sat engrossed in paperwork when something repeatedly hit the window next to her desk—Pow! Pow! Pow!

Betty instantly remembered reading a Purdue police report earlier that day, which stated that someone had shot out the glass in the large palladium window in the Pharmacy Building. Was this same person shooting at Betty's window? The "bangs" continued in rapid fire. Betty crouched on the floor and pulled the telephone down with her. She called Purdue police, explaining who she was and the situation. She asked that a patrol officer come to Hovde as quickly as possible.

Betty hung up, then crawled in her skirt, hose, and heels out the door to the next office down the hall. She stood up in the dark, gingerly approached the window, and peered out. Standing below Betty's office throwing rocks at her window were Dorothy, age eighty-nine, Helen, age eighty-six, Bev, age seventy-two, Barb, age fifty-nine, and Carol Pyle, a visiting alumna. The deans had visited the local frozen custard stand and then stopped by campus to see what their fifth wheel was up to.

Betty cranked open the window and yelled down, "The Purdue police are on their way! You need to leave now! Now!"

The four deans dropped their rocks and scurried off.

The police arrived and looked around the grounds of Hovde but, of course, found no one.

Fifteen minutes later, Betty's office phone rang. It was Bev, feigning meekness. She said, "We meant no harm. It was just a prank."

In her most dean-like voice, Betty said, "That's what all the students say."

The "deans-at-the-window" episode became a longstanding tale and was referenced periodically. In a note she wrote to Betty a couple of years later, Helen said, "Your friends worry about your spending so much overtime. If pebbles at 9:00 p.m. don't stop you, what will?"

The deans were always full of surprises. The next year, Betty had major surgery and was home recuperating. The doorbell rang. She scuffled, weary and worn, to the door. Standing on the front step were Bev and Barb. Bev was holding a get-well gift—a bottle of Old Crow whiskey. Betty said, "Who would have guessed that Beverley Stone's idea of a gift was Old Crow? Nobody else who came to visit brought me bourbon whiskey. Not even a good bottle of wine."

BETTY'S WORK WITH DISABLED STUDENTS over the years made her sensitive to the dangers of head injuries. Some of the students she came to know had sustained life-changing, disabling brain trauma in falls and motorcycle accidents. When she became dean of students, one of her high priorities was related to Boiler Bouts, a fraternity-sponsored boxing competition.

Having no boxing experience, students donned gloves and stepped into a ring set up in the Purdue Armory. Students packed the floor surrounding the ropes, cheering for their favorite contender. Betty said, "I had read enough to know there were some serious brain injuries that occurred as a result of boxing. Certainly, professional boxers were an example. It seemed to me that the risk for Boiler Bouts was far too high. I saw students who experienced brain injuries from automobile accidents, and I saw how hard they had to work, if they came back to school at all."

Boiler Bouts was an event that had been celebrated at Purdue since 1974, when Bev was the dean of students. Many safety cushions were built into the event, including a waiver that the student signed stating that he knew the risks of boxing, and he would not hold the University or his representing group responsible. Students had to wear specified protective helmets and gear. They were required to participate in an orientation before the match. Emergency medical technicians and a Purdue ambulance were on call during the event. A physician from the community had to be ringside.

However, Betty felt it was time to end Boiler Bouts before a tragedy occurred. She prepared a white paper. Betty said, "I consulted several community physicians and the head of the student health center. I obtained statements from them on their assessment of having an event like Boiler Bouts. I read a number of medical journals and research published on injuries, the short-term and long-term impact of those injuries. I covered all the bases that I could. My conclusion was that we should shut down this activity. It was not good for our young people and not good for the institution. The consensus was that the risks were too great from this kind of activity."

Betty's colleagues knew that she was writing the paper and that her initiative to end Boiler Bouts to protect students was of high priority for her, but others would not see her wisdom. Betty said, "In similar fashion to some of Barb's experiences, I presented my white paper to senior administration and was told, 'This is not acceptable. This is not what we're going to do now. This will be a kinder, gentler administration.'"

Boiler Bouts was one of the biggest philanthropic events on campus, raising about $14,000 between 1989 and 1991 as a fundraiser for Big Brothers Big Sisters. The event was held in connection with Purdue Homecoming. To end Boiler Bouts would be reminiscent of shutting down Slayter Center, which was restrictive and unpopular among students. Betty said, "I was told to rewrite the conclusion. Nobody who read all of the white paper would deduce any other conclusion than Boiler Bouts was an unjustified activity. We continued to have Boiler Bouts. With Boiler Bouts, it wasn't a question of *if*, but *when*."

Betty rewrote the conclusion of the white paper as directed, but her assessments from the medical community remained. The evidence did not match the conclusion, but it was a way for Betty to advertise the facts.

Sadly, "when" did occur.

In October 1992, Chris Smith received more than fifty blows to the head at the end of a match when he was so tired that he couldn't keep his arms up to defend himself. One of the blows burst a blood vessel in his brain. He required emergency brain surgery and spent almost three weeks in a coma. He remained in the hospital for two months and required nine months of rehabilitation.

Regarding her white paper and Chris Smith, Betty said, "The University had an opportunity to make a constructive decision to preempt a tragedy. Many of us made visits to the hospital multiple times and tried to be considerate of the student's family. Still, that family had a son who was significantly injured. Such a sad time."

Smith's parents had forbade him from boxing; he boxed without their knowledge that fateful fall day. On April 5, 1993, the *Exponent* ran an interview quoting Smith and his mother discussing a pet bird, their symbol of hope:

> "My first memory is of Thanksgiving," Chris said in a raspy, drawn-out voice. "We watched my favorite movie, *Wild at Heart*. . . .

> Why that was his first recollection over a two-month period is not entirely known, but his recovery is astounding given his odds for survival—which riveted the minds of a campus gripped to the news of the event.
>
> "I don't remember the fight at all," Chris said as he looked at Sailor Ripley, the bird hanging above the kitchen table. The maroon-belly conure is named after the lead character of *Wild at Heart*, a romance movie about a man who won't let anything get between him and his goals. While the bird may seem insignificant, it isn't to the Smith household. Joan Smith, Chris' mom, said the bird has been with her throughout his recovery. She said it helped her get through the times when it appeared her son might not live.
>
> "The doctor told me Chris' chance of survival was like this: You have a lottery ticket, you have about as much chance of winning the lottery as you do of him staying alive," Joan said.
>
> The family was prepared to donate Chris' organs. . . . "At the hospital," Joan said, "They speak of harvesting organs. The word 'harvest' will never be the same to me again."

A long and difficult civil suit against Purdue University was filed. The suit was settled three and a half years after the tragedy. Purdue was not required to pay any money and maintained that it was not liable for Smith's injury. Smith's medical expenses were covered by Purdue health insurance through his father, a University professor.

Smith returned to school and received his Purdue degree in the spring of 1995. He was left with permanent neurological impairments and no peripheral vision. After Smith was injured, the sponsoring fraternity's national board of directors cancelled all of its boxing events nationwide. An April 14, 1993 *Exponent* article quoted Jeff Hackleman, president of the Purdue Interfraternity Council: "The Chris Smith injury was kind of the straw that broke the camel's back," Hackleman said. "It made the whole situation more apparent."

42

To Understand More Than One Knows

BETTY INNOCENTLY PURSUED THE POSSIBILITY of fundraising for Purdue Student Services. She wrote a couple of well-crafted letters regarding the subject and sent them to the administration. She received no response, and the subtle message was that development was an endeavor for the schools and colleges of Purdue, not for Student Services. Then along came an unassuming man—Bob Mauzy.

In 1988, Betty spoke at a Purdue President's Council annual meeting about a popular academic unit in the Office of the Dean of Students, University Division, which provided direction for students who were unsure of what major to choose. Rather than being forced to declare a major, a student could be "unclassified" until he or she determined what academic road was a good fit.

Bob Mauzy, a 1928 Purdue graduate, was in the audience. He understood the perplexities of being a student in the wrong major, and he wished Purdue had offered a University Division program when he was in school. Bob, age eighty-two, was from Middletown, Indiana, and worked part-time in a pharmacy when he was in high school. When he graduated, he followed advice to attend Purdue and major in pharmacy. He had a difficult time with chemistry and two years later changed his major to liberal science.

During his final semester, Bob heard a speech by Earl Beck, director of industrial relations for Eli Lilly and Company. Bob connected with Beck and ended up with a position at Lilly in industrial engineering. Forty-two years later, he retired as general manager of creative packaging.

Once Bob heard Betty speak, his interest was piqued to find out more about Purdue's Student Services. Betty said, "Bob was a low-key fellow. He wore gum-sole shoes, pants with no crease, and a tweed jacket with patches on the elbows. I'm sure if he had taken off the jacket, the sleeves would have kept the shape of his arms. He was just an un-showy fellow."

Bob was fond of the teachings of the ancient Chinese philosopher Lao-Tzu and often expressed this favorite quote in his writings: "Woe is the land where the people *know* more than they *understand.*"

The essence of the quote for Bob was that education held the danger of creating people who think they know a lot but do not truly understand. Lao-Tzu's quote continued: "But happy the land that is ordered so that they understand more than they know."

Bob contemplated a gift to the Office of the Dean of Students. He wrote Betty a letter: "When Purdue deems a person worthy of graduation, hopefully that individual will, indeed, understand more than he, or she knows. I suppose there is no way to insure that qualification. Perhaps it is already being accomplished? If not, how does one go about at least raising the percentage of those who do? Maybe the University Division offers food for thought in that direction."

Betty read and reread Bob's letter, pondering his message. It was an unusual letter full of allegories and depth. Who was this man? He turned out to be a leadership poet. Betty replied, borrowing Dorothy Stratton's favorite line from Lewis Carroll's *Through the Looking-Glass and What Alice Found There*:

> The Purdue environment seems to invite students to focus on their careers, and today's students are interested in activities that will enhance their resumes and help them get the "right" job. Thus, training becomes the focus instead of education. . . . I worry about the missed opportunities to study a new social concept, to hear The Empire Brass or Helen Hayes, or to sit quietly and mediate.
>
> I am concerned that we don't do enough to encourage the development of the Renaissance Person. . . .
>
> Perhaps we can talk about this and "shoes and ships and sealing wax and cabbages and kings" someday when you visit again.

Bob and his wife, Ruth, made a gift to establish the Emily Mauzy Vogel Student Development Fund in honor of their daughter who also attended Purdue. It made possible the Emily Mauzy Vogel (EMV) Sophomore Leadership Conference, held at Camp Tecumseh in Brookston, Indiana, each September. Additionally, this fund helped create a mentoring program, leadership development classes, and a library of resource materials.

The conference became a bonding, electric experience for students. Betty said, "You walked into the meeting room at Camp Tecumseh, and the energy pulsated. The students were so keyed up. They were ready for each new adventure. The first night, there is a big bonfire, and they roast marshmallows and make s'mores. Then, as a surprise, out of the dark come members of the Purdue Marching Band playing 'Hail Purdue.' It's big and unexpected, and it's dark out there."

The 1993 conference brochure described the event for one hundred sophomores "held at Camp Tecumseh, a wonderful treasure just thirty minutes from Purdue. The EMV features topics of racism action and awareness, networking for leadership, etiquette, running meetings, and assertive communication. The 'Almost Anything Goes' teams course emphasizes working together in ways you'll never forget."

Bob wanted an award for the student who took what he or she learned at the conference and put it into action in a leadership capacity on campus the following year. He named the monetary accolade the Betty Nelson Skilled Leader Award. Each year, Bob wrote a welcome letter that was read to participants, which gave a glimpse into the man most of the students never met. One year he wrote, "And never forget that the success of any undertaking rests with the *followers*. Be gracious unto them."

Each attendee was given a lapel pin designed by a student who had attended the first conference. It resembled three interlocking puzzle pieces engraved with "EMV." There was reasoning behind why sophomores were the students chosen for the conference. Betty said:

> Our thinking was that as a freshman, everyone thinks you're wonderful and you glitter and glow. Everything is new and exciting, and you have the energy to take over the world. Your sophomore year, well, there is nothing special going on; you're supposed to know your way around campus, a new group of freshmen come in and they're getting all of the attention, the juniors are beginning to think about careers more seriously. The seniors—they know it all. They're looking at their next life. So, it was the sophomore year that we felt there was not much happening. It would be easy for that to be a down experience.

The EMV Conference nudged students into leadership positions earlier than they may have otherwise. Down-to-earth Bob chose to put his dollars into creating more leaders because of his own experiences. Betty said, "He had been in the corporate world and saw the difference between those who were ready to step forward and do something about the problem areas that they saw and those who would hang back and not do anything. In his own very quiet way, he was a dynamic leader. When he started talking about his packaging business, he would light up. He did all kinds of innovative things for Lilly."

Betty and Bob became pen pals—kindred spirits in the art of letter writing. Neither was fearful of sounding too mystical or lyrical. Betty sent thank-you notes and reported on the events of the EMV Conference, wrapping the facts in emotive quotes and poignant prose. Betty said:

> I felt really close to him. I would receive a notice about one of his gifts, and then I would write him late in the day, maybe nine o'clock at night, or a couple of times after commencement. It was very reflective about what we had just experienced. I would let him know what the day had been like, what the Purdue experience was.

> At one point, the Purdue bells were chiming, and it just felt like the right time to correspond with him about this institution that he loved so much.

Bob's letters to Betty were a welcome balm during stressful times. Betty wrote, "If I find a letter from you in my basket, I save it till last so that my spirits are raised when the day ends. You always include some words that inspire me to think beyond the mundane and today's crisis."

When people did not appear to appreciate or understand the goals of the Office of the Dean of Students, Bob was a beacon of affirmation. Betty wrote in 1990: "I am deeply moved by your belief in the quality of our students, your commitment to future leaders of this country, and your faith in the staff in the Office of the Dean of Students to assist in the development of ethical and mature leaders."

Before he died, Bob methodically began his research to find where his dollars could best be left to ensure that Purdue graduates "understood more than they knew." Bob invited Betty to lunch, although she did not know the real reason why. He asked her what her office did to develop leaders on campus. Two more lunches occurred, and Betty invited students to help answer Bob's question, "How is leadership developed at Purdue?" Betty said Bob was "psyching out the place" only she "had no clue." He had been giving an annual gift to the Office of the Dean of Students for a couple of years, so Betty assumed Bob simply wanted to learn more about students. Betty said, "When the $15,000 gifts came, I thought that was wonderful. That was more than anybody had ever given us. Then I found out about his will from Gordon Chavers, Purdue's general counsel. Bob made a gift of almost a million dollars."

Bob's substantial gift created the Emily Mauzy Vogel Student Development Endowment Fund. Bob's legacy would instill leadership in Purdue students in perpetuity.

After her retirement, Betty stayed in contact with Bob and continued to attend the EMV conferences. In the last years of his life, Bob lived in an Indianapolis retirement community. Betty visited Bob several times over lunch. She took along members of the Office of the Dean of Students staff so that Bob knew the people who were working with the program named after his daughter. It also was Betty's desire to introduce the staff to the quiet man, the "leadership poet."

Betty and staff members visited Bob and conducted a pinning ceremony. Betty pinned the EMV pin shaped like puzzle pieces onto Bob's knit shirt. They brought balloons and took pictures.

Robert M. Mauzy, age ninety-four, died on January 25, 2000. Five months later his daughter, Emily, age sixty-nine, died of cancer.

Betty said, "Bob would walk in a room and be Mr. Cellophane. Folks might not even know he was there, but he'd begin to work his way through, and he would get done exactly what he wanted to do. Bob was really quite a remarkable fellow, and he was a gift from the gods for us. It takes people by surprise; this little old fellow with the funny old clothes and the gum-soled shoes has taken over their world."

BOB'S LETTERS WERE MUCH-NEEDED EMOTIONAL SUSTENANCE in Betty's mailbox in 1993.

In a "banker box" (Betty also called it "Pandora's box") of papers and memorabilia that Betty saved was a collection of newspaper clippings, notes, and cards from supporters regarding an incident when an African American Purdue student was reportedly beaten by white males.

Betty wrapped the assemblage of documents with two papers that look to be copied from a devotional Bible study. The first was titled "God Whispering," and the second was "Blessings in Disguise." The latter document offered these words: "Grapes must be crushed before the wine is made; so too, Lord, I must suffer before my faith is improved, aged, and mellowed."

The incident took place at a fraternity party. A September 22, 1993, Lafayette *Journal and Courier* story, titled "U.S. probing Purdue fight, Racism inquiry to bring visit," stated: "Pearnell Wilson has said he was beaten by white students early April 18 during a party at the Theta Xi fraternity house. Wilson said that during the fight he was choked, stomped on and called 'nigger.' Three Purdue students were disciplined in June by the university in connection with the incident. . . . Three Purdue students also were charged with misdemeanor crimes in connection with the incident."

Shortly after the incident occurred in April, the Purdue chapter of the National Association for the Advancement of Colored People (NAACP) held a discussion panel open to all. An *Exponent* story, "NCAAP to discuss beating of student," stated: "Betty Nelson, dean of students, and Jim Buza, president of Theta Xi, have been invited to speak at tonight's discussion and to answer students' concerns. Nelson said she chose not to attend because she prefers to speak with a smaller group. Buza was unavailable for comment."

Betty believed that speaking to a large group would not be as productive as sitting down with the small number of individuals actually involved in the incident and talking things out. Also, there were other issues surrounding the episode that she was unable to address in order to retain the confidentially of other students. However, her preference to talk openly with the small group involved was perceived as avoidance. A follow-up *Exponent* story regarding the NAACP meeting stated:

> Nelson said earlier that she was not going to attend because she preferred to speak with a smaller group. Some students were incensed by her decision.
>
> "Basically, what it is, is she's weaseling out. They don't want to talk to black students," said Okeafor [Peter Okeafor, advisor to the Purdue NAACP chapter].
>
> "I feel this is indicative of their cowardice, disregard and blatant disrespect of black and minority issues. I feel [Nelson] has an obligation to address students and student issues when she is asked," said Tony Kiene, communications coordinator for the Purdue NAACP chapter. . . .
>
> Eric Smith [president of the Purdue NAACP chapter] said that a meeting between the Purdue NAACP chapter and the dean of students would occur in October.

Michael Walker was charged with assaulting Pearnell Wilson. An *Exponent* story from April 27, 1994 stated: "Walker, a graduate student, is pleading not guilty to charges of misdemeanor battery, saying that he acted in self-defense. Walker was put on suspension by the Office of the Dean of Students."

An all-white jury of three men and three women deliberated for nearly five hours before declaring an impasse. The trial ended in a hung jury.

When the incident first came to light and Betty was painted as a coward hiding in the shadows, the *Exponent* created a cartoon on the Opinions page. A hand-drawn caricature of Betty is shown in her large-framed glasses, her hair a cap of black marker scribbles. The cartoon resembled a wanted poster. It read:

NEWS BULLETIN
Did you know that Purdue has a dean of students?
REWARD
$1,000
Have you seen this woman?
LAST SEEN BEFORE CAMPUS NAACP MEETING

Notes and phone calls of support poured into Betty's office. Lieutenant Brenda King of the Purdue Police Department left a phone message with Betty's secretary: "She did not like the cartoon in the paper today. Bad drawing of the hair. She just didn't like it at all." King also wrote Betty: "The *Exponent* cartoon today was *hateful*. You do not deserve this type of attention! The person who was responsible obviously does not know you—so the joke's on them—right?"

Dale Daniels, of Purdue University Residence Halls, wrote facetiously, "Let me know if there's anybody you want me to beat up or any other way I can assist." One of the most touching notes for Betty was from James Foster, an African American man who was director of the McCutcheon Residence Hall. He wrote: "I'm thinking of you as you continue to face your many challenges, especially those recent ones involving Pearnell Wilson's situation. I applaud your wisdom in such an emotional challenge."

Dorothy, age ninety-two, sent a note to Betty's home:

Dear Betty,

There must be easier ways to earn a living; digging ditches comes to mind. Hope you get combat compensation while serving in combat zone. This, too, will pass, but oh the toll it takes.

No longer in the trenches,
DCS

You know that for whatever good it does you, all of the Ex's are with you 100 percent.

Looking back and reading Dorothy's note twenty years later, Betty said, "I'm pulling this out and thinking, you know, this is the message of the deans' Bible. There are so few people with whom one can talk about what is going on, but this crowd ['the Ex's'] always knew what it was like to be in that position."

43
Hearing What Is Not Said

Betty Nelson handed her 1989 dean of students annual report to Helen Schleman to read. It was a chance for Helen, age eighty-seven, to see the changes in the office since she had retired as dean of women twenty years before. After she read the report, Helen wrote to Betty, quoting a term originally coined by their former colleague, Celie Zissis, and addressing the goal of the office that began with Dorothy Stratton:

> I am overwhelmed by the variety of programs for which your office is responsible. Also, by the work which has gone into the report. Yes, I know computers can help, but can they interpret what the figures mean?
>
> I note that the increase in staff has not kept pace with the increased enrollment. 'Twas ever thus.
>
> I'm happy that the Office of the Dean of Students is no longer primarily the central office for disciplinary cases. It has taken a long time. (Bev

> and I go round and round on this one.) The new grads won't, we hope, say, "I never was called to the Dean's office."
>
> I trust that the Powers that Be will study the report carefully.

As the two Purdue women who knew Amelia Earhart personally, Dorothy and Helen continued to be called upon to speak about the aviatrix. On April 23, 1989, Helen, age eighty-seven, and Dorothy, age ninety, spoke at the Amelia Earhart plaque dedication at the Purdue University Airport. The night before the event, they sat down with pencils and yellow pads of paper to decide what each would say about their mutual friend. They planned that Helen would speak first. Dorothy would follow with her remarks. Sally Watlington, always the willing photographer and chauffer for the two women, said:

> I got them loaded into the car and out to the airport. The plaque dedication began. Helen stepped to the podium and gave the *entire* speech—her portion and Dorothy's! Dorothy was sitting next to me. I could feel her body language while steam was rising. She whispered to me, "She's giving my speech, too!"
>
> I said, "You're just going to have to adlib it."
>
> When Helen finished, Dorothy stepped to the podium and adlibbed for fifteen minutes, never missed a beat, never repeated herself, and did not repeat anything Helen had said. Dorothy was a bright, bright lady.

That same year, Dorothy and Helen attended the forty-sixth SPARs anniversary reunion in St. Louis. A newsletter with a spunky 1940s cartoon of a SPAR reading "Spar Notes, 1989" recapped the event. It said: "Cameras clicked away getting pictures of Captains Dorothy Stratton and Helen Schleman. . . . At the traditional cake-cutting ceremony held under sunny skies at the Sheraton patio, our first Director, Captain Stratton spoke of the planned memorial in Washington to honor all women of all services, of all wars, of all rates and ranks, of all specialties and professions."

Six years later, the groundbreaking occurred in Washington, DC, for the Women in Military Service for America Memorial (WIMSA). It is the only major national monument honoring women who have served in the country's defense during all eras and in all services. The memorial site is a 4.2-acre ceremonial entrance to Arlington National Cemetery, with an education center, museum, and theater. From the terrace, visitors enjoy a panoramic view of Washington, DC. The heart of WIMSA is a computerized record of registered female veterans. Dorothy, Helen, Bev, and Sally Watlington are listed.

Retired Air Force Brigadier General Wilma Vaught spearheaded the very long, arduous fundraising effort for the memorial. Seats in the theater could be purchased in honor of a female veteran, and a small plaque with her name was placed on the chair. When the SPARs celebrated their fiftieth anniversary in 1992, they collected donations for WIMSA. They felt it very fitting to use SPAR funds for a chair in Dorothy's name. A letter sent to Dorothy about the chair read: "The love and respect you engender from all of us make this personal action far more meaningful than just the transfer of funds or donations to WIMSA."

Today, Dorothy and Helen's names are emblazoned on seats in the theater that features *In Defense of a Nation*, a film depicting the roles women played in America's military history.

An editorial about the memorial appeared in the Lafayette *Journal and Courier*: "Recognition has been a long time coming for America's invisible warriors. . . . No matter what their role, they served with courage and dignity. But you would never know it by visiting a military cemetery or touring the United States. Although there are war memorials galore, only the new monument to the women who served in Vietnam at Arlington Cemetery gave Americans a reason to remember the contribution of women in the military. Until now."

Dorothy was invited to attend the groundbreaking but declined because of the physical demands of such a trip. She was asked to send a two-minute speech that was presented at the ceremony with President Bill Clinton and First Lady Hillary Clinton in attendance. Thousands of female veterans who were there heard Dorothy's words. She wrote in part:

> Those who conceived of the project were original thinkers. They stipulated that this memorial should be for all women from any war, regardless of rank or rating. It was to have a strategic location and a distinguished design. It was to be paid for largely by individual contributions.

> When the call goes out, "Your Country Needs You," women, as well as men, respond. Women's service has always been voluntary.
>
> I have a special feeling for the women who offered their services in World War II. The commitment was for the "duration and six months" How long would that be? Of course, no one knew.
>
> As we celebrate this historic day, let us not forget the hundreds of thousands of white markers that lie beyond the gates. To visit this cemetery is a shattering experience. It sears one's soul. The price of keeping the United States free and independent has been high. May we be worthy of the men and women who have helped to keep it so.

TWO SIGNIFICANT STRUCTURES WERE BUILT in 1990 to bear Helen's name and carry forth her life's work and beliefs. The Lafayette YWCA opened the Helen B. Schleman Natatorium, and Purdue built the Helen B. Schleman Hall of Student Services.

The YWCA natatorium was a six-lane swimming pool used as a teaching facility for children and adults. It also was available for those who qualified for the YWCA's social service programs, such as the Women's Crisis Program. A life member of the YWCA, Helen gave financially to the women's shelter, which helped women who had been physically, emotionally, or sexually abused. A story about Helen appeared in the September 1988 YWCA newsletter, stating: "Having chosen a career dedicated to the advancement of women, it seems only natural that Dean Schleman would become closely associated with the YWCA, an organization with mutually held ideals. Dean Schleman's commitment to the YWCA and to women became evident at an early age as she indicates in her telling of this story: 'My father supported the YMCA in Valparaiso and helped them in building their facility. I tried to persuade him to build a joint YWCA–YMCA facility. With no luck, however.'"

The Helen B. Schleman Natatorium was dedicated in February 1990. The *Exponent* ran a story and photo showing Helen at the ribbon-cutting ceremony, scissors in hand and a look of determination on her face. Sally Watlington stands next to Helen, smiling broadly.

Helen was the first person to swim in the pool, accompanied by Sally, who helped her in and out. At ceremony, Helen spoke: "I am honored, indeed, to have this beautiful natatorium named for me. As a matter of fact, it swims awfully well, too. I had the pleasure of being the first non-staff member in the pool on January 2. You all must try it sometime. As an old time physical education teacher, I certainly approve of having a facility that can be used by women, men, and children from all walks of life as they work at being physically fit."

Back in 1968, when Helen Schleman wrote her annual report for the Office of the Dean of Women, she stated, "Purdue needs a physical facility for Student Services comparable to those provided academic work." She wrote that the Offices of the Dean of Women and Men were overcrowded. This was the year of unprecedented unrest on campus, and Helen saw a correlation. She continued, not mincing words:

> There is little criticism these days of the quality of scientific know-how learned by students. There is plenty to worry about in terms of personal standards of honesty, integrity, compassion, self-discipline, and other human qualities that personnel people seem to care more about teaching than do academic departments. . . .
>
> With student unrest—often-unarticulated discontent— . . . it would seem important to strengthen the departments of the University, which work with students directly. . . . Students need time to talk about themselves and someone to listen and discuss their misgivings and apprehensions with them. Someone has got to care, and to show students that he cares, about what kind of persons Purdue students are as well as what they know. . . .
>
> All of the above is said in defense of the proposition that the student personnel services ought to be housed in adequate facilities. A Student Service Building, built and designed to provide an adequate environment for operation of appropriate programs, would enable the Offices to function properly and, at the same time, say for all to hear that Purdue cares about personal development as well as academic excellence.

Twenty years later, the Helen B. Schleman Hall of Student Services was built. The building was named in Helen's honor through the influence of retired Senior Vice President John Hicks and Dean of Students Emerita Beverley Stone.

A gala dedication took place on April 21 in a large tent outside the new building, erected north of Hovde Hall, where the Office of the Dean of Women was first housed during Dorothy's tenure in the 1930s. The dogwood and redbud trees were in bloom. Numerous alumni, former colleagues, friends, and family arrived. Of course, all of the deans were in attendance. Guests greeted each other with hugs and smiles as a string quartet played. A stage was set with chairs and a podium.

Speakers were President Steven Beering, Vice President Richard Grace, Board of Trustees Chairman Bob Jesse, and Trustee Wayne Townsend, acting as Indiana Governor Evan Bayh's representative. Townsend was a former Indiana state senator and 1984 Democratic gubernatorial nominee. He and former U.S. Senator Birch Bayh, Jr. had been classmates at Purdue. In 1977, as a member of the Indiana Senate, Townsend cast the tie-breaking vote to ratify the proposed Equal Rights Amendment. First Lady Rosalynn Carter telephoned Townsend and urged him to switch his vote in favor of the legislation. The ERA passed, and Indiana became the thirty-fifth and final state to ratify the amendment; however, thirty-eight states are required for ratification of a constitutional amendment, and the ERA did not become part of the Constitution.

Helen sat on stage with the five men (video of this event can be found in the Purdue Archives). President Beering began the presentation. Rather than speaking of Helen's many accomplishments as a captain in the U.S. Coast Guard, member of the Defense Advisory Committee on Women in the Services (DACOWITS), her appointment as member of the Education Committee on President Kennedy's Commission on the Status of Women, her presidencies with the National Association of Women Deans and Counselors, her position as a consultant for Richard Nixon's Presidential Task Force on Women's Rights and Responsibilities, and all that she had inspired in female students, faculty, and staff, he said to the audience:

> I welcome you to the dedication of the Helen B. Schleman Hall of Student Services and ask your attention to the program with a biographic sketch of our honoree. Today is more than a celebration of Helen B. Schleman. Today marks the recognition of the women who have in so many very special ways made this University great.
>
> Timing is everything, right? The history of Purdue women unfortunately did not begin in as glorious a fashion as we are celebrating today. I am indebted to Bob Topping for some historical research, which I would like to share with you.

President Beering then listed nine Purdue female students, faculty, and staff beginning from the late 1800s, offering a few sentences of biographical data on each, including Emma McRae and Carolyn Shoemaker. Beering ended with Dorothy Stratton, who was recognized for directing the SPARs and the Girl Scouts of America and "hosting the United Nations." Then the deans were mentioned and asked to stand. Bev, Barb, and Betty stood in the audience. Beering continued: "Helen, I will not repeat and recite here the remarkable career and achievements that you have had because they're known to all of us. You're one of us. We love you."

Vice President Dick Grace spoke next. He held a brass time capsule that would be placed in a special niche in the mall entrance to Schleman Hall. A letter addressing the student body of 2090 was included, along with Helen's curriculum vitae and picture, brochures and reports on student services, archival photographs of Schleman Hall and surrounding buildings, and with symbols of the time, including coinage, stamps, and newspapers.

Chairman Bob Jesse spoke subsequently, giving Helen a plaque that would be installed in the building, along with a small replica for her to keep.

Trustee Wayne Townsend bestowed the highest award given to an Indiana citizen who has distinguished herself through service to the governor or to the state of Indiana. Helen was named the Sagamore of the Wabash. Sagamore was a term used by Native American chieftains to describe great individuals among the tribe to whom the chief looked for wisdom and advice.

Finally, Beering introduced Helen, age eighty-eight. She said, "I don't know whether anyone would ever have believed that Purdue would have a very special building for student services. For a long time, I didn't think so.

As a center, it will facilitate communication among several departments of the University and will stand to serve Purdue's students, even better than they have been. After all, for student personnel workers it is the student experience which is the heart of the educational enterprise."

The doors of the new Helen B. Schleman Hall of Student Services were thrown open to welcome students. Helen's portrait "in blue" was moved from the West Faculty Lounge of the Memorial Union to the lobby. A display case was filled with Helen history: copies of her books, *Group Golf Instruction* and *Your Best Foot Forward;* photos of Helen in her SPAR uniform; another photo of her conferring with students in the Office of the Dean of Women; pictures that show Helen shaking hands with First Lady Pat Nixon on the White House lawn; a picture of her smiling with her dog Trish; and a photo of her with her comrades—Dorothy, Bev, Barb, and Betty—standing in front of the building on the day of the dedication.

Schleman Hall is made of redbrick, Indiana limestone, and enduring ruddy roof tiles. A front portico sports a student-created "green" roof on which plants grow, complete with sedum plantings and picnic tables. On a lunch break, Schleman Hall staff can soak outside in the sunshine, peer past the railing, and see Hovde Hall. Schleman and Hovde will stand side by side for decades to come.

A FEW YEARS BEFORE IN 1987, during the peak of Barb Cook's turbulent tenure, Helen had written to President Beering, as she had written to all of Purdue's presidents since Edward Elliott was in office. It was a four-page handwritten letter—a manifesto, really—just like she had written so many other times, to other presidents, advocating for more women in high levels of administration and on faculty. Helen wrote:

> This is a personal letter to you because you have been so very good to me in many ways, and especially because you have made me feel that you know how I feel about Purdue. You know that I think it is great and that I want it to be as great for women students as it is for men students. . . .
>
> I'm not sure whether churches or universities have been the slower to understand that they are wasting a lot of talent if they don't move toward

> more use of women in high levels of administration. In any case, they have both been slow—and that is one thing that bothers me the most about Purdue. . . .
>
> President Steve, I've thought about this situation for a good many years. It never changes. I take my courage in hand at the moment and talk about it to you because I know that there are several very important appointments to be made soon.

Helen continued her letter by listing seven women she felt were qualified. President Beering replied seven days later in a two-paragraph correspondence thanking Helen for her "thoughtful personal letter," saying he appreciated her "nominations of outstanding women." He said, "I shall submit your nominees to the appropriate committees for consideration."

When the five deans from Purdue walked together into a meeting room at the annual convention of the National Association for Women Deans, Administrators, and Counselors, it was as if royalty entered. A glow followed the famous deans as they greeted other women they had come to know during their fifty-year legacy.

The deans were fabled. No other university had such a heritage of female deans who had served the organization, their institution, and their country. No other university had a woven sisterhood that had accomplished so much for female students, faculty, fellow deans of women, America's women, and each other.

Associate Dean Sandy Monroe remembered attending the annual NAWDAC conventions:

> Some of us who were new to the Office of the Dean of Students, felt like we were connected with celebrities—with Bev, Barb, Helen, and Dorothy. They knew everybody. They would introduce us to people they thought we should know. I always felt like I was very special in the way that I was treated and respected and encouraged. Anyone who had a connection with Purdue— fifteen to twenty people— would go out to dinner together at a marvelous restaurant. That notion of family was so apparent, and the mentoring was happening without us knowing

> it. It was a blessing to work with those women. I feel like they are my professional mothers.

In 1989, the convention was held in San Diego. Helen wrote of the trip in her Christmas letter: "We all went dutifully to meetings and heard good speakers with good professional friends. Then Bev Stone, Barb Cook, Dorothy Stratton, and I rented a car and explored the California coast and mountains from Los Angeles to San Francisco. We stopped here with this friend or that one for lunch and dinner with another one. The 'friends' included a graduate school roommate, former students, and former professional colleagues, so you know that was a variety of visiting!"

In September 1990, the membership of NAWDAC voted to change the association's name to the National Association for Women in Education. In 1991, the organization held its last conference in Boston, and Betty Nelson chaired the event. The farewell session also was the group's seventy-fifth anniversary.

To chair the last gathering of such an organization—one that had advocated for women and minorities, and bolstered higher education since it was established before American women had the right to vote—could have been a daunting task, but highly organized Betty rose to the occasion, and her trusted colleagues assisted her, particularly Lois Wark. Lois had worked in the Office of the Dean of Women when Bev and Barb started in 1956. Lois was the person Barb called the night her husband died.

Betty remembered planning the last convention: "Lois Wark was my wonderful helper for that conference. We worked together with perfect synergy, selecting programs and scheduling. It was a great to have her unfailing support and balanced judgment. Hard now to imagine how we got that conference together with no computer assistance!"

Ironically, the conference was held at Boston's Hotel Lafayette. Although Helen experienced some health problems that year, she was able to attend. All five Purdue deans traveled to Massachusetts on March 15, 1991.

Prior to the gathering, Barb Cook wrote a letter to Pat Rueckel, the executive director of the organization. Barb said, "Hope things are going well for you and for the Association. I do plan to be in Boston—my brother lives there, and I would like to support Betty, and I guess, acknowledge the end of NAWDAC."

After the event, Betty received numerous thank-you notes and accolades. Pat wrote: "What a tour de force. Here is hoping you are on an eternal high for the magnificent program you brought to fruition last week in Boston. It was every inch, bit, and piece extraordinary."

When the deans returned home, the "eternal high" was marked with a natural exclamation point. While the women were in Boston, an ice storm pelted the Midwest. One hundred thousand Hoosiers were without power. Betty returned to piles of downed tree limbs surrounding her home on Hideaway Lane. She said, "The roof had seven holes pierced by limbs that became missiles. One especially large limb was sticking through the dining room ceiling with pink insulation decorating its ragged end like cotton candy. We were without electricity for almost a week. It was such a crazy way to end a wonderful week in Boston."

Western Drive was without power. "Deans' Row" was dark. Sally Watlington received a phone call from the "Deanie Weenies." She said, "They called and said, 'We don't have any electricity. Whoops. We're in trouble.' I had electricity, so I said, 'Come on out to my house.' Now, I had three bedrooms and a cat. There were four of them and a dog. I thought, 'Oh, this is going to be interesting.' I put the cat in the basement. The dog had the upstairs. The dog and the cat never met."

After Sally bustled about preparing and assigning a bed per dean, each somewhat physically feeble at this stage, she threw cushions and blankets onto her living room floor, collapsed, and fell asleep, "exhausted from just refereeing everything."

The final collecting of NAWDAC women also had been the last chance for the group to mingle with Purdue's five deans. One year later, one dean would no longer be living.

44

Helen's Hankie Club

Helen Schleman passed away on February 5, 1992. Bev and Barb were at her bedside. Sally Watlington had left the hospital for a physical therapy appointment because she had just had ankle surgery and was on crutches. Sally said, "I had an appointment, so I loped over there and was sitting on a table, and the nurses said I had a telephone call. I took the call, and it was Doctor Julie Schleck telling me that Helen had passed. In the background I could hear Bev and Barb, but they wanted Julie to tell me. Barb had been outside somewhere, but Bev had been with her."

Sally hobbled back to the hospital. She met Bev and Barb in the parking lot as they were leaving. Sally went to Helen's room for a final goodbye. Dorothy was at home on Western Drive. For pragmatic Dorothy, the death of her friend was best dealt with alone.

A story in the Lafayette *Journal and Courier* described Helen as "former Purdue University dean of women, feminist and community activist." Sally was quoted regarding the greatest lesson Helen gave her: "Women can do and be anything that they want to do and be. There were no limits as far as Helen was concerned." An editorial in the *Journal and Courier* stated: "Many women live Helen Schleman types of lives nowadays. But when she first came to Purdue, action-oriented women convinced of equal abilities and therefore insisting on equal rights and equal opportunities were rare."

Two days after Helen's death there was a Purdue women's basketball game. A moment of silence was observed in honor of the woman who had faithfully supported female athletics. In the stands was Dorothy, who first met Helen while playing basketball in the Purdue women's gym in 1933.

A memorial was held in Purdue's Fowler Hall on February 21. Barb spoke:

> She was to the end, a good Hoosier. To Helen this meant being honest, hardworking, open to everyone, caring about the land, being concerned with every living thing. . . . Perhaps, best of all she loved to walk her dog, be it—Fuzzer, Mr. Coffee, Trish, or Kerry—on the golf course—a time when she and her best friend were free from all of life's traumas and problems. . . . Helen was also the most optimistic person I have ever known. She believed in the innate goodness of every human being. She believed in time that this world would become a place of equality and goodness for all and that sex and color would have no bearing on opportunity. She believed every year that *this year* the Equal Rights Amendment would finally become the law of the land!

In another *Journal and Courier* story, Carol Dewey, then Purdue women's volleyball coach, said, "Every woman student at Purdue has benefited from Helen, and they don't know it."

Sally had promised Helen she would take her dog, Kerry. She, Bev, and Barb sorted through the remains of Helen's house. Sally was cleaning out a closet, and deep in the back she found a poster-sized, black-and-white, frayed photograph tacked to a board. She pulled it out, dust flying. It was a picture of the four directors of the U.S. women's reserves of World War II standing with Eleanor Roosevelt. Dorothy stood next to Colonel Ruth Cheney Streeter of the marine corps. Her good friend Captain Mildred McAfee Horton of the WAVES stood next to Colonel Oveta Culp Hobby of the WACS.

The photo was taken on the grounds of the White House; the directors were shoulder-to-shoulder next to the first lady, who was wearing a fox fur draped over her coat, the paws of the animal dangling, a jaunty hat perched on her forehead. The directors were dressed in their thick wool uniform coats and hats, brass buttons shining, stripes at their sleeves, shoulders back. These were the women who led America's females into World War II military history. Fifty years later, Sally stood next to Helen's closet on Western Drive, blinking at the striking photo.

Dorothy was not a saver. She didn't look back. She lived in the moment. Fortunately, Helen saved everything. Sally had the photo restored and large copies printed.

Bev and Barb wrote their annual Christmas letter to former students: "We, with Sally Watlington's great energy and assistance, cleared Helen's lovely home and finished this task finally in October. Helen saved everything—short string, old rubber bands, letters, books, magazines, one glove, etc. We lovingly chuckled, shed a few tears, and reminisced through it all. She was (is) a great positive influence on everyone she touched. We miss her."

Helen donated her house to the Purdue Research Foundation to sell. Interest on the proceeds went to the Office of the Dean of Students.

Helen owned many books and a well-stocked liquor cabinet. Bev, Barb, and Sally had a "library and liquor" party, inviting friends to come take turns selecting books while enjoying cocktails.

Each woman had a stack of chosen books and thought they were finished with the day, when Sally mentioned there was a box of Helen's handkerchiefs. What was she going to do with them? Betty Nelson said, "The crowd went bonkers: 'Can I have one? Can I have one?'"

Helen always carried a handkerchief. Many she owned were made of linen, embroidered with her initials or her full name spelled in colorful thread. She used man-sized handkerchiefs when she played golf. The day of the party, Sally brought out the box, and the women drew numbers to select a favorite.

Betty said, "It took longer to pick our handkerchiefs than it did to pick the books. We deemed then that handkerchiefs from Helen had extra power. Anytime you're going into a situation where you think this is going to be tense, and you will be challenged, you need to make a presentation to a special group, you take Helen's handkerchief with you. You have the power of Helen with you. You would not believe the number of occasions when we've carried our Helen's handkerchief."

That day, the women christened their group the Helen B. Schleman Society, alias Helen's Hankie Club.

Betty said, "What is this passion? My guess is people outside this group could just think this is all unusual. What is this passing of the Bible, Helen's handkerchiefs, and this building of traditions? But a sense of community comes from that . . . a kind of mystical support. It's affirming that people say you're important. What you do moves the mission on. It matters that you care, and what you do is more than work."

Helen's handkerchief power was put into play in 2000 when Betty's good friend and colleague, Linda Ewing, was dying of renal cell carcinoma. Linda was the coworker who had an office across from Betty's in the 1960s. The two women could finish each other's sentences. Betty described Linda as "one of these solid, firstborn, capable individuals."

Linda was a hankie-carrying member of the Helen B. Schleman Society. The week before Linda passed away, Betty was at her bedside. She asked, "Linda, do you know where Helen's handkerchief is?" Linda could not remember where her handkerchief might be, so Betty brought her own to the hospital and placed it on Linda's pillow.

Linda passed away with Helen's handkerchief next to her. Afterward, the family took the handkerchief with Linda's belongings. Betty no longer had her Helen hankie. She was happy that her original had been with Linda when she left this world, but Betty needed her own. She asked Sally for another from the large box still brimming with the power of Helen in the form of a square cotton cloth.

After Helen's death, Sally helped Dorothy move from Western Drive to Westminster Village in West Lafayette. Bev and Barb wrote of Dorothy's move in their 1992 Christmas letter: "She seems to like it but reports that it's like living in a dormitory. (Perhaps we are destined to keep re-living our lives!)"

Both Bev and Barb were aging, feeling the aches and pains of arthritis and a bad back, respectively. They wrote: "We do nightly exercises together—a floorshow, which would be the best entertainment in Tippecanoe County if our 'showings' were public. Bev will have arthroscopic surgery on both knees on January 7. She expects to be bunny hopping by springtime."

The challenge in living a long life is that you watch your friends go before you. In 1994, Mildred McAfee passed away. Dorothy admired "Captain Mac"—the former president of Wellesley College—for her brilliant mind. In a speech after the war, Mildred criticized the "folly of a national policy of discussing manpower in a national emergency as though it were only male power," adding that such an attitude put women in the "category of a national luxury instead of a national asset."

After Mildred's passing, Dorothy, age ninety-five, wrote, "Her death has hit me hard" and listed their similarities: "Both born in Missouri, less than one year apart; Both born to Protestant ministers; Both chose education as their field of work; Mildred was Dean of Women/Students at several colleges, including Oberlin, and D.C.S. was Dean of Women at Purdue; Mildred was Director of WAVES during WWII, and D.C.S. was Director of SPARS."

Dorothy thought Helen, being a few years younger, would outlive her. After Helen passed on, Dorothy began to think seriously about her memorial service. She had wanted to have it in Helen's living room near the pond and the flowing water of the Isabel Bloom sculpture, but that was no longer possible. Dorothy wanted a simple service, and she made one specific request—she asked friend Bob Griffiths to sing a favorite hymn, "How Great Thou Art."

Another aspect to living a long life is the pleasure of seeing events come full circle. In 1992, Dorothy wrote a letter to Purdue's Dean of Liberal Arts David A. Caputo. The school had just changed its name from Humanities, Social Science, and Education (HSSE) to Liberal Arts. Dorothy was quite pleased. The initiative she attempted to cultivate for women in the late 1930s blossomed in the 1990s. She wanted Caputo to know about it.

Accompanying the letter was an April 1946 bulletin that Helen had saved highlighting the liberal science curriculum for women. Dorothy wrote:

> Before World War II, Purdue could not give the B.A. degree. According to Dave Ross, this was by Gentlemen's Agreement with I.U., [and] gentlemen don't break their agreements. I don't know when this agreement was declared null and void. My guess is it was when the G.I.'s began hording the campuses after World War II.

What is important about this is it was the first attempt to broaden offerings in the liberal arts. Why just for women? There was more "push" on that front. President Elliott appointed a committee on the Education of Women. . . . When I came in the middle of the Great Depression from California, I was appalled by the lack of a School of Liberal Arts. Women were the real minority on campus. A significant percentage wanted Liberal Arts Courses.

Needless to say, I am delighted with the current developments. Please accept my best wishes to you, personally and professionally, and to the success of the School of Liberal Arts.

45

Betty's Blast Off and Bible Hand Off

After thirty years working for Purdue students, Betty M. Nelson retired in 1995. Betty decided to retire early at age sixty because her parents and brother had all developed cancer, and only her brother survived. She said, "So I pulled out my warranty and checked the small print. I realized I didn't have a guarantee. There comes a time when the reality of that sinks in and one decides to live differently."

Betty wanted to volunteer for causes beyond Purdue. After she retired, she worked one more semester as chairman of Purdue's United Way campaign. She said, "That was a good bridge activity for me—it allowed me to make contacts in the community."

A story about Betty's retirement appeared in Purdue's publication *Perspective,* with a photo of her sitting in her sunny office in Schleman Hall, smiling brightly for photographer Dave Umberger, the same photographer who took the photo of "Five Deans Walking" in 1987. A vase of red carnations sat on her well-ordered desk, which was decorated with Purdue paperweights. The headline read: "Magic touch, Betty Nelson recalls that some needs never change." Betty was quoted: "I've learned that one thing remains the same: Students thrive on personal attention. Last year, Martha Dungan Nichols, B.S.H. '34, gave me a letter postmarked August 4, 1930, sent to her by Dean Carolyn Shoemaker, Purdue's first dean of women. In this handwritten letter of welcome to an incoming student, Dean Shoemaker greeted her warmly as 'my dear Miss Dungan,' explaining that a 'big sister' would contact her soon, and closed by stating, 'Please come to my office so we can get acquainted.'"

An *Inside Purdue* story described Betty as a young sixty-year-old woman: "Retiring seems out of character for Nelson—known for working long days, doing several things at once and always having something good to say about someone. A member of her staff gave her a retirement gift that's more in keeping with her style—roller blades. 'I was an avid roller skater when I was younger, so I'm looking forward to getting on these,' she says. . . . But remember, Betty—use the curb cuts, and no jumping off retaining walls with those things!"

Photos taken the day Betty received her rollerblades show her in her Schleman Hall office unwrapping a box as staff members gather around. She pulled out a rollerblade, smiling broadly as the staff laughed. She then placed the rollerblade in the crook of her arm like the winning trophy and looked around as if she was about to make an acceptance speech. Another snapshot shows Betty in her maroon blazer, skirt, and hose with a roller blade on her right foot and a black pump on the left. She clings to a staff member's arm while others lean out their office doors watching their retiring dean of students skate away on one foot.

Dorothy, Bev, Barb, and Sally hosted a retirement party for Betty at the Lafayette Country Club in May 1995, with nearly 150 people invited. The title of the event was "Betty's Blast-Off, Celebrating Dean Nelson's Past, Present and Future."

When she announced her retirement, Betty received flowers from her husband, Dick, with a card that said, simply, "To Betty from Dick. I know this is difficult."

Dorothy wrote Betty a note:

> I'm sure you're glad the Big Decision is behind you. Helen said she loved retirement. I hated it, but New York City is different from West Lafayette. You'll now have some time to do what you want to do. Sixty is a good age. You still have time to do what pleases you. Moreover, you and Dick will have more time together. . . . When I read about the complexities of the office, I realize how the job has changed.
>
> One thing I wish you would do—assemble your speeches so that your friends can read them. Each one is carefully crafted.
>
> You know how much I admire you.

Barb Cook wrote Betty. She was thinking about the Bible:

> There are many things you will surely miss, and there are many others, which you will never need to think about again. Ah—
>
> All one can do is feel delight in knowing that one has given one's best effort and somehow that effort will be acknowledged by future leadership in the office. We will have to plan a Shoemaker Bible initiation!
>
> Well, good friend, good luck in your last months on the job. You will find these months strange and often uncontrollable—but as Bev says, "Keep your tail up!"

Betty's campus retirement party was not the traditional reception typically held in a quiet, reserved room of the Memorial Union. Instead, Betty had an ice cream social in the spacious lobby of Schleman Hall. The invitation was a sherbet-hued card depicting heaps of ice cream atop a cone with the words, "Here's the Scoop!" The copy read: "Please join the Office of the Dean of Students in celebrating Dean Betty M. Nelson's retirement, the topping of her distinguished career, which added many rich flavors to the Purdue community."

Ice cream stations were parked in the corners of the lobby. A sign in purple, pink, and brown hung from the ceiling above the guest registry that said, "You make each day a Sundae!" Another sign read, "It's a sherbet you'll be missed."

Well-wishers lined up to greet Betty, standing on the gold and black terrazzo tile of the Schleman Hall lobby with Purdue's giant official seal underfoot.

Of course, Dorothy, Bev, and Barb attended Betty's ice cream social. Helen Schleman's portrait hung in the corner over a cozy nook of lobby chairs.

Betty received numerous letters upon her retirement. One particularly telling note was from retired Vice President John Hicks:

> In my forty-eight years at Purdue, I have known no one who has worked harder, or been more dedicated to her responsibilities than you. Nor have I known anyone more organized, so as to make use of every minute of the day and often the night, too.
>
> Your goal has always been to determine what is best for each individual student, and act accordingly. If only everyone connected with Purdue had this same goal!
>
> I have enjoyed working with you over the years, beginning with your contributions to disabled students, and culminating with your work as Dean. How many other universities have had a parade of stars like Dorothy Stratton, Helen Schleman, Bev Stone, Barbara Cook and Betty Nelson? The answer is: "none"!

ONE YEAR AFTER BETTY LEFT HER OFFICE, Tony Hawkins was officially appointed Purdue's fourth dean of students. Tony had been an associate dean of students and had worked at Purdue for twenty-one years.

Betty invited Tony to lunch at her house. Dorothy, Bev, and Barb were there. Bev wore her gold Purdue pendant watch. Celestial Chicken Salad was served. Betty presented Carolyn Shoemaker's Bible to the first and only man who would hold possession of the secret symbol of the Purdue dean of women/students.

When Betty served Key lime pie, photographer Vincent Walter arrived to enjoy dessert and record the moment in pictures. Dave Umberger was unavailable that day. The group gathered at Betty's dining room table for photographs. The deans were getting older, and they were battling health problems, especially Bev. Betty, Tony, and Barb stood behind Dorothy and Bev, the seated elders. Bev looked off to the right. Vince snapped the picture.

Betty opened the Bible to the page where she had tidily written her name and the initials of her predecessors in July 1987, and she wrote: "Psalms 117 / Psalms 118:24, 28–29 / Passed to L. Tony Hawkins / August 7, 1996 / By DCS, MBS, BIC, BMN."

For the first time since 1947, Helen Schleman's initials were not written down as the Shoemaker Bible was passed.

Psalms 117 is the "Psalm of praise." The New American Standard version reads: "Praise the Lord, all nations; Laud Him, all peoples! For His loving kindness is great toward us, And the truth of the Lord is everlasting. Praise the Lord!"

The Life Application Study Bible interprets the theme of the above passage: "God's love is unchanging in the midst of changing situations. This gives us security."

Psalms 118:24 tells the reader to make the most of each moment, and to do it joyfully: "This is the day which the LORD has made; Let us rejoice and be glad in it." Psalms 118:28–29 reads, "You are my God, and I give thanks to You; You are my God, I extol You. Give thanks to the Lord, for He is good; For His loving kindness is everlasting."

The theme of Psalms 118 according to the Life Application Study Bible is: "Stay true to God and his word no matter how bad the world becomes. Obedience to God's laws is the only way to achieve real happiness."

Betty's chosen passages are fitting for how she lived her retirement life, her head bent slightly forward, scurrying to the next volunteer meeting, community art show, Purdue reception, Purdue retiree event, or alumni gathering. Betty always said, "I don't want to miss a thing." She swirled through a room of Purdue community members or civic friends, talking with each person, remembering tidbits of their lives, including personal triumphs and challenges. She was never afraid to speak to the heart of a matter with fearless candor softened with humor and her serene grace. Wherever Betty was, she was *there*—in the moment, listening to the person standing before her.

After Betty retired, the Dean Betty Nelson Service Award was created, which honors Purdue students who have demonstrated outstanding community service in the Lafayette area. The students selected are the ones who often go unrecognized due to their servant nature.

Betty stayed true to her conviction of supporting students, Purdue University, society, and humanity. Nightly, into the wee hours of the morning, Betty exchanged e-mails with hundreds of alumni, friends, and family. The quotes she placed on her e-mail signature are all Betty:

> "I am at an advantage if all citizens are doing well."
> Claire Gaudiani, Purdue University presentation on 3/4/11
>
> "God is a verb, not a noun."
> Buckminster Fuller

46

Hugging the Purdue Campus

On August 29, 1997, the "Deans' Tea" was held at Duncan Hall in Lafayette, where Dean Carolyn Shoemaker had been expected to give a talk the day she passed away in 1933. The event was to celebrate Dean Carolyn Shoemaker for "her heritage of strength and warmth as a life member of the Community House Association Board." The event also honored her inspiring speech, "Civic Needs," given in 1915, which galvanized a group of women to raise funds to purchase a building to be used as Lafayette's first community center for women and girls.

Dorothy, Bev, Barb, and Betty attended the tea. A portrait of Carolyn Shoemaker was unveiled on the stage. She looks wistful in the painting, her pearl necklace a striking contrast to her black dress with lace sleeves. A photo was taken of the four deans standing two-by-two like powerful pastel bookends embracing the portrait. The only dean missing was Helen.

A member of Purdue's Shoemaker Cooperative spoke at the tea. The house bears Carolyn's name through a bequest that was accepted by the group in 1940.

For the first time on the day of the tea, the deans spoke publically about Carolyn Shoemaker's Bible with a Lafayette *Journal and Courier* reporter. The subsequent article revealed the story of Dorothy finding the Bible in Carolyn's desk in 1933. Characteristically to the point, Dorothy said, "We have always passed it down."

The newspaper deemed the collection of the four surviving deans at Duncan Hall "a rare gathering."

An award was created by the Community House Association Board and announced that day—the Carolyn Shoemaker Achievement Award. It was to be given in April to a woman who effectively "Celebrates the Art of Communication as did Carolyn Shoemaker." In 1999, Bev Stone received the honor.

At the Deans' Tea, Betty spoke on guardian angels: "Some don't believe. Some have one; some feel the force but don't know what the angel looks like. I have at least three—I need more than one. I know the appearance of mine. Dorothy Stratton, Beverley Stone, Barbara Cook have been mentors, guides, friends, models, and guardian angels. Except for Dean Shoemaker and Helen Schleman, you see Purdue's lineup of student personnel deans who served until 1995."

The same year that Bev, age eighty-three, was honored with the Carolyn Shoemaker Achievement Award, she moved from Western Drive to George Davis Manor in West Lafayette. The retirement village was named after Dr. George E. Davis. Davis had been the executive director of the Indiana State Commission on the Aging and Aged during the late 1950s to early 1970s. He also was the man who became dean of students back in the 1940s while Dorothy and Helen were on unpaid leave from Purdue to serve during World War II. For six years, Helen had to remind Davis that he did not have jurisdiction over the Office of the Dean of Women.

Barb had been attempting to care for Bev in their home. Barb had her own physical handicaps. She had broken both hips and her back was in terrible shape, yet she continued to lift Bev into chairs and the car. Finally, the decision was made to move Bev to the retirement village. Barb visited two or three times a day.

As Bev and Barb were dealing with the changes in their lives, Betty wrote:

> I did some work with Bill Bridges, author of "Transitions," and one of the biggest things I learned from him is that people are not resistant to the change in and of itself but to the psychological reorientation that accompanies any type of change. He also said there must be an ending before there can be a beginning. . . .
>
> The time in between known as the middle . . . is like being in the air between trapeze bars or when Linus's blanket is in the dryer! I think both Bev and Barb have had a major psychological reorientation.
>
> It reminds me that soon the "blanket comes out of the dryer" and one can feel secure again! I do hope that Bev and Barb have reached a new and better stage in this transition process—I think so but am holding my breath!

Betty and Sally Watlington looked after Barb, who was looking after Bev. They hosted an eighty-fifth birthday party for Bev in a gathering room at George Davis Manor, with cake to Bev's specifications—chocolate with pink roses. Barb wrote an essay of thanks on June 13, 2001, entitled, "Thoughts for Betty and Sally." It revealed Barb's struggle with her memory:

> Once upon a time, there were two friends named Sally and Betty who both lived in the village of West Lafayette. . . .
>
> Somewhere along the line, Sally and Betty (in their spare time!) decided to care for two of the rattled disabled named Barb and Bev. Bev is physically disabled, and Barb is absent-minded and, in general, rattled most of the time. . . .
>
> It is believed by Betty and Sally that Bev and Barb need "Keepers," so they appointed themselves to this task. They stop by to see Bev and tell her what is going on in the community and the social event of the day. They offer nourishing meals to Barb who keeps losing inches in height, and call to remind her of appointments she has promised to keep. . . .
>
> Bev and Barb think that Sally and Betty are the greatest and best things that happen to Lafayette, but especially to the two of them!
>
> So many, many thanks dear friends for all you do for us!

On March 24, 1999, Dorothy C. Stratton celebrated her one hundredth birthday. Dorothy asked for no fanfare. Sally planned a party hosted by Dorothy's niece and nephew from California and held at the Lafayette Country Club. Friends and family from around the country attended Dorothy's party to honor the woman who had led such a full life and was far from calling it quits. Two senior World War II coast guard SPARs traveled from Washington, DC, to honor Dorothy and make remarks.

The cover of the *Reservist* coast guard magazine featured a World War II-era photo of Dorothy with the words, "Capt. Dorothy Stratton, the First Director of the SPARs, reaches . . . 100!" The editor wrote inside: "One of our own, CAPT Dorothy Stratton, first Director of the Women's Reserve (SPARs), turns 100 years old March 24. Wow! I first put this special event on the long-range schedule back on October 18, 1997. That's the day the Women in Military Service to America (WIMSA) memorial was dedicated at Arlington National Cemetery. While covering that event, two World War II-era SPARs approached me and reminded me of this special occasion."

The colors of the March issue were gold and black in honor of Dorothy's time as Purdue's dean of women. A four-page story about Dorothy appeared. Author Susan Shanahan wrote, "I believe it was no coincidence that Dorothy Stratton was born on the heels of a new century and in March—the month in which we celebrate women's history."

The magazine also put a call out for birthday greetings and received two hundred e-mail greetings and fifty cards "from every nook and cranny of our nation, and several from overseas." One e-mail suggested that the coast guard change its core values during Dorothy's birthday week to "Honor, Respect, and Devotion to Dorothy!"

Dorothy drafted a thank-you note and sent it to the coast guard. She wrote, "You have demonstrated the true meaning of Semper Paratus, Always Ready. I salute you!"

Dorothy was interviewed for an article in the *Journal and Courier* about her century of living. Still well read, Dorothy commented on the status of women in 1999 and how to face change: "I think it's more acceptable for women today to do any job, which wasn't always the case. But there is still job discrimination. It's much better for women today, but it's not perfect.

There are hard choices. You know, you roll with the punches. You forget about things that were different. You adjust to things as they are. And that's what you have to do."

REDBRICK, INDIANA LIMESTONE, words cast for eternity in a fortress of concrete—three gateway markers to Purdue University honor Dean of Students Emerita M. Beverley Stone, Dean of Students Emerita Barbara Ivy Wood Cook, and Dean of Students Emerita Betty M. Nelson. The markers hug the campus, stating boldly—*this* is Purdue University.

Bev's marker was the first to be built near the Purdue Memorial Union at the corner of Grant and State Streets, the most common thoroughfare leading to campus. Purdue's Panhellenic Association surprised Bev with the sign. The organization spent five years raising money through their popular plant sale held in the Memorial Union. When the gateway marker was erected in 1984, Panhellenic's gift was the single largest donation given to Purdue by a student group. Once they decided to donate the sign, The Panhellenic Association kept the identity of the person to whom they would dedicate it a secret until they invited her to speak at one of their meetings. When Bev finished talking, she was told the new gateway marker was to be dedicated in her honor.

The accompanying plaque states, "In honor of M. Beverley Stone, Dean of Student Emerita, for her 24 years of loving concern for students and for her exemplary leadership to Panhellenic, the sororities, and the University—Donated by the Purdue Panhellenic Association, October 1984."

Barb's Purdue marker was built in 1989 at Northwestern and Stadium Avenues. Members of the Barbara Cook Chapter of Mortar Board, along with friends and former students, donated money to build the symbol, a 47.5-ton, 70-foot-long precast concrete marker just east of Lambert Fieldhouse. The plaque reads in part: "The power of her warmth extends to all." Designer and landscape architect John Collier called the piece an "earth sculpture," fitting for Barb, a woman who loved all things flora and fauna.

Betty's marker is at the corner of Grant Street and Northwestern Avenue near Knoy Hall of Technology. Jane Hamblin and Sandy Monroe spearheaded the project. The sign stands nine feet tall and is ten feet long, with a small limestone seat and built-in planter. The bronze plaque quotes Betty: "Every job is a self-portrait of the person who did it. Autograph your work with excellence."

At her marker dedication on October 19, 1996, Betty said, "If I had a plane today, I would attach a huge trailer sign and take off from the Purdue Airport. And the sign would read, 'Thank you, dear friends. I love you!' I'd circle and tip my wing in salute and circle again and again. . . . I am especially appreciative of Sue Hudson, the designer, and John Collier, the landscape architect, who has plans for the plantings for this area. These two routinely create magical effects for Purdue's huge front yard."

Barb Cook also spoke at Betty's gateway marker dedication. She said:

> Beverley Stone, who preceded me as dean of students, is honored by a marker at State and Grant Streets. . . . Mortar Board and others honored me with a marker at Northwestern and Stadium in 1989. Bev and I always say to one another that we are symbolically hugging the campus one end to the other. Now that Bev and I are getting somewhat feeble, we welcome the addition of a vital, "young" retiree to help us support the campus middle. As ol' Purdue continues to grow, more hugs will surely be needed. We think Betty Nelson fits this role perfectly.

BEVERLEY STONE PASSED AWAY on April 16, 2003, at the age of eighty-six. A "Service of Worship and Memorial" was held at First United Methodist Church in West Lafayette. The program was printed on pink paper. For U.S. Navy Lieutenant Commander Stone, the minister read "Crossing the Bar." In his poem written after a serious illness while at sea, Lord Alfred Tennyson compares death to crossing the "sandbar" between the tide of life and the ocean that lies beyond death, the "boundless deep."

A member of the Purdue University Glee Club sang the "Purdue Hymn."

Barb wrote a eulogy for her friend of more than fifty years, but Sally stepped to the podium and read Barb's words. Her tribute ended with this message to Bev: "To you we pray for 'Fair Winds and Following Seas.'"

Former student Mark Lubbers, who had named his daughter after Bev, spoke: "I cannot even *begin* to speak completely for the thousands of students whose lives she touched. She lived for us. Cared deeply for us—

not in a syrupy sort of way, but rather in a wise way—as the arbiter of that strange and difficult period between leaving home and making your way in the world."

Bev was buried alongside her family in Forest Lawn Cemetery in the city where she was born, Norfolk, Virginia. In 1991, Bev had written her "suggested funeral and burial arrangements": "I do not want an expensive casket and shall select one at Hippensteels while living. . . . If he is willing to do so, I would like Mark Lubbers to speak briefly of Purdue alums. . . . As a veteran, I would like to have an American flag on the casket."

In 2004, three Purdue alumni commissioned the creation of a sculpture honoring Bev and Barb. Marylu McEwen, Barbara B. Stonewater, and Barbara G. Watts, of the class of 1968, spent their careers in student services. Stonewater said: "Deans Stone and Cook modeled for us what it was like to be professionals in student affairs. These women were a step ahead of women like them all over the country, and they impacted us all on a personal and professional level as to what it meant to be a strong, assertive, wonderful, smart, professional woman."

Dave Caudill, a sculptor from Louisville, Kentucky, crafted *When Dreams Dance,* a flowing spiral of metal unlike any other sculpture on Purdue's campus. Located on the west side of Schleman Hall, *When Dreams Dance* is feminine and free-form. The sculpture sits among ivy and is rooted in the earth. It is strength. It is grace. *When Dreams Dance* is Bev and Barb.

On December 11, Barb spoke at a dedication ceremony. For several years, she had struggled to care for Bev until her death the previous year. Barb was still grieving. She said:

> While thinking of this special day, I was visited by two spirits: Helen Schleman and Beverley Stone, who came to reminisce about the importance of student affairs in the lives of Purdue students, and conversely, the joy students brought to those of us lucky enough to have worked in the student affairs area.
>
> "We were not always recognized as 'educators,'" they said, "but we always knew we were, and our goal was steadfastly to assist students individually

> and in groups to become, as the saying goes, 'to be the best each can be,' and we also believed we had other responsibilities to make Purdue the best it could be." . . .
>
> I wish to quote something that the "oldest spirit" one said at the end of a speech to her contemporary women deans: "Like a lion, I roar with pride in our profession!"

Barb was quoted in a Lafayette *Journal and Courier* article about the sculpture: "I was so touched to hear about this lovely gesture from my former students, who were later my colleagues. Beverley Stone was a dear friend of mine, and I'm sure she, too, would've been flabbergasted."

Dave Caudill said, "My sculptures' lyrical twists of stainless steel have become metaphors of the paths we take in life."

47

By Your Leave, Sirs

She said she was "going to hang around forever," and she was nearly right. Dorothy C. Stratton passed away peacefully on September 17, 2006, at the age of 107.

Newspapers and Internet sites throughout the United States, from the *New York Times* to the Girl Scouts of America, printed memorials to Dorothy. Her "former" lives were splashed across the media: "Former Dean of Women dies at 107"; "Memorial Service for Former Executive Director of GSUSA Held Oct 1 in Indiana"; "Purdue pioneer Stratton dies at 107"; "Dorothy Stratton, Coast Guard Leader, Dies at 107." Photos of Dorothy in her SPAR uniform or Girl Scout uniform accompanied the news of her passing.

The commandant of the United States Coast Guard released a bulletin with the subject line, "Death of First Director of Women's Reserve (SPARS)."

On October 1, the day of Dorothy's memorial service in West Lafayette, national ensigns flew at half-mast at coast guard units around the globe.

As she requested, Dorothy's memorial service was a simple, private family burial. Sally Watlington, retired navy captain, read the same poem that had been recited at Bev Stone's service, "Crossing the Bar." Dorothy's niece and nephew spoke. "How Great Thou Art" was sung. After the presentation of the flag, Dorothy was buried alongside her parents at Grandview Cemetery.

It was suggested that memorial contributions be made to the donor's favorite charity, or the Dorothy C. Stratton NROTC Scholarship Fund. The annual scholarship had been created in 1999 to be given to a female student in the Purdue navy ROTC program. A plaque bearing Dorothy's name and the names of recipients hangs in the Purdue Armory.

In the book written soon after the end of World War II, *Three Years Behind the Mast: The Story of the United States Coast Guard SPARS,* Dorothy wrote a message to the coast guard under the heading "The Skipper Speaks": "We shall always think of the Coast Guard with loyalty and affection. Our 'Three Years Behind the Mast' have been a never-to-be-forgotten experience which we shall always cherish. A hearty wish for smooth sailing goes with our final salute and our 'By Your Leave, Sirs' as we bow out of your gallant company."

DOROTHY WAS A DILIGENT STUDENT OF LATIN. When Purdue University bestowed the honor of naming Betty M. Nelson as the dean of students e*merita*, Dorothy took exception. Betty said:

> In her quiet but emphatic way, Dorothy let me know there was no Latin word "emerita." That was absolute—she was positive! I told Dorothy what I read about "emerita" in the *Merriam-Webster Unabridged Dictionary*; it made no difference. She would not argue about the matter—it was settled for her. I finally took the very, very large *Merriam-Webster Unabridged Dictionary* to the Quality Copy Shop and had the page copied that included "emerita" and its gender-specific meaning. Even the copy of the page did not cause Dorothy to acknowledge that I could appropriately be titled DOS emerita. She graciously accepted the page I offered but with little comment.

After Dorothy's death, Betty and Sally cleared Dorothy's sparsely kept room at Westminster Village. Sally was sorting the few things that remained in Dorothy's desk. In the back of a drawer, Sally found an 8.5-by-11 sheet of paper folded four times. She unfolded the document, read it, and handed it to Betty. It was the copy of the page from *Merriam-Webster*, several years old by then. Betty said, "Dorothy seemed to have left the message that she would have the last word on the 'emerita' matter and was smiling from her heavenly perch at our discovery."

In 2008, the coast guard announced that it would name a new National Security Cutter in honor of Dorothy Stratton. A cutter is a ship over sixty-five feet in length. For more than two centuries, the U.S. Coast Guard has been America's maritime guardian, employing cutters to protect oceanic borders, save those in peril, and safeguard interests around the globe. The coast guard is "Always Ready" to answer all hazards and all threats.

The Legend-class National Security Cutter would be the first named in honor of a woman. First Lady Michelle Obama sponsored the new cutter, which meant she would christen the ship when construction was completed and later participate in the vessel's commissioning.

It was the first time in history that a first lady sponsored a coast guard or navy ship. Dorothy, a dyed-in-the-wool Democrat, would have been proud. It also was fitting that an African American woman would champion the ship named for the World War II director of the SPARs. During the war, when Dorothy took leave from her position as dean of women at Purdue, Interim Dean Claire Coolidge had denied housing to black women.

On July 23, 2010, in Pascagoula, Mississippi, home of Ingalls Shipbuilding, Michelle Obama christened a National Security Cutter in honor of Captain Dorothy C. Stratton. Betty and Dick Nelson and Captain Sally Watlington, in her white navy uniform, attended the christening with a contingent of Dorothy's family and friends. By this time, Barb Cook lived in University Place and was unable to attend this unprecedented event in the life of her chosen family.

From the 11,000 SPARs who served during World War II, more than twenty surviving women attended from across the United States. The coast guard band played as the audience waved American flags in the hot summer air and waited for the first lady to speak.

The backdrop to the podium was a billboard-sized banner with an image of Dorothy in her SPAR uniform. When the first lady was introduced, the crowd stood and applauded for several minutes. As Dorothy's ship and her image towered behind Michelle Obama, she said:

> I wasn't fortunate enough to know Captain Stratton personally. But I have come to know her story. And as a woman, and as a mother of two daughters, as an American, I stand in awe of her life of service. . . .
>
> Captain Stratton taught us first about love of country. See, she didn't come from a military family. And she certainly didn't dream of wearing the uniform. Instead, she distinguished herself first in academia. But what happened? Pearl Harbor was bombed, and our country was at war. So she volunteered. And when a colleague at Purdue University said—and this is a quote—"Dorothy, you can't afford to do this," her reply was simple. She said, "I can't afford *not* to."
>
> Captain Stratton also taught us about perseverance. See, for all its opportunities, the SPARs were still limited. They couldn't give men orders, which is an absolute problem. [Laughter.] They couldn't serve overseas, or even go to sea. Later in life, she would say, "I'm sometimes referred to as the commanding officer of the SPARs. Actually, I had no command authority. All I had was the power of persuasion." . . .
>
> The legacy of Captain Stratton and her SPARs lives on in all those who followed in their footsteps. After World War II, it would be another thirty years before women started to be fully admitted to the coast guard and other services. But ask any of those women—including those here today—and they'll tell you that it was Captain Stratton, the SPARs, and the women of World War II who opened the door so that they could walk through and proudly serve this country.

The first lady was escorted to Dorothy's cutter. She took the tethered champagne bottle—covered in a knit sock to prevent glass from exploding into the air, as red, white, and blue banners waved in the breeze—and said, "In the name of the United States of America, I christen thee *Stratton*. May God bless this ship and all who sail in her."

The first lady then struck the bow of Dorothy's ship, and "fump!"—the bottle bounced off. It was as if Dorothy—always no-frills and direct—said, "I'm not going along with all this hoopla that easily."

With a second whack, the bottle broke, splattering champagne onto Michele Obama. The crowd cheered. The band played the coast guard marching song, "Semper Paratus."

Betty and Sally stood in the audience clapping, tears in their eyes, the two people who knew Dorothy the best.

Fast-forward two years, and on March 31, 2012, a rainy and gray day, the United States Coast Guard Cutter *Stratton* was commissioned to head out to sea from Alameda, California. Again, Sally, Betty, and a gaggle of friends and family attended, including many of the SPARs from World War II who loved Dorothy as their fearless leader. They sat in the stands wearing ponchos and holding umbrellas.

The massive, gleaming white *Stratton* was docked behind a stage filled with coast guard dignitaries and Michelle Obama. The cutter was wrapped in a giant red, white, and blue ribbon. A banner of maritime signal flags was strung across the top of the ship, waving in the drizzle, a colorful punctuation in a colorless sky.

A seal was created for the new cutter. Each color and image of its shield and crest bears meaning to Dorothy. Depicted is the coast guard motto "Always Ready." Hawthorn branches signify the state of Missouri, where Dorothy was born. There also is a crest showing the cutter sailing between the continents, with Dorothy's famous 1942 words to Purdue Trustee Kathryn McHale, "We can't afford not to"—a slight modification from Dorothy's original words, "*I* cannot afford not to."

The afternoon before the commissioning, Betty, Sally, and their group walked onto the deck of the cutter. They toured Dorothy's ship from stem to stern. A cutter is like its own small city, serving those who sail the seas while they protect the United States coastline. That evening, Betty presented a framed photo of Dorothy's portrait to the cutter's first commanding officer, Captain Charles Cashin.

On the day of the commissioning, the *Stratton* crew marched up the gangway onto the cutter. During training, the crew had already sailed to several East Coast ports. They had navigated the *Stratton* through the

Panama Canal, south to the equator, and up to California. While traveling north from the equator, the *Stratton* responded to a Colombian fishing vessel in distress, saving eight lives. Before it was even commissioned for service, Dorothy's ship had navigated uncharted waters to help others.

Michelle Obama gave the orders: "Lay aboard and bring our cutter to life!"

Engines roared. The United States Coast Guard Cutter *Stratton* was alive and ready for the sea.

48

The Place Just Right

Barb Cook moved from her home at 1807 Western Drive, the last dean on "Deans' Row," to University Place Retirement Community in 2007. She took her black cat, Coalie, and settled into an apartment with the help of Betty Nelson and Sally Watlington. Her memory was slipping away. Barb, always the prolific writer, kept journals from the late 1980s until her first year in her retirement apartment. The latter writings revealed her awareness of fate's shadowy death grip on her scholarly mind.

In November 2010, Betty and Sally moved Barb to the Memory Unit at Mulberry Health and Retirement Community in Mulberry, Indiana. In one of her journals written before her memory was too diminished, Barb wrote, "As I think about my life, I believe I have done my best. . . . I have been rewarded most by former students who still keep in contact. I thank them and Purdue for giving me this opportunity."

Betty and Sally continued to look after Barb, serving as her guardians and overseeing her care. In subtle, gentle ways, Betty would remind the nursing staff on the Memory Unit that Dr. Barbara Ivy Wood Cook, who sat before them unaware of the world beyond her room, was Purdue's dean of students emerita. It was a prompt to consider the real Barb, the woman who had lived with much depth.

Betty and Sally continued to send a yearly Christmas letter with an update to nearly 150 Purdue alumni and friends who were on Barb and Bev's address list. Many who received the letter also had known Dorothy and Helen.

On April 10, 2013, Barb, age eighty-three, passed away. A memorial service was held on May 17 at St. John's Episcopal Church in Lafayette. Betty and Sally sent a letter announcing the service to the names on Barb's Christmas list. Betty found apropos postage. She said, "The absolute highlight was finding the perfect postage stamp for the mailing—love having Barb continue to make a personal political statement with the Rosa Parks stamp! Barb's spirit lives on and continues to promote equality of gender and race."

Barb wanted to be buried in Memorial Park Cemetery in her hometown of Memphis, Tennessee, near her parents and two of her aunts. The weekend after Barb passed, Betty and Sally drove to Memphis to bury Barb. They stayed in Barb's favorite hotel—the Peabody. The elegant hotel is synonymous with southern hospitality and delta style, built in downtown Memphis in 1869, the same year Purdue University was founded.

When Betty retired to her room at the Peabody, she found sitting on a table a vase of flowers—a fragrant white lily tinged in pink and a couple of red roses with a spray of pink snapdragons—along with a plate of chocolate-covered strawberries. The gifts were from Purdue alumni Ann and Bill Moreau. Bill was the *Exponent* editor who in 1974 printed the cartoon of Bev Stone "magically" becoming Purdue's dean of students with a wave of the wand by Vice President Fischang. Bill had been Bev and Barb's lifelong friend. After Barb's death, Bill wrote a letter to her brother, Pete. He said:

> During . . . my time as an undergraduate and later when I did a year of graduate school, Bev and Barb were my frequent lunch and dinner companions and my idols. I felt especially close to Barb, probably because of her height, her grace, and her amazing ability to indicate that everything I said—however banal—was interesting and worthy of consideration. She urged me in every encounter to follow my passions and change the world. . . .

> In the 1980s and early 90s I got involved in Indiana government, which permitted me to reach out frequently to Bev and Barb. . . . Barb was one of the founding members of the Governor's Commission on Women, certainly one of the smartest appointments Governor Bayh ever made.
>
> In 1991, I was fortunate enough to be appointed by Governor Bayh to a seat on the Purdue Board of Trustees. This time around, I found myself a part of the Purdue administration at a time when Bev and Barb were retired and quite able—and willing—to voice their opinions about the operation of their beloved Purdue. Once again, I found myself seeking forgiveness from Barb for decisions she thought didn't take the interests of students sufficiently into account. She thought universities ought to be focused on the students. Typical Barb!

The next morning, Betty and Sally packed the car and drove to Memorial Park Cemetery. Betty took along the vase of flowers from the Moreaus.

They turned the car into the cemetery. It looked like a park. The grave markers were flush to the earth; only rolling landscape with a smattering of large trees and a few benches could be seen. The sky was cloudless; the azaleas, dogwood, and redbud trees were in bloom. It was a perfect day for Barb, who as a child had walked in the Memphis woods with her father, learning the names of wildflowers and birds.

A green tent was set up over Barb's casket, and four rows of chairs sat waiting, vacant. Two men in suits who were handling the burial stood outside the tent. The committal service was conducted by Reverend Eyleen Farmer of Calvary Episcopal Church, the church of Barb's childhood. Barb would have been quite pleased that a female priest conducted her service.

Betty placed the vase of flowers from the Moreaus on a ledge in front of Barb's casket. The heavy glass vase and colorful spray added an understated touch.

Barb wanted to be buried in her Purdue academic robe. Inside the closed casket, she was in full regalia, wearing her black gown of heavy faille fabric and rich velvet. Embroidered in gold at each shoulder was the Purdue University seal with the griffin, a symbol of strength. She held her mortarboard cap and her Mortar Board National College Senior Honor Society pin was attached to her robe.

Barb's cat, Coalie, passed away when Barb lived at University Place. The cat was cremated and the ashes placed in a can. Sally glued a photo of Barb holding Coalie onto the can and tucked it inside the casket.

Reverend Farmer began reciting the traditional Episcopalian memorial service. Betty and Sally sat on the front row, looking at Barb's casket. A red Japanese maple served as a backdrop. On what was an otherwise windless day, a breeze entered the tent and whipped at the vase of flowers, knocking it to the ground. Betty said, "There was this little clutch of flowers on the ground in the middle of all this glass. So Sally leaned over, picked up the flowers, dusted off the glass, and laid the bouquet across the top of the casket, a little mini blanket of flowers. Barb probably liked that better—get them out of their container, have them look a little freer."

Sally remembered her reaction: "I said to myself, 'Barb is giving us a signal—Get on with this. Get the thing over with.'"

The rector stopped talking midsentence, looked at the shattered vase and strewn flowers, and then continued with the service. Betty said, "I don't think the priest was accustomed to vases exploding off her caskets."

IN 1991, BARB WROTE A TWO-PAGE AUTOBIOGRAPHY, reflecting on her life and how it could have turned out differently. She wrote, "I have loved my professional life and the Purdue students, and have felt singularly blessed in this experience. Yet I sometimes wonder what my life would have been if Salem had lived. I am sure it would have been different as it has been for many of my classmates at Syracuse University in 1954. Life takes strange turns. . . . I am, in retrospect, proud of myself as a professional; I wonder how I would have done as a long-time wife and mother?"

In his letter eulogizing Barb, Bill Moreau ended with this: "I keep a picture under the glass of my desk. It has followed me to at least ten offices and a couple of career moves. It is a snapshot of four people. The year is 1979. From left-to-right are Mark Lubbers, Barb, Bev, and a very skinny and mustachioed me. Barb and Bev were in DC for a Mortar Board convention and wanted to see their two friends who were working on Capitol Hill. Barb is beaming, and has her arms swung wide apart, and she has all three of us in her embrace. I will keep that picture in sight until I have no more sight."

49

Epilogue

Carolyn Shoemaker's Bible was passed from L. Tony Hawkins to Dean of Students Danita Brown on June 23, 2011.

To commemorate the hundredth anniversary of Carolyn's appointment as Purdue University's first dean of women, Danita Brown transferred the Bible to Purdue University's Susan Bulkeley Butler Women's Archives on June 17, 2013.

Now a preserved artifact, the deans' Bible symbolizes the professional and personal bond between six indomitable Purdue women.

In 2009, Purdue's Barbara Cook Chapter of Mortar Board commissioned portraits of M. Beverley Stone, Barbara I. Cook, and Betty M. Nelson to commemorate the deans' achievements and their fifty years spent working with the chapter. Indianapolis-based artist Mark Dillman painted the portraits that are displayed in the Purdue Memorial Union West Faculty Lounge.

No portrait, marker, or building graced Purdue's campus to honor Dorothy C. Stratton until March 2012. Purdue Libraries celebrated Women's History Month by unveiling a portrait of Dorothy painted by Mark Dillman and contributed by Sally Watlington. A Purdue Archives and Special Collections exhibit in Dorothy's honor opened the month before. Betty and Sally spoke at the reception hosted by Dean of Libraries James L. Mullins, telling tales of their dear friend. A video of this ceremony is housed in the Purdue Archives.

FROM HER HOME ON WOODED HIDEAWAY LANE, Dean of Students Emerita Betty M. Nelson and her husband, Dick, continue to enjoy a jam-packed retirement filled with Purdue University and community events. Betty remains well-connected with Purdue students, both past and present, and with retired colleagues through her work with the Purdue University Retirees Association. Currently, she is president of the Greater Lafayette Mortar Board Alumni Chapter.

Sally Watlington volunteers in her community, where she serves as board chair of Franciscan St. Elizabeth Health/Hospitals. She also serves as secretary-treasurer of the Mortar Board National Foundation and treasurer of the YWCA Foundation of Greater Lafayette. She spends free time in her terraced garden where Helen Schleman's Isabel Bloom statue holds court.

Betty and Sally share much history, memories, and affection for the four "Deanie Weenies" who once lived on "Deans' Row."

Index

Access to Public Records Act (APRA), 334
Adaptive Learner Program, 348
Ade, George, 4
agriculture, 271; women majoring in, 5, 80, 176
Agnes Scott College, 329
airport, Purdue University, 101, 291, 432; Amelia Earhart and, 57, 86, 88, 89, 404; Robert F. Kennedy at, 276
Akeley, Anna (professor), 329
Albjerg, Marguerite, Dr., 199
Albjerg, Victor, Dr., 199
Aldrin, Buzz; 303–4
Amelia Earhart Fund for Aeronautical Research, 87
Amelia Earhart Plaque dedication, 404
American Association of University Women (AAUW), 117–18, 155; journal of, 209–10
American Counseling and Personnel Association, 275
American Standards Association, 211
American Women's Association, 70
Anderson, Charles Albert, 97–98
Arbuckle, G. O. (director of university residences), 173
Arkansas Agricultural, Mechanical and Normal (AM&N), 161
Armstrong, Janet Shearon (Mrs. Neil), as Purdue student, 304
Armstrong, Neil, as Purdue graduate, 303–4
Army Specialized Training Program (ASTP), 135–36
Arnsman, Betty, 295–96
Arvin, Janie, 342, 347
Association of Women Students (AWS), 172, 229, 334
ASTP (Army Specialized Training Program), 135–36
astronauts: from Purdue, 303–4, 305; women as, 303, 305
Athletic Conference of American College Women, 40
Auburn Automobile Company, 59, 60
Auburn University, 358
Avery, George, 371
AWS (Association of Women Students), 172, 229, 334
Ayres, W. L., 84–85

Baldwin, James: *The Fire Next Time*, 282
Ball State University, 256
Bankoff, Joe, 265–66
Banta, K. Vernon, 211

Baptists, 32–34, 36, 182
Barbara Cook Chapter of Mortar Board, 381, 445
Barnard College, 273–74, 277
Barnes, Sarah, 83
Bates, Daisy, 225
Beard, Mary Ritter, 101–2
Beauvoir, Simone de, *The Second Sex*, 299
Beck, Miriam, 60
Bell, Vereen, *Swamp Water*, 148
Beering, Steven (president): disparages Office of Dean of Students, 372; Nude Olympics and, 370–71; readmits dropped football player, 374–77; Slayter Center closing and, 371
Berg, Chris, 341
Big Sister Movement, 9
Big Ten, 172, 290, 310, 328, 329, 374
Bill of Student Rights, 276
birth control, 256, 274, 286
blacks: activism of women, 9, 226–27, 293–95; Delta Sigma Theta and, 279; discrimination against, 141–44, 161–63, 274–75, 299, 398–99; men in military, 135–36, 144; student demonstrations and, 280–82, 293–95
Black Purdue, 142–43, 280
Blalock, Marion Williamson, 279–80
Blanton, John W., 290
Bloom, Isabel, Helen Schleman's fountain by, 234, 446
Boiler Bouts, 390–93
Bovee, Dorothy, 82; "Women and Women's Work," 83
Boyk, Sol, 82
Boy Scouts of America, 10–11
Boy's Life, 11
Branch, Frederick C., 135–36
Breyfogle Ranch, 39
Brown, Danita (dean of students), 445
Brown, Herbert C., as Nobel Laureate, 207
Brown, James R., 63
Brubaker, Guy, 290
Brucker, Edmund, paints Helen Schleman's portrait, 309
Brynjulf, Strandenaes, paints Amelia Earhart's portrait, 102
Bunting, Mary, Dr., 217, 221
Burke, Marshall, 224
Burns, Ken (executive vice president and treasurer), 346
Burns, Lucy, 9–11
Butz, Earl, 271–72, 301, 308–9
Butz, Keith, 361
Buza, Jim, 399
Byrkett, Sharon Arvin, 342–43, 347

Caesar, Sid, *Tars and Spars*, 126–27
Cantor, Eddie, Hollywood Canteen and, 140
Caputo, David A. (dean of liberal arts), 419
careers: counseling for, 37, 59, 61, 97; marriage and, 71, 109–10, 139, 168, 263; for women, 58, 93–94, 136; women as overqualified in, 138–39; women's education and, 6, 175, 206, 220
Carlyle, Mr., as caretaker of Ross Hills Camp, 236
Carlyle, Mrs., as Helen Schleman's housekeeper, 236
Carnegie, Andrew, 7
Carnegie Corporation of New York, 7
Carnegie Foundation, 7
Carolyn E. Shoemaker Scholarship, 29
Carter, James E., 211
Carter, Rosalynn, 408
Cary, Frank, 20
Carey, Ernestine Gilbreth, 72
Catholicism, Catholics, 28, 255–56, 312
Caudill, Dave, 433
Cedarville University, 159
Central Presbyterian Church, 7, 28
Chapman, Sally Putnam, 104
Chavers, Gordon (general counsel), 397
Chayes, Antonia, 220
Chicago, 275; 1933 World's Fair in, 44
Chisholm, Shirley, 307
Christmas parties of Helen Schleman, 236–37
civil rights, 223, 224, 243; of disabled, 214, 340; legislation for, 323; Martin Luther King Jr.'s assassination and, 275–78; President Kennedy and, 242; women and, 306–7
Civil Rights Act of 1964, 230–31, 323, 336–37
Civil Rights Act of 1968, Title VIII (Fair Housing Act), 174, 231
civil rights movement, 320, 340; James Baldwin and, 282; Free Speech Movement and, 265; Jesse Jackson and, 295; women in, 225–26, 230
Civil War: Purdue Memorial Union and, 21; Dorothy Stratton's grandfather and, 32
cohabitation: on college campuses, 273–74; premarital, advocated by Helen Schleman, 259–60
Columbia University, 31, 34, 163–64, 187; student unrest at, 274, 281; Teachers College, 96, 187
Committee on Scholastic Delinquencies and Readmissions, 374–75
Committee on the Education of Women, 81
Community Center for Women, 16
Community House, 16–17, 27, 29
Community House Association, 16, 27, 427, 428
Congressional Union (National Woman's Party), 9

Cook, Barbara Ivy Wood (Barb) (dean of students), 1, 157–66, 270, 444; as associate dean of women, 301, 314; Black Salute controversy and, 294; blindfolded for Handicap Awareness Day, 344; childhood of, 157–59; communist book collection of, 164–65; Salem Cook and, 166, 188–93, 197; *Counseling Women*, 318; as dean of students, 357–58, 365–77, 391; deans-at-the-window episode, 389; on Deans' Row, 359–60, 363–64; death of, 442–44; as director of Placement Service for Women, 197–98, 240, 257; favorite book of, 198; on *The Feminine Mystique*, 230; in "Five Deans Walking" photo, 382; on future, 314–15; gateway marker of, 431; at Girl Scout camp, 158–59; Grand Prix Girls and, 373; hair of, 262; at Helen B. Schleman Symposium, 358; as Helen Schleman Gold Medallion Award winner, 272; integration and, 162–63; Ph.D. thesis of, 257, 263–64; on President Kennedy's assassination, 240–42; Sonya Margerum and, 355–56, 370; marriage of, 166, 188–91; monitors student rallies, 291, 292; Mortar Board and, 25, 317, 325–26, 380, 445; as Mortar Board Leadership Conference speaker, 367; Betty Nelson and, 389; Nude Olympics and, 370–71; papers and speeches by, 314–18, 335; parties hosted by, 200, 353, 355; portrait of, 445; private life of, 314; at Purdue University, 187, 194, 197–98, 229, 261, 299; readmission of dropped football player controversy and, 374–77; retirement of, 372, 379–81, 441; on Helen Schleman, 416; Carolyn Shoemaker's Bible and, 358, 381–82; Slayter Center closing and, 371–72; Beverley Stone as friend and housemate of, 188, 191, 195, 197, 236, 353, 355, 356, 358–60, 373, 432, 433–434; Dorothy Stratton and, 363; student alcohol abuse and, 369–72; at Syracuse University, 164–65, 190, 191; at University of Arkansas, 160–63, 188, 191; Sally Watlington and, 362–63; as Woman of the Year for 1971, 316; as YWCA Salute to women in Education Award nominee, 369
Cook, Salem: death of, 192–93, 197; as husband of Barbara Cook, 166, 188–91
Coolidge, Clare (assistant dean of women), 106, 142–43; Amelia Earhart collection and, 104; as interim dean, 113, 135–36, 140, 171; Office of Student Affairs debacle and, 149–52
Copland, Aaron, 166
Córdova, France A., as first woman president of Purdue, 308
Cornell University, 25
Cosmopolitan, 65
Coulter, Lucy Eunice, 16
Coulter, Stanley (dean of men), 4, 13, 15, 16, 29, 36
Creek, H. L. (English Department head), 6
Curtiss-Wright Engineering Cadettes, 136–38

DACOWITS (Defense Advisory Committee on Women in the Services), 205–8, 222, 258–59
Daniels, Dale, 400
Davidson, Clara, 95–96
Davis, Bette, Hollywood Canteen and, 140
Davis, George E., Office of Student Affairs debacle and, 149–53, 155–56, 170, 221, 295
Dean Betty Nelson Service Award, 425
Deans' Bible, The, 2, 3, 35, 36, 401, 445; tradition of, 167–68, 283, 265–66, 358, 381–82; in Susan Bulkeley Butler Women's Archives, 445
deans of men, 15, 16, 106
deans of women, 14, 15; compassion of, 107, 298; dual role of, 8; entertaining students, 200–201; *The Feminine Mystique* and, 230; functions of, 13, 37, 107–8; office space of, 106; standards of conduct for, 109–10. *See also names of individual deans*
Deans' Row (Western Drive), 2, 364, 381, 384, 413, 441, 446
Debris (yearbook), 107, 111, 210; "A Look Back: Tragedies," 368; "The Coed's Plea," 17; on Greek Week, 195; Helen Schleman in, 173
Defense Advisory Committee on Women in the Services (DACOWITS), 205–8, 222, 258–59
DeFrantz, Faburn, 143
Delta Sigma Theta, 10, 279
Denton, Wallace, 315
Detroit, Michigan, racial unrest in, 275
Dewey, Carol, on Helen Schleman, 416
Dickens, Charles, 258
Dietrich, Marlene, Hollywood Canteen and, 140
Dietz, Howard, 126
Dillman, Mark, 445–446
discrimination: Amelia Earhart on, 64; against blacks, 142, 294; against black women, 10, 142–43; Civil Rights Act and, 230, 231; against disabled, 215; in housing, 174; Helen Schleman against racial, 49, 274–75; Title IX and, 323–24; against women, 105, 110, 163, 204, 210, 224–25, 305–6, 334, 336; in workplace, 224, 430
Division of Education, 77
Division of Intercollegiate and Intramural Athletics, 84

Donohue, Robert, Admiral, as Dorothy Stratton's supervisor, 123–24
Dostoevsky, Fyodor, *The Idiot*, 198
Dow Chemical Company, 296
Duhme, Ophelia Fowler, 47
Dukes, Vernon, 126
Duncan Electrical Manufacturing Company, 27, 76
Duncan Hall, 27–28
Duncan, Sarah Ely, 27
Duncan, Thomas, 27
Durant, Henry, 41
Durant, Paula, 41
Durante, Jimmy, Hollywood Canteen and, 140

Earhart, Amelia, 55–68, 86, 201, 207, 220; as catalyst; for clothing and, 59, 64; disappearance of, 101, 104; dormitory life and, 63; dreams of mechanical training for women, 88; encourages liberal arts degree, 85; faculty appointment of, 55–58; Lillian Gilbreth and, 75, 76; historical materials of, 102–4; *Last Flight*, 87; last flight of, 88–92; mealtimes and, 63, 64; Nancy Drew and, 246; plaque dedicated to, 201; as poet and writer, 65, 66; portrait of, 102; George Palmer Putnam and, 56, 86, 101–3, 104; as role model, 110; Eleanor Roosevelt and, 56; Helen Schleman and, 404; speeches of, 56, 61; study of aviation and, 86–88; weekly waffles with Dorothy Stratton, 66, 67
Ecker, Carol, 202–3
Eckles, R. B., 84
education: marriage and, 6, 175, 177; motherhood and, 6; women and, 6, 174–75, 227–29
Eikenberry, Kevin, 367
Eiler, Sue Daniel, 291–92, 301, 316
Eisinger, C. E, 290
Eisenhower, Dwight D., 77, 212, 271
Elliott, Edward C. (president), 28, 36, 48, 106, 113, 285; Amelia Earhart and, 55–58, 88–89, 102–4; Office of Student Affairs debacle and, 149–51, 153; George Putnam and, 56, 57, 89–91, 101, 102–3; on segregation, 141; Dorothy Stratton and, 31, 34, 49, 81
Emily Mauzy Vogel (EMV) Sophomore Leadership Conference, 395–98
engineering: civil, 236; women in, 5, 64, 80, 136–38, 305–6
England, Bill, 350
English Department, 4, 6–7, 290, 359
Ephron, Nora, 327
Equal Employment Opportunity Commission (EEOC), 336
Equal Pay Act of 1963, 224
Equal Rights Amendment (ERA), 24, 218, 408; introduced into Congress, 310; not mentioned in *American Women* report, 224; sponsoring of, 130, 231
ERA. *See* Equal Rights Amendment
Ewing, Ken, pastor at University Church, 258
Ewing, Linda Hurd, 258–59; death of, 418
Exponent (Purdue student newspaper), 115, 208, 291, 307, 310, 347, 384; administrative consolidation and, 329–30; on black student beating incident, 399–400; cartoons in, 330, 379–80, 400, 442; on Coed Canteens, 139; Barbara Cook in, 165, 193, 380; black salute coverage in, 293–94; editors of, 286, 298, 316; letters to editor of, 287–89; on readmission of expelled football player controversy, 376–77; Helen Schleman in, 337; on Chris Smith Boiler Bout, 391–92; Bill Smoot controversy and, 286–90; Beverley Stone in, 320, 349–52, 366; student unrest in, 265–66, 296; on *Your Best Foot Forward*, 181

Fair Housing Act of 1968, 174, 231
Feldt, Irene (acting director of Women's Residence Halls), 135, 151
Fels, Anna, 24
female students: advising and counseling of, 106–7; book of regulations for, 54; careers and, 61–62, 220; concerns about, 8; curfew of, 171–73; curriculum for, 82; as doctoral students, 263–64; dress code for, 179–80; Amelia Earhart and, 58–62; education of, expected to prepare for marriage and motherhood, 41, 139, 175, 178, 228–29; enrollment increases of, 79; liberal science program for, 83–84; motivation for, 222; need for a Bachelor's degree, 80–81; orientation for, 174–78; residence hall and, 49, 63; progress for, stalled, 170–71; in loco parentis and, 81; welfare of, 37
Fischang, Bill, (vice president for student services), 330
Fisher, Jody, 236
Fisher, Martin L. (dean of men), 36
"Five Deans Walking" photograph, 1, 382, 421
Forrestal, James, Secretary of the Navy, 115, 123
Forrestal, Josephine: SPARs and, 124; WAVES uniform and, 115, 123
Foster, James, 400
Franciscan St. Elizabeth Health/Hospitals, 28, 446
Frank and Lillian Gilbreth Collection, 77
fraternities and sororities, 172, 201–2, 372, 431; alcohol abuse and, 369; Boiler Bouts and, 390–92; Delta Sigma Theta, 10, 279; Greek Week and, 195–96; housemothers and, 54, 191, 286; houses of, 136, 139, 191; rush and, 19, 52–53, 201; Theta Xi, 398–99

Frazier, James T., 248–49
Frazier, Marian, 65
Freedman, Estelle, 273
Freehafer, Lytle J., 354
Free Speech Movement, 265
"Freshman Folio, The" (1937–38), 106
Friedan, Betty: *The Feminine Mystique*, 226–31

Gambrell, Mary Latimer, 321
Gangone, Lynn M., *The National Association for Women in Education*, 155
Garfield, John, Hollywood Canteen and, 140
Gass, William, Professor, 287
Gas-well Farm, 39
Gates, Ralph, 143
George Palmer Putnam Collection of Amelia Earhart Papers, 66
Gilbreth, Frank, Jr., 72
Gilbreth, Frank, Sr., 71–73, 210
Gilbreth, Lillian Moller, 69–78, 361–62; acknowledged, 109; as authority in industrial engineering and management, 70; in *Cheaper by the Dozen*, 71; donates papers to Purdue, 77; Amelia Earhart and , 75, 76; Amelia Earhart collection and, 104; Edward Elliott and, 69, 75; encourages liberal arts degree, 85; family life of, 71–72, 76; on Girl Scouts of America Board of Directors, 181; honored by Helen Schleman, 78; husband's death, 73–74; portrait of, in National Portrait Gallery, 362; on President's Committee on Employment of the Physically Handicapped, 210, 215; as role model, 110; Dorothy Stratton and, 69, 75, 361; in World War II, 112–13
Gillespie, Beulah V., 221, 223
Girl Scouts of America, 181–82; *American Girl* magazine, 131–32; Camp Kiwani, 158–59; Dorothy Stratton as executive director of, 114–15, 205, 208
Goldwater, Barry, 130
Goodman, Ellen, 387–88
Goudge, Elizabeth, *Green Dolphin Street*, 148–49
Graduate, The (movie), 287
Graham, Katharine, 307
Graham, Martha, *Appalachian Spring*, 166
Graham, W. R., 29
Grand Prix Girls, 373
grants for student wives, 270
Great Depression, 31, 34, 38, 44, 47, 94; teens needing counseling during, 96; insecurity of young women during, 107
Green, Edith Louise Starrett, 324
Green Guard, 9; controversy at 1968 ice cream social of, 285–92, 371
Gregory, Dick, 280
Grier, Daniel (assistant dean of men), 261
Griffiths, Bob, 419
Griffiths, Martha W., 230–31
Gunderson, Susan, 261

Haas, Phil (provost), 374
Hahn, Mark, 347
Hall, Helen, 66
Hamblin, Jane, 26, 325
Hamerschlag, Vera, as commanding officer in LORAN, 131
Hand, Helen, 28
handicaps, people with, 210, 339–48; barriers to, 211–15; learning disabilities and, 348
Hansen, Arthur (president), 351; appointment of, 308; inequalities of female faculty and, 333, 336–38; at retirement of Beverley Stone, 353
Hardy, Thomas, 95
Harvard University, Education Review, 107, 153, 158, 254
Harvey, as Beverley Stone's favorite play, 198
Hawkins, Tony, 424
Hazelton, Helen, 81, 82
Height, Dorothy, 226
Helen B. Schleman Gold Medallion Award, 272–73
Helen B. Schleman Natatorium, Lafayette YWCA, 406–7
Helen B. Schleman Symposium, 358
Hepburn, Katharine, WCWA and, 101
Hicks, John, as executive assistant to President Hovde, 281, 333, 335; as executive vice president, 314, 341, 375, 424
Higginbotham, A. Leon, Jr., 141–42
Hilton, Eunice, 164–65, 191
Hobby, Oveta Cup, 112, 125
Hollywood Canteen, 139–40
home economics: classes at Ladies Hall, 5; dean of, 18, 32, 220–21, 335; male as dean of, 221–23, 295; school of, 77, 85, 169, 177, 220, 221; students of, 104, 304, 198, 304; teachers of, 169; women and, 80, 82, 139, 176–77
Home Economics Society (Virginia C. Meredith Club), 24
honor societies, 24–26. *See also* Mortar Board
Hood, Nicholas Hood, Sr., Reverend, 142
Horton, Douglas, Reverend, as Mildred McAfee's husband, 153
Housemother Training School, 54; Barbara Cook at, 191–92
Hovde, Frederick L. (president), 83–84, 169, 206, 281; consolidation of residential systems under, 295; housing issues

and, 173; male dean of School of Home Economics controversy and, 220–23; Office of Student Affairs debacle and, 156; retires, 307; Helen Schleman and, 156, 183, 202–3, 267–68; Schleman-Hovde Golf Classic, 361; segregation and, 142, 282; Bill Smoot controversy and, 288–89; Beverley Stone and, 283, 352; student unrest and, 283, 296
Hovde Hall of Administration (Executive Building), 167, 188, 366, 388–89; construction of, 106; first Indiana wheelchair lift in, 342; student protests at, 280–81, 316
Hoover, Herbert, 74
Hoover, Lou, 74
Howard University, 10, 279
Hudson, Rock, 368
Humanities, Social Science and Education (HSSE) School, 85, 375, 419
Hunt, Silas Herbert, 161–63
Hunter College, 123, 147, 321
Hutchings, L. M. (dean of the School of Veterinary Medicine), 202–3
Huxhold, David, 346

Iacocca, Lee, 387
Indiana Higher Education Committee on Disabled Students (Indiana AHEAD), 340
Independent Living Movement, 214
Indiana Dunes National Lakeshore, 240
Indiana University, 80, 94, 161
Industrial Management Society, 71
Industrial School and Free Kindergarten, 16–18, 29
in loco parentis policy, 273; students opposed to, 276
International Federation of University Women (IFUW), Dorothy Stratton and, 208–9
International Monetary Fund (IMF), Dorothy Stratton and, 154–55, 167
Iran hostage crisis, 209

Jackson, Jessie, 280, 295
Jefferson, Frieda Parker, 143
Jessie Levering Cary Home for Children, 20
Jim Crow laws, 141
Johnson, Lyndon B., 211, 224, 230, 242
Jones, Sandy, 347
Journal and Courier (Lafayette, Indiana), 299, 303–4, 357, 371, 376, 387–89, 398, 405, 415–16, 428, 430, 434

Kampen, Emerson, 234
Kampen Golf Course (North Golf Course), 2, 234, 235
Kansas Collegiate Athletic Conference, 33
Kelly, Grace, 183
Kennedy, John F., 211, 213; assassinated, 214, 229, 240–42; Civil Rights Act and, 230; President's Commission on the Status of Women, 217–18; as Roman Catholic, 255–56; space race of, 304; at Women's Conference on Civil Rights, 224
Kennedy, Robert F., 287; assassinated, 277, 297; at Purdue, 276; Indianapolis speech of, 275–76; as U.S. Attorney General, 224
Kennedy, Rosemary, 213
Kentucky Deans of Women (KADW), Dorothy Stratton addresses, 106–7
Kettelhut, Karl H., 50
King, Bernice, 226
King, Billie Jean, Bobby Riggs vs., 326–28
King, Bob (athletic academic advisor), 376
King, Brenda, 400
King, Martin Luther, Jr., 225, 279; assassination of, 275, 280, 297
King, Pamela Tyson, 293–94
Kirincic, Karen, 288
Klein, Mary Jane, 124
Korean War, 207

Ladies' Home Journal, 181
Lake Michigan, Helen Schleman's cottage on, 237–40
LaMar, Kris, 317
Lamarr, Hedy, Hollywood Canteen and, 140
Lanczos, Cornelius, 82
Landers, Ann, 354
LaRue, Homer, 281
LeClair, Linda, 273–74
Leslie, Harry G., 29
Liebman, Max, 126
Little Rock Nine, 226
Lloyd-Jones, Esther McDonald, 96–97
Lubbers, Elizabeth Stone, 351
Lubbers, Mark, 350–51
Lubbers, Teresa, 351
Lucretia Mott Amendment, 23, 24
Lyne, Mary C., 131–32

Maas, Melvin J., 211, 212
Mackey, Guy "Red" (athletic director), 294
Mainbocher (Main Rousseau Bocher), designs WAVES' uniforms, 115
male chauvinism, 327, 328
Mallett, Donald R. (vice president and executive dean), 206, 296, 308, 309–10
March on Washington, 225–26
Margerum, Sonya, campaigns for mayor, 355–56
Marine Corps Women's Reserve, 129
Marland, William, 251–52
marriage: education and, 6, 170, 177, 268; in coast guard, 122–23; pressure on women to, 174–76; women's careers and, 109–10, 170, 177, 255, 268

Marshall, George C., DACOWITS and, 205
Martin, Gertrude S., 13
Martin, William, 221
Massachusetts Institute of Technology (MIT), 131
Matthews, Mary L. (dean of home economics), 18, 32
Mauzy, Bob, 393–98
McAfee, Mildred: death of, 419; as Director of WAVES, 115, 123, 129, 132–33, 146; marriage of, 153; Dorothy Stratton and, 117, 119, 120
McCarthyism, 164
McCray, Warren T., 18
McCutcheon, John T., 4
McEwen, Marylu, 231, 275; at Auburn University, 358; Beverley Stone and, 300, 313–14; PhD of, 263–64; Helen B. Schleman Symposium, 358; Mortar Board and, 272
McGinty, Lynnda, 305–6
McHale, Kathryn (trustee), 114, 285; Office of Student Affairs debacle and, 151–53
McRae, Emma Montgomery (unofficial dean of women), 4–7
Mead, Margaret, 299
Meeks, Anna, 255
Meloney, Marie Mattingly, 56
mentoring, mentors, 24, 125, 253, 259, 411, 428; Clara Davidson as, 96; Lillian Gilbreth as, 114, 210; males as, 163; of Betty Nelson, 258, 259, 386; program for, 395; Bev Stone as, 300; Dorothy Stratton as, 38
Meredith, Virginia Claypool (trustee), 18, 285; Home Economics Building and, 19; Purdue Memorial Union and, 21; women's housing and, 19, 41, 48
Meriwether, Lee, as Miss America, 182
Methodists, 39, 246–47, 255–56, 432
Metzler, Cindy, 334
Michigan State University, 172
Milholland, Inez, 9
Millay, Edna St. Vincent, 94–95
Miller, Basil, *Patty Lou in the Coast Guard*, 126
Miller, Sally Downham, *Mourning and Dancing*, 203–4
Millet, Kate: *Sexual Politics*, 321–22; visits Purdue, 322
Mink, Patsy, 324
Miss America Pageant, 182–85
Miss Purdue Scholarship Pageant, 317
missionary barrels: Dorothy Stratton and, 33
Miss Michigan Contest, 183
Mitchell, Betty. *See* Nelson, Betty Mitchell
Mitchell, Emory, as father of Betty Nelson, 244–45, 248–49, 251–52, 385
Mitchell, Lewis "Bud," as brother of Betty Nelson, 245
Mitchell, Margaret, *Gone with the Wind*, 247
Mitchell, Margaret "Peg" (Betty Nelson's mother), 245, 246–48, 251–52
Monroe, Sandy, 331, 385, 411–12
Moreau, Bill, 329–30, 442–43
Morgan, Sallie Payne, 94
Mortar Board, 24–26, 199; alumni chapters of, 446; calendars of, 196–97, 373; Barbara Cook and, 317, 324–25, 373; Gingham Gallop and, 26; Leadership Conference, 36, 367–68; national foundation of, 446; officers of, 104; originally Mortar Board National College Senior Honor Society, 25; Purdue University and, 26; quarterly of, 206–7; research assisted by, 108; Helen Schleman and, 40, 49, 206
Mott, Lucretia, 6, 23
Mr. Coffee, Helen Schleman's cocker spaniel, 236
Ms. Magazine, 320
Mulberry Health and Retirement Community, 441
Mullins, James L., 446
Muncie McRae Club, 4–5
Mundel, Marvin, 77

Nancy Drew, 246
Nargi, Nancy Norton, 299
NASA (National Aeronautics and Space Administration), 305
National Academy of Engineering, 71
National Association for Crippled Children and Adults, 211
National Association for the Advancement of Colored People (NAACP), at Purdue, 398–400
National Association for Women Deans, Administrators, and Counselors (NAWDAC), 324, 411; Barb Cook as president of, 325
National Association of Deans of Men (NADM), 15
National Association of Deans of Women (NADW), 13, 14, 24, 108, 155; conferences of, 165; conventions of, 169–70; in military, 121; networking at, 191; protection of dean of women position, 170. *See also* National Association of Women Deans and Counselors
National Association of Women Deans and Counselors (NAWDC): civil rights and, 242, 276; Betty Friedan at convention, 230; *Journal of*, 315, 317–18; mentoring in, 259; newly named, 206; 1968 conference of, 275; Helen B. Schleman Symposium, 358; Betty Nelson as chair of, 388; Helen Schleman addresses, 269, 270; Helen Schleman as president-elect of,

210, 222, 223–25, 230. *See also* National Association of Deans of Women
National Collegiate Athletic Association (NCAA), 324
National Council of Negro Women, 226
National Education Association (NEA), 13
National Industrial Recovery Act, 47
National Organization for Women, 203
National Panhellenic Conference (NPC), 52, 201–2
National Women's Council, 230
National Youth Administration (NYA), 38
Nelson, Betty Mitchell (dean of students), 1, 196, 235, 237, 441; as assistant dean of women, 215, 248, 262, 281, 297–98; as associate dean, 367; black student beating incident and, 398–401; Boiler Bouts and, 390–92; childhood of, 243–50; Barbara Cook on, 423; as dean of students, 381, 383–86, 388–401; deans-at-the-window episode, 388–89; early career of, 253–60; in "Five Deans Walking" photograph, 382; gateway marker of, 431–32; Ellen Goodman and, 387–88; EMV Sophomore Leadership Conference and, 393–98; Helen B. Schleman Symposium and, 358; as Helen Schleman Gold Medallion Award winner, 272; makes campus handicapped accessible, 339–48; Bob Mauzy and, 393–98; on Kate Millett, 322; meets and marries Dick Nelson, 254; as Mortar Board Leadership Conference moderator, 367; National Association for Women Deans, Administrators, and Counselors chair, 388; portrait of, 445; president of the Greater Lafayette Mortar Board Alumni Chapter, 446; at Radford University, 245, 250–51; readmission of dropped football player controversy and, 374–77; retirement of, 397, 421–26; Helen Schleman and, 385; at Schleman Scholars award ceremonies, 270–71; Carolyn Shoemaker's Bible and, 381–82; on Slayter Center closing, 371–72; Beverley Stone and, 200, 312–13, 353–54; Dorothy Stratton and, 388, 446; student sit-ins and, 297–98; United Way campaign, 421; work with Purdue University Retirees Association, 367, 446
Nelson, Richard "Dick," 384, 422, 446; meets and marries Betty Mitchell, 254
Newell, Barbara W., 307
New York Herald Tribune, 56, 65
New York Times, 65, 311; on Span Plan program, 270
Nineteenth Amendment: ratification of, 11, 23, 306; fiftieth anniversary of, 310
99ers (women flyers), 103
Nixon, Richard M., 306, 323
nontraditional students, Span Plan for 268
North Golf Course (Kampen Golf Course), 2, 235; Helen Schleman and, 234
Northwestern University, 40, 41, 281
Nuclear Test Ban treaty, 242
Nugent, Tim, 345

Obama, Michelle: dedication of cutter *Stratton*, 437–440
Oberlin College, 117
Office of the Dean of Men, 13, 36; becomes Office of the Dean of Students, 328
Office of the Dean of Schools of Engineering, 36
Office of the Dean of Students, 26; merger in 1974, 328; Bev Stone and, 328–29
Office of the Dean of Women, 35, 36, 38, 328
Ohio University, Athens, 254, 253
Ohio State University, 24–26, 43, 256
Ohio Wesleyan University, 13
O'Keefe, Georgia, WCWA and, 101
Old Masters program, 208, 290
Osmun, John, committee of, 289–90
Ottawa University (Ottawa, Kansas), 33

Page, Robert L., 295
Pahlavi, Farah, Queen of Iran, 209
Pahlavī, Mohammad Rezā Shāh, 209
Panhellenic Association, 431
pantsuits, 311–12
Parks, Bert, 184–85
Parks, Rosa, 226
Patton, Leslie, K., 98
Paul, Alice, 9–12, 23, 101, 230
Peace Corps, 242
Pearl, Francis, 347
Pearl Harbor, attacked by Japanese, 98, 112
Pepper Shakers, 27
Perkins, Frances, 48, 101
Perry, Edna, 247
Peterson, Esther, 210–11, 217–20, 224–25
Philip Morris, 318–20
Phillips, Kathryn Sission, 13
P.H.T. ("Putting Husband Through") degree, 269
Physical Education Department, 37
pill, the, 256
Pi Sigma Alpha, 25
Pi Sigma Chi, 24
polio, 210, 213
Pollack, Shepard P., 319–20
Poorman, Gregg, 346, 347

portraits: of Barbara Cook, 445–46; of Amelia Earhart, 102; of Lillian Gilbreth, 362; of Kate Millett, 322; of Betty Nelson, 445–46; of Helen Schleman, 270, 309,

410, 424; of Carolyn Shoemaker, 427; of Beverley Stone, 445–46; of Dorothy Stratton, 439, 446. *See also* "Five Deans Walking" photograph
Porter, Cole, Hollywood Canteen and, 140
Potter, Andrey A. (dean of schools of engineering), 36, 74, 150–51, 285
Presbyterians, 7, 28, 306, 321
Presidential Task Force on Women's Rights and Responsibilities, 306
President's Commission on the Status of Women, 217–19, 222; *American Women* report, 224–25, 226–27, 229
President's Committee on Employment of the Handicapped, 213–15
President's Committee on Employment of the Physically Handicapped, 210–13, 249, 344–45
Prohibition, 18
Psychology Department, 77, 257
Public Works Administration (PWA), 47, 106
Purdue Exponent. See *Exponent*
Purdue Memorial Union Association Board of Governors, 21
Purdue News, the University Handbook, 136
Purdue Research Foundation: Earl Butz and, 271; Helen Schleman's bequest to, 270, 417
Purdue Student Services, 393–95
Purdue University: accessibility at, 215; administrative organization of, 49; alcohol abuse at, 369–72; black students at, 279–82, 293–85, 398–99; deferred rush at, 201–2; fraternities at, 398–99; handicapped accessibility of, 339–48; inequality of female faculty, 333–38, 352; military training at, 136; NAACP at, 398–400; racism at, 141–44, 282, 294, 398–400; student clubs and organizations at, 4–5, 9, 24–26, 27, 53, 54, 66, 104, 285–92, 371; student demonstrations at, 265–66, 277, 280–82, 285–92, 293–95, 296–300; student newspaper of, 115, 139, 165, 181, 193, 208, 265–66, 286–98, 307, 310, 316, 320, 329–30, 337, 347–52, 366, 376–80, 384, 391–92, 399–400, 442; yearbook of, 17, 107, 111, 173, 195, 210, 368
Purdue University, campus sites and buildings: Armory, 206; Beering Hall, 257; Cary East, 20; Cary Hall, 53; Cary Quadrangle, 20, 136, 370–71; Purdue Creamery, 63; Duhme dormitory, 47, 52, 102; Education Building, 257; Eliza Fowler Hall, 29, 35, 106, 416; Elliott Hall of Music, 276, 342, 343; Engineering Administration Building, 20, 36, 343–44; Executive Building, 106; George Dexter House, 20; Hall of Music, 342; Heavilon Hall, 105; Helen B. Schleman Hall of Student Services, 406, 408–10; Home Economics Building, 19; Ladies Hall, 5, 17, 19; Mackey Arena, 294, 342; Memorial Mall, 136, 290; Memorial Union Building, 21, 103, 289, 310, 446; North Hall dormitory, 51; Ross-Ade Stadium, 342; South Hall, 102; Stewart Center, 50, 342, 343; University Hall, 6; Windsor Halls, 47, 51. *See also* airport, Purdue University; Hovde Hall of Administration; Slayter Center; Women's Residence Hall
Purdue University Board of Trustees, 18, 19; Green Guard controversy and, 288–89; raising tuition, 265; Beverley Stone at, 313–14; students on, 299; women on, 114, 308, 335
Purdue University Libraries: Archives and Special Collections, 109, 268, 291, 334, 446; Amelia Earhart collection and, 103, 104; Lillian Gilbreth papers at, 362
Purdue University Retirees Association, 446
Purdue Women's Caucus, 336–37
Purdue Women's Club, 334, 338
Putnam, George Palmer (Amelia Earhart's husband): donates wife's materials, 101–3, 104; Edward Elliott and, 56, 57, 89–91, 101, 102–3; life in Women's Residence Hall, 51, 63, 65; *Soaring Wings*, 57, 86
Pyle, Carol, deans-at-the-window episode, 389

Radcliffe College, 221
Radio Corporation of America (RCA) Engineering Cadettes, 136–38
Radford University, 253; Betty Nelson at, 245, 250–51
Randolph, A. Philip, 225
Randolph-Macon Women's College, 93
Read, David, 321
Reagan, Ronald, 209, 265
recipes: Celestial Chicken Salad, 2; Dean of Women Punch, 200–201, 347
Rehabilitation Act (1973), 215, 339–42, 344
Reid, Helen, 56
Reid, Ogden, 56
residence halls, 48, 160; Amelia Earhart and, 201; reorganization of, 295–96; women's hours in, 171–72, 174, 259–60, 273
Richards, Cindy, 193
Ride, Sally, as America's first woman astronaut, 305
Rieger, Linda, 203
Riesser, Bill, 349–50
Riggs, Bobby, Billie Jean King vs., 326–28
Ritchie, Sharon Kay, 185
Roark, Eldridge "El," 297
Roberts, Edward V., 213–14
Roberts, Flora, 387

Roche, Teresa, 236, 314
Rogers, Edith Nourse, 112
Rolling Quads (University of California, Berkeley), 214
Roosevelt, Eleanor, 38, 56, 146, 416–17; as chair of President's Commission on the Status of Women, 217–18, 224; Lillian Gilbreth and, 76; visits University of Arkansas, 160–62; WCWA and, 101
Roosevelt, Franklin D., 38, 48, 146
Ross, David, 48, 285; Amelia Earhart and, 87–88; donates land for airfield, 86; Dorothy Stratton and, 80, 81, 109
Ross Hills Camp, 236
Rout, Dorothy Wurster, 138
Ruml, Beardsley, *Tomorrow's Business*, 148–49
Russell, Phillip, 20

Saarinen, Eero, Helen Schleman's table by, 235
St. Elizabeth Hospital, 28, 446
Salter, Stephanie, 316
San Bernardino, California, 31, 34
Sandler, Bernice R., 105
Sanger, Margaret, WCWA and, 101
Santmyer, Helen Hooven, *And Ladies of the Club*, 159
Sarah Lawrence College, 228
Schleman, Blanche Hollett (Helen Schleman's mother), 39
Schleman, Delos (Helen Schleman's brother), 39
Schleman, Helen B. (dean of women), 2, 39–51, 55, 258; advocates for more women in administration, 410–11; ahead of her time, 110; *American Women* report and, 224, 226–27, 229; articles by, 107–8; awards of, 206, 309; battles discrimination, 49, 171–74, 202–4; bequests of, 270, 272; biography of, 39–45; Isabel Bloom statue and, 446; Earl Butz and, 271–72; career change of, 43, 64; Christmas parties of, 236–37; as consultant for Nixon's Presidential Task Force on Women's Rights and Responsibilities, 306; Barbara Cook and, 191–93, 318, 359, 368, 369, 380; on Clare Coolidge, 143; as coauthor of *Your Best Foot Forward: Social Usage for Young Moderns*, 108–9, 111, 180–81; crisis of consolidation of residential systems and, 295–96; crisis of man as dean of School of Home Economics and, 220–23, 295; DACOWITS and, 205–6, 208, 222; as dean of women, 155–56, 168, 169, 170–73, 174–78, 194, 195, 197, 231, 261, 263, 264, 265, 281, 301; in deans-at-the-window episode, 389; on Deans' Row, 359, 362–64; death of, 270, 415–16; deferred rush established and, 201–2; Amelia Earhart and, 58, 88–90; Amelia Earhart plaque and, 201, 404; earns master's degree, 43; *The Feminine Mystique* and, 228–31; in "Five Deans Walking" photograph, 382; freshmen women's conference and, 174–78; Lillian Gilbreth and, 361; golf and, 234, 236, 361; Go-to-Hell Fund, 179–80, 247, 248, 385; as grad student, 37; hair of, 262; handkerchiefs of, 417–18; Helen B. Schleman Symposium and, 358; housing difficulties of, 173–74, 206, 233–34, 359; housekeeper of, 236; Lake Michigan cottage of, 237–40; at launch of *Newsletter of the Athletic Conference of American College Women*, 41; liberal science program and, 85; Sonya Margerum's campaign and, 355; memorial for, 416; as mentor, 259, 355; Miss America Pageant and, 182–85, 317; Miss Michigan Contest and, 183; on NAWDAC convention, 412; Betty Nelson and, 385, 389; new house of, 233–35, 237, 270; on Nude Olympics, 371; NYA initiative and, 38, 48, 180; Office of Student Affairs debacle and, 155–56, 170, 221, 295; organized and implemented Housemother training, 54; parties hosted by, 200, 235–37; podiatric health of, 268; portrait of, 309; as president of NAWDC, 210, 222, 225, 230; President Kennedy's assassination and, 241–42; as president of Northwestern's Women's Athletic Association, 41; on President's Commission on Status of Women, 217, 218, 222, 224; on President's Committee on Employment of the Physically Handicapped, 210, 215; private life of, 314; referees women's basketball at Purdue, 45; retirement of, 267–77, 283, 308–10; salary of, 50, 201; as salary watchdog, 333–38; Schleman-Hovde Golf Classic and, 361; Carolyn Shoemaker's Bible and, 167–68, 283, 381; in SPARs, 100, 119–20, 131–32, 147–49, 153, 180; Beverley Stone and, 187–88, 283, 353, 359; Dorothy Stratton and, 37–38, 49, 321, 362–63; urges women students to plan for full life, 62, 174–77, 219, 229, 231; Virginia Slims American Women's Opinion Poll and, 319 visits White House, 223–24; Sally Watlington and, 362–63; women's hours in residence halls and, 259–60; writes *Group Golf Instruction*, 44, 234
Schleman, Herbert (Helen Schleman's brother), 39, 184
Schleman, William (Helen Schleman's father), 39

Schleman Hall, 270
Schleman-Hovde Golf Classic, 361
Schleman-Morton Company, 40
Schleman Scholars, 270–71
Scholer, Walter P., 50
Schools of Engineering, 77
School of Home Economics, 77, 82, 85
School of Management, 77
School of Science, 80, 82, 84
School of Veterinary Medicine, 202–3
Schwartz, Robert A., "How the Deans of Women Became Men," 14, 15
Scudder, Jeanette: dean of women at University of Arkansas, 160; hires Barbara Cook, 163, 165–66; gives recommendations, 187–88, 191; Beverley Stone and, 163–64, 166
segregation: Civil Rights Act and, 234; in classrooms, 162–63; in higher education, 14, 164; in housing, 141–44; Little Rock Nine and, 226; racial, 141–42, 282, 296, 369; in Southern colleges, 161–63
Seneca Falls Women's Right Convention, 6
Seward, Doris M. (assistant dean), 185
sexual harassment, 254–55
Shearon, Janet. *See* Armstrong, Janet Shearon
Shoemaker, Carolyn Ernestine (dean of women), 3–13, 35, 285, 311; assists students financially, 9; Bible of, 35, 106, 167–68, 215, 283, 365–66, 381–82, 424–25; "Civic Needs" speech, 16; commemoration of hundredth anniversary, 445; Community Center for Women and, 16–17, 41; concerned about female students' needs, 19; death of, 28, 427; Amelia Earhart collection and, 104; as English Literature professor, 6; as member of Central Presbyterian Church, 7; memorial service for, 29–30; Mortar Board and, 25; office and home at George Dexter house, 20; as part-time dean of women, 7, 8; rapport of, with students, 18; "Women's Building," 17
Shoemaker, Charles (brother of Carolyn Shoemaker), 4
Shoemaker, Jesse (brother of Carolyn Shoemaker), 4
Shore, Dinah, Hollywood Canteen and, 140
Shriver, Eunice Kennedy, Special Olympics and, 213
Shropshire, Jackie Lamond, 162, 368–69
Simon, Mary Lou, 214
Sims, Araminta Elizabeth, 94
sisterhood, of deans of women, 14
Skelton, Red, Hollywood Canteen and, 140
Slayter Center, 285; closing of, 371–72, 391
Smart, James H. (president), 5
Smith, Chris, Boiler Bouts tragedy and, 391–92
Smith, Clyde, as husband of Margaret Chase Smith, 130
Smith, D. Robertson, 50
Smith, Howard W., Civil Rights Act and, 230
Smith, Margaret Chase, 130
Smith, Marion L, 8, 29
Smith, Robert J., designs Helen Schleman's new house, 233
Smoot, Bill, 298; as editor of *Exponent*, 286; Green Guard speech of, 286–88, 371
social graces of college students, 107–8
Society of Women Geographers, 103
Span Plan program, Helen Schleman and, 268–71
SPARs (Women's Reserve of the U.S. Coast Guard), 121–33; blacks in, 144; creation of, 118–19; first anniversary of, 145–46; LORAN involvement of, 131; naming of, 118; pay of, 122; recruitment for, 119, 121, 122, 124–26, 128; Helen B. Schleman in, 100, 119–20, 131–32, 147–49, 153, 180, 404; stations of, 146–47, 149; Dorothy Stratton as director of,100, 117–33, 145–46, 154, 167; *Tars and Spars* revue, 126–27; uniform of, 119–20
Special Olympics, 213
Speech, Language, and Hearing Sciences Department, 105
Springvale Cemetery, 29
Stage Door Canteen, 139
Stanford University, 324; first woman astronaut from, 305
Stanley, Winifred, 130
Stanton, Elizabeth Cady, 6, 23
Steer, Max (Mack), 105
Steer, Ruth, women's restrooms and, 105
Steinem, Gloria, 180, 320
Stewart, James "Jimmy," 198
Stewart, Lillian, 50
Stewart, Robert Bruce (chief financial officer), 32; Helen Schleman and, 49–51; Office of Student Affairs debacle and, 151
Stimson, Henry L., 11
Stobaugh, Donita, 257
Stockton, J. J. (dean of School of Veterinary Medicine), 203
Stone, Marguerite Beverley (Bev) (dean of women; dean of students), 1, 93–100, 310–11; Charles Albert Anderson and, 97–98; as assistant dean at Purdue University, 172, 187–88, 193–94, 195–97, 261; biography of, 94–95; at Board of Trustees meetings, 313–14; on campus unrest, 281; as City Council member, 354–56, 365, 370; as coauthor of *Counseling Women*, 318; on Committee

on the Status of Women, 335, 338; compassion of, 349–50 Barbara Cook and, 262, 428–429, 380; Clara Davidson and, 95; as dean of students, 328–29, 349–51, 365–77, 390; as dean of women, 283, 294, 297–301, 313–14, 317, 330; in deans-at-the-window episode, 389; on Deans' Row, 359–60, 363–64; death and funeral of, 198, 432–33; described as a lady, 93, 99, 262, 350; as Distinguished Purdue Women Award winner, 352; Doctor of Humane Letters degree of, 373; *The Feminine Mystique* and, 229–30; in "Five Deans Walking" photograph, 382; as friend and housemate of Barbara Cook, 188, 191, 236, 241, 331, 356, 373, 358–60; gateway marker of, 431; Green Guard counseling program and, 196; *Harvey* as favorite play, 198; Helen B. Schleman Symposium and, 358; as Helen Schleman Gold Medallion Award winner, 272, 316; illness of, 300–301, 320; Iron Key member, 199; Sonya Margerum and, 355–56; M. Beverley Stone Award and, 352–53; Esther McDonald Lloyd-Jones and, 96–97; Edna St. Vincent Millay and, 94–95; Mortar Board and, 196–97; Betty Nelson and, 257, 389; Old Masters program and, 195, 208; parties hosted by, 200, 353, 355; Leslie K. Patton commends, 98; portrait of, 445; President Kennedy's assassination and, 242; private life of, 314; at Randolph-Macon College, 93; retirement of, 331, 352–54, 428; Carolyn Shoemaker's Bible and, 283, 365–66, 381; Dorothy Stratton and, 107, 285; student unrest and, 297–98, 300; teaches chemistry to premed students, 98–99; teaches high school, 96; at Tusculum College, 97; at University of Arkansas, 160–61, 163–64; Sally Watlington and, 362; in WAVES, 99, 127–28, 132, 146–47, 160, 163; "Women and Civil Rights," 306–7; Women's Panhellenic Association and, 195–96

Stone, Mary, 94

Stone, Winthrop E. (president), 7, 311, 330

N.S.C Stratton, 437–440

Stratton, Anna Troxler (Dorothy Stratton's mother), 32, 109; death of, 112

Stratton, Dorothy C. (dean of women), 2, 31–38, 40, 45, 50; articles by, 107–8; awards of, 215; as coauthor of *Your Best Foot Forward: Social Usage for Young Moderns*, 108–9, 111, 180–81; biography of, 31–34; career change of, 64; changes rush structure, 19, 52–53, 201; Barbara Cook and, 363, 381; on Clare Coolidge, 143; as dean of women at Purdue University, 31–32, 34, 37, 188; in deans-at-the-window episode, 389; on Deans' Row, 363–64; death and memorial service, 419, 435, 436, 437–440; death of parents of, 148; as director of SPARs, 117–33, 140, 144, 145–46, 154, 167; Amelia Earhart and, 58 66, 67, 88–92, 404; Amelia Earhart collection and, 103–4; Edward Elliott and, 81; encourages female enrollment, 85; as executive director of Girl Scouts of America, 114–15, 181–82, 205, 208; exhibit on, 446; in "Five Deans Walking" photograph, 382; Lillian Gilbreth and, 74–75, 114, 181, 361; housemates of, 353; instituted Housemother Training School, 54, 191; as interesting, 111, 210; International Monetary Fund and, 154–55, 167; liberal science program and, 82, 85, 419–20; Mortar Board and 36; Betty Nelson and, 388, 423, 400–401; Office of Student Affairs debacle and, 150–53; office space of, 106; one hundredth birthday of, 430; as pioneer, 114; portrait of, 446; on President's Committee on Employment of the Physically Handicapped, 210, 215, 244; private life of, 314; pushes for women's restrooms, 104–5; religion and, 182; resignation of, 154–55, 167, 168–69; in Retraining and Reemployment Administration, 153–54; David Ross and, 81, 109; Helen Schleman and, 48, 180, 321, 363; on segregation, 143–44; Carolyn Shoemaker's Bible and, 35, 106, 167–68, 283, 365–66, 381; total education and, 174–75; in WAVES, 113–17; United Nations and, 208–10; waffles served by, 74–75, 66, 67; in Washington, DC, 116–17; Sally Watlington and, 208, 263; "Women on Women," 209–10; at WIMSA memorial dedication, 405–6

Stratton, Richard (Dorothy Stratton's brother), 32

Stratton, Richard Lee ((Dorothy Stratton's father), 32; death of, 109, 112

student demonstrations: administration's monitoring of, 291; 264–66, 280–82, 296–300; black salute and, 293–95

student fees, 291

students, handicapped, 342–43

student teachers, 207

Sturges Senior High School, 31

Susan Bulkeley Butler Women's Archives, 445

Sutton, Mary, 245

Swarthmore College, 24, 25

Syracuse University, 25; Barbara Cook at, 164, 190, 191

Tarbell, Ida, "Fifty Foremost Women of the United States," 69
Tehran, Iran, 209
"temporarily able-bodied," 341
tennis, 326–28
Tereshkova, Valentina, as first woman in space, 304–5
Thomas, Robin J., interviews by, 124
TIAA-CREF, suit against, 335–38
Time magazine, 327; Purdue in, 291
Title IX, 323–26
Tomahawk Service and Leadership Honor Society, 342
tomato aspic, 208
Topping, Robert W., *A Century and Beyond*, 84, 106, 142; *The Hovde Years*, 84
Truman, Harry S., 152–53
Turner, Lana, Hollywood Canteen and, 140
Tusculum College, 97

Umberger, Dave, 2; "Five Deans Walking" photograph, 382
uniforms: of female faculty, 179, 261; of female students, 179–80; of WAVES, 115–16
United Nations (UN), Dorothy Stratton and, 208–10
United States Army, WACS and, 112
United States Army Corps of Engineers, 239
United States Army's Patriotic Civilian Service Award, to Helen Schleman, 206
United States Cadet Nurse Corps, 140
United States Coast Guard, 117, 118, 435. *See also* SPARs
United States Department of Health, Education, and Welfare, 210
United States Naval Institute, oral history interviews, 112
United States Naval Women's Reserves. *See* WAVES
United States Navy, women in, 207–8
United States Senate, subcommittee hearings on suffrage march mistreatment, 11
United Way campaign, 421
University Church, 258
University of Arkansas, 160–63; Barbara Cook at, 191; segregation at, 368–69; Beverley Stone as assistant dean of women at, 187
University of California, 40
University of California, Berkeley, 213–14, 265, 277
University of Chicago, 24, 34
University of Illinois, 214, 345
University of Maryland, 335
University of Michigan, 25, 335
University of Minnesota, 268
University of North Dakota, 201
University of Wisconsin, Madison, 50, 117
U-Sing, 272

V-12 Navy College Training Program, 135–36
Vail, Gladys E. (dean of School of Home Economics), 223
Vallely, Lloyd M., 53
Valparaiso, Indiana, 239
Valparaiso University, 229
Vassar College, 228
Vaught, Wilma, 405
veterans: disabled, 345; return to college, 83, 161–62, 170; support for, 154, 171
Vietnam War: effects of, 290; student unrest and, 264–65, 274, 280, 290, 291, 296–97
violence, Helen Schleman on, 277
Virginia C. Meredith Club, 24
Virginia Kelly Karnes Archives and Special Collections Research Center: Amelia Earhart Papers in, 104; Helen Schleman papers in, 268; student demonstrations documented in, 291; *Your Best Foot Forward: Social Usage for Young Moderns* in, 109. *See also* Purdue University Libraries
Voss, Janice E., as Purdue's first woman astronaut, 305
Voting Rights Act of 1965, 231

WAACs. *See* Women's Army Auxiliary Corps
WACs. *See* Women's Army Corps
Waesche, Russell R., Admiral, 124
Walbaum, Dick (assistant dean for administration), 331–32
Walker, Michael, 398–400
Wark, Lois, 192–93
War Manpower Commission, 112, 113
Washington, Booker T., 143
Washington, DC, 116–17
Washington Post, 56, 203
Watergate, 330
Watlington, Sally, 66, 199–200, 206, 331, 346, 362, 404, 44, 446; Barbara Cook and, 359, 362, 381; on deans' hair, 261–62; Deans' Row and, 362–64; naval career of, 207–8, 362; as salary watchdog, 333; Helen Schleman and, 203, 235, 333; Beverley Stone and 353, 359, 263, 366–67; Dorothy Stratton and, 208
WAVES (United States Naval Women's Reserves): barracks of, 127, 132; interactions with other branches, 119, 129; Mildred McAfee as director of, 99, 115, 123, 129, 146; pay of, 122; representatives visiting universities, 140; singing in, 128; size of, 127; stations of, 146; Beverley Stone

and, 99–100, 207; Dorothy Stratton in, 112–17, 120; uniforms of, 115–16, 119–20, 128; view of, 125
Weber, Mary E., 305
Wellesley College, 42–43
Wells-Barnett, Ida B., 10
Western Society of Engineers, 71
White, Margaret, on Board of Trustees, 308
Wickes, Jeannette Tremlin, 138
Wilson, Mindwell Crampton, 4
Wilson, Pearnell, 398–400
Wilson, Woodrow, 9
Women in Military Service for America Memorial (WIMSA), 404–6
women: in agriculture, 5; armed forces and, 205–6, 207; careers and, 6, 61, 64, 170, 220; "chilly climate" for, 105; civil rights and, 306–7; as college presidents, 307–8; concerns about, on college campus, 8; curriculum for, 82; discrimination against, 210, 219; earning college degrees, 6, 25; in engineering, 5, 64, 80, 136–38, 305–6; fear of recognition of, 24; lower wages for, 110, 333–35; Modern Training for Modern Women, 82; service of, in World War II, 112–33, 207; sex and, 287, 288; sexual harassment of, 254–55; in space program, 304–5; standards of conduct for, 109–10; in tennis, 326–28; as wives of male students, 269–71; as workers in World War II, 112–13
Women's Army Auxiliary Corps (WAACs), 120; bad press and, 125; creation of, 112; interaction with other branches, 129; representatives visiting universities, 140; uniforms of, 115
Women's Army Corps (WACs), 112
Women's Conference on Civil Rights, 223–24
Women's Equity Action League (WEAL), 334
women's history: intellectual, 6; women's archives and, 101–4
Women's Interhall Council, 310
women's liberation, 305, 327; at Purdue, 306–7
Women's Reserve of the U.S. Coast Guard. *See* SPARs
Women's Residence Hall, 20–21, 101; becomes Amelia Earhart's home, 59, 102; built with PWA funds, 47, 48, 106; designed by Scholer, 50; mealtimes at, 62; opening of, 49, 51; as potential site of Amelia Earhart collection, 103; renamed South Hall, 5, 102
women's rest rooms, 104–5; Lillian Gilbreth on, 112
women's rights, 130, 210, 274, 320, 337; in Iran, 209; Nixon's presidential task force and, 306, 408; President's Commission on the Status of Women and, 218; Seneca Falls convention and, 6. *See also* Equal Rights Amendment
Women's Self-Government Association (WSGA), 53, 54, 66, 104
women's suffrage, 9, 18, 210, 299; parade for, 9–11
Wood, Karl (Barbara Cook's father), 157–58
Wood, Pete (Barbara Cook's brother), 158
Wood, Thelma Champaign (Barbara Cook's mother), 2, 158
Works Progress Administration (WPA), 48
World Center for Women's Archives (WCWA), 101–3
World Institute on Disability, 214
World War I, 16, 21; disabled veterans of, 210
World War II: atomic bomb dropped during, 152–53, 158–59; demobilization after, 153–54, 171; in Europe, 102; higher education and, 136;implications of, for women, 155, 170; Pearl Harbor and, 98; Purdue's war efforts during, 113, 135–41; United States enters, 112; veterans of, 27, 83, 170, 345; women's service in, 112–33, 207

Young Men's Christian Association (YMCA), 143
Young Women's Christian Association (YWCA), 9, 17, 40, 78, 406–7
Your Best Foot Forward: Social Usage for Young Moderns (Dorothy Stratton and Helen Schleman, 1940), 108–9, 111; second edition, 180–81
YWCA Foundation of Greater Lafayette, 446

Zissis, Celie, 258, 339, 403; Span Plan and, 269–70
Zwierlein, Paula: Amelia Earhart collection and, 104

Reading Group Guide

The Deans' Bible is a book that opens doors to a variety of discussion topics that are relevant for women and men today: the call for more women in administrative positions, equal pay for equal work, equality in higher education, the example of women helping other women, and the courage to wear the mantle of inclusion regardless of gender, sexual orientation, color, or physical disability.

The women of *The Deans' Bible* started the conversation. You and your group can continue the still necessary dialogue.

The Deans' Bible Discussion Topics

1. The deans experienced an extraordinary friendship that lasted throughout their lifetimes. Why are relationships between women important? Have you experienced such a sisterhood? Do men form similar woven bonds?

2. How did the military experiences of three of the deans affect their lives and the lives of their students and colleagues?

3. Helen Schleman said she was born fifty years before her time. As dean of women in the 1940s–1960s, Helen experienced challenges to convince female students and the male administration that a college degree was important for women. Is there still a stigma, perhaps covert, for women in college today?

4. Helen Schleman was a wonderful mentor to her staff and her students. She was willing to "share," via lunches and parties in her home, the influential women she knew who visited the Purdue campus, such as engineer Lillian Gilbreth. Have you experienced similar mentoring?

5. The deans led with integrity, and as a group they acted as the "checkpoint" for one another as to the rightness and wrongness of a situation. It's easier to stand your ground when you know you have someone behind you supporting your stance. How can women today change the world by being a "checkpoint" for others?

6. Through forthright actions and eloquent speeches, the deans were stellar role models as effective change agents. Compare the deans' methods of calling for change with the notorious speech and actions by *Exponent* editor Bill Smoot in the fall of 1968.

7. Helen Schleman emphasized "life planning" for women students. How do you juggle a life plan while also remaining open to seizing opportunities that come along?

8. Discuss the significance of the icons of connection shared by the deans and others: Carolyn Shoemaker's Bible, Purdue pendant watches, Celestial Chicken Salad, Dean of Women Punch, and Helen's Hankie Club.

9. Discuss the impact of legislation on the story arc of *The Deans' Bible*: the 19th Amendment giving women the right to vote, creation of the World War II Women's Reserves, President Kennedy's Commission on the Status of Women, the Civil Rights Act of 1968, the proposed Equal Rights Amendment, President Nixon's Task Force on Women's Rights and Responsibilities, Title IX, the Rehabilitation Act of 1973, the Americans with Disabilities Act, and the Freedom of Information Act.

10. Discuss the books that were important to the lives of the deans: *Gone with the Wind, Nancy Drew, And Ladies of the Club,* poems by Edna St. Vincent Millay, *The Idiot, The Feminine Mystique,* and *The Velveteen Rabbit.* What books made an impact on your life?

11. The deans were role models in retirement. Helen continued to monitor salaries and positions for women at Purdue, Bev entered politics, Barb was a founding member of Indiana Governor Birch Bayh's Commission on Women, and Betty transformed the Purdue University Retirees Association. Through modeling, the deans' final quest for equality was for those victimized by ageism. Discuss ageism in our culture.

Additional Resources

Reading Group Guide: docs.lib.purdue.edu/deansbible/1

***The Deans' Bible* Bibliography:** docs.lib.purdue.edu/deansbible/2

Author Narrative Video: docs.lib.purdue.edu/deansbible/3

Purdue University Virginia Kelly Karnes Archives and Special Collections "Quest for Equality": collections.lib.purdue.edu/womens-archives/quest-for-equality